ABOVE THE BOTTOM LINE

FINANCIAL
MANAGEMENT
IN
HUMAN
SERVICES

ROGER A. LOHMANN

NASW PRESS

National Association of Social Workers
Washington, DC

Darrell P. Wheeler, PhD, MPH, ACSW, *President*
Angelo McClain, PhD, LCSW, *Chief Executive Officer*

Cheryl Y. Bradley, *Publisher*
Stella Donovan, *Acquisitions Editor*
Julie Gutin, *Project Manager*
Sharon Fletcher, *Marketing Manager*
Sue Harris, *Copyeditor*
Stefanie Salazer, *Proofreader*
Lori J. Holtzinger, Zinger Indexing, *Indexer*

Cover by Britt Engen, Metadog Design Group
Interior design and composition by Xcel Graphic Services
Printed and bound by Sheridan Books

First impression: September 2016

Library of Congress Cataloging-in-Publication Data

Names: Lohmann, Roger A., 1942– author.
Title: Above the bottom line : financial management in human services / Roger A. Lohmann.
Description: Washington, DC : NASW Press, 2016. | Includes bibliographical references and index.
Identifiers: LCCN 2016022302 (print) | LCCN 2016029564 (eBook) | ISBN 978-0-87101-498-6 (paperbook) | ISBN 978-0-87101-499-3 (eBook)
Subjects: LCSH: Human services—Finance. | Social service—Finance. | Social work administration.
Classification: LCC HV41 .L6326 2016 (print) | LCC HV41 (eBook) | DDC 361.0068/1—dc23
LC record available at https://lccn.loc.gov/2016022302

Printed in the United States of America

For my grandchildren,
Brandon T. Lohmann and Madison Elizabeth Romano

Contents

About the Author

Roger A. Lohmann, PhD, is professor emeritus of social work at West Virginia University, Morgantown. He received his BA from St. Cloud State University, MA from the University of Minnesota, and PhD from the Heller School at Brandeis University.

After a term as the youngest director of a Community Action Agency in the War on Poverty, Lohmann developed one of the first courses on financial management in social work education, and his earlier book, *Breaking Even: Financial Management in Human Service Organizations*, was the first book-length discussion ever published on the topic. He is the author of numerous other publications, including several *Encyclopedia of Social Work* entries on financial management and related topics; *Social Administration* (coauthored with Nancy Lohmann); the award-winning *The Commons: New Perspectives on Nonprofit Organization and Voluntary Action*; and his latest electronic book, *Voluntary Action in New Commons: Democracy in the Life World Beyond Market, State and Household*. These last two books lay out a perspective on nonprofit organization and civil society that he calls the commons theory of voluntary action.

Lohmann has received a number of awards and recognitions for his work, including lifetime achievement awards from the Association for Community Organization and Social Administration and the Association for Research on Nonprofit Organizations and Voluntary Action, a *Nonprofit Times* listing as one of the 50 most influential people in the nonprofit sector, and designation as a Benedum Scholar at West Virginia University.

Acknowledgments

Each time I sit down to write something on financial management, I am reminded of Gene Flaten, who first recruited me to the War on Poverty and introduced me to community action in rural Minnesota; the late Robert Morris, who indulged my fascination with financial and managerial economic issues at the Heller School; and Ed Pawlak, who recruited me to a faculty position at the University of Tennessee specifically to teach financial management to social work students.

In recent years, I have been grateful many times for my colleagues in the Civil Society Design Network (CSDN, known colloquially as the Over the Hill Gang)—a group of retired faculty colleagues and friends from around the world who keep in touch with and keep tabs on one another as the retirement years go by. Jon Van Til and I founded the group more years ago than I care to remember, and Jon has done more than his fair share to keep the CSDN flame alive. Also important for my continuing intellectual health are the Queens University (Kingston, Ontario) third-sector theory group, particularly Jon, Laurie Mook, Jack Quarter, Wenjue Knutson, Adelbert Wagner, and numerous others.

I would also particularly like to thank George McCully, founder and leader of the *Catalogue for Philanthropy*, for his continuing advice and support on the meaning of philanthropy in American and world history. George has single-handedly brought about a transformation of our understanding and called our attention to the paradigm shift of this profound idea from the conventional "donations and foundations" view to a much richer, more nuanced, and historically grounded view steeped in human betterment. When Jane Addams spoke of philanthropy, it was this larger vision to which she referred.

Connecting philanthropy to enterprise may strike some in social work as little short of a clash of ideologies. The embrace of enterprise in this book has many sources, none more important than Dennis Young and Michael Sherraden, who were extolling this idea many years before it was taken up by others. My intellectual debts to them and to Larry Martin, Karen Harper-Dorton, and Ginny Majewski should be clear in the text. Each of them has contributed to the view laid out in this book, although none will necessarily agree with what I have written. The same can certainly be said for the colleagues I met through the Donors Forum (now Forefront), especially Lenore and Steve Ealy, Gus DeZerega, and the late Richard Cornuelle. I frequently disagreed with them, but listening closely was a rewarding experience, nonetheless. I would also like to thank George Ginader for providing useful information for the discussion of accounting at a crucial time in the genesis of this book. George and other "snowbird" members of our Monday morning coffee group provided many hours of enjoyable conversation in recent years.

Furthermore, I would like to thank several people at NASW Press who made this publication experience particularly enjoyable, especially Cheryl Bradley, Stella Donovan, Julie Gutin, Susannah Harris, and Sharon Fletcher.

Finally, heartfelt thanks to Nancy, my wife and best friend for more than half a century, who enabled me to complete this book in relatively short order. In all cases, the help was much appreciated, but responsibility for errors and omissions remains mine alone.

1

Introduction

This book is about managing the finances of human services programs and organizations. It is directed primarily to an audience of social workers—students and working professionals employed in the full range of human services settings.

SOCIAL WORK

According to the National Association of Social Workers (NASW, n.d.-b), *social work* is the professional activity of helping individuals, groups, or communities enhance or restore their capacity for social functioning and creating social conditions favorable to this goal. Although useful and widely accepted, umbrella terms such as "social functioning" and "social conditions" cover the full range of efforts (and perhaps a great deal that falls outside the profession) but may require some further clarification for those seeking to capture the essence of social work as a financial endeavor. In July 2014, the International Association of Schools of Social Work General Assembly and the International Federation of Social Workers approved a definition of *social work* that elaborated on the NASW definition:

> Social work is a practice-based profession and an academic discipline that promotes social change and development, social cohesion, and the empowerment and liberation of people. Principles of social justice, human rights, collective responsibility and respect for diversities are central to social work. Underpinned by theories of social work, social sciences, humanities and indigenous knowledge, social work engages people and structures to address life challenges and enhance wellbeing. (International Association of Schools of Social Work, n.d.)

At this writing, these are the most current and universal in a series of organized and official efforts to capture in words the essence of the large, open-ended, and continually changing complex of individual and collective activities that is contemporary social work. It is tempting to try to define the field by stringing together long lists of important keywords.

When the breadth of what social workers do is combined with the places where and ways in which they do it, as in the study of financial management of human services, the whole situation can easily appear unwieldy. In focusing on managing the finances of social work, we need not address directly in any detail the distinctive nature, purposes, or activities that define contemporary social work other than the fundamentally ethical nature of the professional tasks and challenges. Instead, we can focus almost exclusively on the human and financial resources necessary to do those deeds. With that peculiar focus in mind, let us address briefly two additional definitions: *human services*, which is the generic term used here for what social workers (and others) do, and *financial management*, which is the generic term for what they require to do (or deliver) human services.

HUMAN SERVICES

In marked contrast to economics, finance, and general management, social work has always been an idealistic, goal-oriented, value-driven enterprise with only limited attention to the means necessary to attain those ends (Barney & Ouchi, 1986; Jegers, 2008; B. Keating & Keating, 2009; Speckbacher, 2003; Steinberg, 2004; D. R. Young, 2007; D. R. Young & Steinberg, 1995). Social work practice consists of the professional application of social work values, principles, and techniques to one or more of the following ends:

- helping people obtain tangible services
- providing counseling and psychotherapy with individuals, families, and groups
- helping communities or groups provide or improve their social and health services
- participating in relevant legislative activities (NASW, n.d.-a)

This list offers what is, in effect, a typology for the term "human services." Under these four categories we can fit virtually all of the services and activities whose financing we are concerned with. There are other such lists, notably the typology found in the second version of the United Way of America Service and Information System (UWASIS II) (Sumariwalla & Levis, 2000; United Way of America, 1974) and the less complete human services section of the "National Taxonomy of Exempt Entities" (NTEE) (National Center for Charitable Statistics, n.d.). Another approach is the traditional Aristotelian humanist view of philanthropy deployed by George McCully (2008), which divides philanthropic targets into three types: nature, culture, and human services. A complete and up-to-date listing of McCully's (2015) "Taxonomy of Philanthropy" is available online at the *Catalogue for Philanthropy* Web site. A listing of the NTEE is available online at the Urban Institute Web site. For perspective on the reemergence of philanthropy as a subject of study and teaching, see the volumes of the Filer Commission study (Commission on Foundations and Private Philanthropy, 1970). Brilliant (2000) provided a history of the Filer and Peterson commissions that sets the reemergence in histori-cal context. As the definitions above suggest and the various typologies illustrate, contemporary human services include a broad range of service programs, events, and activities promoting social change, human development, and the empower-ment and liberation of a variety of individuals, groups, and communities.

FINANCIAL MANAGEMENT

Financial management is one important facet of the larger challenges posed by human services. Within social work education, a small contingent of researchers, teachers, and writers working under the banner of community organization and social administration have been writing on financial and other management topics for decades (see also C. Alexander, 1977; D. M. Austin, 2002; Ezell, 2000; Ginsberg, 2008; Lohmann & Lohmann, 2002; Patti, 2009). Financial management in human services refers to "the control and use of money and other scarce resources to fur-ther organizational goals, consistent with law, ethics, and community standards" (Lohmann, 1980, p. 292). Managing the financing of human services involves "a variety of concepts, principles, and tools designed to improve the use of resources to accomplish in an efficient and effective manner the mission goals, [and] objec-tives of human service agencies and programs" (Martin, 2001, p. 1).

The need for better understanding of the financial situation of human services has never been greater. Perhaps the greatest threats facing every human service organization today come from the financial instability of the contemporary prac-tice environment. Nonprofit organizations are particularly vulnerable because of the instability of the funding climate, whereas independent private practitioners, in particular, have all of the threats and challenges faced by small businesses in a tight economy (Braswell, Fortin, & Osteryoung, 1984; Forsythe, 2000; Gross, 1995; Herzlinger, 1979; Jegers, 1997; Kingma, 1993; Martin, 2006; Wedig, 1994).

This need for improved financial understanding is particularly acute among nonprofit organizations, and a substantial literature generalizing to the entire range of nonprofit organizations has developed (McLaughlin, 2002; McMillan, 2000a, 2003; Ritchie & Eastwood, 2006; Ritchie & Kolodinsky, 2003; Worth, 2009; D. R. Young, 2007; Zietlow, Hankin, & Seidner, 2007). A survey of 5,451 nonprofit organizations funded by the Bank of America Charitable Foundation concluded that the nonprofit fund-ing system (based on donors and grants) was "chronically brittle" (Lindsay, 2015). One-third (32 percent) of nonprofit organizations surveyed reported problems with financial sustainability. Table 1.1 shows other results of the survey. Thus, although nonprofit human services are the central focal point of the following discussion, effort is made to extend the discussion to other public and private settings as well.

In the chapters of this book, I address in detail various aspects of the theory and practice of managing the finances of human services organizations, ranging in size from small to large. I refer to the most basic understanding of financial opera-tions and concerns as *financial literacy*, which, like all literacy, is both an individual and a collective concern. It would be inaccurate to suggest that social workers alone are concerned with financial management in human services. Many others— accountants, bankers, lawyers, managers from other professional backgrounds,

Table 1.1: Survey of Nonprofit Organizations

Response	%
Financial sustainability	32
Staff retention/payroll	25
Funding that covers full costs	19
Unrestricted income	16
Community engagement	13
Cuts in government funding	13
Managing or pursuing growth	13
Meeting demand for services	13
Not enough staff	12
Developing cash reserves	12
Reliable cash flow	12

Note: Results are from a survey of 5,451 nonprofit organizations funded by the Bank of America Nonprofit Sector Fund during January and February, 2015, which posed the following question: "What are the top challenges facing your nonprofit?" (Multiple responses were allowed.) Nonprofit Finance Fund, 2015, *State of the Sector Surveys: 2015 Survey.* Retrieved from http://www.nonprofitfinancefund.org/state-of-the-sector-surveys

board members, volunteers, grant makers, and more than a few clients—are also concerned with aspects of this topic in various situations. All of these individuals are referred to in what follows as stakeholders. They come with varying degrees of financial literacy, ranging from very high to low. Many social work students and even some social work practitioners tend toward the lower end of financial literacy. Yet, it would be misleading to assume that only a few social workers in specialized management positions are concerned with financial management issues and questions. In the modern human services organization, every decision by every worker can have important resource implications, and some measure of financial literacy is a basic requirement of informed, evidence-based practice.

A NOTE ON THE BOOK TITLE AND OTHER TERMINOLOGY

What is the meaning of "above the bottom line" in the book title? "The bottom line" is a common phrase in business jargon that refers to the final result of a set of financial calculations. The management guru Peter Drucker was fond of asking of human services and other nonprofit organizations, "What is the bottom line where there is no bottom line?" (Drucker, as cited in Martin, 2001, p. 6). This question and situation apply directly to many human services.

The word "above" in the title has two simultaneous meanings. In one sense, the word means previous, preceding, or going before. The second sense of the word here is over and beyond: For members of the social work profession, financial bottom line concerns are never sufficient in themselves. There will always be more to delivering human services than whether or not costs are covered or the enterprise is making money.

Monetization and Metaphor

To manage finances, it is necessary to "translate financial matters into meaningful and relevant information" for policymakers, decision makers, and leaders (Hildreth, as cited in Martin, 2001). In the following pages, human services organizations are considered not in the usual way they are handled in the social work literature but from a particular, monetized viewpoint. To highlight this perspective, the term "human services organization" is generally not used. Instead, "human services enterprise" (HSE) is the preferred term here to highlight and emphasize the monetized perspective, the fact that we are following the money.

Monetization is the expression or presentation of data, resources, concepts, findings, evaluations, and other conclusions in terms of money—regardless of whether as dollars, pounds, euros, or some other currencies. In human services, monetization is always partial and incomplete, and many important values cannot be expressed in terms of money. Every social worker knows this, and there is nothing inherent in managing human services finances that should require this to be ignored or forgotten. Monetization in human services finance also means that those seeking to manage the financing of service delivery must pay attention to the differences between terms used literally—where actual monetization is involved—and a range of figurative or metaphorical uses of the same terms. We may speak metaphorically of staff members as assets, of the human cost of injustice, of trying to better budget our time, or of the impact of new ideas without invoking any actual monetization and without any intention of assigning actual monetary values to them. In this book, the uses of such metaphorical expressions are deliberately held to an absolute minimum to highlight the role of actual monetization, limit confusion, and maintain the emphasis on the monetized meanings. There is no suggestion intended here that such metaphoric and nonmonetized connotations are incorrect, unimportant, or wrong. American English is bursting with them. However, the point of this book is to focus on the monetized meanings.

Most references in the text are monetized in dollars and cents, as the principal intended audience of this book is North American. However, the basic ideas hold equally well when monetized as pounds, euros, rupees, wons, renminbis, or any of the world's other currencies.

Finances

For purposes of this book, *finances* is another name for the monetized resources that make *service delivery*, or the production of human services, possible. To finance something is to take action to secure and organize the resources necessary to achieve a result or carry out an action. The term *capital* can serve as a synonym for financing, and *capitalization* describes the processes involved in locating new *income*, a term that refers to monetized or financial inputs into any enterprise in human services. *Expenditure* and *expense* both track monetized outputs. Other terms, such as *service, outcome, and product,* typically refer to nonmonetized outputs of human services (Dalton & Morelli, 1988; Martin, 1997).

Stocks and Flows

A good way to think about monetized resources, according to both economists and accountants, is as the management of systems of stocks and flows, which is also a beginning definition of the term *enterprise*. The *assets* of an enterprise—its bank balances, investments, and various forms of anticipated income—constitute its stock in this sense. (The notion of stocks as shares of ownership is actually an offshoot of this idea.) In HSEs, flows consist of two types: *inflows*, all types of which can be called "income," and *outflows*, which also are of two (monetized) types, that is, expenses and services. Many of the challenges of financial management in human services involves attention to the quantitative relationships between those two types of outputs, both with one another and with income. Later chapters take up the tricky subject of the relationships between measurable, quantitative stocks and flows and the more elusive, difficult to quantify, and even unmeasurable domains of human capital.

The flow of monetized resources through an HSE are tracked by transactions recorded in the accounting system and laid out in the enterprise's plans and budgets. Such flows are controlled and directed by the processes of making decisions and changing those plans. Budgets generally outline expected future income and expenditures, usually for a fiscal year. Monthly, quarterly, and annual financial statements track actual monetized performance after the fact. A range of specialized studies, or *financial analyses*, may be conducted using either future-oriented budget or historical financial statement information.

Profit

Finally, it is necessary to offer a brief comment on the meaning of "profit." The connection of human services and social work with the idea of profit is a complex one, beginning with the misunderstanding that nonprofit organizations are organizations unable or unwilling to make profits. This (false) meaning results from confusion stemming from a failure to note the difference between financial surpluses and profits. The term *profit* actually refers only to the portion of a financial surplus distributed by an explicit act or decision to owners or shareholders. All types of enterprises, including for-profit businesses, can have undistributed surpluses, but nonprofit human services are forbidden by law from making such distributions. In all cases for both profit and nonprofit enterprises, except perhaps single-owner unincorporated businesses, some formal decision and declaration or resolution is required for surpluses to be distributed as profits. Without the decision to distribute, potential profits remain as surpluses. Thus, the difference between for-profit and nonprofit enterprises is not whether or not they have more income than expenses (surpluses) but whether it is legal for them to distribute such surpluses as profits to owners or shareholders. Thoroughly understanding this point is increasingly important in social work because of the growth of private practice. Social work can be conducted as a profit-making venture, whether by individuals, groups, or corporations and whether in the form of a private, public, or nonprofit organization. There is no requirement of any sort, however, that the private practice of social work must be a profit-distributing activity.

Lumping or Splitting?

The understanding of profit has many implications. It is sometimes said that there are two types of people: *lumpers,* those who focus on the similarities among different things, and *splitters,* those who focus on differences and distinctions. Past social work treatments of financial issues and topics have often emphasized the uniqueness of social work financial concerns in public and nonprofit settings.* The growth of private social work practice in recent years has rendered that approach largely obsolete. Mayers (2004, pp. 24–28) has created a list of the supposedly unique characteristics of nonprofit human services, accompanied by a far more convincing list of their common characteristics. Nonprofit and for-profit organizations, he suggests, both acquire external resources to produce goods and services; are subject to scarcity; and may incur financial obligations, charge fees for their services, and seek to market their services, which may be similar. Note that this list applies not only to private nonprofit and conventional for-profit organizations but also to public nonprofit agencies and an entirely new set of social enterprises, which is introduced in more detail in chapter 2. In chapter 5, two leading authorities suggest that there are really only two financially important differences between nonprofit and for-profit enterprises: nondistribution constraints and handling of donations. It would appear that many forms of contemporary HSE are minimizing those differences in the name of social enterprise, the sharing economy, and the third and fourth sectors.

   This book is an exercise in lumping—specifically, recognizing the many similarities and a few important differences among the financial concerns of large and small, public and private, nonprofit and for-profit settings. Just as social work practice is a unique and definable enterprise across a vast range of situations and settings, the financial management of human services can be seen from a singular, unified perspective. However, in lumping together the full range of types of organized financial entities, it is also necessary that we keep in mind essential splits or differences. Yet, when it comes to financial management of human services, these are increasingly seen as variations on a theme rather than essential distinctions.

---

*Feit and Li (1998), Martin (2001), Lohmann (1980), and Mayers (2004) all embraced a kind of limited version of the splitting approach, with a core focus on tax-exempt nonprofit organizations and forays into the special issues or concerns of public agencies. The journal literature on financial management has long been more heavily focused on publicly funded nonprofit settings. Meanwhile, outside influences, including accounting and federal and state policies, have acted to downplay all but the most essential differences.

Delivery of human services is typically a collective, organized activity. Thus, the question is, how best to refer to the organized entities that deliver human services? For historic and theoretical reasons, the most common casual reference for social workers is the term "social agency." A growing professional literature grounded in social administration and the social science of organizations prefers the term "human services organization" (see, for example, M. J. Austin, Regan, Gothard, & Carnochan, 2013; Hasenfeld & Garrow, 2012; Patti, 2009). Both of these terms have strong connotations of public and nonprofit organizations and do not quite connect directly with the full range of the concerns of financial management.

In this book, the term *human services enterprise* (HSE), is used for two principal reasons: First, the term can represent the full range of possibilities that includes private practice along with nonprofit and public organizations. Second and most important, the term *enterprise* is used to signify explicit emphasis on monetized perspectives and financial concerns, consistent with common usage. For example, the Web site of the American Public Human Services Association asks, "How does IT [information technology] fit within the larger context of the health and human service enterprise?" Several state health and human services departments refer to contracts with non-state agencies as "enterprise agreements." The Australian Department of Human Services also has enterprise agreements with its various contractors. The U.S. Department of Health and Human Services operates what it calls an "enterprise architecture" in which financial management is listed as one of the domains. All in all, the term "HSE" is already in widespread use.

In its most general meaning, *enterprise* refers to an undertaking or a project of extensive scope, difficulty, complication, or risk, especially one with economic and financial implications. In that general sense, all human services organizations; social agencies; and public, nonprofit, and for-profit programs, as well as numerous other human services projects and ventures, can thus legitimately be termed enterprises. In the following chapters, *HSE* is used as an umbrella term to refer to all forms of human service organization viewed from an explicitly monetized or financial vantage point. HSE can apply not only to formal and informal groups of practitioners in public, nonprofit, or for-profit settings and to assorted formal human services organizations and corporations but also to monetized views of assorted social work groups and departments in other host settings and forms of individual, group, and corporate private practice of social work (Auslander, 1996; Jansson & Simmons, 1986).

HSE can also be used to refer to the financial dimensions of committees and community collaborations, freestanding programs and campaigns, membership associations, community organizing efforts, community development ventures, and community-changing projects. Additional applications include the financial domains of schools and departments of social work and human services educational programs, social work departments within non–social work host settings, and all modes of private practice. *HSE* can further refer to all other settings where resources are gathered and leveraged to deliver human services, provided that they maintain budgets, financial records, or accounts; use financial analysis techniques; or engage in operational decision making to implement their plans and carry out

Figure 1.1: General Systems Model of Human Services

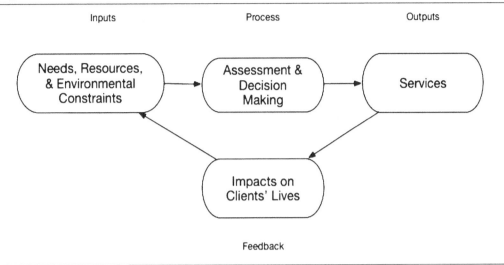

their missions. Last, but not least, HSEs all benefit from strategic thinking about where they are going and how best to get there.

Strategy

"Strategy" is a fundamental term in financial management, particularly for budget planning and financial evaluation and analysis. The term *strategy* is used here to denote the highest-level understanding of the means of pursuing a mission to achieve a goal or result (the ends). Missions, goals, and objectives speak to the who, what, and why of purposeful action, whereas strategy and tactics speak to the how, when, and where questions. Thus, for example, the general HSE mission is to deliver services to meet clients' needs. The companion strategy involves how to do so in the most appropriate manner possible.

The idea of strategy is important for HSEs as an avenue of individualization. The approach of each enterprise to its own strategic financial concerns is unique and may vary under differing conditions. There is no blueprint for enterprise strategy and it is impossible to list all of the possibilities. Followed to its extreme, individualization of each enterprise makes general knowledge of financial management impossible, so some compromise is necessary. In this book, a simplified approach to core matters of financial strategy is followed, one that focuses on essential elements addressing two essential strategic dimensions. The first of these is resource, or *inflow strategy*, which is about finding the proper balance of income sources, process, and operational tactics involving such matters as staffing, inventories, and cash flows and special expenditure issues in particular contexts. The second strategic dimension is expense, or *outflow strategy*, which is concerned with connections between the missions, goals, and objectives of the human services organization and the expenditure of financial resources to achieve those purposes. There are several essential strategic concerns that are so fundamental that they cannot be overlooked, for example, (a) commitment to effective and efficient performance, (b) continual adherence to generally accepted accounting principles (GAAPs) and the ways in which HSEs provide for efficient use of resources and effective performance, and (c) commitment to ethically informed practice. A case is also made here for income strategies emphasizing the pursuit of multiple (and diverse) sources of funding. A rationale for this strategy is outlined and supported by evidence in the discussion on fiscal distress, in chapter 10.

OTHER IMPORTANT PRELIMINARIES

A few other important matters need to be noted before we dive into managing human service finances. First, the assumptions of social work as a self-governing profession and the fundamental role of ethics in all aspects of social work practice, including in the financial arena, are important in guiding and shaping the presentation here. Three important ethical (and legal) concerns are transparency, fiduciary duty, and self-dealing.

Transparency

Transparency of financial information is one general strategic dimension to which great lip service is paid today. It can represent either a very real strategic commitment of an HSE or a mere cliché.* An HSE with genuine commitment to transparency will routinely make its budgets and financial statements available to its stakeholders in a timely manner and demonstrate a willingness to answer questions and discuss the implications of what is found there at board meetings and budget hearings and in other venues (Aranoff, 2003). The Internal Revenue Service's (IRS) annual release of Form 990 tax returns for public charities and Web sites such as Guidestar.org have, to some extent, resolved many questions of legally mandated transparency. Even so, some enterprises may claim to be transparent but still fail to produce or distribute financial statements or make copies of their budgets available in a timely manner.

Fiduciary Duty

Another important general strategic consideration is *fiduciary duty*, the bundle of ethical and legal requirements for someone handling other people's money, one of the most important expressions of ethical practice in HSE settings. A *fiduciary agent* is anyone who handles other people's money, and *fiduciary duty* is concerned with the obligations of doing so. The key consideration in HSE financial management is that those handling the finances of a group, partnership, corporation (whether

---

*Each year of the many years that I taught financial management to social work students, at least one student, and in tough times several, would report reluctance or outright refusals from social work administrators to share information about finances with them.

profit making or nonprofit), or government organization have ethical and legally enforceable duties to act with care and due diligence in the management of those finances. This includes abiding by all appropriate local, state, and federal laws; avoiding *self-dealing,* or profiting from inappropriate personal gain; and the need to report such violations by others. Regardless of to whom accountability and fiduciary duty are owed in specific cases—colleagues, board members, stockholders, citizens, clients, community members, the general public, or others—acting in a manner consistent with care and due diligence in financial concerns is the bedrock consideration of the practice of financial management.

Self-Dealing

Public charity is a historical term reaching back centuries in Anglo-American law. It is used by the IRS to refer specifically to tax-exempt and tax-deductible 501(c)(3) corporations, and it is also the source of an important moral precept for all forms of HSE, an idea referred to as the prohibition against self-dealing. Examples would be an HSE administrator who is also a partner in a private company that has a sole source contract with the HSE to carry out its fundraising or a board member whose firm sells supplies to the HSE. Both for those nonprofit HSEs organized as public charities and for other public agencies or for-profit corporations with shareholders who are not involved in the day-to-day operations of service delivery, avoiding the actual practice of self-dealing is very important. Even the appearance of insider transactions between the enterprise and individuals involved in its governance and operations can be extremely damaging to an HSE. Djankov, La Porta, Lopez-de-Silanes, and Shleifer (2008) have constructed a cross-cultural Index of Self-Dealing, which they claim is applicable across at least 73 countries.

Administrative Ethics

Both transparency and self-dealing highlight the importance not only of lawful behavior but also of administrative ethics as a general concern. Social work practice in all settings is guided by ethical principles and standards that place people above profits. That perspective and the ethical posture it implies extend into the management of finances in all cases, including private practice. Although the NASW (2008) *Code of Ethics* provides only limited guidance for administrative matters, it does offer a solid universal starting point for all social work and human services concerns (see Lohmann & Lohmann, 2002, pp. 468–484, for a detailed discussion of administrative ethics in the code). Ethical principles such as (a) doing no harm and (b) putting clients' interests ahead of the individual self-interest of workers or the collective agency create a general ethical environment in which it is possible to address most financial strategies and concerns. But one should not assume that the ethics of human services finance will always be easy, simple, or straightforward. In fact, dealing with ethical questions in the financial context is difficult and challenging work! Nonetheless, members of the social work profession are obligated to take on these challenges.

OVERALL DESIGN

This book is organized using a general systems perspective to the extent feasible (see Figure 1.1). The systemic elements of diverse financial systems associated with many different agencies, programs, and services in all modes of practice make it possible to discuss the broad range of contemporary HSE in a single volume. In the chapters that follow, HSE accounting and budgeting systems are demonstrated to be already well organized, and two additional systems—of financial analysis and operations management—are observed to be emerging.

All of the major financial management texts in social work education have used systems as an organizing framework (Feit & Li, 1998; Lohmann, 1980; Martin, 2001; Mayers, 2004). In particular, the concept of information systems is fundamental. It is important to be clear, however, that some aspects of financial management are more systematic, regular, codified, and monetized than others, whereas others remain downright chaotic!

Another guiding framework of this book is the proposition that there has been a quiet revolution in our understanding of the structure and function of financial management in human services in recent decades. That revolution can be understood in terms of the emergence of coherent HSE accounting and budgeting systems and the beginnings of a similar coalescence in the two other systems. The phrase "quiet revolution," however, deserves to be in quotation marks for several reasons. Most important, the changes that are detailed in this volume have hardly been quiet, and they have been much more gradual than the kind of sudden, dramatic changes often brought to mind by the idea of revolution. As the seemingly superannuated dates of some of the sources cited in this book suggest, this evolution is the buildup of many small changes over more than a half-century of work by a relatively small body of specialists in several disciplines. Taken together, however, for those who know and understand them, these changes add up to nothing less than an intellectual revolution—a paradigm shift in our understanding of financial management in human services. Regrettably, however, another reason for the quotation marks is that, to date, awareness of this paradigm shift has been largely limited to management researchers and specialists. The actual impact on financial management practice in human services has been minimal, at best. In fact, to choose but one thread, actual budgetary practice in most human services

Figure 1.2: Financial Systems Model for Human Services

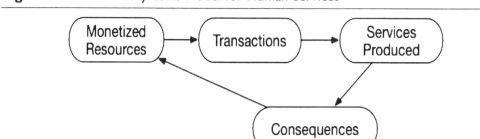

today is far more indebted to developments in the 1920s or 1930s than to any more recent developments (see, for example, Purdy, 1921). The reasons for this lack of impact of the revised paradigm of financial management are highly complex. One of the most important is the continuing strength of the apprenticeship model of human services management. The vast majority of human services managers continue to rise through the ranks, promoted from the direct services for which they were professionally trained, with little or no formal financial management training and no time on the job to master this repertory of new knowledge and skills. So they do what apprentices have always done: learning as quickly and thoroughly as possible to do only the things already being done and doing them in the way things have always been done in their particular organizational setting. Thus, the real revolution in financial practice remains to be finished, a theme that is taken up in the final chapter.

Chapters 2 through 4 discuss necessary background details about the intellectual or theoretical revolution itself. Chapter 5 details current understanding of the nonprofit accounting system, with occasional forays into business and government accounting. Chapter 6 details emergent understanding of budget systems, with further emphasis in the final chapter on resolving the continuing discrepancies between incrementalist (or political) and synoptic (or rationalist) approaches (Wildavsky, 1973). Chapters 7 through 11 focus on various modes of financial analysis, and chapter 12 focuses on financial operations. In chapter 13, the various pieces of these existing and emerging systems are pulled together in a postrevolutionary perspective termed the syncretic financial management system.

In addition to the practical details of financial management practice in these various areas, a small amount of history and theory is necessary to understand the current practice theory of financial management in human services. The gradual revolution in financial management practice in recent decades has arisen from many causes and resulted, with little or no fanfare, in a vastly more sophisticated practice than anything previously existing in human services. Yet, the vast majority of new social workers enter practice in this brave new world with almost no understanding of these systems or their role and scope.

NUMERICAL IMAGINATION

Social workers often mistakenly assume that some advanced knowledge of highly esoteric mathematics is required to understand human services finance. Nothing could be further from the truth. In most cases, basic arithmetic skills are all that are needed, although some limited understandings of basic algebra may be helpful. Perhaps the single greatest talent required in financial management might be termed *numerical imagination*: the ability to mentally link the substantive program activities of the agency with the abstract, monetized numerical world of financial amounts, statements, budgets, analyses, and all the rest. This talent consists, in brief, of the ability to visualize or conceptualize in real (that is, practical, program, and professional) terms the implications of changes in the various numerical qualities of a budget or financial statement.

Balance

Among the most important imaginings in the history of financial management has been the discovery of various dimensions of balance. The core operation of modern accounting, double-entry bookkeeping, originated in Florence, Italy, during the Italian Renaissance, with the publication in 1494 of *Summa de Arithmetica, Geometria, Proportioni et Proportionalita* [Summary of Arithmetic, Geometry, Proportions and Proportionality] by the Franciscan friar Luca Pacioli, a contemporary of Leonardo da Vinci and Niccolò Machiavelli. For an economic historian's discussion of Pacioli's contribution, see Braudel (1986, pp. 573–574). Double entry is, in essence, a system of compiling self-correcting quantitative information in ways that numerical series (noted in right- and lefthand columns known as debits and credits) must always remain in balance (that is, have equal totals in each column), as in the trial balance shown in Table 1.2.

In this way, the Renaissance ideal of a balanced universe was translated into a highly effective system for isolating routine arithmetic errors of addition and subtraction that still influences us today. Such errors will become apparent in a procedure called the "trial balance" (see Table 1.2), so that they can be isolated and corrected. In the case of modern, computer-based accounting systems, balancing accounts is built directly into the code, and the traditional human errors of notation and arithmetic are automatically highlighted for correction. The trial balance presented in Table 1.2 shows left (debits) and right (credits) columns that are equal and likely free of inadvertent arithmetic errors (because the two columns equal or balance one another). The trial balance has numerous other uses as well. For the manager who has learned how to read one, a trial balance offers an early and easy overview of much of the key information shown separately in later, more finished financial statements. One should be aware, however, that this method is named "trial" for a reason, as it is a fundamental test of the accuracy of basic accounting entries. When that test fails (that is, the right- and lefthand columns are not equal, or balanced), it means there are errors that could be anywhere and the information is not reliable until these errors are identified and corrected. This Renaissance idea of balance permeates all aspects of accounting and extends to budgeting, financial analysis, and operations, as is illustrated in later chapters.

CONCLUSION

It may not be self-evident or easy to discern from predominant perspectives on social work theory, but financial management topics reach directly into the heart of professional interests today. Whether it is a question of finding the means to serve clients or discovering the evidence to justify the claims of efficient and effective practice to supporters and skeptics alike, financial management perspectives are important parts of the overall picture. The ability to approach important topics and questions in monetary terms, to deal with important questions of strategy, and to visualize the financial significance of important policy decisions are just some of

Table 1.2: Trial Balance

<Name of Enterprise>
<Date>

Account No.	Line Item	Debits ($)	Credits ($)
	Assets		
101	Cash in bank	49,718.71	
102	Petty cash	150.00	
103	Pledges receivable	8,650.00	
104	Allowance for uncollected pledges	41,112.71	865.00
105	Accounts receivable—client fees	6,141.19	4,712.00
106	Allowances for uncollected fees	4,142.32	4,781.17
107	Inventories		6,118.79
108	Prepaid expenses		917.42
	Liabilities		
201	Accounts payable		95,172.23
202	Payroll withholdings		
203	Accrued expenses		
	Net Income	6,000	
	Income and Support		
301	Unrestricted contributions		78,219.54
302	Allocations from local United Way		98,674.78
303	Contract income		57,241.43
304	Grant income		43,717.48
305	Income from fees		91,366.19
	Expenditures		
401	Wages and salaries	261,487.41	
402	Health insurance	7,844.61	
403	Employer's share FICA tax	22,749.36	
404	Professional fees	31,393.31	
405	Supplies	6,275.68	
501	Communications	12,551.37	
502	Postage and shipping	2,562.57	
503	Office rent	9,924.00	
504	Printing and copying	187.50	
505	Local travel	10,895.29	
506	Trial balances	481,486.03	481,486.03

Note: FICA = Federal Insurance Contributions Act. In financial management, it is often used as a shorthand label for social security–related withholdings from employees' paychecks.

the essential skills required of the contemporary social worker. In the 11 chapters that follow, the reader is guided through the most essential financial considerations driving contemporary practice in human services today. Together, these add up to a quiet revolution in financial management practice that has transformed the handling of financial issues from top to bottom. Finally, in the last chapter the various threads of the existing accounting and budgeting that have emerged and the financial analysis and operational systems that are emerging are pulled together into a single, syncretic model of contemporary financial management practice. An important key to this transformation is the emergent role of the HSE introduced and discussed in chapter 2.

2

Rise of Enterprise in Human Services

A key feature of this book, tying all the chapters and the diverse, multidisciplinary theories and concepts together into a unified whole, is the concept of the HSE. The term is used here to define a single, consistent financial entity that brings together perspectives from organization theory, law, accounting, economics, politics, and other fields. Basic to the enterprise concept is a single lens through which to view money or financial resources and the monetized aspects of people and their behavior, or what is referred to here as *human capital*. Also basic to the enterprise concept is the accounting entity, a concept akin to the unit of analysis in social research that refers to the particular object, fund, group, corporation, or organization for which accounting data are collected, organized, and presented. This could be a corporation, foundation, organization, or program (Martin, 2001, pp. 10–17) or some other collection of valuable resources or assets. With all of this diversity, the term *enterprise* (as in private enterprise, nonprofit enterprise, social enterprise, and public enterprise) offers a common reference point for referring to any human services organization, corporation, program, service, department, or institution as a collective entity.*

THE QUIET REVOLUTION

An ongoing quiet revolution during the past several decades in social administration practice, involving the handling of human and financial resources, has transformed how we view basic financial entities. The delivery of human services becomes more complex each year, but for those who rise to the occasion, this

---

*In the decades-long buildup to the current situation, other entities—notably funds, grants, projects and programs—have at times served as accounting entities in social work. However, major advances in accounting, organization, and community theory now enable the current enterprise, or organization-as-entity, perspective embraced by the accounting profession and the IRS as well as the social work profession.

transformation has also brought a range of new tools to keep the task manageable. Financial options continue to expand, and the range of tools available to deal with finances has become considerably more extensive and refined. Major changes in this area have often gone unnoticed because most have occurred in small, piecemeal, periodic adjustments. However, the cumulative impact on practice has been considerable. Entirely new species of organized service delivery have been added alongside traditional community social agencies, and refinements in managing finances have been close to the core of many of these new practices. Computerized accounting and budget systems and electronic spreadsheets are small but crucial components of the change. Traditional voluntary agency income sources such as donations, foundation grants, and allocations from United Way or other annual federated financing campaigns have been supplemented, first by public grants, later by performance contracts, and then by an ever-increasing variety of financial instruments in managed care, including many arrangements too complex to deal with here (Meezan & McBeath, 2011). Meanwhile, growing numbers of private practitioners have found both solo and group practices and practice in nontraditional host settings to be financially viable. Many different organizing options are available alongside traditional public and nonprofit agencies, including partnerships, trusts, commons, cooperatives, corporations, collaboratives, employee-owned companies, limited profit (Type B) corporations, and others. Services are increasingly categorized not only into public or governmental and community nonprofit agencies but also into third (nonprofit) sectors and fourth (social enterprise) sectors and numerous mixed, blended, or hybrid combinations (for example, collaboratives and public–private partnerships) (Billis, 2010; Ivery, 2008; Poole, 2008; Smith, 2014).

FINANCIAL MANAGEMENT PROCESSES

All of this financial diversity threatens to mask and obfuscate the underlying clarity and universality of certain basic financial management processes. The concept of enterprise offers a unifying way of seeing clearly the common features of this diversity. It is the intent of this book to highlight and detail as clearly as possible the basic processes of HSE as they operate across the full spectrum of contemporary social work practice. Managing the finances of the HSE consists of three types of operations: First are the accounting and budgeting systems. There is almost no possibility that you will ever encounter an existing, operational HSE that does not have clearly established systems, supported by policies and practices in both areas. Even in the most casual and informal group settings, as long as there is a program or project to be pursued, someone will be tasked with the responsibility of projecting anticipated expenses, locating income, and reporting on financial activities. Much of the existing literature on financial management has begun with the start-up process of organizing such systems (see, for example, Lohmann, 1980) and such tasks as defining programs (Martin, 2001, pp. 10–17). We generally forgo that step here. The processes are by now relatively straightforward, well understood, and well documented, and there is no need for another discussion of them here.

There is, at present, enormous variety in how HSEs implement their accounting and budget systems, however. Some are fully electronic; others still use the traditional paper-and-pencil methods used by those who first applied Pacioli's 15th century double-entry bookkeeping. Many (perhaps most) HSEs function comfortably with traditional line-item budgets. Others strive to expand the frontiers of practice with experiments in program budgeting, performance management, zero-sum budgeting, social accounting, innovative investment strategies, and other areas (Fry, 1998; Zietlow & Seider, 2007). Some (especially smaller) nonprofit HSEs continue to function on a strictly cash basis or even use archaic systems of fund accounting (Vatter, 1947).* Many might like to embrace stewardship accounting as well, if only there were such a practical reality (P. Block, 2013; Brinckerhoff, 2004; Caers et al., 2006; J. H. Davis, Schoorman, & Donaldson, 1997; Engdahl, 1991; Levine, 1994; Natarajan, 1996). Although a vast range of tools of financial analysis and operations, such as those discussed in chapters 7–12, are available today, many HSEs fail to take even minimal advantage of the analytical potentials available to them.

In the aftermath of an extended period of innovation—reaching in some cases back to the 1970s and beyond—the principal challenge facing students of financial management today is to accurately understand, describe, and discuss what exists in particular HSEs and why and how to apply this vast repertory of knowledge, skills, and techniques to financial practice in the HSE.

SMALL BITS OF THEORY

In the remainder of this chapter and the chapters that follow, a range of contemporary organizational, accounting, and budgeting concepts and practices are examined. In preparation, several levels of organization theory are pieced together, from the organization of individual enterprises to the organization of communities and sectors. Some of this will be familiar terrain for readers, and no attempt is made to present anything other than the barest of cursory sketches. Then, in the next chapter, we look at a variety of legal forms and economic organization.

Organization Theories

Most authorities agree on the underlying importance of organization theory to an understanding of the general management context. The concept of human services organization offers theoretical context, and organization theory in general explains many aspects of individual behavior and group action. The connection between theories of human services organizations and financial matters, however, is less clear-cut. Nevertheless, there are important connections to be drawn here.

Hasenfeld and English (1974) introduced the perspective of human services organizations as technologies and drew a distinction between people-processing organizations, with their information processing technologies, and people-changing

---

*Note that in the smallest HSEs with only a single program supported by a single funding source, such distinctions are, for most intents and purposes, meaningless.

organizations, with their educational, therapeutic, and transformative technologies. Hasenfeld (2010) seemed to set people-processing technologies aside when he defined *human services technology* as procedures that are "legitimated and sanctioned" by an organization "aimed at changing the physical, psychological, social or cultural attributes of people" (p. 110). These were later characterized as moral, gendered, and "indeterminate" (Hasenfeld, 2010, p. 7). These technologies are said by others to be organized as "open systems" (Scott, 1998), and they may function as repertories of both resources and outputs (Lohmann, 2015).

Selection of particular repertories of technologies represents a strategic choice for the HSE and typically has important resource implications. Thus, people-processing tasks (for example, eligibility determination, voter registration, scheduling, or billing) can often—but not always—be structured as series of simple, straightforward, discrete steps, whereas people-changing tasks are often closely interrelated—in Hasenfeld's terminology, they are moral, gendered, and indeterminate—and involve larger measures of unpredictability, discretionary judgment, and interpersonal continuity. Some of the major implications of Hasenfeld's (2010) distinction are likely to be evident in cost studies, such as those dealt with in chapter 8.

Political Economy

Financial understanding of HSEs is not only concerned with internal organizational dynamics, however. There is also the need to understand aspects of the larger environment. David M. Austin (1981, 1988, 2002) was the principal advocate of political economy perspectives for understanding human services organizations. At its essence, the *political economy perspective* is the view that political and economic as well as other social and cultural factors can be brought to bear to understand organizational functioning. In recent decades, diverse political economy views have been applied to a number of different settings and problems relevant to human services (Chamlee-Wright, 2010; Chamlee-Wright & Storr, 2010).

One of the important questions arising from political economy perspectives involves the structuring of institutions (Ostrom, 1990), and this question has been one of the entry points for the now massive literature on the third sector (Smith, 2014; D. R. Young, 2007). More recently, an entirely new category of socially aware and conscience-driven businesses has emerged and been called by some a *fourth sector* (http://www.fourthsector.net/learn/fourth-sector) (Harper-Dorton & Majewski, 2015).

Nonprofit Financial Research

Kirsten Grønbjerg, at the Indiana University Center on Philanthropy, has authored numerous case studies of the financing of nonprofit human services. For example, Grønbjerg (1993) identified a condition of "reciprocal dependency" between nonprofit human services and community development organizations and their funders and strong continuity in enterprise funding patterns once a particular mix had been developed. A key element in this mix was said to be the reputation of the agency. Grønbjerg (1993, p. 181) concluded that patterns of funding continuity,

Figure 2.1: A "Fourth Sector"?

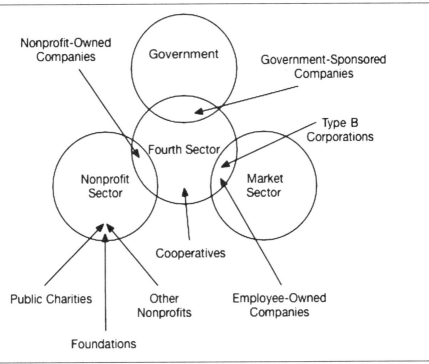

cost sharing, demands on management, and limits on enterprise discretion and autonomy explain why leaders of most HSEs view government funding positively but with some ambivalence. In that same study, Grønbjerg (1993, p. 183) distinguished government funding sources by degrees of discretion, intensity, predictability, mission relatedness, and general assessment.

Nonprofit Organization Theory

Lester Salamon (2015) defined *nonprofit organizations* as formal, voluntary organizations that are not *profit-distributing*, not governmental, and self-governing. This distinction implicitly points to a number of other possible kinds of organizational enterprises: for-profit, governmental, and those that are not self-governing. In Salamon's analysis, nonprofit organizations in the United States are trending away from informal, voluntary associations such as the social work agencies of the late 19th and early 20th centuries and toward more formal organizations staffed by paid, professional employees. They are also moving away from management by citizen volunteers and toward professional management. This history also receives support from Anheier and Themudo (2005), Holland and Ritvo (2008), and numerous others. The perspectives emerging from this and other nonprofit management and organization research offer a useful and reliable characterization of contemporary nonprofit HSEs that distinguishes them from both public sector bureaus and for-profit firms.

Stakeholders

Another of the useful concepts guiding contemporary financial management practice in human services that comes to us from the nonprofit literature is the concept of *stakeholders*, which constitute certain groups or interests of strong, even critical, importance to the programs or services to whom some measure of accountability is due. The classic stakeholders of private practice are the owners or shareholders, whose "stake" is their investment in the business, which brings with it the expectation of a profitable return on investment (R. E. Freeman, 1984). A wide variety of newer forms of stakeholders are also found in and near HSEs today, such as those associated with Type B corporations, the sharing economy, efforts to capture underutilized capacity (for example, food banks, ride sharing, housing material recycling) and other forms of what might be called capitalism without capitalists.

Determining the stakeholders of HSEs can be more complex than identifying shareholders of a publicly held corporation. For ethical reasons, clients are usually given pride of place by social workers as the most important stakeholders of human services. In addition to clients receiving needed services, employees whose livelihood is dependent on the fortunes of the HSE are also among the most important stakeholders of most HSEs. Another important set of stakeholders in nonprofit services are the donors and grant makers whose gifts help the organization to flourish. In the case of purchase of service contracts, those with whom the service providers have contracted are also stakeholders. In the classic voluntary sector model, volunteers are also important stakeholders (Beito, Gordon, & Tabarrok, 2002; Harris, 1996). Board members, community residents, and others may also function as stakeholders. Regardless of the particular configuration of stakeholders in an enterprise, a concern for stakeholders usually leads directly to concern for accountability. In all cases, those who have donated money or in other ways provided important resources will expect to know what was done with their contributions to the cause.

Careful, thoughtful analysis of the stakeholders of an HSE is an essential part of building an effective constituency and transforming stakeholders from the like-minded to active participants in the enterprise. Once an organized constituency has been identified, efforts must be made to maintain their support. An initial strategy can be keeping these constituencies fully informed of the range of benefits they receive to encourage vigorous support for the agency's budget. There simply is no substitute for a large group of satisfied clients and constituents to fall back on. Once the constituents have been identified and courted, there is always room to expand the base of support and increase its role. Furthermore, among large agency followings, there may be some value in identifying specific constituent groups and directing special attention to them. It is important to note that savvy constituency builders always attend to feedback from constituent groups. Many agencies maintain special files of letters of support and testimonials and include these in grant proposals or with budget documents. It is certainly not unreasonable to request such letters from those who already may have offered their verbal support.

Often among novice administrators the question of how to approach constituencies for their support arises. "I can't just beg them to help me, can I?" many a recent graduate has been heard to plead. Indeed not, and carefully working out an approach is one of the elements for success in working with constituents. One commonly used strategy involves the structuring of programs and projects to encourage greater constituency support. The use of advisory committees to generate support is one of the least recognized strategies in many communities. Advisory committees nearly always ask for more resources.

Accountability

Accountability of the HSE to assorted stakeholders is one of the established principles in modern social administration (Lohmann & Lohmann, 2002). However, the details regarding management accountability, to whom and for what, can be highly complex questions (Ebrahim, 2003; Elisha, 2008; Elkin, 1985; E. K. Keating & Frumkin, 2003; Kettner & Martin, 1993b; Martin & Kettner, 1997; Nitterhouse, 1997; Quarter, Mook, & Armstrong, 2009, chapter 9; Sloan, 2009; Steinberg, 2008). Public and nonprofit HSEs do not have owners, partners, or stockholders, whose interest is primarily financial or can be easily addressed in profit-and-loss statements. Nonprofit HSEs are also unlike government agencies, which have precise accountabilities to bureaucratic overseers and legislative bodies and less clear obligations to the tax-paying citizenry. In each case, however, the modern HSE is likely to have assorted groups and individuals in the community and elsewhere to whom it owes responsibility in a range of different ways, financial and otherwise. An important part of financial management involves identifying those various stakeholders and groups and communicating effectively with them. A number of social work agencies may be accountable only unto themselves; that is, professional staff and volunteers may be accountable only to the organization's own trustees and officers. That is not an especially desirable position to be in, however, and such self-sufficient entities might be well served by becoming less so.

In the smallest HSEs, questions of accountability can be woven directly into the fabric of the interpersonal relations among board members, professional and paraprofessional staff, volunteers, and other interested stakeholders. This dynamic is often a key part of the general concern today with social capital. Even so, accountabilities in the small social enterprise can be difficult to sort out, in large part because of the informality of relations. In moderate-sized and large agencies, such "informal organization" accountabilities are often joined by a range of formal obligations spelled out in position descriptions, policy and procedure statements, and other ways. In the largest HSEs, these formal accountabilities can become even more complex. For example, a chief financial officer (CFO) may supervise a department of bookkeepers and others and, in turn, report to the chief executive officer (CEO) individually or to a management committee or group. In every case, it behooves the social work manager to develop as thorough an understanding as possible of who is expected to be accountable to what person or entity, when, for what, and even how and why. The only real principle operating in most cases, other than the need to know and abide by legal requirements, is to understand the individual organization and respect its unique accountability environment.

Outputs, Outcomes, and Performance

Another of the themes woven throughout the remaining chapters involves defining, classifying, and measuring the results of efforts in HSEs. Within the frame of the systems model shown in Figure 1.1, the term *output* is used to designate any of the discrete episodic, timed, or material units of service produced or provided by an HSE (Auslander, 1996; Martin, 1997). Consistent with Hasenfeld's people-changing perspective, the term *outcomes* is used to designate changes in the life-worlds of clients "achieved, at least partially, as a result of their participation in a human service program" (Martin, 2001, p. 66).

Martin (2001, p. 70) includes a very useful distinction between different types of outputs as performance measures. He distinguishes material units (for example, meals, prescriptions, food baskets, vouchers) from episodes (for example, visits, appointments, rides, sessions) and time units (hours, days, weeks, months, quarters, or years). Martin also distinguishes two types of quality performance measures: outputs that meet a stated quality standard and client satisfaction (Martin, 2001, p. 71). Lohmann (1980, pp. 239–241) focused primarily on time units and time-related measures such as the input measure of the service hour and outcome measures such as the problem-free interval.

Together, outputs and outcomes track the performance of an HSE. Kettner and Martin (1996) reviewed the literature and concluded that performance measures should be evaluated in terms of five criteria: their utility or usefulness, precision or specificity, feasibility or ease of collection, costing or ease of cost reporting, and consensus among stakeholders. From this, they made a connection directly between performance and cost concerns: "Any performance measure that cannot be costed out (cost per output, cost per quality output, cost per outcome) will not meet [the Government Accounting Standards Board's service efforts and accomplishments] reporting; thus its utility is low" (Martin, 2001, p. 73). It probably will not be particularly useful for nonprofit or for-profit human services, either.

Together with sometimes elusive notions of quality, performance measures define service effectiveness. Performance can be said to be a composite measure—actually, a kind of magnet—bringing together concerns with the effectiveness of outputs and outcomes, productivity, and the efficiency of resource use (an input consideration). As Martin (2001, pp. 67–69) noted, the Government Performance and Results Act (GPRA) and the Service Efforts and Accomplishments (SEA) initiative of the Government Accounting Standards Board (GASB) impose some very specific measurement and reporting responsibilities on government human services organizations (see also Grasso, 1994; Kautz, Netting, Huber, Borders, & Davis, 1997; Moynihan & Kroll, 2015). The expectations for nonprofit, social enterprise, and for-profit human services are still more diffuse and indirect and less focused. Even so, it is fair to say that there are also very definite accountability concerns with outputs, outcomes, and performance in those enterprises as well. Thus, it is assumed in this book that every HSE has some interest in measuring outputs, outcomes, and performance. Such concerns are woven throughout the discussions of chapters 7–12.

The Voluntary Agency

The earliest form of professional social work practice was in the HSE generally known as the voluntary agency, the ideal type from which contemporary nonprofit human services evolved. As a type, voluntary agencies such as settlement houses and charity organization societies blended characteristics of voluntary associations with formal organizations capable of sustained service delivery (Beito, 2000; Vincent & Plant, 1984). Gathering individual social workers together into a formal organization with a collective accountability to donors and grant makers was a key financial aspect of scientific charity. Prior to the New Deal, as social work became a career rather than a calling, the term *social agency* covered a fairly narrow range of donative and volunteer-driven human services organizations, including charity organization societies, settlement houses, community centers, family services, and programs of hospital and school social work. Each voluntary agency was an informally organized (that is, unincorporated) mixture of volunteers and paid employees operating on the basis of individual donations or grants from foundations, for example, the Russell Sage Foundation. After the 1920s, most voluntary agencies came to rely on annually approved budgets that remained fixed throughout the fiscal year. Such common pool budgets, which divide up and assign known pools of available resources, are still in use today. Accounting practices in voluntary agencies were guided by no GAAPs or audit standards until the 1970s. Accountability was largely effort based (rather than results based) and an abundance of detail about spending patterns substituted for reporting of outcomes or evidence-based results.

The term *social agency* refers explicitly to this history and the voluntary HSE as an actual (rather than purely symbolic) agent of the community and its donors, volunteers, supporters, and other stakeholders (see Figure 2.2). Many of these voluntary sector entities still exist in communities everywhere. From a financial perspective, social agency began long ago in the financial exchanges between wealthy

Figure 2.2: The Triple Exchange of Voluntary Agency Transactions

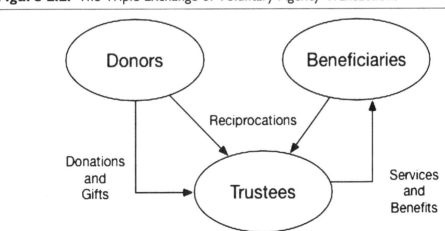

donors and the voluntary social work agencies that accepted their donations. This is a different and more complex configuration from the sales–purchase relations of ordinary business. When a donation is accepted, the HSE becomes the agent, legally and ethically, of the donor.

The central problem of this principal–agent relation in human services is how the *principal* (that is, the individual donor or grant maker whose money is given to the agency, where it becomes fungible, or indistinguishable from every other contribution) can assure that the *agents* (that is, the social workers receiving the donations) are carrying out the donor's intent. The accountability context framed by the GPRA and SEA is designed to deal with public variants of this general problem. Nonprofit incorporation imposes nondistribution constraints, and establishing budgeting and accounting systems are also parts of the answer to that question that have evolved over the past century. A major question posed by both social enterprise and the private practice of social work is the extent to which those principal–agent expectations carry over into those contexts.

Established case law recognizes and reinforces the principle of *donor intent*, that acceptance of a donation for a specific purpose implies a legal obligation to use the donation only in that way. In nonprofit financial management, respecting the difference between such *restricted* and *unrestricted donations* is fundamental (Baker, 1988). Whereas the same norms and laws regarding donor intent apply to donations to for-profit organizations, oversight and enforcement in that area is nearly nonexistent. (Try tracking the donation you make to your favorite charity at the grocery or big box store checkout counter sometime.)

In the movement from agency to enterprise, donations have gone from being the major income stream to one of many sources of income in most human services organizations. Figure 2.3 shows the range and proportions of a typical multiple-funding-source configuration. Sadly, just as a vast range of other types of nonprofit organization, including college and university foundations and hospitals, were discovering the value of donations, human services nonprofits were, by and large, moving away from donations as a major source of funding (Ferreri & Cowen, 1993). Nonetheless, the situation of donations to social agencies marks the historic departure point for HSE concern for financial management.

Financial Management Defined

Management of financial resources, or simply *financial management*, refers to decision making and direction in human services organizations for identifying, locating, collecting, and using money, time, and other fungible resources to facilitate delivery of organized human services and maintain appropriate accountability. The term *fungible* refers to physical or symbolic objects that can be exchanged, traded, or substituted for other things. Money is the ultimate fungible resource. Look in your wallet or coin purse, try to remember where you received each bill or coin, and think about why it might matter (most likely, you can't and it doesn't). Money is entirely fungible, in that any bill or coin can be substituted for any other, and thus there is no reason to attempt to distinguish among or individualize them. People may also be important resources, but they are nonfungible, and remembering

Figure 2.3: Pie Chart of Sources of Income for a Typical Multiple-Funding-Source Organization

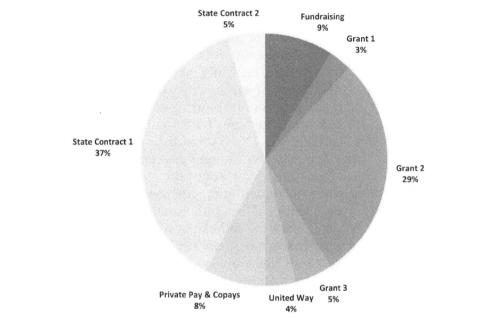

things such as where you met them and what they have done for and with you is vitally important.

Fungibility is sometimes limited in managing finances in human services. Although money is fungible, there are instances, as with some restricted donations, grants, and contracts, where it matters a great deal where certain funds came from (because the people it came from matter) and how they can be used. In this sense, the opposite characteristic of fungibility is designation, or *earmarking*, of selected resources.* Although some income will remain fungible, other income must be tracked closely and accounted for. One of the most fundamental ways in which managing human services resources can vary from ordinary business is in the more pervasive role of earmarking.

Accumulated changes over the past three decades in the management of finances in social work practice have been dramatic. Perhaps most visible to the majority of social workers are those changes related to the spread of public contracting; the introduction of managed health and mental health care; and, more recently, the Patient Protection and Affordable Care Act and the Health Care and Education Reconciliation Act of 2010. As various sources have noted (for example, M. J. Austin & Hopkins, 2004, pp. 3–4; Franklin, 2001; Lohmann & Lohmann, 2002; Munson, 2012; Sowers & Ellis, 2001), these changes have largely obliterated what

---

*The term *earmark* refers originally to the practice of marking the ears of animals (such as a cat having the upper triangle of one ear trimmed off to signify it has been spayed). In financial terms, the term *earmarking* may refer to the practice in banks of folding over a corner (making an ear) of a bill in order to mark it for some purpose.

once was a clear line of demarcation between administrative decision making on financial matters and the resource-directing decisions of therapists, counselors, case managers, and other direct service social workers who could previously practice with little regard for direct fiduciary effects of their actions.

When case managers, therapists, or group workers are given quotas for billable hours or asked to write grants or solicit donations to develop or continue their practice activities with clients, they are explicitly involved in the financial management system, and the demarcations of earlier times between direct and indirect practice become blurry and unclear. A similar blurring of the lines occurs when such service providers are asked to select the type of intervention based on what can be reimbursed. M. J. Austin and Hopkins (2004) provided a succinct summary of the changes in social work practice that have brought direct practice into this mode.

Although most social workers are aware of the continuous daily manifestations of these developments—contracts and agreements, insurance reimbursements, grants of many types, client-paid fees, individual donations, liability issues, and other financial considerations—the full extent of this transformation in the social economy of social work practice may not yet be clear. The quiet revolution in social work financing has transformed financial management slowly over many decades along numerous pathways, mostly by adding entirely new options to the original donation-based "gift economy" of social agencies that formed the more or less exclusive financial structure of social work practice prior to the adoption of the Social Security Act in 1935. Financial arrangements for public human services, such as those described by White (1940) and MacMahon, Millett, and Ogden (1941), have been in almost continuous evolution. This environment of continual exchange is one of the things that gives larger historical significance to the practice of incremental budgeting described in chapter 6. Each increment of change left aspects of the older practices intact, transformed others, and occasionally added entirely new financial arrangements and possibilities.

The result is a financial system of constantly accumulating complexity. The revolution may now be complete in some respects (for example, the accounting and reporting infrastructure known as GAAPs),* while it is still underway in others (for example, measuring outcomes and performance management). It may not be important for students and new professionals to remember all of the key steps of this revolution in detail. Its general outline is recognizable as a transition from agency to enterprise and the blending and blurring of such ideal types (hybridity) that characterize the present reality (Billis, 2010; Harper-Dorton & Majewski, 2015; Smith, 2014).

Voluntary Social Agencies

In large urban communities in the United States, remnants can be seen of what were once known as voluntary social agencies, which were supported by individual donors (whose leaders were sometimes derisively labeled "mother bountifuls"); each agency's fundraising efforts; or the "federated financing" of Community

---

*GAAPs are a set of national and increasingly international principles and standards governing the accounting practices of nonprofit social enterprises. See chapter 5 for details.

Chests, United Way, and other less well known but similar campaigns. Where remnants of this voluntary sector remain in place, these social agencies continue to function much as they have for more than 100 years (Johns, 1946). Since the 1980s, older surviving donor- and volunteer-supported agencies have been joined by a variety of new gift-based charitable agencies responding to new needs but still largely eschewing government grants and third-party contracts for practical, ideological, or other reasons. Some of these new agencies are engaged in service delivery, whereas others are primarily planning and advocacy programs (Gibelman & Kraft, 1996). As financial entities, these organizations still fit with the original meaning of the term *social agency* as agents and stewards of their donors and grantors.

Stewardship, the careful, thoughtful concern for the interests and assets of others, is a primary concern in social agency practice, and as stewards of donations and gifts from others, these are service operations supported financially by what can be characterized as *common resource pools*, a concept discussed in chapter 4. Even today, many free clinics, food programs, and other voluntary social agencies exist, and their true agency financial arrangements are much like the original charity organization societies and settlement houses, out of which 20th century professional social work arose.

These voluntary agencies are, typically, small, nonprofit, and community based, with limited professional staff and ample roles for volunteers and nonprofessionals. Some (for example, religious missions and some more recent faith-based providers) have arms-length relationships at best with the contemporary social work profession, whereas others are fully staffed by professional social workers. Regardless of such permutations, the legal obligations of fiduciary relationships and the financial model of voluntary social agencies remains intact. This is especially evident in the core concern for periodically refreshing through individual gifts and institutional donations, and even subscriptions and memberships, the common resource pools that are subsequently spent down to support their operations. In some respects, the American Red Cross, the Salvation Army, and their many local affiliates, large as they may be, are still exemplars of this type of voluntary agency. Most of the contemporary human services community, however, has shifted to other income models and, in the process, has been transformed.

THE AGE OF GRANTS

It is difficult for students today to understand the social economy of voluntary social agencies as it existed before the current regime of hundreds of different public programs and thousands of foundations making grants. Indeed, in the three decades after the passage of the Social Security Act in 1935 and before the variety of federal grant programs adopted during the Great Society legislative onslaught of 1963–1968, the term *grant* referred almost exclusively to (a) unilateral transfer payments from one level of government (federal) to other levels of government (state, local, or both) or (b) unilateral transfer payments from foundations or federated charitable organizations (for example, United Way) to a nonprofit charitable organization.

First Steps toward Enterprise

Over time, some of the oldest and best known of these voluntary social agencies, some of which predate World War I, have taken quite different and distinct financial paths that led them far beyond the donation-based common resource pools of the traditional voluntary agencies. Some, including numerous YMCAs and Goodwill Industries, recognized their changing economic position early and began developing quasi-commercial funding strategies (often provoking significant controversy), transforming themselves into social enterprises long before that term and the associated notion of a fourth sector arose to characterize them. The many complex practical, ideological, and other reasons for such adaptations are not a primary concern of this discussion (see Gidron & Hasenfeld, 2012; LeRoux, 2005; Lohmann & Lohmann, 2008; Steinberg, 2004; D. R. Young, 1983). Here, we are concerned with the resulting shifts in the financial basis of social work practice. In this vein, a *social enterprise* can be defined as any "business with primarily social objectives whose surpluses are principally reinvested for that purpose in the business or in the community, rather than being driven by the need to maximize profit for share holders" (Department for Business Innovation & Skills, 2011). This definition includes those HSEs that have had to scramble to define new services and new funding sources; those that have had to replace lost grant income; controversial public programs that find themselves in longer and longer arms-length relations with legislators or politicians seeking to distance themselves from controversy; and a wide assortment of private practices that have forged complex networks of support with insurance vendors, statutory public programs, and others. In all of these cases, having to hustle for funding or support is a consistent theme running through their efforts.

The shift from "agency" to "enterprise" terminology deployed here is not a matter of ideology, idiosyncrasy, or intent. It is not a virtue or a curse. It stems from a practical concern for how best to characterize the financial arrangements necessary to support human services and has been evolving for several decades (Frankfather, 1981; LeRoux, 2005; Martin, 1997; D. R. Young, 1983). When Congress backed away from the Economic Opportunity Act (1964), the Revenue Sharing Act (1972), Title XX of the Social Security Act (1975), and other social legislation, it became clear that human services in general would no longer be publicly funded in the United States. All human services organizations realized that without the embrace of a more entrepreneurial attitude, they might be in trouble. Of course, the rise of enterprise is only one thread in the very mixed tapestry that is the funding environment for HSEs, but it is an important one.

For those not comfortable with the term "enterprise," the definition above can be fitted to traditional social work agency terminology with little loss of meaning. *HSE* is a mission-oriented, surplus-applying (that is, not profit-distributing) human services organization of assets that draws on a variety of capitalization strategies, including donations, gifts, grants, volunteer efforts, and various types of sales of its services, to underwrite current operations and generate surpluses for reinvestment in the enterprise and the communities it serves. Note that this definition explicitly includes the social enterprise and community investment modes of private practice in which the proprietors take their own salaries as an expense and plow profits—that is, operating surpluses—back into the practice. Human services practices that place profits over service and seek to maximize returns on investment, where they exist, are outside the purview of this book.

Adoption of a fundamental entrepreneurial posture—often referred to as having to hustle for funding—is one of the key characteristics driving the transformation of social agencies into social enterprises, arising directly out of the twin desires of social workers to provide service and to meet needs. This has sometimes occurred despite—even in the face of—residual antibusiness or anticapitalist attitudes of managers, boards, or the social workers employed there.

Most adopted this posture not so much to make money but to enhance their ability to serve. Contract-based entrepreneurship has been the most direct route to an increased ability to provide services. Funded purchase of service contracts, based as they are on contractual obligations to deliver specified numbers of units of service, quietly, almost surreptitiously, also put many human services into an entrepreneurial posture of capital acquisition (Kettner & Martin, 1985a, 1985b, 1986, 1987, 1988, 1990, 1993a, 1995; Smith, 2014; Smith & Lipsky, 1992). The financial challenges of accurately budgeting resources keyed to the rate of service delivery, actively managing accounts receivable collections, and monitoring the flow of cash into and out of the bank account are basically the same concerns as the typical small service business—including the social worker in private practice trying hard to make a go of it. Despite the slow, organic evolution into social entrepreneurship in human services, many in social work are still wedded to a fundamental distinction between morally elevated nonprofit or charitable social service and morally debased for-profit business (Vincent & Plant, 1984).

Events across a broad front have acted to undermine this once meaningful difference; this can be seen in everything from the development of enterprise accounting for nonprofits, to the shift away from grants to performance contracts, to the increased focus on outcome measurement, to the growth of more robust, educated, and licensed professionalism in social work. The implications of this for managing the finances of the HSE have been little short of revolutionary. As a pair of accounting authorities noted recently, financially speaking, "there are only two fundamental differences between for-profit and nonprofit organizations. First, for-profit businesses have transactions with shareholders, whereas nonprofit organizations do not. Second, nonprofit organizations [can] receive contributed capital* which businesses do not" (Anthony & Young, 2005, p. 468).[†] These authors wrote that statement more than a decade ago. The only part of it that is no longer fully true is the last sentence. Since that comment was published, a growing array of retail establishments have discovered that, in fact, they can collect all manner

---

*The phrase *contributed capital* here means gifts, grants, and donations—the benchmarks of the income base of voluntary social agencies. In social enterprises, such contributed capital functions in combination with other ways of acquiring capital from fees, earned income from investments, capitation payments, and income from an increasingly wide variety of other sources.

[†]Some social workers may not agree with the simple nature of this distinction or may wish for a more complex formulation. Because the authors of this statement are among the leading authorities on nonprofit accounting, the burden of proof currently rests with the doubters to identify other, more essential differences.

of donated capital at the checkout counter as self-appointed agents acting in the name of assorted public charities.

Orphans of Public Policy

The rise of enterprise in human services organizations is particularly evident in one group of HSEs, where risks associated with limited, uncertain, and insecure financial bases have given rise to a particularly aggressive form of social enterprise.* This group of social agencies includes community action agencies, community mental health centers, housing authorities and bodies, local and regional agencies for older adults, diverse community-based agencies, and other *orphans of public policy* originally established during and after the Great Society period and subsequently abandoned by public funders as programs were eliminated or defunded. In a broader sense, this category also includes public and state universities, whose proportion of public funding has fallen from nearly 100 percent in the past to percentages in the low teens or below, forcing them to adopt entrepreneurial strategies, including the current tuition funding regime. The common trait of all of these social enterprises is that they were created or reformed in response to one or more federal policy initiatives and subsequently abandoned by public authorities.

Many community-based service programs did not survive changes in their original or subsequent missions. Others, including hospices and Head Start programs, have been able, through organized political advocacy, to establish newer and more-or-less reliable federal and state income streams through such historic sources as Title XX and revenue sharing or more current sources such as Social Services Block Grants; Medicare; Medicaid; and, most recently, the Patient Protection and Affordable Care Act (Conlan, 1984; Hargrove & Melton, 1987). Agencies in this category responded to the loss of their initial public funding sources by moving into full social entrepreneurial mode, as reflected by the literature on grantsmanship defunding, decentralization, and cutbacks (Coley & Scheinberg, 2008; M. S. Davis, 1999; Dykstra & Aitken, 1984; Geever & the Foundation Center, 2012; Lauffer, 1997). These enterprises engaged in repurposing themselves as necessary by using classic goal displacement maneuvers such as those described by David Sills's (1957) classic study and more recent work on that topic.† They became financial chameleons changing their colors and stripes to adapt to the changing policy environment.

The Chronically Underfunded Agency

A distinct subset of this group found its way to social enterprise by a slightly different route. The central financial fact of life for one group of HSEs is that although public funding gave birth to them, their tax-exempt status still allows donations,

---

*It is worth noting also that in the uncertain environment of the contemporary social enterprise, managing or dealing with risk is one of the essential characteristics. Such risk management is a characteristic often integrally tied to notions of enterprise and entrepreneurship. Thus, in this additional sense, contemporary human services managers are entrepreneurs.

†The contemporary literature of goal displacement studies is vast—and far too large to cite here (see Abramson, 2009; Froelich, 1999).

and their discovery of new and more limited public funding allows them to survive, none of these sources have been adequate to support robust pursuit of the missions these organizations set for themselves. Additional funding is both desirable and necessary. Such circumstances also put a whole group of additional human services organizations in a limited entrepreneurial mode. United Way funding, independent donations, or a narrow spectrum of public allocation or contracts would allow them to survive, but they can thrive only by leveraging the funding they already have to secure additional support.* Moreover, that pursuit requires them to become more entrepreneurial. This group includes a substantial number of multifunded nonprofit human services, whose leaders have elected to pursue mixed income strategies combining gifts and donations, grants, and fee-based services (perhaps also including sliding scale fees and offers of what are, in effect, discounted and pro bono services) (J. Hall, 1975).

TIME

By convention, accounting and budget planning for all of these enterprises both generally occur within a fiscal year framework. This is a simple social convention brought on earlier by the assumption that the social agency is an ongoing enterprise, but it continues to be an important one in practice. A fiscal year for these purposes can be any regular 12-month period. It is usually set by board action, remains consistent over long periods, and is coordinated with the end-of-year closing processes of accounting, IRS, and other state and corporate reporting requirements (Krishman, Yetman, & Yetman, 2006). A major part of what makes financial information comparable is consistency, allowing current data to be compared with last year's figures and next year's projections. Such comparison is only possible if data are organized on a consistent basis over time, which gives rise to two of the essential elements of enterprise budget theory.

A useful time convention that is slowly gaining recognition is the practice of setting data for the fiscal year in a context of a three- or five-year time span that also includes the year or two before it and the year or two after. The advantages of thinking in three-year or five-year, as well as one-year, intervals are many and discussed elsewhere in the text.

CONCLUSION

Key to understanding the rise of enterprise thinking in human services is the way in which, between the 1970s and the 1990s, a large number of social agencies created as agents of public policy were cut adrift by public policymakers, in the

---

*Some funding sources have even translated that into a positive income-support strategy, for example, "we hope that you will use our funding as matching funds as you pursue additional funding." Foundations are well known for offering start-up funds for brief multiyear periods with the full expectation that after the start-up period, replacement funding will somehow appear from somewhere.

full expectation that they would simply disappear. Although many programs and agencies did disappear, unable to survive without the public financial support that was their original raison d'être, those that survived did so by discovering their own forms of enterprise—captured by words such as "hustle," "grantsman-ship," "initiative," "devolution," and "resourcefulness." The long-term effect of this transformation—which is still unfolding—has been to transfer the initiative in human services policy from centralized federal and state public policy and community voluntary leadership to the stakeholders of human services organizations, particularly board members, executives, and key staff members. Along with this aspect of the gradual revolution has been a major shift in ideology, the consequences of which are still unfolding. We look more closely at the legal and other ramifications of this in chapter 3.

3

Human Services Enterprise:
Current Trends

The term *HSE* serves as a linguistic marker for the organization of financial assets and human capital.* The focus in this chapter is on describing and explaining different HSEs, including the range of financial arrangements, and introducing human capital as a factor in human services delivery. Focusing on HSEs as organizations of resources, rather than as organizations of people and their relationships, enables us to bring a consistent financial perspective to the full range of settings of contemporary practice. Current HSEs include everything from the resources brought to bear by individual private practitioners to for-profit, nonprofit, and public enterprises. In the following sections, we look more closely at these options as organized monetized resources. The HSE is an ideal type that can be distinguished abstractly from a human services organization, allowing us to see differences in resource patterns that may not otherwise be clear. Thus, the endowment of a human services organization may be just part of that organization or may be organized as a trust or foundation, that is, a completely separate legal entity controlling its own assets with no corresponding staff or organization.

Many of the references to nonprofit organizations in the social work literature are too imprecise and nonspecific to be of much use in understanding the actual financial organization of HSEs. There are, in fact, more than 25 types of nonprofit organizations identified in the U.S. tax code, where the term "nonprofit" originates. They range from congressionally created nonprofit institutions such as the American Red Cross to cemeteries and black lung trusts. The term "nonprofit" also extends to credit unions (which are, in essence, nonprofit banks); agricultural, horticultural, and labor organizations; business associations (or trade groups);

---

*The discussion in this chapter touches on a variety of complex legal issues or concerns that vary by jurisdiction. The approach is consistently from a management perspective. None of this discussion is intended to offer legal or accounting advice for specific organizations. Dealing with real cases or problems of this sort requires competent professional advice.

political parties; retirement funds; and numerous other possibilities. (For the full list of tax-exempt entities, see http://www.irs.gov/Charities-%26-Non-Profits/Types-of-Tax-Exempt-Organizations.)

In general, the nonprofit focus here is exclusively on three of the largest categories of tax-exempt nonprofits. The most important groups for human services are tax-exempt 501(c)(3) public charities and private foundations to which donations are also tax deductible. Also of limited interest are tax-exempt 501(c)(4) social welfare organizations to which donations are not deductible but that cannot be forced to reveal their members or donors. Following the *Citizens United v. Federal Election Commission* decision by the U.S. Supreme Court in 2010, this group of misnamed nonprofit organizations, which have no necessary connection to social welfare as that term is understood in social work, has become the most important vehicle for funding political campaign advertising.

Looking at finances also necessitates distinctions among organizations in the for-profit category. Most financial organizations identified in the social work literature as for-profit businesses are one of three types of financial organization: (1) *sole proprietorships*, or *solopreneurships*, with assets owned and controlled by a single individual; (2) *partnerships*, or group practices owned collectively by two or more individuals; or (3) *joint stock corporations*, which are incorporated, owned by their shareholders, and managed and controlled by some combination of paid management and a board of directors. This latter category may include closely held corporations owned by a single stockholder, a group of business associates, or family members, and publicly held corporations whose stock sells openly on the world's stock exchanges. Two special types of for-profit corporation that could receive wider attention in human services are member-owned cooperatives and various Type B corporations, with missions of social good and limits on profit distributions.

In the category of public agencies, the range of possible types of organizations is wide and includes legislatively created agencies or *bureaus*, with prescribed missions, annual or regular appropriations, and mandated service programs, parts of which may be delegated or contracted to nonprofit or commercial HSEs, and a growing range of public–private partnership arrangements and blended HSEs (Billis, 2010). Also of interest are those public HSEs that are legislatively created bureaus, that is, departments or programs that have legislatively enacted missions but no ongoing appropriations—a category that includes at least some state social work (and many other professional) licensing operations that are expected to support themselves with fee income. A final category about which little systematic data are presently available is the large and growing range of public–private partnerships; collaborations; and assorted other blends of market, third-sector, and public enterprises. One such arrangement that has been fairly extensively studied is when components of public programs have been contracted out to nonprofit corporations (Boris, 2010; Boris & Steuerle, 2006; Smith & Lipsky, 1992). Such contracting of public services extends far beyond human services to the military; prison management; and a wide range of human services missions in adoptions, foster care, and other public functions. Each of these types of HSE has its own characteristics. The remainder of this chapter examines some of their key features.

SOLOPRENEURS

Theoretically and practically, new human services typically begin in the initiatives of individual practitioners, who act as helpers, founders, advocates, philanthropists, and leaders, as well as in other ways associated with the terms "enterprise," "entrepreneur," or "social entrepreneur." There are many special issues, including "founders' syndrome," associated with solopreneurs in enterprises, issues that have yet to be clearly documented in the social work literature.* From an enterprise perspective, a key resource utilization decision is associated with such individual enterprises. It can be called the *serve, advocate, or organize choice*: Those who discover any social problem in a community may use their personal financial, intellectual, mental, emotional, social, political, and other resources to serve those directly in need; to alert, inform, and advocate for others; or to organize the services needed. Individual services, advocacy, and organized service delivery are all forms of social enterprise, each with its own interesting financial implications. Such individuals—whether acting to simply support themselves; to make a profit; or as unpaid volunteers, community leaders, contractors, or self-employed service providers—form an important category of sole proprietorship or *solopreneurship*. Individuals involved in solopreneurship cannot really be called human services organizations in the usual sense, but they are a form of HSE. Solopreneurs remain in control or ownership of all of the necessary resources—basically, their own money and time. Thus, social workers who supplement their regular salaries by serving as paid consultants, conducting training sessions for which they are paid, or receiving other supplementary income are essentially functioning as sole proprietors, or individually owned and controlled businesses.† In this same category is the social worker who undertakes the entrepreneurial challenges of creating a new organization, program, or service. Many social workers who engage in private practice or advocate for change on the side, that is, in addition to regular employment, do so as solopreneurs.

Solopreneurs are the simplest form of HSE. A solopreneur engaged in private practice can usually rely on the tools and resources of personal financial management to manage the practice. Following a personal budget to keep track of expenses and filing the necessary tax forms pretty well sums up what is necessary; everything else described below is optional. Readily available software applications such as Quicken have all of the resources needed to manage the various kinds of personal accounting systems of solopreneurship; to establish a budget and track bank accounts, credit cards, savings accounts, and investments; and even to process the information needed for personal tax returns. It should be possible to fully manage such an individual private practice, whether full- or part-time, using these resources. Income earned from private practice would be fully taxable; the practice of social work is not inherently a tax-exempt activity, and an individual cannot

---

Founders' syndrome refers to the enduring social and psychological effects (particularly negative ones) of founders who overstay their involvement as programs and services outgrow them (S. R. Block, 2004).
†One financial test is a measure of how others perceive the efforts of solopreneurs and how they perceive it themselves: Do they receive IRS Form 1099 or file a Schedule C on their tax returns for human services–related activities? If so, they are engaged in solopreneurship.

incorporate as a tax-exempt corporation. Taking on additional employees, whether as partners, regular employees, or incorporators, complicates the situation, and professional accounting and legal advice should be sought. The larger and more established such an HSE becomes, the more important the considerations detailed in the following chapters become—from preparing a budget and financial statements to managing cash flows and all the forms of financial analysis discussed. However, on the basis of our current understanding of solopreneurship in human services, there is usually only a single financial stakeholder.

ASSOCIATIONS

Possibly the most fundamental fact of HSE, however, is the social nature of most service delivery—and the underlying necessity of collective choice. No one really does social work or human services alone; even solopreneurship involves a professional and one or more clients. Human services thus always involves others, and that reality—association in its most fundamental sense—is critical in defining the nature of the financial organization of all other HSEs. The major possibilities for organizing the collective assets needed for human service delivery include trusts, partnerships, voluntary associations, nonprofit corporations, cooperatives, joint stock corporations, social enterprise corporations, and foundations. Each of these types of economic and legal organization has unique characteristics, advantages, and disadvantages and may be useful under different circumstances. In the following paragraphs, we briefly review some of the most important of these characteristics and implications.

TRUSTS

One of the most fundamental and long-standing ways of organizing monetized resources, or *assets*, is the *trust*, a legal instrument whereby a donor (the *principal*) sets aside a certain body of assets to be managed by another individual (the *agent*) or group (*agents*). A trust is typically not a formal human services organization in the usual sense, but it can be a financial organization, or HSE, in the sense used here. A trust typically involves a small association of donors, agents, and beneficiaries. It is the most fundamental form of the tripartite financial exchange, or third-party transaction shown in Figure 2.2 (Weber, 1991). Large trusts might result in the establishment and operation of formal human services organizations, for example, when they specify conditions paralleling those of an operating foundation (discussed later). Trusts are a legal form that stretch back to the 1601 English Statute of Charitable Uses and even further through the European Middle Ages, ultimately to the foundations of ancient Roman law. Marion Fremont-Smith suggested that trusts might have been a more appropriate form for the financial organization of modern human services than the ubiquitous nonprofit corporation (Fremont-Smith, 2004, pp. 19–114, 133–148). This did not occur, however. From the start, federal discretionary grants mandated tax-exempt nonprofit 501(c)(3) corporations rather than trusts as conditions of eligibility. Thus, in the current financial world, human services managers are likely to encounter trusts only in the form of bequests, living or other wills, formal endowments, and other such forms (Wymer, Scaife, & McDonald, 2012). An essential characteristic of an HSE financial trust is *fidelity*, the degree to which the trustees act in conformity with the stated wishes of the principal. This same principle, termed "fiduciary responsibility," is applicable to corporate board members and directors, which is the reason they are sometimes also called "trustees."

GROUP PRACTICE: PARTNERSHIPS AND PROFESSIONAL CORPORATIONS

One of the most fundamental forms of association is the small group, as most social workers are aware. Boards, committees, task forces, coalitions, collaborations, and working groups of many kinds fall under this heading.* An important option for a solopreneur wishing to organize is to seek out others and to form or join a group including them. A special, enduring form of such coalitions is one in which an individual practitioner joins with others in the collective effort that accountants and lawyers call *partnership*. An organized partnership may consist of social worker partners only or may involve medical or other professionals. Partnership was the traditional preferred form of monetized organization for both physicians and lawyers. Partnerships are ordinarily governed by agreements that specify what monetized assets (cash, securities, intellectual or other property, and so forth) each member of the group, or *partner*, brings to the practice and how profits are to be distributed among the partners. An HSE partnership agreement in which it is stipulated that partners will be paid salaries and all (or most) financial surpluses will remain in the partnership is possible.

As a form of monetized organization, the most important characteristic of partnerships is that partners are all jointly liable for the actions of the partnership. Thus, if one partner engages in illegal or unethical conduct, all partners in the group could be held accountable for the resulting fines, penalties, or damage awards. For this reason, it is difficult to see why any social workers might establish such partnerships and why they would not prefer the legal advantages of professional corporations or professional limited liability corporations. The particular legal advantages and disadvantages of partnerships and professional corporations for human services are beyond the scope of this work, however.

UNINCORPORATED ASSOCIATIONS

The most distinctive form of HSE in the early history of social work up until the 1960s was, in fact, not a monetized organization at all. Before federal grants on a larger scale

---

*Group theory is important for understanding this form of HSE but is not covered here. Several good guides to group theory are available, although most do not deal with the financial aspects of group practice.

highlighted the nonprofit corporation and before purchase of service contracting expanded the range of HSEs to include private practice and for-profit organizations, most HSEs simply existed or functioned as voluntary associations with no formal legal status or financial or economic organization. The legal term for this arrangement is "unincorporated association." The sociological term is "voluntary associations," which for the most part also fits easily into the social work designation of "groups."

Until quite recently, the major financial characteristic of all unincorporated associations has been their lack of legal standing; they could not, for example, be sued, sue, enter contracts, or have their own tax liability. It has not always been feasible or cost effective to establish formal trusts, partnerships, or corporations for all forms of human service, but laws in many states now recognize certain limited rights for unincorporated associations, which are still found in a variety of forms of community practice. Examples of these include various development- and neighborhood-organizing committees or efforts; disaster response efforts; and advocacy, mobilization, and social justice efforts. Sometimes, the membership of a shifting alliance of groups, networks, and relations is just not clear. In other cases, protecting the anonymity of participants may be an important strategic concern. In the early stages of some organizing efforts, there may be a strong reliance on human capital factors such as innovative ideas, connections, and networking, with little or no financial capital involved.

Unless an association owned or received property or large bequests or had some other reason to act, many early human services enterprises simply got together and carried forth, with little or no thought of the legal or financial ramifications. The same may be true today more often than is generally realized or acknowledged. The unincorporated association model was a very workable arrangement for earlier times, and we should be reluctant to be too critical of it today.

In recognition of this reality, a number of states have recently extended legal rights and restrictions to unincorporated associations, including the ability to sue, to be sued, and to enter contracts. Since 1987, many state legislatures have adopted the Uniform Unincorporated Nonprofit Associations Act (1996) and, in 2008, the National Conference of Commissioners on Uniform State Laws endorsed the more expansive Revised Uniform Unincorporated Nonprofit Associations Act (National Conference of Commissioners on Uniform State Laws, 2011), since adopted by a number of states. The major impact of these statutes is the creation, in more limited forms, of something like the legal personality feature of corporations and limit setting on the liability of individual members of the association. Thus, associations may, under some conditions, be able to enter contracts, sue (and be sued) in court, and possess some other features of collective legal identity. Unincorporated neighborhood and grassroots community associations are among the largest beneficiaries of these new arrangements.

Even though the members of an association, task force, or collaboration may all be employed by other HSEs, such an unincorporated association may have its own financial resources and engage in decisions with financial implications. As a form of monetized organization, the most important characteristic of voluntary human services groups is that all members of the group could, under certain circumstances, be individually liable for the actions of the group, or the association itself may be treated as a separate legal persona, much like a corporation. Prudence dictates finding out the legal implications that hold in a particular state. For those social workers who regularly serve on such groups, it may be advisable to gain a clear understanding of such practical matters as the applicable state law and whether the professional liability insurance coverage of the social worker or employer extends to such instances.

FUNDRAISING CAMPAIGNS

One form of association that is sometimes conducted as an informal association is a fundraising campaign. In the past two decades, the professional literature on fundraising has grown enormously (see, for example, G. D. Alexander & Carlson, 2005; M. R. Hall, Sowell, & Institute for Governmental Service, University of Maryland, College Park, 1994; Kelly, 1998; Marx, 2000). One of the more unusual and difficult to classify forms of HSE is the federated fundraising campaign.

Fundraising can be difficult to fit within contemporary organizational and enterprise perspectives. It tends to exist in a variety of distinct forms. One form is the permanent staff member or fundraising department of a larger organization. Most contemporary colleges and universities have quasi-independent foundations, development staff, or both. Although some contemporary HSEs have similarly established fundraising programs or organizational units, most do not. In fact, in small nonprofit organizations, which may be the most pervasive organizational form of HSE, the executive director may simply put on her fundraising hat and add fundraising to many other duties.

The most pervasive form of HSE in fundraising practice is probably the campaign, a time-limited temporary social and financial organization. Other important fundraising organizations are special events. American fundraising is typically invested in a simplified sociology of stratification that distinguishes large and small donors and tailors different fundraising techniques to each stratum. We explore some of the implications of this in the discussion of income strategies.

CORPORATIONS

Corporations are one of the most interesting, complex, and pervasive forms of organized HSE. As an HSE, a *corporation* is a legal enterprise that has been granted a state charter recognizing it as a legal person with rights and responsibilities distinct from its members. The peculiar Anglo-American legal doctrines of incorporation only began to assume something of their current form in the 1930s with the adoption of the Revenue Acts. Incorporation is a state-level action that allows corporations to be taxed and parties to sign contracts, sue, and be sued in court and possess other characteristics as legal and financial actors. Among these are the recognition by federal and state tax authorities that certain corporate missions or purposes are exempt from taxation and the provision that donations to a subset of tax-exempt corporations may also be tax deductible for the donors.

After more than 100 years of little notice or controversy, the idea of corporations as legal individuals (which dates from an 1880-era court decision) suddenly became politicized when two highly divisive Supreme Court rulings granted corporations not only the traditional legal rights of individuality (to sue and be sued, to represent themselves in court, and so forth) but also the rights of political citizens (that is, free speech, considering that money is a form of speech), thereby effectively decimating the existing system of campaign finance reforms.

Despite its clumsy and misleading label, the doctrine of legal personality will probably survive the current controversy out of sheer necessity, as there is currently no other way under U.S. law to deal with collective action. Major portions of the entire U.S. economy, including most of the human services system, currently rest on the structure and actions of corporations. Several separate types of corporations are of greatest interest for human services: several types of tax-exempt nonprofit corporations; two types of joint stock corporations, namely, those that are closely held (or privately owned and controlled) and those that are publicly traded; and new Type B, or limited profit and limited liability, corporations. A few comments on each are in order here.

NONPROFIT CORPORATIONS

With few exceptions, corporations are chartered under state laws (which tend to vary somewhat) but categorized by federal tax law. In the current categorization, Sections 501(c)(1) through 501(c)(28) of the Internal Revenue Code all refer to various forms of nonprofit entity. Section 501(c)(3) (tax-exempt and tax-deductible) is the single largest of these categories. Contemporary HSEs typically operate as 501(c)(3) corporations, various forms of for-profit corporation, or public agencies. Community action agencies, community mental health centers, area agencies on aging, family services, local chapters of the Boys & Girls Clubs of America, United Way chapters, and thousands of other HSEs have all been incorporated as 501(c)(3) corporations.

501(c)(3) Corporations

The IRS further divides tax-exempt 501(c)(3) corporations into two types: public charities and foundations. Public charities are generally HSEs that pursue some purpose (including most human services) historically defined as public charity work; have an active program of generating income from contributions by the general public, government sources, private foundations, or other public charities; or actively work to support other public charities. Foundations, by contrast, are generally organizations that receive the majority of their funding from a single source or a small number of sources and make grants to public charities.

The key financial feature of 501(c)(3) corporations is the *nondistribution constraint*, which has two parts: To be incorporated by their states, nonprofit corporations typically must include a provision in their articles of incorporation that none of the funds they receive may be distributed as profits or returns on investment to shareholders or owners. The second and equally important part, termed a *dissolution of assets clause*, specifies that in the event of the closure (or dissolution) of the corporation, any remaining assets after all obligations are paid must be distributed only to another legitimate 501(c)(3) entity. This is both a recognition of original donor intent (known as the *cy pres doctrine*) and a way to prevent the creation of bogus tax-exempt nonprofit groups or solicitation and receipt of donations for allegedly charitable purposes followed by quick dissolution and distribution (or cashing out) to the creators of untaxed profits. Whereas such a possibility may seem farfetched to the typical honest social worker, the IRS and the courts deal regularly with many such actual cases, and receiving a 501(c)(3) designation from the IRS involves proving that both provisions are in place.

501(c)(4) Corporations

A related IRS category is that of 501(c)(4) corporations, known by the misleading label of "social welfare organizations." The term "social welfare" here has no connection to the ordinary social work uses of the term. Chambers of commerce, Rotary clubs and other civic leagues, incorporated neighborhood associations, community betterment groups, homeowners' associations, and volunteer fire departments all fall under the 501(c)(4) designation. These corporations are exempt from state and federal taxes, but donations to them are not tax deductible. One reason for this is that in 501(c)(4)s, those donating to the organization typically also receive important benefits from the corporation—membership benefits, neighborhood services, fire protection, and so forth—in ways that donors to 501(c)(3)s do not. In 501(c)(3)s, the presumed benefits—apart from the warm glow of charitable contributions—go to others as in the three-way transaction shown in Figure 2.2. In addition, however, 501(c)(4)s, like 501(c)(3)s and other types of associations, are allowed to keep their donors confidential, which is where their strategic use in political campaigns arises. The origins of this doctrine are usually traced to the civil rights movement in the late 1950s and to efforts of segregationist states to disrupt civil rights organizing by obtaining the membership lists of civil rights groups. In *NAACP v. Alabama* (1958), the U.S. Supreme Court first upheld the right of private membership associations to withhold their membership lists from public authorities.*

THE THIRD SECTOR

Transformation of the voluntary agency into a nonprofit enterprise is just one of the many pathways that have brought large numbers of social agencies into increasingly entrepreneurial postures today. Most local affiliates of major national voluntary agencies—the Salvation Army; Catholic, Lutheran, and Jewish social

---

*It is important to note here that under current doctrines of constitutional law, any differences between "for-profit" and "not-for-profit" associations or organizations are (or ought to be) a matter of indifference to government, except as it involves tax policy.

services; the Boys & Girls Clubs of America; Family Service Associations of America; and Travelers Aid International, for example—have made this transition. Since the 1980s, recognition of an underlying coherence arose out of the sheer variety of these voluntary, quasi-public, contract-based, entrepreneurial, multifunded non-profit agencies through the growing popularity of the third-sector concept. The third sector is distinguished from the market (or private, for-profit) sector and the governmental (or public) sector. In addition to *third sector*, this grouping is also sometimes referred to as the nonprofit, nongovernmental, independent, philanthropic, voluntary, or social sector and civil society.

The transformations of the rise of enterprise and the growth of the third sector are closely related to larger trends in the economy, polity, and society. At first, a phenomenon termed "cutback management" achieved a great deal of attention in the social work management literature during the first flush of what American sources call the "new conservatism" and Europeans call "neoliberalism" in the Reagan–Thatcher era of the 1980s (Angelica & Hyman, 1997; Baker, 1988; G. Barber, Slavin, & Barnett, 1983; Brooks, 1995; Demone & Gibelman, 1984; Finch, 1982; Friedman, 1995; Glazer, 1984; Haynes & Mickelson, 1992; Jamieson, 1982; Mason, Wodarski, Parham, & Lindsey, 1985; Nakamoto & Altaffer, 1992; Pawlak, Jeter, & Fink, 1983; Reisch & Taylor, 1983; Stoesz & Karger, 1993). In some respects, the era of cutback management and devolution also signaled the dawn of new and relatively greater austerity for human services and the beginning of a more complex financial environment for HSEs.

A national classification scheme of third-sector enterprises, the NTEE has gained acceptance with diverse national peak associations such as NASW, the United Way of America, and Independent Sector as well as state attorneys general, the IRS, and the National Accounting Standards Board. Organizations such as the Foundation Center, the National Center for Charitable Statistics, Guidestar (http://www .guidestar.org), Charity Navigator (http://www.charitynavigator.org), ProPublica's Nonprofit Explorer (https://projects.propublica.org/nonprofits/), and a growing body of researchers use the third-sector concept to advantage. Journals such as *Human Service Organizations* (previously *Administration in Social Work*), the *Journal of Community Practice, Nonprofit and Voluntary Sector Quarterly, Nonprofit Management and Leadership*, and *Voluntas* have published studies based on this organizing rubric. The underlying idea that much contemporary human service is not quite governmental in auspice and not profit-oriented places it squarely in this other realm called the *third sector*.

The model of an organized third sector juxtaposed against state and market leads easily to a more expansive view of a sector consisting of more than simply tax-exempt service delivery organizations. Recently, an older concept has been revived: the *social economy*, which in the current American context refers to public charities, foundations, cooperatives, and financial mutual organizations such as credit unions and housing funds (Lohmann, 2007; Mook, Quarter, Armstrong, & Whitman, 2015; Quarter, Mook, & Ryan, 2010; Van Til, 1988). The third sector, civil society, and the social economy are not the only such new rubrics to have been recently suggested, however. Two others are the notion of a fourth sector of social enterprise and a category of faith-based services.

THE FOURTH SECTOR

The fourth sector is an attempt to capture a variety of real-world fusions of traditional philanthropic, charitable, social welfare, human services, and other missions with the language, worldviews, and profit-oriented objectives of business. This is still a very unstable, even volatile idea, and the fourth-sector concept has been prolific in generating labels in an attempt to categorize the various entities thought to be included therein, including cooperatives; social businesses; ethical corporations; new profit companies; blended value, chaordic, and community wealth organizations; civic, municipal, faith-based nonprofit, social economy, sustainable, and social enterprises; and community development, common good, and community interest corporations (Harper-Dorton & Majewski, 2015). A fourth sector might also include elements of the sharing and social economies discussed in later chapters.

Although the idea of numbering may be growing stale, the economic concept of sector—as in the information sector, the transportation sector, the entertainment sector, and so forth—is actually very useful, and the prospect of seeing many additional sectors proclaimed under the heading of the social economy is very real (Mook et al., 2015).

FAITH-BASED SERVICES

One of the enduring conundrums posed by current sector approaches concerns how to categorize religious organizations. Upward of half of all 501(c)(3) public charities in the United States are religious organizations, and many more are unregistered. Many other religious organizations are incorporated in their states. Does that make them eligible for inclusion in the third sector, along with all of the various secular public charities? Or do they form a separate, distinct sector—a fifth, a sixth, or some other number? Regardless, there are some significant differences between religious and other organizations over and above differences in religious belief. Notably, religious nonprofit organizations are exempted on First Amendment grounds from having to report their financial activities to the IRS on Form 990. Even so, many still complete the tax return, and from these at least a partial picture of religious charities is obtained. Further clarifying this picture is emerging research by nonprofit scholars, a few of them closely associated with social work, including Ram Cnaan, Bob Wineburg, and Stephanie Boddie, among others (see, for example, Cnaan, Wineburg, & Boddie, 1999; see also other work by Harris, 1996). There are also a few specialized forms of financial organization that apply only to religious organizations—for example, tithing and fundraising by offerings—that are beyond the scope of this study.

THE EVANGELICAL COUNCIL FOR FINANCIAL ACCOUNTABILITY CODE

There is little question that financial concerns weigh heavily on religious organizations, and this has given rise to the pursuit of best practices and also the only code of financial standards and practices in the field today (Zech, 2010). The Evangelical Council for Financial Accountability (ECFA), established in 1979, has established a set of financial standards for religious organizations.* (The language of the code bears every sign of having been drafted by a committee, so it is reworded slightly here for readability.) In addition to a required initial statement of commitment to religious doctrine, the ECFA code includes roughly a dozen basic standards that can be applied equally well to most ethically minded HSEs. There is currently no other body comparable to the ECFA in setting financial and compensation expectations for the remaining half of the U.S. nonprofit community nor anything as explicit as the ECFA standards and compensation policy anywhere in human services. In addition to the important connections many people draw between religion and morality, the ECFA financial standards can, in important respects, be said to speak to both.

To meet ECFA standards, enterprises must be managed by a board of at least five independent members that meets at least twice a year to establish policy and review results. The numbers here are somewhat arbitrary but also provide specificity in standard setting. The board must provide financial oversight that includes regularly preparing complete and accurate financial statements. The board or a financial committee consisting of a majority of independent members must also provide for an independent audit, review the annual financial statements, and maintain appropriate communication with an independent certified public accountant, who is expected to inform the board of any material weaknesses in internal control and any other significant risks. The board, its finance committee, and designated employees are also expected to exercise the appropriate management and introduce sufficient internal controls to provide reasonable assurance that all of the organization's operations are carried out and resources are used in a responsible manner and in conformity with applicable laws and regulations, such conformity taking into account biblical mandates (Coe & Ellis, 1991; Stevens, 2004; Wooten, Coker, & Elmore, 2003). (The reference to biblical mandates is one of only two explicitly religious references in the ECFA code.) This includes transparency, such as providing copies of current financial statements upon written request and any other disclosures required by law (Aranoff, 2003). In addition, organizations are expected to set the salaries and other benefits of their top leaders and address related-party transactions (self-dealing) in a manner that demonstrates integrity and propriety and conforms to a separate code, the ECFA's Policy for Excellence in Compensation-Setting and Related-Party Transactions. Finally, organizations are expected to be good stewards of funds and truthful in communications. They are to honor donor intent, guide and advise givers to "adequately consider their broad interests," avoid knowingly accepting gifts from or contracting with givers in a manner that would "place a hardship on the giver or place the giver's future well-being in jeopardy," and not base compensation of fundraising contractors and consultants or its own staff directly or indirectly on a percentage of charitable contributions raised. This latter point is one of the oldest provisions of fundraising ethics: Fundraisers should not be rewarded for their efforts with incentives or percentages of donations.

---

*The complete code can be found online at the ECFA Web site (http://www.ecfa.org/Content/Standards).

JOINT STOCK CORPORATIONS

Most comparisons of for-profit organizations with nonprofit organizations are, in reality, comparisons of public charities, 501(c)(3)s, with joint stock corporations that make no attempt to deal with important nuances such as the issues raised by the nondistribution constraint or new forms of capitalism in evidence in various fourth-sector organizations and the sharing economy. In the context of financial management, such differences are vital and have many ramifications that have yet to be explored.

Joint stock corporations may be closely (that is, privately) held or publicly traded on various stock exchanges. There are three types of joint stock corporations: ordinary (or Type C) corporations, which are legally obligated to maximize shareholder returns on investment; Type S, or pass-through corporations; and social enterprise corporations of Type B (for benefit), whose corporate charters may place limits, restrictions, or conditions on maximal profit seeking. Human services are provided by social workers in all types of corporations, and those social workers are subject to the same orientation to be profit-minded as all other corporate employees. Whether this is problematic depends on many factors. The economic and financial implications of social work in private, corporate practice have yet to be thoroughly analyzed, and whether there are important differences from the financial perspectives presented here remains to be seen.

COOPERATIVES

Human services provided by cooperatives are one of the types of enterprise currently claimed by both third- and fourth-sector enthusiasts (Harper-Dorton & Majewski, 2015; Mook et al., 2015; Rothschild & Whitt, 1986). Cooperatives are member-owned businesses, and some are also publicly traded corporations. It may be reasonable to think of them as joint stock corporations in which stock ownership is conditional upon participation in the company. (Another potentially related category is employee-owned corporations.) When they first appeared in Europe and North America in the 19th century, cooperatives were generally partisan, ideological forms of economic organization, with a strong emphasis on economic cooperation, and often organized in direct opposition to market monopolies, conglomerates, and other actors powerful enough to hold down prices to independent producers (farmers, for example) or to overcharge consumers (electrical utility or grocery customers, for example). In this context, Johnston defined cooperatives as "self-help organizations, formed voluntarily . . . by groups of people wishing to meet a common need. Ownership and control rest equally with all members" (Johnston, 1950, p. 1383).

In Canada and some parts of the United States, cooperatives are common, particularly in agriculture, food services, retail industries, energy, housing, and childcare. At one time, cooperatives were also proposed as potential solutions to the shortage of health care in rural areas (Johnston, 1950). Some health care economists have suggested that private hospitals are de facto doctors' cooperatives. There is a substantial international professional literature, including publications on general practitioner cooperatives in health care (see, for example, Giesen, Ferwerda, & Tijssen, 2007), even though such coops are virtually unknown in the United States.

A keyword search of Guidestar.org on July 6, 2015, found 932 references to human services cooperatives, but the majority of these appeared to be 501(c)(3) public charities with the words "cooperative" or "cooperation" in their titles. Perhaps typical of these is the Cooperative for Human Services in Lexington, Massachusetts, founded in 1981 with a focus on disabilities programs in accordance with the Americans with Disabilities Act in 1990 and preceding legislation. Cooperative Home Care Associates in the Bronx, New York (http://www.chcany.org), is a worker-owned human services provider with a dual focus on service provision and job creation. A national nonprofit organization called Green America, formerly Co-op America (http://www.greenamerica.org), is a source for further information on human services cooperatives.

There are several kinds of cooperatives. For example, purchasing cooperatives jointly purchase services or supplies for their organization members as a way to lower operating costs. In the business world, Ace Hardware is a cooperative of independent hardware stores that pool their buying power to purchase inventory. Two other fundamental forms of cooperatives are producer and consumer cooperatives, in which the costs of production—and the resulting profits—are shared among a membership of producers. Several large food producers, including Land O'Lakes, Florida's Natural, and Ocean Spray, are examples. Consumer cooperatives are organized by consumers seeking to achieve better prices or improved quality in the goods or services they purchase. In human services, many childcare cooperatives begin as solutions to the problem of finding affordable childcare faced by the working mothers who are members. A number of feminist providers of human services have also pursued cooperative organization principles at times in their history. Although cooperative ideas such as worker ownership and economic participation of clients in services are very appealing, the cooperative as a form of human services delivery has never spread very widely.

TYPE B CORPORATIONS

Type B corporations are the most important recent addition to enterprise types, owing to the growing social enterprise movement. At the time of Lohmann (1980), such possibilities were still far in the future, with discussion constrained to the possibility of limited dividend corporations. Since then, a great deal of practical activity, organizing, and policy making has brought this new type into reality. Starting with certain pioneering ventures, such as Paul Newman's food products and Ben & Jerry's ice cream, a variety of conventional businesses declared, in effect, that "we want to make money, sure, but we don't need to maximize profits and, more important, we want to do some good at the same time."

This is also now a viable option for the private practice of social work. In 2010, Maryland became the first state to allow benefit (or Type B) corporations, and, since that time, at least 27 other states have followed suit. In contrast to the nonprofit corporation, prohibited by law from distributing profits; the ordinary business corporation, mandated by law to maximize returns on investment for its shareholders; and the cooperative, expected to reap benefits for its membership; the Type B corporation is created for profit-oriented public benefit, is not tax exempt, and is not required to do more than clarify for its owners and shareholders its intent. For example, "Our corporation will contribute 50 percent of its gross operating surplus to charities of the board's choosing." Of course, public charities, business corporations, cooperatives, and benefit corporations are all ideal types, and the possibilities of combining them in various ways are nearly endless.

PUBLIC SOCIAL AGENCY

The last major category of contemporary human services enterprises to be mentioned here are public agencies—primarily in state and local governments with a smattering of federal and local public agencies—with human services missions. There are an estimated 3,000 to 4,000 public human services agencies in the United States. They are located in all 50 states and the five populated U.S. territories, most of the 3,144 counties in the United States, and an unknown number of civil subdivisions in the territories. In addition, there are 310 federally recognized Native American reservations with some measure of public service powers and an undetermined number of metropolitan, city, town, and village public agencies. This is not counting the assorted other incorporated nonprofits created by governmental action or as public–private partnerships.

The principal characteristic of public enterprise is the need for explicit delegation of authority: Services offered by public agencies and public officials are generally legal only if conducted under the auspices of a specific law, statute, or ordinance, with a clear chain of authority between the law and the service. This is in marked contrast to the latitude granted to nonprofit and for-profit enterprises to engage in any actions consistent with their mission that are not explicitly illegal. Within their mandates, public agencies may either conduct their own programs or make grants or enter contracts with others to do so. In the context of efforts to reduce the size and scope of government, such contracting out has, in fact, become a major dynamic of governmental action.

The move to contracting has brought fundamental changes in the public social agency financial model of practice. Notably, an entire class of social workers working in public agencies is now engaged in management of contracts with actual service providers. This has also lent a practical necessity to the case for outcome and effectiveness measurement as reflected in the expectations of the GPRA and SEA requirements.

FEDERATED FINANCING AND ENTERPRISE

One of the most interesting forms of HSE has a somewhat oblique connection to formal organizations. Beginning with such enterprises as the U.S. Sanitary

Commission during the Civil War, continuing through the Community Chest movement* during World War I to the present, there is a long history of public–private partnerships, interagency collaboration, shared funding, and a host of similar arrangements (Boris & Steuerle, 2006; Ebaugh, Chafetz, & Pipes, 2007; Hardy & Phillips, 1998; Snavely & Tracy, 2000; Tropman, 1972). A brief history of United Way, a well-known example of federated financing, is provided on the organization's Web site (http://www.unitedway.org/about/history; also see Russell Sage Foundation, 1919). The dimensions of such activities are many and varied, but the notion of federated financing is common to many of them. The fundamental idea of federated financing is that of a collaboration—a group or network of service providers working together with other stakeholders in a collective fundraising effort and allocative planning arrangements for dividing the collection (Kleinman, 1985).

The principles of federated financing were already well understood before World War I. The basic idea is that scale and scope economies that are not otherwise possible can be achieved when large groups of enterprises raise funds together (Mester, 1987). Scale economies are saved and lower costs realized with shared resources or increased volume of output. The scale economies of federated fundraising take advantage of the reality that many fixed costs of a fundraising campaign will be the same whether the campaign is conducted for one enterprise or dozens. Using previously unused capacity (like underutilized employees who serve as "loaned executives") is one of the most familiar strategies of these scale economies (Eschman, Schwartz, & Austin, 2011; Kane, 1993). Federated financing as an HSE is a seriously understudied phenomenon that could benefit from more research (Aft & Aft, 2009; Barman, 2006; Brilliant, 1990; J. S. Glaser, 1994; Marx, 2000).

The two largest examples of federated financing for human services are the 4,000 community members worldwide of the United Way Worldwide network (formerly United Way of America) and the Combined Federal Campaign for employees of the U.S. government. Some states also have their own state employees' campaigns modeled on the Combined Federal Campaign. One of the reasons for the long-term effectiveness of all of these examples is the focus on workplace giving, but the concept itself may be evolving (see Barman, 2006). Traditional federated workplace giving programs may be losing ground to other workplace-centered giving. H. Art Taylor, president and CEO of the Better Business Bureau Wise Giving Alliance, observed, "Many businesses offer other alternatives ranging from matching payroll contributions designated for community charities selected by employees to engaging staff with electronic and social media donation activities" (Taylor, 2015, para. 1). Note that the first option identified by Taylor represents a kind of in-house federated financing campaign for those organizations. The United Way approach may also face increasing pressures associated with the growth of social enterprise businesses if the business representatives on local United Way boards support preferential funding for these more businesslike activities over more conventional human services. Whether federated funding becomes a historical footnote or continues to be an important income stream for many human services in the future is currently an open question.

––––––––––––––

*It's the same Community Chest as named on the Monopoly board!

MANAGEMENT SUPPORT ORGANIZATIONS

The idea of enhancing scale and scope economies through collaboration is also an idea behind many activities of management support organizations (MSOs), those organizations that provide assistance to HSEs with various management responsibilities. There are many possibilities, and some communities and regions are better served in this respect than others. For example, an accounting firm that specializes in assisting HSEs with their tax returns or conducts audits would be an example of a relevant MSO. Likewise, a law firm that provides pro bono legal assistance with incorporation, tax, property, and other issues to nonprofit clients would be another. Technology-related services and consulting are other important management support activities. The published research literature on MSOs is very limited, and little is known about the availability of management support services nationwide (Brown & Kalegaonkar, 2002; Connor, Kadel-Taras, & Vinocur-Kaplan, 1999). Connor et al. (1999) proposed that management support organizations should take on the task of coordinating community collaborations.

MSOs also provide assistance with board development, mentoring programs, advancement of best practices, education and training workshops, information technology, help desks, client referrals, investment assistance, marketing and promotion, and consultation on a wide range of topics, including accounting, budgeting, fundraising, and financial analysis.

FOUNDATIONS

Foundation grants provide an important category of management support and are also a major funding source for nonprofit and public HSEs, especially those in metropolitan urban settings with strong traditions of philanthropy. Some foundations also provide assorted management support services, either formally or informally. For HSEs in nonmetropolitan settings everywhere, foundation funding is relatively less significant for HSEs, if only because it is less available and correspondingly more difficult to obtain. There has been tremendous growth, both in numbers and in total assets, of foundations in the last 30 years. Although in the early years of the 20th century, foundation funding played an important role in shaping social work and human services, it has been relatively less important since the rise of public funding for services in the 1960s.

In 2012, there were an estimated 86,192 foundations in the United States, with total assets of $715 billion, gift income of $52.1 billion, and grants of $51.8 billion.* For several decades, foundations have been a major area of growth. A decade earlier, in 2002, there were 64,845 foundations (75 percent as many as in 2012), with total assets of $431.8 billion (60 percent), gift income of $22.1 billion (42.1 percent), and giving totaling $30 billion in grants (57.9 percent). Two decades earlier, in 1992, there were fewer than 50,000 foundations.

---

*Statistical information in this section was retrieved from the Foundation Center Web site on June, 9, 2015.

Of the current number, 78,582 (91 percent) of these foundations are classified as independent foundations, 4,218 (<5 percent) are listed as operating foundations, 2,629 (3 percent) are corporate foundations, and 763 (<1 percent) are community foundations. Community foundations held gift income of $7.4 billion, with total assets of $64.9 billion, and made grants totaling $4.9 billion.

The top 1,000 foundations made 42,000 grants to human services for a total value of $3.5 billion (average grant >$83,000). This was second only to education, where the number of grants was fewer (31,040) but the value was larger ($4.9 billion; average grant >$187,800). The top 1,000 foundations gave 2 percent of their grants to benefit older people; 24 percent to help children and youths; 3 percent for crime and abuse victims; 28 percent for economically disadvantaged people; 11 percent for racial and ethnic minorities; 1 percent for lesbian, gay, bisexual, transgender, and questioning individuals; 2 percent for immigrants and refugees; 2 percent for men and boys; 7 percent for women and girls; 1 percent for military veterans; 1 percent for offenders or ex-offenders; 1 percent for people with HIV/AIDS; 5 percent for people with disabilities; and less than 1 percent each for terminally ill individuals, workers in sex trades, single parents, and those with substance abuse problems.*

Distribution of foundation grants is very skewed geographically, with the states with the largest populations also making the largest number of foundation grants: 15 percent of grants were made in California, 3 percent in Florida, 4 percent in Illinois, 4 percent in Colorado, 4 percent in Massachusetts, 11 percent in New York, and 8 percent in Texas. Among the remainder, 30 states (including all of the smallest and poorest states) received 2 percent or less of total foundation grants. A more detailed portrait of foundation funding can be obtained from closer examination of the major types of foundations.

INDEPENDENT FOUNDATIONS

Independent foundations are consistently the largest single category of foundations, with 78,582 independent foundations holding $584 billion in assets, including $32.2 billion in gifts received and $34.5 billion in giving (2012 Foundation Center data). The Gates Foundation is by far the largest, with over $40 billion in assets. The Ford Foundation is next with $12 billion, whereas the smallest of the top 100 has "only" around $850 million in assets. The remaining 78,482 independent foundations, although smaller, still have sizeable assets, and together independent foundations provide substantial funding to HSEs.

OPERATING FOUNDATIONS

There were also 4,218 operating foundations in the United States in 2012 holding $43.3 billion in assets, with $7.7 billion in gifts received and $6 billion in total giving. Operating foundations in human services are often advocacy foundations. The

---

*This is not an exhaustive list and these are overlapping categories (for instance, immigrants and refugees can be economically disadvantaged, disabled, military veterans, and so forth) and other possible categories are omitted, so the numbers do not total 100 percent.

best known and most important of these in social work history was the Russell Sage Foundation, which from its founding in 1907 to its reorganization in 1948 was known colloquially as "the social work foundation" and subsequently has been an important source of funding for social problems research (Chambers, 1971; Hammack, 1988; Hammack & Wheeler, 1994). In some respects, the Russell Sage Foundation also tells the story of the growth of American foundations. It began with two initial gifts from Margaret Olivia Slocum Sage, the wife of Russell Sage, which totaled $15 million (in 1907 dollars). After more than 100 years of operations and thousands of grants, the Russell Sage Foundation today has assets of $323 million (in 2014 dollars). Much of that increase in size came about not through additional giving but from returns on foundation investments.

A search of Guidestar.org on the terms "social work" and "operating foundation" (on June 9, 2015) produced no results, but a search of "operating foundation" and "human services" turned up 1,468 results. Organizing an HSE—perhaps with the engagement of a major donor—as an operating foundation, such as the original Russell Sage Foundation, offers possibilities that should not be dismissed lightly. As this foundation demonstrated for several decades, an operating foundation can be a highly effective base for advocacy and social reform activities.

CORPORATE FOUNDATIONS

The Foundation Center Web site also reports that in 2012 there were 2,629 corporate foundations with $23.2 billion in total assets, $5.5 billion in total giving (23.7 percent of total assets), and $4.6 billion in gifts received. New York State had the most corporate foundations with 226 (<9 percent). California had 176 corporate foundations and Illinois, Pennsylvania, Ohio, Massachusetts, Texas, Wisconsin, and Minnesota all had more than 100 each. Nine states reported 10 or fewer. As the comparative percentage of gifts figures above show, corporate foundations appear to be much more heavily engaged in giving than are independent foundations; some may be little more than "pass throughs" for channeling corporate giving (Adams & Hardwick, 1998). However, they also have substantially fewer total assets than independent or operating foundations do.

Corporate foundations are often significant sources of smaller gifts and grants, for example, corporate contributions to United Way and federated fundraising campaigns, and for incidental expenses. Thus, a bank foundation or the company foundation of a local big box retail store may be called upon to fund an annual meeting or other special events. The record of corporate foundations providing major ongoing support for programs is much spottier.

COMMUNITY FOUNDATIONS

The type of foundation likely to be of greatest future interest for the largest number of HSEs is also the smallest of the four major types. Community foundations are an old, established form reaching back to the original community foundation established in 1920. The basic idea amounts to something like combining a local

community network of trusts and a federated campaign with an MSO dedicated
to professional grants and investment management. Instead of relying on traditional community arrangements whereby individual lawyers and bankers manage
smaller trusts—some as small as $10,000, and many with very specific restrictions—
the community foundation provides a central repository for consolidating such
purposes communitywide.

The six main characteristics of a community foundation are

1. grantmaking
2. broadly defined mission (for example, to improve the quality of life in a
   community)
3. service to geographically defined communities—a city, state, region, dis-
   trict, or province
4. support from a broad range of private as well as public donors and seeks
   philanthropic contributions primarily from inside the community
5. governance by local boards reflecting a broad range of the community
   interests
6. building capital endowments, which is an important element of financial
   sustainability

There are more than 700 community foundations in the United States and
nearly 2,000 worldwide. The community foundation movement began with the
formation of the Cleveland (Ohio) Foundation in 1920 but remained relatively small
until the economic boom of the 1990s and the associated groundswell of foundation
formations. Several large national foundations coordinated their staff initiatives
and used highly targeted grant giving in a coordinated campaign (an example of
federated financing in itself) to create the present network of 700+ community
foundations blanketing most major metropolitan and many micropolitan communities and smaller communities and rural areas throughout the United States. (For
example, Doddridge County, West Virginia, with a total population of less than
10,000 people, has its own community foundation, managed as a regional affiliate
by the nearby Parkersburg Area Community Foundation.)

In addition to offering sources of funding for HSEs and ways to create an
endowment income stream without having to administer and invest the funds
themselves, community foundations also offer a broad range of creative solutions
for a number of chronic funding problems. Conventional perspectives framed as a
choice between conventional grant writing and a fundraising campaign in which
the HSE asks donors to contribute do not begin to exhaust the potentialities of
community foundations. For example, some community foundations have specific
funds created to underwrite the administrative costs of an HSE in that community,
thereby allowing the HSE to engage in cost sharing and legitimately budget higher
program cost percentages in its grant applications.

Community foundations typically have minimal requirements for establishing specific programs ($10,000, $25,000, and $50,000 are common figures), and all
of the conventional rules governing foundations (for example, minimal payouts)
apply. In this way, potential philanthropists with limited funds can establish lasting

legacies, for example, the Lily Laguna Memorial Fund of Peterson County for the Personal Care of Recovering Substance Abuse Victims. In a community foundation, such funds might be custom designated specifically for supporting a particular program in an HSE. Essentially, in such cases, the community foundation does not review a grant application or make a grant to the agency. Instead, it manages the donor's investment, making payments to the HSE as appropriate, collecting a small management fee along the way.

Program support, administrative support, and endowments for small agencies are just three of many specific types of foundation grants. Some community foundations have agency-specific funds at their local community foundations to cover some or all of their administrative costs. These were probably established by sophisticated donors who understood the ways in which the ever-present drive to keep administrative costs low represents a false and constricting economy and wished to free an HSE from the burdens of such expectations. With such funds covering part or all of an HSE's administrative costs, the HSE can legitimately claim lower administrative costs and higher portions of additional funding directed to programs.

In the long run, the targeted specificity of community foundation funding has some of its own problems, in particular, the problem known as *the dead hand of philanthropy*: what to do with problem-specific funding when the problem no longer exists or when the program changes and the donor's intent can no longer be honored. There is a large body of case law regarding the *cy pres* (meaning, roughly, "as near as possible") doctrine, governing what to do when philanthropic purposes have gotten so out of touch with current realities that legally spending restricted funds is no longer possible. One might consider the historical context, for example, funds established to support the families of merchant sailors injured by harpoons or factory workers run over by horse-drawn carriages. Similarly, many funds were established to aid city street corner newspaper sellers. The *cy pres* guidance in general is that in such cases, funds may be dispensed to the next nearest purpose, although judicial action may be necessary to make this happen.

CONCLUSION

The quiet revolution in human services financial management has many different threads that together weave a new and unprecedented tapestry that has gone largely unnoticed in social work. The new discoveries in organization theory, new political economy, stakeholder theory, and accountability have, among other things, laid the groundwork for completely new understandings of the relation between money—financial capital—and what social workers have traditionally called "knowledge, skills, and values"—or human capital. However, to begin to fully grasp the significance of those developments for financial management, a distinction must be made between the human services organization as a network of interpersonal relations and the human services *enterprise* as a set of economic or financial relations—networks of assets, commitments, income, and expenses. There are today numerous ways to legally organize an HSE, including legislatively created public agencies; private practice in solo enterprises or solopreneurships; partnerships; trusts; numerous types of corporations, including public, nonprofit, and for-profit organizations; and cooperatives. Among the more important features of the quiet revolution opening up this panoply of possibilities have been the vicissitudes of fickle public social policies that, over a period of decades, created large numbers of new human services organizations, only to cut them adrift and leave them to find their own resources. Such agencies of the public will were effectively transformed into social enterprises. So numerous have these new HSEs become that the nonprofit community services constitute a major component of the third—or nonprofit—sector and private practice enterprise could in the very near future constitute a component of an emerging fourth—or social enterprise—sector.

4

Income and Human Capital

Income, according to Merriam-Webster's online dictionary, is a gain or benefit from capital or labor measured in money. This definition points out some of the more subtle features of the social work approach to HSE. In business, an *income statement*, also known as a *profit and loss statement*, reports on net income available to the owners, because a for-profit enterprise is, theoretically and practically, a financial organization of capital for generating income for owners. A business, in this view, is a machine for the distillation of owners' income. From a financial vantage point, owners' profits are, we are told, the point. By contrast, the foremost objective of all human service is not generating wealth for owners; in fact, in public and nonprofit service delivery, such distribution is explicitly forbidden. The key objective is providing high-quality human services. As such, the ultimate destination of income changes. Income for human services is primarily the gathering of resources into the enterprise for the purpose of service delivery.

In this vein, capital can be seen as the sum of all resources held or controlled by an HSE and available to produce services. Such capital is of two types: monetized financial resources in the form of money and credit and nonmonetized labor, effort, or *human capital* in the form of the efforts, knowledge, skills, and values of the people engaged in delivering direct and supportive services. The mere mention of capital in human services may provoke grand theory discussions or sociopolitical critiques of capitalism as an economic system (see, for example, Walters, 2011). Our sole interest in the concept of capital here is more mundane.

Within the terminology of the systems framework, *capital* is a useful and convenient term for inputs to the financial management system, and *financial capital* refers to the sum of all monetized inputs, that is, the financial assets owned or held by an HSE. That leaves open the question of the other component mentioned in the dictionary definition: labor. Conventional economic treatments of *resources*, or factors of production, tend to categorize them as land, labor, and capital. Recent economic approaches to capital in management economics have added another dimension, called *managerial* or *entrepreneurial capital*, which is a type of human capital. Using this as a starting point, a human capital perspective should enable discussion of other, similar factors that also influence human services production, including the knowledge, skills, and values; social and political networks and influences; and levels of trust of *labor*, or nonmanagerial workers. In what follows, this distinction between management and labor will be elaborated in the discussion of costs and reflected primarily as the three-part distinction among administrative costs, fundraising costs (one type of labor and associated costs), and program costs (service delivery and related costs). In this way, the capital resources of HSE can be divided into two basic types: financial and human capital.

RESOURCES: HUMAN AND FINANCIAL CAPITAL

In this chapter, we detail some of the major systematic implications of this rather simple insight. At the most basic levels, not only efforts and activities but all of the features of interpersonal relationships—friendship, collegiality, influence, competition, trust, and many others—between coworkers, stakeholders and managers, workers and clients, and just about every other conceivable human connection are capable of serving as human capital resources to facilitate human service delivery. A fully robust approach to financial management in HSEs ought to take into account this full range of human capital. The primary question has long been, how can this best be done?

It is one of the insights of modern understanding of HSE that the simple act of organizing can generate its own resources. Certainly, this is true for the relatively straightforward insight that employees are important resources and HSEs can employ managers and professional personnel specifically to pursue resources. This may include the labor of fundraisers, grant writers, and contract negotiators, among others. Community organization and group work practitioners have also long been aware of and practiced with other dimensions of this same idea. Since its debut in conjunction with Robert Putnam's discovery of declining civic participation in the United States, the concept of social capital—in particular, trust and social networks—has captured the imagination of a generation of social, economic, and political researchers (Hanifan, 1916; Putnam, 2000). One of the insights of social capital for HSEs was initially highlighted by community organization researchers decades ago: The mere act of initiating an HSE—to meet a need, deal with a problem, and offer a service—creates relationships and improved trust and extends into the existing social networks of those involved (D. M. Austin, 1981; Brager & Specht, 1973; Buell, 1952; Dunham, 1970; Johns & De Marche, 1951; Warren, 1987; Zald, 1967). In some respects, social capital and other forms of human capital may be as important as financial capital to the success of an HSE, but they are also a good deal more esoteric and difficult to quantify and measure. Human capital comes in many forms, only a few of which are noted here. In addition to *social capital*, people one knows and trusts, there is *cultural capital*, the resources of language, culture, art, and history that people can bring to bear on the service experience, and *political capital*, those social and cultural resources with particular cogency in government settings and political arenas (Bielefeld & Corbin, 1996; Lindeman, 1936/1988).

In this sense, *human capital* is an umbrella term for all of the individual and group resources that people bring to HSE situations. Concepts of human capital in HSEs are covered in greater depth in chapter 11. For the present purposes, the various forms of financial capital important for HSEs are considered. Financial capital can be counted, measured, recorded, and manipulated in the accounting, budget, and analytical systems of an HSE. Human capital involves situational factors that, although very real, can ordinarily only be noted and taken into account indirectly and informally. Table 4.1 shows a human capital budget (sometimes called a personnel or human resources budget). It is a type of sub-budget that lists all of the human capital–related expenses separately, and, in most human services, it is the largest portion of the total, all-funds, or enterprise budget.

Table 4.1: Human Capital Budget

Brown County Rehabilitation Center
November 20XX

Item	Budgeted		Year to Date	
	Income ($)	Expenses ($)	Income ($)	Expenses ($)
Executive salaries	274,000	274,000	256,428	251,166
Professional staff	2,859,650		2,941,387	
Education program		476,800		437,066
Counseling program		167,500		153,541
Sheltered workshop		228,750		209,687
Cafe		814,500		746,625
Legal Aid		244,500		224,125
Paraprofessional staff				
Education program		127,600		110,000
Counseling		760,000		696,666
Cafe		40,000		36,666
Total wages and salaries	3,133,650	3,133,650	3,197,815	2,865,542
Additional human capital costs				
Fringe benefits (+21%)	658,070	658,070		603,230
Staff travel and conferences	187,700	187,700		172,058
Consultants	47,800	47,800		43,816
Liability malpractice insurance	162,710	162,710		149,150
Total additional human capital costs			1,056,280	
Unbudgeted surplus			67,428	
Total human capital	4,189,930	4,189,930	4,254,095	3,833,796

CLASSIFICATION OF INCOME

It is possible to classify HSE financial capital into different types of income using a number of different classification schemes. In this section, we look at three different classification systems: the revised IRS Form 990 exempt entities tax return, an approach grounded in classifying income by source, and an approach based on distinguishing the characteristics of types of income themselves. None is inherently superior or preferable to the others, and different HSEs may use each of these and other approaches to classification for different purposes.

THE IRS TYPOLOGY

In the current revised IRS Form 990 for nonprofit tax-exempt entities, the IRS uses the term *income* to characterize all financial inputs. Another possible term—*revenue*—is the middle word in the name of the agency and has often been used in the past. A third term—*resources*—is also sometimes used. Although not all forms of human services delivery are tax exempt, and there are other issues involved, we consistently use the term *income* throughout this book for clarity. Lines 8–11 of IRS Form 990 return identify four distinct categories that together comprise total income for tax-exempt entities:

1. contributions and grants
2. program service income
3. investment income
4. other income

Note that from the IRS's perspective, the original and primary reason for IRS Form 990 is to determine the tax liability (if any) of HSEs and other nonprofit entities. In IRS Form 990, the category of contributions refers to what are also called *donations or gifts*: unilateral (or one-way) and nontaxed transfers of resources to the reporting enterprise. What the IRS calls *program service income* has traditionally been designated in HSEs with the terms *fees* and *fee income* (Goldberg & Kovac, 1973; Goodman, 1960, 1970; Lohmann, 1980; Sax, 1978; Shireman, 1975; Wernet et al., 1993). These are usually not taxed, provided that the service for which the fee is charged is associated with an enterprise mission that fits within the broad umbrella of the IRS public charities. That vision is inherited from the Statute of Charitable Uses, which originated in England in 1601 (Fishman, 2008). One of the legal and financial characteristics of HSEs is the impermeable membrane that exists between those activities designated nonprofit and those characterized as for-profit. Funds may flow into a tax-exempt 501(c)(3) enterprise in any of these forms but may flow out only in the form of services fitting comfortably within a public charitable mission or transfers to other 501(c)(3) enterprises. (On the general subject of nonprofits and taxation, see Blazek, 2012; Cordes & Weisbrod, 1998; McMillan, 2000b; Vowell, 2000; Webb, 1996.)

It is important to note that the IRS exercises no control over missions and this is not a prohibition of particular types of services. From the IRS perspective, an HSE with tax-exempt or tax-deductible status is completely free to operate a travel agency or a restaurant as a revenue or profit center without threatening its tax-exempt status. However, income generated by such a non–tax exempt activity is subject to federal income taxation as an unrelated business income tax (UBIT). Nonprofit Travelers Aid services are a major exception to this. Their mission is to provide free travel-related services within the meaning of the law. For most HSEs, the fees a travel agency charges would be classified as "other income" and most likely subject to UBIT. Finally, investment as an income stream refers to interest earnings, rents from rental properties, earnings, capital gains on stock portfolios, or other income from investments.

These IRS classifications are useful for several purposes. Their original purpose is for the IRS to determine tax liability. For HSE financial management, they show how the IRS classifies income and expenses. For instructional purposes, they illustrate also that even beyond the choice of terminology, there is no one universal way of classifying income. Classifications vary depending on the intent of the classifier.

What the IRS calls "program service income" is usually referred to in the social work literature as "fees" and "fee income." Social work programs have a long and distinctive history with fee collection, beginning with an extensive discussion in the 1950s casework literature, which concluded that social workers could legitimately charge fees to clients who could afford to pay but that in some cases, sliding scale fees might be necessary to adjust fees to clients' ability to pay. Such issues do not matter in the IRS categorization. The IRS is only interested in determining tax obligations, and these categories of income do just that. Note, for example, that all program, management, and general expenses are summarized as "other expenses," whereas fundraising expenses are given two separate lines. Line 7 of IRS Form 990 explicitly asks the reporting entity to report its unrelated business income subject to taxation.

Note also that the IRS classification only applies to monetary resources. Even though the efforts of volunteers have long been an important form of human capital for human services, the IRS has not tracked those efforts for decades. Likewise, in-kind resources (works of art, automobiles, and other valuable commodities) are generally only of interest to the IRS when a fair market value can be established.

Classification by Source

The financial statements shown in chapter 5 suggest additional ways to classify income. It is possible, for example, to categorize by the sources from which it comes. This is the approach taken in the statement of cash flows (see Table 5.3). In this approach, income in a period (labeled *cash receipts*) may come from (a) clients, (b) grant makers, (c) contractors, (d) insurance companies, (e) donors, or (f) other sources. Presumably, those would be labeled (a) *fees*; (b) *grants*; (c) *contracts*; (d) *insurance payments*; (e) *gifts, contributions, or donations*; and (f) *other income*. In some cases (that is, where sliding scale fees are important in the income picture of an HSE), it might also be useful to categorize total income by income class or merely to distinguish between income from sliding scale fees and that from full-fee clients. Likewise, when large grants are involved, it may be helpful to list each separately on a sources of income table (as in Table 4.2).

Additional, detailed listings might also be appropriate in some cases for contracts, insurance companies, Medicaid, and other third-party vendors. Under various circumstances, it would also be possible to separate out grant makers into public grants, foundation grants, and corporate grants or even grants from individuals (where *grants* is another term for large donations, especially those accompanied by restrictions). Finally, federated funding organizations and other HSEs receiving large numbers of donations frequently categorize them by the size of the donations (often attaching colorful names for each category) and publish lists of some or all donors by size of gift.

Classification by Income Characteristics

There are other ways to classify income. One such schema is classification by the characteristics of the income itself, for example, (a) contributions, (b) memberships, (c) program fees, (d) fundraising, (e) grants, (f) contracts (purchase of service contracts), (g) investments, and (h) reclassifications. *Contributions*, or donations, are gifts to the HSE received from the community or general public. Memberships are also voluntary contributions, but ordinarily they are offered in exchange for participation in an organization. Contributions can usually be distinguished from memberships by the prospect of *member benefits*, or financial advantages flowing back to the member in exchange for the membership payment. The same, of course, may sometimes be true of contributions, particularly large contributions, where the donor may be awarded status or recognition. For tax purposes, memberships may

Table 4.2: Sources of Income

Source	Amount ($)	%
Fundraising	78,241.00	9.36
Grant 1	25,000.00	2.99
Grant 2	241,000.00	28.82
Grant 3	8,270.00	0.99
United Way	31,200.00	3.73
Private pay and copays	68,270.00	8.16
State Contract 1	341,700.00	40.86
State Contract 2	42,653.00	5.10
Total income	836,334.00	100.00

not be tax deductible, or, when they are, members may only be able to deduct the net amount of the contribution less the value of benefits received. Program fees may be distinguished by program, by the previously mentioned sliding scale/ full-fee distinction, or on some other basis. Distinguishing between contributions and fundraising makes sense in some (but not all) circumstances but requires some explanation. The most likely distinction to be drawn here would be between (unsolicited) contributions that just come in "over the transom" and donations resulting from an organized fundraising program or campaign. If nothing else, unsolicited contributions typically involve no trackable expense to the HSE, whereas contributions to an organized campaign are net income, taking into account the costs of the campaign. In those cases where the fundraising campaign is conducted for some specific purpose (like a building or renovations), it may also be necessary to make a further distinction between restricted donations and unrestricted ones. All of this would allow a more exact comparison of the costs of fundraising to the amounts raised.

The comments on grants and contracts in the previous section also apply in this listing. The classification of investments is an item obviously useful only in those cases where the HSE has an established investment program generating significant returns. If the HSE earned $0.89 last month as interest on its checking account, that would probably not require inclusion in a listing of income sources. The final item, reclassifications, is likely only to be used periodically and is reserved for assorted reassignments of income to different categories from their original locations. For example, in a situation where differences between solicited and unsolicited donations may be controversial among donors, stakeholders, or board members, a category such as this may come in handy as a kind of pressure release valve to assure all concerned that efforts are being made to get the classifications right and to make adjustments in classification when necessary.

CONTRIBUTIONS

As a category, *contributions* can be said to be those donations, small grants, and other miscellaneous income with no restrictions. They are ordinarily not memberships or subject to any of the conditions or restrictions involved in grants or special purpose fundraising campaigns. Of course, any distinction between contributions, fundraising, and grants can, at times, be a rather artificial one. All three of these categories represent some form of unilateral transfer payment (one of the principal meanings of *grants*), and there may be no reason to distinguish among them. In such cases, collapsing two or even all three of these together into a single category (the United Way calls this category *public support*) may be the most prudent course. Nevertheless, for purposes of discussion here, we approach contributions as undesignated income, including both unsolicited gifts and regular, annual, or other periodic donations made spontaneously by donors. For example, the category of contributions may include all unsolicited donations. It is a fairly widespread practice, for example, for published obituaries to specify gifts to particular public charities "in lieu of flowers," and at least some individuals organize part of their individual giving around making such donations. Many HSEs will find such contributions a miniscule source of income and thus not bother to track them. In other cases, monitoring these gifts as a separate category of income may be worthwhile.

In this sense, contributions as a source of income may correspond most closely to the type of income identified below as "found money." It is ordinarily impossible to predict how much may come in during any given period, and there is no particular reason to attempt to do so. One use of such found money would be to apply it to the current fundraising goal, discussed in a section that follows. That approach would not necessarily be inconsistent with other approaches, such as setting these funds aside by board or management decision for some special purpose, for example, adding them to income for a particular program, to the investment pool, or to an endowment in the local community foundation.

MEMBERSHIPS

The difference between a contribution and a membership is ordinarily quite straightforward: Memberships are not unilateral transfers, while contributions are. Memberships ordinarily involve some return to the individual member. Anything can be labeled *member benefits*, starting perhaps with the right to attend membership meetings. Membership may also involve opportunities to use members-only facilities, such as lounges, health clubs, swimming pools, and so forth; member services, such as free admissions; magazines; access to members-only Web sites; or free tickets to an annual luncheon.

In most cases involving member benefits, only the contribution portion of a payment is tax deductible; member benefits are not. In recognition of this, the IRS requires that, on receipts for contributions from donors, the amount of the donation must be specified as a net amount, less the value of any member benefits or other benefits received. Thus, a $100 contribution to an HSE may only be deductible as a $50 donation if the donor receives a pair of "free" tickets worth $25 each for a benefit concert in recognition of the donation.

PROGRAM SERVICE INCOME

Program service income, or *fees* for short, is money received directly either from clients or from third parties such as purchase of service contractors, Medicaid agencies, or insurance companies. Program service income is typically received in exchange for services to clients. From an HSE budget standpoint, program service income has the advantages of simplicity; fairness; enhancement of administrative flexibility; and, to the extent that they offer clients a choice of service vendors, feedback on client preferences (Lohmann, 1980, p. 82). Fees are also metered; that is, they rise and fall with changes in the volume of services delivered. Fees also have two disadvantages as income sources. First, total returns expected from program service income tend to be unpredictable as an income item, making the challenge of budgeting more complex. This issue is a major focus of chapter 9. In addition, charging fees may be unrealistic in a wide range of human services programs, settings, and situations, including poverty, disasters, and many emergency and crisis situations. Once highly controversial in social work, program service fees have become a standard income practice throughout health and human services systems, although they are certainly not universal.

There are several distinct types of program service income. *Participation fees* involve the collection of nominal amounts from clients, primarily as a good faith gesture on the part of the client rather than for the purpose of generating financial support for the services delivered; in essence, participation fees serve as a symbol of commitment to the program or service. *Fair share fees* are often used for special events and activities. The amount charged is determined by dividing the total cost equally among the participants. *Flat rate fees,* or standard charges, are the types of program service income most often arising in budget discussions. The amount of a flat rate fee is ordinarily determined by estimating the total number of service units to be delivered in a given period (for example, in a fiscal year) and the estimated cost to be covered, which may be the full cost or some type of cost sharing in conjunction with some subvention. In chapter 9, for example, the fee income ordinarily predicted in a break-even analysis consists of flat rate fees. In theory, another type of fee is the *capitation fee*, which is periodically discussed in health care reform, but I have found little evidence of its actual use in human services or social work, at least in the published literature.

Finally, a distinctive (some would suggest peculiar) fee important in some settings dealing with poor clients is the *sliding scale fee*, an adjustable charge to clients (Wernet et al., 1993). As the name suggests, a sliding scale fee is one that increases or decreases in relation to a client characteristic, such as residency or income. Thus, for example, many state universities charge differing tuition for state residents and nonresidents on the theory that in-state residents (or their parents) have already paid for a larger share of university costs through general taxation. The most common sliding scale factor in an HSE is the ability to pay. Table 4.3 shows an income- and expense-based sliding scale fee for an HSE using two variables:

Table 4.3: Sliding Scale Fees

	Fee ($) Based on Family Size			
Income Level	One Child	Two Children	Three Children	Four or More Children
200% of poverty level or higher	100	80	60	40
150% of poverty level	50	40	30	20
100% of poverty level or lower	0	0	0	0

Note: Full fee = $100.

family income and family size. The fee schedule shows a 20 percent reduction for each additional child and no fee charged at all for those families at or below the current poverty line.

An HSE operating entirely on the basis of program service fees is, for all intents and purposes, operating like a small business, except that human services are not ordinarily in a position to estimate or calculate demand. Establishing fixed fees are as close as any HSE comes to setting prices. For further details on the management of fees, see the discussions of fees in Lohmann (1980, pp. 80–97) and Mayers (2004, pp. 152–155).

GRANTS

One of the analytical methods of financial management with a strong practice base and only a tenuous foothold in the knowledge base of the modern university system—and one with a much closer connection to the social work profession and human services organizations—is what is variously called *grant writing* and *grantsmanship*. Many universities offer practical and technical grant writing courses, but these are usually freestanding isolates, and the general subject of grants is not subsumed neatly under any traditional field of knowledge or social science discipline. It is an outlier everywhere. Grant theory, such as it is, might also be termed *soft money theory* or perhaps just *how to find money*. Unlike the companion topic of fundraising, grants are still something of an orphan. Efforts by Kenneth Boulding several decades ago to bring grants into mainstream economics were largely unsuccessful, and no other discipline or profession has made the topic its own in the way that, for example, accounting departments have embraced nonprofit accounting and public administration has embraced nonprofit management. Even the research literature on the subject of grants is very spotty.

The practice theory of grants may be said to have its origins in the work of the Foundation Center in the mid-1950s, notably through the efforts of people such as F. Emerson Andrews of the Russell Sage Foundation and John Gardner. Modern grants are not the same as donations; they are not just gifts but rather a special species of purposeful, directed (and often solicited) gifts. At the core of grant theory is the proposal and the grant writing process. Grants—particularly land grants—reach deep into American colonial history and beyond. Human services grants got their start with the numerous land grants Dorothea Dix was able to secure for state hospitals from assorted legislatures. Grant activity took a giant step forward with the Social Security Act of 1935 and the provisions for intergovernmental grants-in-aid from the federal to state and local governments for public welfare. These were all intergovernmental transfer payments, formula based, and for the most part noncompetitive (that is, one state's receipt of a grant and the grant's size were not dependent on any other state going unfunded). By contrast, the federal grant programs that emerged in the 1960s were new and unprecedented public policy: nonformulaic, often highly competitive, discretionary grants capable of going away nearly as quickly as they arose.

Discretionary grants are one-way transfer payments. In the most general terms, *grants* are unilateral transfers of money, goods, or services from one entity or organization (the funder or grant maker) to another (the recipient or grantee) behind the previously discussed nonpermeable membrane of the nondistribution constraint. They are an important source of income for the full spectrum of nonprofit, public, community, and grassroots HSEs. There is no particular reason HSEs in private practice could not also receive grants from some sources (for example, another individual or a business). However, once funds are received by a 501(c)(3) organization, they enter the protected domain of the nondistribution constraint on tax-exempt public charity and nonprofit HSEs, private foundations, and other tax-exempt entities that would likely face tax liabilities, civil penalties, or worse for making such grants.

Mayers (2004) defined a program grant as "an allocation of funds from a governmental agency, a private foundation, or . . . a federated funding source, to a human service organization for a specific program or project" (p. 125). Grants are often made for the pursuit of a specific program of objectives or policy agendas, but there is nothing inherent in the grant financial model that demands this. Grants can include not only direct money awards but also unilateral transfers of land, equipment, software, or supplies. The three largest and most general types of grants by source are government and foundation grants and those from federated funding systems such as United Way and the Combined Federal Campaign.

Grants are, for some, the paramount feature in human services financing. Careers are made and broken on the success of grant-getting efforts. Grants are sometimes seen as the only hope of coming close to meeting human needs in the community, although as the discussion of other income sources in this chapter makes clear, this is far from true. On the negative side, some see grants as the epitome of nonaccountability and wastefulness, the tools of elitist domination, or the agents of reduced autonomy in the voluntary sector (see, for example, Boris & Steuerle, 2006; W. G. Hill, 1971; Rice, 1975; Smith & Lipsky, 1992; Stock, 1969).

Categorical grants, the largest of which is federal Title XIX (Medicaid) assistance to the states, are legislatively enabled, recurrent, and dependable income streams, distributed across the board to all recipients willing to accept them. Such grants are noncompetitive and formula based. *Program grants*, whether from federal, state, or foundation sources, are program specific, often one-shot funds or soft funding with limited possibilities of repeat funding. They are direct expressions of social policy initiatives and create incentive structures to induce recipients to behave in a manner encouraged by the grant maker. Revenue sharing gave way to "block grants" designed to shift discretionary authority away from federal decision makers to state and local deciders (Conlan, 1984; Hargrove & Melton, 1987). Although a ubiquitous phenomenon in some HSE income streams, block grants fit well with the earlier suggestion of grants as a form of orphan knowledge. The research literature on block grants in human services is very spotty, perhaps subject to overgeneralization from a very few cases. The best way to learn about what is happening with block grant funding in a particular state or community is to talk with the people involved.

CONTRACTS

Martin (2001, p. 161) introduced the language of the Federal Grant and Cooperative Agreement Act to categorize the motives of governmental grant makers into
two main types of financial relationships and three distinct financial instruments.
Procurement relationships, Martin noted, are distinct from assistance relationships.
In the former, a federal agency expends funds to purchase goods and services for
its own purposes. The financial instrument for this purpose is usually a contract.
In the latter assistance relationship, a federal department provides funds to a state
or local governmental or a private nonprofit human services organization to assist
that entity in pursuing its own agenda or mission. The financial instruments for
this purpose are usually either grants or cooperative agreements. In the language
of federal procurement, grants are always and only a form of assistance. Martin
(2001) asserted that "the distinction . . . is more than just semantics" (p. 161), and
his distinctions are convincing.

The distinction between procurement and assistance is a useful and important
one for those thinking about government grants and contracts and can sometimes
even be applied generally. The U.S. government uses procurement relationships
and contracts to pursue a wide variety of purposes, from building federal high-
ways, military equipment, and hardware to managing national parks and wildlife
refuges. In the case of human services, however, this can also be a somewhat artificial distinction that dissolves immediately once the grantee or contractee adopts
or embraces the relevant federal policy objective and makes it their own.

The reasons for this are that, unlike submarines or tanks, the U.S. government
does not purchase human services for its own use or consumption but rather as
a third party on behalf of others (clients) (Levinthal, Meijs, & Hustinx, 2009). Furthermore, human services are always local to some specific social environment and
cannot be inventoried, warehoused, or transported away from the local environment of the client and service provider. Thus, once the human services contractor
agrees in good faith to carry out the federal objective in that environment and the
federal procurement entity agrees, much of the distinction between procurement
and assistance largely disappears. It becomes a distinction without a difference,
albeit still a useful one in many other contexts. This distinction is, as Martin (2001)
observed, embedded in law and policy, including IRS Form 990's categories of
revenue discussed above. Furthermore, adopting the stance of a purchaser rather
than an assistant has empowered the federal government with a strong set of
weapons in efforts to define and measure outputs. Thus, we uphold this distinction—artificial though it may be in some ultimate sense—in the rest of this chapter
and throughout the book.

FUNDRAISING

Although probably very few HSEs can sustain themselves at present with only
contributions and donations generated through their fundraising efforts, there are
a number of reasons why every nonprofit HSE ought to generate at least a portion

of its total income in this way.* Most important of these is the role a diversity of income sources plays in a sustainable operation. There is evidence that higher numbers and diversity of income sources help ward off fiscal distress, as discussed in chapter 10. As the research results profiled in Table 1.1 suggest, financial sustainability is the greatest concern for a wide variety of nonprofit organizations, including those providing human services. Finally, in recent decades, there have been massive increases in private philanthropy in the United States—as evidenced by the growth of foundations—and individual giving is always the largest category of philanthropic giving. Yet, whereas schools, colleges, universities, and other causes receive billions of dollars each year through private giving, many HSEs do not raise any funds this way, and others are limited to what is generated through United Way, the Combined Federal Campaign, and other federated funding arrangements. Every HSE would be well served by having at least a limited fundraising operation in its total income picture.

Some readers may be skeptical of the distinction drawn between contributions and fundraising income. The principal reason for maintaining a distinction between income from contributions and fundraising income is most evident in cases where fundraising is being conducted for some specific purpose, for example, a capital campaign to raise funds to purchase a building or a fundraising campaign to endow a particular program. Traditionally, there have been two principal approaches to organizing fundraising in HSEs: as an ongoing part of the organization (cultivating donations and accepting contributions) and through specially organized and time-limited fundraising campaigns. In recent years, the research literature on fundraising has grown exponentially.† Whereas much of the literature remains in the form of highly practical how-to guides written primarily by experienced practitioners, there is also a growing evidence-based literature and a small body of philanthropy theory. Available guides include the two-volume encyclopedia *Philanthropy in America* (Burlingame, 2004), a variety of textbooks (G. D. Alexander & Carlson, 2005; Kelly, 1998), a history by Olivier Zunz (2012), or the cultural theory of philanthropy by George McCully (2008).

PHILANTHROPIC PARADIGM SHIFT

Philanthropy is an old term of ancient Greek origin that is often used by fundraisers as a synonym for fundraising and foundations. It is also a key term in what George McCully and others believe is an emerging shift in the philanthropic paradigm that grew out of voluntary sector origins and evolved over the course of the 20th century (McCully, 2008). Philanthropy, and not just fundraising, in McCully's rendition is deeply woven into American history and culture (see Appendix A). One of

---

*It may be a small point, but in current usage, the term "fundraising" (one word) is preferred over "fund raising" (two), according to the Association of Fundraising Professionals.
†For a perspective on the recent emergence of fundraising as an academic field of study by one of the founding figures, see the essays in Rosso (1996).

the simplest definitions of *philanthropy* is Robert Payton's (1988) private action for public good or, as McCully prefers, private initiatives for public good, focusing on quality of life. This approach places emphasis on the ends of philanthropy (public good and quality of life) rather than the means (foundations and fundraising). McCully estimates that only roughly one in 10 nonprofit organizations is engaged in actual philanthropy. This covers the efforts of individuals working alone as well as a range of private (that is, nongovernmental) group activities. As Jane Addams argued, human service is a fundamentally philanthropic ideal. Whereas the term *fundraising* puts the accent on the practice of asking for and accepting funds, *philanthropy* places giving in the larger context of good works linking financial means with larger ends.

THE AMERICAN PLAN

A distinctive American model of philanthropy arose between the Civil War and World War I (see Zunz, 2012). This model involves several unique elements, one of which is the bilevel campaign (McCully, 2015). Although philanthropic deeds by aristocratic, wealthy, and powerful social elites have a history stretching back to the ancient world and across many cultures, it was only in the late 19th and early 20th century United States that ways of successfully reaching out to middle- and lower-class donors were developed. The recent worldwide growth of philanthropy began with the initial creative burst of American-run nongovernmental organizations (NGOs) that also included the rebranding of United Way as United Way International. When coupled with the growth of knowledge of the history and philosophy of philanthropy, all of these trends have reinforced the paradigm-shifting view of philanthropy as derived from a "classical humanistic culture of philanthropy [that is] seen as quintessentially American" (see Appendix A). As McCully (2008) observed, this view of philanthropy informed the building of American colonial society, underlay the American Revolution and the U.S. Constitution, and fueled the antislavery and women's suffrage movements.

Some potential indicators of the paradigm shift in philanthropy have already been noted or alluded to: diverse taxonomies and IRS-related and other Web-based data sets that enable various forms of data mining, including prospect research; changes in the nature of workplace giving; radical growth in the number, size, and diversity of foundations; the emergence of community foundations; donor-advised funds and charitable remainder trusts; a creative reformulation of nonprofit social agencies into social enterprises in a third sector of human service and other nonprofits with growing demands for new income; an emerging fourth sector driven in part by a trend McCully called "new wealth-creators emerging as risk-taking donor-investors [willing to] explore unconventional modes of giving and volunteering" (see Appendix A). This paradigm shift also embraces a number of factors not yet discussed. Important among these are younger, systematic, and data-driven donors who reject key features of the old paradigm and want to act creatively to improve the human condition—the classic conception of philanthropy (as more than just fundraising) dating back to the ancient Greeks.

CROWDFUNDING

One of the dimensions of the paradigm shift in philanthropy is the emergence of the unprecedented philanthropic dynamic known as crowdfunding, a completely new form of capitalization that straddles all existing boundaries and limits. *Crowdfunding* is the practice of funding a project—whether private, public, charitable, or moneymaking—by generating small contributions from large numbers of people via the Internet. A development noteworthy to HSEs is that the traditional distinction between donative nonprofits and nondonative ones, described by Anthony and Young (2005) and referenced above, appears to be blurring. Donors today appear to be less concerned with who is asking for their contribution than whether their contribution is put to good use.

In the face of this new form, the traditional financial profile of philanthropy remains largely unchanged. According to the IRS, charitable contributions account for around 2 percent of the gross domestic product—roughly the same proportion as in 1940. Fewer than one in five estates greater than $650,000 probated in the United States include charitable bequests. Only about one-quarter of taxpayers itemize their charitable contributions, and various tax reforms have been proposed to eliminate the charitable deduction entirely. This is the context in which crowdfunding emerged.

Kickstarter was an early platform for crowdfunding and is still one of the largest. Estimates are that the crowdfunding industry has grown to be a multibillion-dollar enterprise, with many different possible arrangements. Just like third-party funding, crowdfunding models illustrate the tripartite exchange shown in Figure 2.2. In crowdfunding, a *project initiator* lists and describes a project idea at a crowdfunding Web site (*the platform*) and links the idea with the *crowd* willing to support the idea. It is clear that at least some social workers and human services are already using crowdfunding. A search (on July 17, 2015) of the GoFundMe site using the search term "human services" listed over 13,000 current projects, and a search for "human services" and "social work" found 1,700 projects.

Kickstarter does not allow personal fundraising and charges processing fees of 3 percent to 5 percent. GoFundMe claims to be an even larger site and allows personal fundraising. Campaigns asking for help for flood, fire, and other disaster victims are as likely to be found there as the projects of HSEs. Another site, Indiegogo, charges 9 percent but, in an apparent effort to discourage hopeless projects, returns 5 percent to those listings whose goal is reached. DonorsChoose is a crowdfunding site devoted to classroom education projects. It charges 15 percent, but donations are entirely tax deductible. Indiegogo is an international site, available in English, German, French, and Spanish. GiveForward charges initiators 5 percent and a 2.3 percent processing fee (information from http://crowdfunding.com downloaded on June 9, 2015). These are just a few of the rapidly proliferating crowdfunding sites.

Advancement

Two other fundraising-related ideas merit mention here: advancement and prospect research. *Advancement* is a catchy word for a rather arcane common law doctrine that deals with gifts to one's heirs or successors during one's lifetime that can be viewed as an advance on an inheritance. This has a history reaching back to the English Statute of Charitable Uses, a legislative companion to the Elizabethan Poor Law. Advancement as law linguistically links the terms *advancement* and *institutional advancement* as synonyms for broader, programmatic, and philanthropic views of fundraising as a component of general enterprise management and American culture. In addition to fundraising, it embraces generous doses of marketing, stakeholder, or constituency development and human capitalization. An enduring challenge for HSEs, particularly smaller ones, is that of founding and maintaining a credible institutional advancement effort; where available person power is limited, the task may seem overwhelming. In many agencies, a finance committee such as the one detailed in chapter 13 may also be the focal point (and mandate a new name) for enterprisewide efforts at institutional advancement.

Prospect Research

Prospect research is the name for a set of research methods used to gather and analyze relevant information about potential donors. Under the new philanthropy paradigm noted by McCully (2008) and in the context of institutional "friend finding" and related activities in social media, the focus of prospect research develops into a full-time, year-round constituency-building effort. In the past, it has been very rare for human services agencies to use or rely on even the narrowest forms of prospect research. However, there is no reason for that to continue and countless reasons for it to change. The Association of Professional Researchers for Advancement (http://www.aprahome.org) is the professional association for prospect researchers. The focus of this association is on finding and vetting potential large donors. Prospect research is partially a historical search based on finding those who have already established a track record of giving. Even more effective, however, is the prospect research that finds potential donors before they have made large gifts to others. "Rich lists" are one of the common prospect research tools. (For example, the rich list published in the Sunday edition of the *New York Times* is often mentioned, but its value has also been questioned.) Prospect researchers often work with wealth indexes and assorted financial algorithms, many of which rely heavily on such factors as real estate holdings. Prospect researchers often rely extensively on information found only in subscription databases such as Factiva, LexisNexis, and the Forecasting Analysis and Modeling Environment (FAME); the fees to these sources may constitute a positive barrier to small HSEs in particular. Nonetheless, human services could be doing a great deal more—and some already are seeking to reach out—in the area of prospect research in their communities and beyond.

INVESTMENTS

A successful fundraising program that generates more income than can (or should) be expended in the current period may also open up unprecedented issues of where, how, and when to invest surplus funds. There may be some HSEs where the board or finance committee insists, whether for good reasons or not, on directly managing the portfolio of investments for the enterprise. In general, however, there are other options that may be more worthwhile. One of these better options would be to place invested funds with a local community foundation, assuming they have the capability to provide the oversight and active management of the profile in question. In that way, the specialized knowledge and skills of the community foundation board and staff can be leveraged to the benefit of the HSE. In other cases, the HSE may seek out a trustworthy private investment firm. For those HSEs hardy (or foolhardy) enough to attempt to manage their own investments, there are some resources, including a small body of research-based theoretical work, available today to deal with the challenges involved (Fry, 1998; D. R. Young, 2007; Zeitlow & Seider, 2007).

MANAGEMENT OF "FOUND MONEY"

An unexpected twist on the notion of investments is what personal financial counselors sometimes call the theory of found money. The basic idea is that in a household—or an HSE—occasionally and unexpectedly (relatively) small, unbudgeted amounts of money committed to no particular purpose or income center may become available. If such found money is recognized when it occurs, it can be put to good use, for example, as an addition to the enterprise's investments or for some other special purpose. Unsolicited contributions may constitute the largest amount of found money in an HSE, but there may be many other sources. Depending on the scale of the enterprise operations, there can be many different sources of found money: small donations; refunds and rebates; class action settlements; inheritances and bequests; coupons; frequent flyer miles; income from bake sales, yard sales, and smaller special events; and numerous others. This category does have its limits, however. Ordinarily, public or foundation grant funds, for example, cannot legitimately be laundered through any type of expend-and-rebate arrangement—whether accidentally or deliberately—so that it is reclassified as found money. By contrast, foundation officials in particular may be prone to say to grantees, "Just keep the unspent funds," together with an admonition such as, "And use them wisely." Public grant officials may be precluded by law from allowing this and expect unexpended surpluses to be returned to the public treasury. In any case, it is not a bad practice to obtain confirmation in writing of such a decision to keep found money.

The best approach to management of found money is to be content with accumulating small sums for distinct purposes, and the best way for found money to really amount to something would be to place it in a special account (it may be called a *rainy day fund*, a *future opportunities fund*, or some such label). It may even be feasible to set up a separate savings account, for example, and become very diligent about putting found money into it. Develop a plan so that there is not only a reason to keep finding this extra money but also clear ideas about intentions for using it. It is a good idea to run this idea initially by the board or the finance committee or even to get formal board action on it to present to HSE auditors. Otherwise, it can all too easily appear as some kind of private deal or "skimming" operation and even lead to an accusation of embezzlement. As with many aspects of HSE financial management, the key here is openness and transparency.

With found money, of course, one cannot count on regular deposits; a found money income stream is, by definition, unanticipated and unpredictable. But a certain discipline and commitment to this approach can still be applied, starting small and working toward a specific goal. Working with found money requires not only transparency but also patience. One should expect to take small, incremental steps initially. For a found money strategy to work, one must fight the urge to raid the account for anything other than the original purpose. However, it can produce rewards. In one instance a number of years ago, an HSE was able to finance the initial purchase of computers for all of its staff from unearmarked funds redirected by a project to reduce copier costs.

A NOTE ON EXPENDITURE CLASSIFICATION

Earlier in this chapter, a variety of ways to categorize income were introduced. Expenses can also be classified in any of several different ways. The conventional line-item budget is only one such way (a detailed chart of accounts is the usual beginning place for identifying line items). For both enterprises and regulatory bodies, classification has traditionally been geared to solving particular problems; as a result, a variety of approaches to classification have arisen. The IRS has its own system of classifying revenues, and the cost principles outlined in the Office of Management and Budget (OMB) Circular A-122 go in yet another direction. There have been recent efforts to reconcile at least some of this variety, however.

The Urban Institute Web site (http://nccs.urban.org/projects/ucoa .cfm#Agreement) contains a spreadsheet that lists a complete Unified Chart of Accounts (UCOA) and tracks their relationships to IRS Form 990, OMB A-122 cost principles, and United Way of America reporting requirements. This standard chart of accounts is a beginning effort at uniform classification for nonprofit organizations and is available from the National Center for Charitable Statistics for use by any nonprofit organization, accountant, or consultant. The system is designed for nonprofit organizations and their consulting accountants to easily and reliably translate their financial statements into the categories required by IRS Form 990, the federal OMB, and into other standard reporting formats. The UCOA also seeks to promote uniform accounting practices throughout the nonprofit sector. Complete information on the UCOA and a printed copy of the chart are also available in the book *Unified Financial Reporting System for Not-for-Profit Organizations: A Comprehensive Guide to Unifying GAAP, IRS Form 990, and Other Financial Reports Using a Unified Chart of Accounts* (Sumariwalla & Levis, 2000).

Perhaps because they are still fewer in number, there has been much less attention paid to standardized charts of accounts in public, for-profit, and fourth-sector social enterprises. For nonprofits, IRS Form 990 offers another such classification, related but also distinct because of its role in tax identification and collection. Note that the IRS divides 501(c)(3) nonprofit organizations into two categories: public charities (including most nonprofit HSEs) and private foundations. Under what we might call the IRS's *impermeable membrane doctrine,* any 501(c)(3) can be a grant maker, but only to another 501(c)(3). It remains a public charity as long as such grant making is not its principal activity. Contributions (donations and gifts) made by (rather than to) the reporting entity would be covered under expenses, which IRS Form 990 categorizes beginning in line 13:

- grants and similar amounts paid
- benefits paid to or for members
- salaries, other compensation, and benefits
- professional fundraising fees
- total fundraising expenses
- other expenses

This classification serves the IRS's primary purpose of identifying taxable income. It is useful for HSEs to understand mostly in the context of filing (and understanding) their IRS Form 990 tax returns. Many other expense classification schemes are also possible in addition to the conventional line-item classification that most readers will have encountered at some point. In some of the exercises in chapters 6 and 13, for example, a variety of lumping and splitting exercises are introduced to classify expenditures under the three main headings of administrative, fundraising, and program expenses; as two main headings, human capital and current expenses; and in other ways.

Income in HSEs comes in many shapes, forms, sizes, and quantities. It is possible to characterize all forms of HSE capital as two types: financial capital (money and credit) and human capital (knowledge, skills, and values). The conventional economic categories of land, labor, and capital are not especially useful for human services purposes, although a common recent addition to that listing, managerial capital, can, by extension, offer a useful starting point for human capital. The social work formulation of knowledge, skills, and values is also useful in that regard.

A range of different classifications of income and expenses are useful for different purposes. Readers are urged to understand the IRS classifications of income and expenses, for example, as a way of further understanding the intent of the IRS's Form 990 exempt entities tax return, which nonreligious 501(c)(3) corporations are expected to file annually.

On the basis of the evolving understanding of the role of HSE, the variety of types of enterprises currently involved in producing or delivering human services, and the various types and sources of income involved to enable service delivery, the next chapter delves into a detailed examination of the accounting system and, in particular, the range and types of financial statements that are part of the GAAPs that have evolved as a key component of the quiet revolution.

CONCLUSION

There is enormous variety in the resources that are brought together to enable delivery or production of human services. In general, however, these can be subsumed under two overarching headings: those resources that are monetized or financial and the human resources—the knowledge, skills and values—that social workers bring to the task of delivering human services. The umbrella concept of capital offers a useful rubric for bringing these two very different types of resources together under a single heading.

5

Statements: Accounting for Human Services

Accounting is a self-governing profession, like social work, and, like social work, is heavily defined by actual practice and by principles intended to define and codify that practice. There is currently no universally agreed-upon theory of accounting (Riahi-Belkaoui, 2003, p. ix), and there are numerous definitions of "accountancy." GAAPs tend to converge around the issues and definitions identified in chapter 1. Thus, the question of what organizations are doing in applying concepts and practices matters a great deal.

GAAPs and accounting standards for businesses and nonprofits are defined by the Financial Accounting Standards Board (FASB), and audit standards are established by the American Institute of Certified Public Accountants (AICPA). The American Association of Accountants is the professional organization for practitioners that is most analogous to NASW for social workers. However, accounting also has developed a certification-based system for certified public accountants (CPAs) at the top of the professional hierarchy. (In Canada, Great Britain, and elsewhere, CPA is an acronym for *chartered public accountant*.)*

Financial accounting is the information core of human services accountability in the modern HSE. Those involved in human services practice often treat it as either dauntingly unintelligible or meaningless background noise. Accountability and related concerns with transparency and sustainability involve both financial and nonfinancial concerns. Adoption of an enterprise accounting model for nonprofit health and human services by all of the relevant accounting bodies has led to stabilization and uniformity in nonprofit human services accounting for the first time. The enterprise model in business accounting has been stable for much longer.

---

*Readers of this chapter can be forgiven for concluding that accounting is a field besotted by acronyms. This chapter contains too many. Unfortunately, in contemporary HSE practice, such alphabet soup is used with great regularity, and it is therefore important for the student to begin to understand what the various acronyms refer to.

For governmental accounting, GASB is a seven-member board established in 1984 to develop a new model of government accounting and to oversee the definition of GAAPs for state and local government, including public human services. This board took over the function of the National Committee on Governmental Accounting, and a third body, the Federal Accounting Standards Advisory Board (FASAB), issues the Statement of Federal Financial Accounting Standards (SFFAS). While these regulatory bodies—FASB, GASB, and FASAB—are nonprofit organizations, necessary legislation allowing governmental units to participate in the governmental accounting regime is fundamentally different from the voluntary compliance of nonprofit organizations. Key features of the government accounting regime include the Chief Financial Officers Act (1990), numerous state legislative enactments, the Government Performance and Results Act (2000, with major amendments in 2010), and the Service Efforts and Accomplishments reporting design established by GASB (see Martin, 2001, pp. 65–75). The Chief Financial Officers Act mandates annual audit statements for the federal government as a whole and for cabinet-level departments. It also established FASAB. Unlike nonprofit accounting, which has abandoned fund accounting entirely, current government accounting has partially embraced enterprise accounting while retaining a number of elements of fund accounting. Sorting out the many details of government accounting is beyond the scope of the present discussion; instead, the primary focus of the chapter is on current approaches to nonprofit accounting (R. J. Freeman, Shoulders, Allison, Patton, & Smith, 2009; D. W. Young, 2005).

ACCOUNTING DEFINED

In general, *accounting* is the art and practice of identifying, gathering, measuring, summarizing, and analyzing information on financial activities and positions necessary to support economic decision making of a recognized group or organization (American Accounting Association, as cited in Mook, 2013, p. 17). Professional accountants usually approach accounting as a rational, technical, quantitative, and value-free practice (Mook, 2013, p. 18). Such a stance is inconsistent with much social work theory and practice, which is strongly value based; an approach shared with some critical theorists in the accounting profession is discussed in chapter 11 (see also Mook, 2013, pp. 18–19). Even so, the pursuit of value-free objectivity remains the dominant perspective in the practice of accounting, and the human services manager must learn to recognize and work within its assumptions and limits. Accounting is a very precise practice with great attention to many details of little concern to others. The social work manager of the small private or nonprofit HSE who must master the details of accounting is fairly rare and will undoubtedly need to consult a recent accounting textbook or manual (and probably more than one!) for the answers to questions left unanswered here (see, for example, Bryce, 2000; Finkler, 2013; Zietlow & Seider, 2007). Fortunately, such details are not the usual concern of human services managers, who work primarily with the resulting reports and analyses without involvement in the details of their preparation.

TYPES OF ACCOUNTING

The recognized types of accounting include financial and management accounting, as well as tax accounting and auditing, expense accounting, cost accounting, and a new and still controversial type called social accounting. *Financial accounting* refers to standardized ways of recording the actions of programs and services as additions to (income) and subtractions from (expenditures) a stock of financial resources (*capital*, or assets). A basic assumption of financial accounting is that financial reporting is for stakeholders, beginning with boards of directors and also including grant makers, donors, and other funders, among others. *Managerial accounting* is a more limited subset of financial accounting in which reporting represents feedback to enable managers to better perform their day-to-day duties and fulfill their responsibilities.

For a long time, and until quite recently, nonprofit HSEs were largely left to their own devices to devise accounting standards and practices. However, in the last quarter of the 20th century, the rapid growth of public funding in social work and dramatic increases in the number of human services organizations delivering services led to a movement within the accounting profession for the development of uniform standards (known as GAAPs). This movement began in the United States but has since spread worldwide.

All HSEs and programs are required to engage in financial accounting to the extent that they accept funding from outside sources or wish to hold tax-exempt status. Over and above this mandatory dimension, accounting technology can be very useful if approached as a helpful tool rather than merely an obligation. The trial balance was originally designed only for use by bookkeepers in error correction, a task made largely superfluous by computerized accounting systems. From a managerial perspective, the trial balance also serves as a kind of early warning system to detect a range of potential issues and problems. There is a general lack of cost accounting schemes for human services like those used in modern hospitals. As a result, general managerial accounting strategy in HSEs requires extra steps to conduct, prepare, or oversee special cost studies developed from basic accounting data, a topic explored in chapter 9.

Figure 5.1: Human Services Accounting System

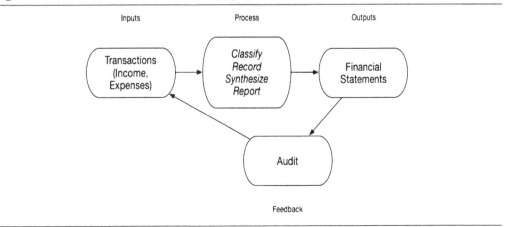

In the typical HSE, managerial accounting includes attention not only to financial accounting, cost monitoring, and fiscal control but also to budget preparation, monitoring, and reporting over and above any financial reporting required by outside funding sources. It is usually a simple procedure to prepare regular monthly comparisons of the approved budget with actual expenses taken from the trial balance. The principal focus of tax accounting in social work entities holding 501(c)(3) tax-exempt status is twofold: accurate completion of the annual IRS Form 990 report and compliance with UBIT requirements where necessary. Finally, *auditing* is the process of examination of financial statements and supportive records to determine their accuracy. The current GAAPs for all nonprofit, commercial, and government entities require regular, periodic audits. In sum, all of the major types of accounting have at least some role to play in the modern HSE.

DEFINITIONS AND DEPARTURES

One of the problems for human service accountability in the past was the neglect of human services programs by accountancy at all levels. This meant for a very long time that accounting in social administration was very much a do-it-yourself enterprise. This led to an unstandardized hodgepodge of approaches, financial standards, and inventions. Some of the resulting developments (for example, workplace giving and federated financing campaigns of Community Chests and United Way) were important innovations that have survived and thrived. Some (for example, specific budgeting and fund accounting practices) have survived in dramatically modified and restricted form, whereas others (for example, systems of stewardship and fund accounting) have been replaced entirely.

By the late 1950s, national human services associations, including Family Services of America and United Way of America, developed their own accounting handbooks, charts of accounts, and financial standards for practice. Local community services unaffiliated with any national networks were largely free to devise their own practices and standards or to not engage in any financial reporting at all. This laissez-faire approach was undermined by the arrival of public federal and state funding in the 1960s. Each federal grant-making agency sought to impose its own standards on the rapidly proliferating social agencies and programs. Such an approach proved to be less problematic for social administrators than it was for the CPAs tasked with auditing the rapidly expanding universe of social agencies and programs and attesting to the accuracy of their financial statements.

By the early 1970s, a committee of AICPA had devised accounting standards for voluntary health and welfare entities and, by 1974, the first-ever national set of uniform accounting standards.* In addition to kick-starting the general movement toward national GAAPs, one of the most useful developments resulting from this AICPA initiative was the three-part distinction of administrative, fundraising, and program costs that remains in effect and useful today (see Table 6.5). A few years later, the FASB and the GASB refined the original AICPA standards into the GAAPs

---

*See chapter 2 of Lohmann (1980) for a review of that development.

for nonprofit and public entities. This trend toward universal accounting standards for nonprofits may not have fully run its course. Recently, a number of European countries have signed on to a set of International Financial Reporting Standards promulgated by the International Accounting Standards Board.

The original focus was on distinct accounting and audit principles and standards for voluntary health and welfare entities and permitted such traditional practices as fund accounting, program entities, and cash selection or modified accrual accounting. The FASB adopted a broader, more uniform and far-sighted approach to tax-exempt nonprofit organizations in general, beginning with the radical redefinition of the basic accounting entity from funds (and the companion concepts of grant and program) to the enterprise as a whole. Thus, the discussion of enterprise concepts in prior chapters was prompted by this shift in accounting entities, which laid the basis for an entirely new set of theoretical understandings, including the social enterprise perspective presented in chapter 1 and a new budget type discussed in chapter 6, the "all-funds," or enterprise, budget.

Some limited accommodation of funds accounting may still be necessary for the handling of restricted funds, where large donors or grantors may require specific accountability for the moneys they have contributed, but such accounting is now done within the overall rubric of the enterprise as a whole. Thus, an HSE is expected to have a single, uniform, integrated accounting system and the ability to produce reports for the entire organization as well as for separate funds for each major program, as it might have in the past.

The current GAAPs promulgated by FASB did away with many idiosyncratic fund accounting practices for nonprofits. In fact, this transformation in accounting may be the most real, concrete meaning of "becoming more businesslike" for contemporary nonprofit human services. The result is often something of a mixed blessing. GAAPs also mandate accrual accounting and annual financial audits, practices that can place outsized financial burdens on small, underfunded agencies.

ACCOUNTING ASSUMPTIONS

An important feature of the combined efforts of the GAAPs has been the emergence and gradual embrace of a set of uniform standard assumptions over and beyond those already discussed on which social work accounting is based, regardless of whether accounting is for a nonprofit or for-profit organization or a governmental entity. The most fundamental accounting assumptions have already been mentioned. Of core importance is the entity assumption. Enterprises as accounting entities are assumed to be ongoing or continuous operations, with a definite beginning, reports at regular intervals over the entire period of operations, and explicit legal and administrative provisions for ending or termination.* Monetization, as

---

*The most critical of these in the case of nonprofit organizations is the membrane of tax deductibility, behind the nondistribution constraint and the disposition of assets clause. In general, the nondistribution constraint applying to tax-exempt nonprofit organizations requires that such assets can only be distributed to a public or other nonprofit entity.

previously discussed, is another assumption. A third, closely related assumption is *periodicity*, that periodic financial reports in a series are for the same entity and are, in that sense, comparable. Reporting periods may be days, months, quarters, or years, and specific line items in recurring reports for those periods are the basic units of comparison. The most basic periodical unit is the *fiscal year*, which may be any 365-day period, corresponding with the calendar year, federal or state fiscal years, or another period of the organization's choosing.

    Materiality, or the likelihood that the presence or absence of a piece of accounting information would alter a decision or course of action, is also important, as it makes clear what is and is not covered by accounting data. The *consistency* assumption that named items being measured or assessed are defined similarly over time provides the basis for valid and reliable period-to-period comparison.

FIVE CATEGORIES AND THE BASIC EQUATIONS

A typical chart of accounts includes an indefinite number of individual items divided into five basic categories. This presents another important case of lumping and splitting: Although there are dozens of possible accounts, they are always grouped into five basic categories that appear in financial statements of all types of nonprofit entities. The five categories deal with two fundamental measures: financial position and changes over time. The conventional names for the three groups of accounts that deal with financial position are "assets," "liabilities," and "net income." The last of these is simply the difference between the first two and is a measure of the working capital available at the end of an accounting period. The final two categories record changes and are termed "income" and "expenses." Regardless of level of detail, these five categories relate to one another in consistent, reliable ways that date back hundreds of years to Pacioli and summarize the financial position and activity of an HSE in consistent, monetary terms.

Assets

The key to understanding all five categories and the centerpiece of nonprofit financial accounting is the concept of assets. The other four basic categories all represent adjustments of one kind or another to this most fundamental category. The term is the accounting word for the resources or capital available before outstanding expenses have been paid and all debts have been settled. Assets are most easily thought of as what the entity, the HSE, owns. This may be in the form of cash in the bank, land, buildings, vehicles, investments, or other assets. Most of us recognize also that many of the most vital assets (or more accurately, perhaps, strengths) of human services, such as the knowledge and experience of staff, the use of experience-tested methods of doing things, and networks of trusted relations, cannot be monetized or measured, even though they are fundamentally important. Whereas we may, at times, speak of such strengths as assets, they are not, strictly speaking, assets in a financial accounting sense, regardless of how essential they may be to the operation of services—unless they can be monetized. Efforts to do so are within the domain of contemporary social accounting, and we discuss one contemporary example of this in the discussion of the basic accounting equation later in this chapter and variations in chapter 11.

Not all financial assets are always immediately at hand; some are only within reach. Thus, distinctions are often made between *liquid assets* or *current assets*, which are available for more or less immediate use, and those that are not, labeled with such terms as *nonliquid assets* and *long-term assets*. Another essential category of assets for any HSE, *accounts receivable*, may include grants or contracts awarded but not yet paid or donations that have been pledged but have not yet been received. In fee-for-service contexts, services that have been delivered and billed but have not yet been paid are likely to be the most important category of accounts receivable (sometimes also referred to just as *receivables*).

Liabilities

We cannot fully appreciate the current asset position of any entity without also considering the liabilities, which are those financial obligations that the enterprise owes to others (Mattocks, 2008). The typical type of liabilities for most HSEs are those termed *current liabilities*, such as unpaid bills for rent, utilities, or other similar short-term obligations. Another type, *long-term liabilities*, are those obligations that continue over long periods of time, including mortgages on buildings and property; bond issues; or long-term, secured loans. Current liabilities are usually listed in the accounts payable section of financial statements. Furthermore, if there are routinely enough liabilities over an extended period of time, these may require a separate accounts payable journal. An accounts payable line in the trial balance offers a useful reminder of the outstanding current liabilities, comparable from month to month and year to year.

In accounting theory, liabilities are commitments that offset or subtract from the assets held by an entity. This gives rise to the basic formula of nonprofit accounting: assets − liabilities = net income. Under the terms of double-entry bookkeeping, this equation will always be true and any statement of financial position should be in balance at all times. (This is primarily why that statement is called a "balance sheet.")

Net Income

Application of the basic equation—subtracting liabilities from total assets—produces the third and most problematic basic category, labeled "net income." This has always been the single most inconsistently labeled and difficult to interpret of the five basic categories. It used to be called the "fund balance," "surplus," "equity," and a variety of other names, and few nonaccountants can say with certainty what its real significance is. Regardless of what it is called, it is always the result of subtracting total liabilities from total assets. In business accounting, this same result is often identified as "owners' equity," or, more simply, "capital." In the next section, an important use of this item in constructing a basic financial ratio is discussed.

Income and Expense

The last two of the basic categories, income and expenses, can also be a bit confusing in HSE settings. In accounting terms, *income* refers to financial inflows adding to the stock of assets held by the enterprise, and *expenses* refer to decreases, subtractions from, or reductions to assets. Together income and expense accounts are used to gather and report financial activity data. There is a certain amount of ambiguity in terminology between net income on the balance sheet and the financial activity recorded by income, but these distinctions become clear with use. The combined effects of income and expenditure over time are reflected not only as activities in themselves but also as changes from one time to the next in the stock of assets and liabilities or the claims against that stock. Just as financial position is always reported for precise moments in time, financial activity is reported across specified periods or intervals of time, and financial activity reports, including all income and expense statements (as well as budgets), must note in their headers the period for which financial activity is reported or the period for which future activity is projected. As is shown in the next chapter, budgets are customarily prepared as reports of anticipated or expected financial activity rather than as anticipated future financial position, and thus they are also made for periods of time rather than specific points in time.

Likewise, *expense* is primarily used as a noun to describe the financial result of transactions. Furthermore, *expense* can also be used as a verb for the action of spending, for example, by saying that something is expensed or that an expenditure was made. *Expenditure* is initially a term describing the process of spending, although it too can be and is used separately and in some cases as a synonym for expense. For example, "that was a large expenditure."

Receipts and *disbursements* traditionally have served as other names for income and expense. *Revenue* is a term borrowed from governmental accounting. In human services settings, it is most often used, if at all, as a synonym for income or receipts.

The entire financial history and current position of a human service is told in terms of the assets, liabilities, net income, income, and expense. These five terms also are the basic elements used in construction of the basic financial statements defined in the GAAPs. Unlumped, they are subject to almost infinite variety, as shown in the sample chart of accounts.

BASIC FINANCIAL STATEMENTS

The basic financial position and activity of any nonprofit enterprise are assumed to be adequately captured and summarized by three basic financial statements that summarize key information captured by the enterprise's accounting system. According to Financial Accounting Standard (FAS) 117, these statements are (a) a statement of financial position, (b) a statement of activities, and (c) a statement of cash flows. FAS 117 further mandates a fourth statement, (d) a statement of functional expenses for all voluntary health and welfare organizations, and recommends it for other nonprofits (Wing, Gordon, Hager, Pollak, & Rooney, 2006). These four financial statements, together with IRS Form 990, are built from information recorded within the five basic categories of accounting data.

Statement of Financial Position

The basic formula (total assets − total liabilities = net income) defines the structure and contents of the statement of financial position, also widely known as a balance sheet. As its name suggests, this statement is used to document the financial position of an enterprise at a particular point in time. Thus, the date noted on a statement is very important and one of the first places to look. The specific day on which the reporting occurs may vary, but the continuity and periodicity assumptions remind us that consistency over the long haul matters. A reviewer should be able to look at a series of balance sheets and reconstruct with a high degree of confidence changes in the assets held by the enterprise. Thus, the differences between two consecutive statements of financial position, one dated the first of a month and the next dated the 15th of the following month, are not actually monthly reports, as the difference between them actually reflects a six-week interval. Analysts of balance sheets need to train themselves to always check the dates of such statements before looking for other information.

The statement of financial position may be the easiest place to begin any financial analysis of a set of human service operations. There are typically three major pieces of information to be found there: What assets did the organization hold at this time? What liabilities did it have? What was the *net income*, or the difference between those assets and liabilities? Other questions can be asked of this statement as well: What is the nature of those assets? Do they represent cash, investments, accounts receivable, or something else? What is the nature of the liabilities? Are they accounts payable, short-term loans, or long-term mortgages? Are the liabilities small or large in comparison with the assets? How subject are they to being demanded or called in on short notice? As is demonstrated in chapter 10, it is also possible to construct a variety of interesting and meaningful ratios from the data in this statement that add to its usefulness.

Statement of Functional Expenditures

The statement of functional expenditures is the principal statement for tracking financial activity over a period of time (see Table 5.2). As the name suggests, this statement reports on financial outflows or expenditures. This is also the statement in which some version of standard charts of accounts in effect in the enterprise is likely to come into play in the list of expenditures shown. Thus, the statement of functional expenditures is likely to be used in any of a number of ways in preparing a budget, for example, providing the actual expenditures column to compare with budget projections.

This statement is useful to gain further insight into the operations previously referred to as "lumping" and "splitting," or, more formally, "aggregation" and "disaggregation." *Aggregation*, or lumping, refers to consolidating a longer, more

Table 5.1: Statement of Financial Position (Balance Sheet)

<Name of Enterprise>
April 30, 20XX

Account Type	Total ($)	Operations ($)	Unrestricted, Board Designated ($)	Restricted ($)	Prior Year
			Year to Date		
Assets					
Current	370,000	70,000	300,000		321,000
Fixed	1,843,296		1,843,296		1,794,187
Long-term	2,438,291		438,291[a]	2,000,000	2,224,743
Total assets	4,651,587	70,000	2,581,587	2,000,000	4,339,930
Liabilities					
Current	18,491		18,491		37,281
Long-term[b]	743,298			743,298	821,247
Total liabilities	761,689		18,491	743,298[c]	858,528
Net assets[d]					
Unrestricted					
Undesignated					
Board designated					
Property, plant, and					
equipment					
Restricted					
Temporarily					
Permanently					
Total net assets	3,889,898	70,000	2,563,096	1,256,702	3,481,402
Total liabilities and net assets	4,651,587	70,000	2,581,587	2,000,000	3,339,820

[a]The value of board-directed investments.
[b]Long-term liabilities designate an endowment fund, 35 percent of which is donor restricted.
[c]Amount of long-term mortgage.
[d]Several possible detailed listings for net assets are shown in italics, but details are omitted to simplify the statement. Monetary amounts are shown only for total net assets.

detailed list of items into a few or even one item, while *disaggregation* refers to the opposite operation of breaking open or splitting a single item into a longer list of composite operations. It is very important to remember that lumping and splitting in accounting always involve an implicit addition problem ($A = a^1 + a^2 + a^3 \ldots + a^n$, where A is the aggregated amount and a^n represents the individual split items). The complete listing of financial transactions recorded in accounting journals is

Table 5.2: Statement of Functional Expenditures

<Name of Enterprise>
for the Year 20XX

Category	Division				
	Adult Services ($)	Children's Services ($)	Management and General ($)	Fundraising ($)	Total ($)
Human resources	387,429	641,237	78,318	55,420	1,162,404
Building and grounds[a]	46,492	76,948	9,400	6,651	139,488
Other expenditures[b]	147,223	243,670	29,761	21,060	441,714
Total expenditures	581,144	961,855	117,479	83,131	1,743,606

[a]As the statement of financial position shows, this enterprise owns its own building, for which it has a mortgage. Thus, titling this category "rent" would not be accurate. Costs of the current mortgage payments and maintenance are prorated across the four categories.

[b]In this example, all expenditures other than personnel costs and mortgage expenses are lumped together in a single line. Many enterprises may prefer more detailed listings of expenditures. This is mostly a matter of traditional practice and does not affect the overall statement.

fully disaggregated. The trial balance (see Table 1.2) that lists the current value of each ledger account is up one level of aggregation. The amount of detail, or *aggregation*, shown on the statement of functional expenditures is a matter of both convention and the nature of the problems to be solved.

Statement of Cash Flows

In the 1974 accounting standards for voluntary health and welfare entities, the original version of this statement had the very colorful but descriptively accurate name of "statement of receipts, disbursements, and changes in fund balance." The current statement of cash flows (see Table 5.3) is essentially the same statement, but with a simpler title. This statement can be a highly useful tool for human services managers who learn how to read and use it. The version shown in Table 5.3 has several useful pieces of information. Table 5.3 includes a column for percentages here to give readers a start in grasping its usefulness. Another useful piece of information in this statement summarizes payouts to employees, in the form of wages and salaries as well as additional fringe benefits such as the Federal Insurance Contributions Act (FICA) tax, health insurance, and retirement. Again, the percentages can be particularly useful in making comparisons over time. The ratio of human capital expenses to total expenses is also useful. Such ratios typically run above (and sometimes well above) .5, and for any HSE where that is not the case, analysts might well ask, "Where is all the money going? It isn't going into salaries for services!" Finally, this statement provides a place to note any taxes paid (for example, UBITs) and the differences between inflows and outflows of

Table 5.3: Statement of Cash Flows

<Name of Enterprise>
<Date>

Cash Flow, All Operating Activities	This Year ($)	This Year %	Last Year ($)	Last Year %
Cash receipts, source				
Clients	386,421	19.09	351,643	18.11
Grants	718,227	35.47	790,050	40.67
Contracts	841,316	41.55	681,466	35.08
Insurance	27,494	1.36	57,737	2.97
Donations	51,265	2.53	61,518	3.17
Total cash receipts	2,024,723	100.00	1,942,414	100.00
Cash disbursements				
Cash paid to employees	1,295,823	65.56	1,295,794	65.63
Cash paid for employees	362,830	18.36	365,729	18.52
Taxes paid (UBITs, etc.)	0	0.00	0	0.00
All other cash paid	317,800	16.08	312,742	15.84
Total cash disbursements	1,976,453	100	1,974,265	99.99
Net cash (deficit) from operating activities	48,270	2.38	−$31,851	−1.64

Note: UBITs = unrelated business income taxes.

cash. Studying successive versions of this statement, for example, may be a good beginning point for cash flow analysis, as discussed in chapter 12.

Statement of Financial Activity

The statement of financial activity is the last of the four basic financial statements (see Table 5.4) The rules for its preparation and use are spelled out in FASB Standard 117 but will likely not be initially clear to novice social administrators. For anyone who is prepared to study and understand it and make use of its insights, it can be a valuable tool whether prepared quarterly or monthly. Structurally, it is a statement noting the combined effects of income and expenses, broken down by the three basic cost categories of administrative, fundraising, and program expenses. Given the controversy that has engulfed HSEs for more than a century, having a ready measure of administrative costs available at all times can be a useful strategic weapon, and being able to compare fundraising costs with income from fundraising is also highly useful (Clark & Jordan, 2001).

Finally, direct program costs (and the indirect costs of administration and fundraising) are a useful starting point for monetary measures of outputs.

Table 5.4: Statement of Financial Activity

<Name of Enterprise>
April 30, 20XX

Category	Unrestricted ($)	Temporarily Restricted ($)	Permanently Restricted ($)	Total ($)
	Type of Assets			
Income				
Client payments	2,512,449			2,512,000
Grant income		250,000		250,000
Contract income		410,000		410,000
Investment income			29,449	29,449
Insurance payments				
Expenditures				
Program	1,987,428	625,000	25,687	2,638,115
Management and general	184,726	25,000		209,726
Fundraising	57,281	10,000		67,281
Changes in net assets	283,114	10,000	3,762	296,876
+ Beginning net assets	2,031,256	704,287	867,479	3,603,022
− Ending net assets	2,314,370	714,287	871,241	3,899,898

Note: This statement must agree with the total net assets on the statement of financial position.

ANALYTICAL NOTES

The full information value of financial statements begins to become apparent, as the examples above suggest, when the social work manager ceases merely looking at or reading the information already encoded in the financial statements (Wacht, 1987; Wolf, 2001). The greater value becomes apparent through comparing two or more items found there. Some comparisons can be done in terms of more and less. A variety of systematic ways of making such comparisons are the subject of chapter 10 and termed "ratio analysis." Before undertaking a systematic analysis, however, the budding financial analyst might just want to sit down with a set of financial statements and tease out the basic information to be found there. For example, by viewing the total assets listing on the balance sheet and the total income shown on the cash flow statement in several successive reports, it is ordinarily fairly easy to note which amounts are greater and which are smaller. It is straightforward and relatively easy to compare any item for this year (or this quarter or this month) with the same item in a previous period: "Our total assets are up over a year ago, but total expenses are down." Many such simple comparisons can be extracted from any set of financial statements, and their usefulness as management guidance is straightforward. Even more useful information can be extracted from a set of financial statements through the simple arithmetic exercises known as ratio analysis. A financial ratio is most often expressed as a decimal fraction derived from a numerator drawn from one financial statement item and a denominator from another.

Managing accountability concerns is a fundamental process of social administration. The first steps are generally in the hands of accountants, but social work managers need to know something of the process in order to make use of the outputs of the accounting system. This chapter is intended to give an overview of some of the most fundamental terms and concepts of accounting. Subsequent chapters focus on various facets of the process of management analysis of basic accounting reports, including a review of a range of developments in the area of *social accounting*: a set of efforts to monetize a broader range of concerns for accountability, sustainability, transparency and auditing.

AUDITS

The accuracy of financial statements is a constant concern in financial management and a great deal rests on the assumption that they are, indeed, accurate. *Audit* is a general term for a periodic (usually annual) investigation of financial statements to determine their accuracy and fidelity with law and policy. There are two principal types of audits: internal and external. An *internal audit* might be conducted at any time by any stakeholder of an HSE, including the treasurer or other board members, the finance committee, a special audit committee, the bookkeeper, or another staff person, and it is usually done for a specific purpose (McMullen, 1996). An *external audit* is conducted by a CPA, includes a certified set of financial statements, and ends with a formal opinion regarding the accuracy of the included financial statements. An audit committee may be formed to accept and oversee the HSE response to the auditor's report (McMullen, 1996). That opinion typically will be either an *unqualified* opinion (the best result), stating that the financial statements are accurate and conform with GAAPs with no qualifiers or exceptions, or a *qualified* opinion, detailing areas of concern where the CPA cannot definitely say that the statements are accurate or conform to GAAPs and notes a list of exceptions.

CONCLUSION

The transformation of the basis of nonprofit accounting from fund accounting to an enterprise model is the centerpiece of the quiet revolution in human services financial management. Among the implications for social work is that the enterprise basis of accounting brings nonprofit and private practice more closely into line and creates a greater separation than ever before between private and public nonprofits. The sharp dividing line created by the nondistribution constraint between nonprofit and for-profit practice and the limited likelihood that others will make donations to the latter are both still very important. The four financial statements are mandated by FASB Standard 117.

Most important for financial management, however, is that the changes wrought in recent decades in nonprofit and public accounting provide an important base for future accountability in human services that is not only conceptually stable and mature but is also grounded in GAAPs, which are increasingly universal and consistent across all modes of practice—and across national boundaries. As such, GAAPs provide the conceptual linchpin for consistent approaches to accountability across all modes of social work practice in human services in different communities with differing cultures, histories, and traditions. In the future, this reliable base will be increasingly important not only for human services accounting but also for improved measurement in budgeting and financial analysis as well.

6

Plans: Budgeting in Human Services

The term *budget* comes from the old French term *bougette*, meaning a little bag, sack, or pouch suitable for carrying coins.* Both the term and the practices it describes come to us by way of British parliamentarians, who adopted the term *budget* to describe presentations by the Chancellor of the Exchequer of an annual financial report to Parliament (United Way of America, 1975). This presumably led to discussions of what had been done and what might be done in the future and thus to something very much like contemporary budget discussions. Budgeting is the principal form of financial planning undertaken in most HSEs today (Blazek, 1996; Fos, Miller, Amy, & Zuniga, 2004; Gambino & Reardon, 1981; Maness & Zietlow, 2005; Wymer et al., 2012). For HSEs, *financial planning* is the process of preparing a set of financial decisions for action in the future, and *budgeting* is the monetized dimension of such planning. In this chapter, we examine aspects of budgetary planning and two distinct approaches to budgeting that come together in a perspective referred to as "enterprise budgeting."

BACKGROUND

Financial planning and budgeting at the organizational level have a significant history, both in general management and in human services. In the early decades of the 20th century, scholars and practitioners of scientific management were actively involved in developing key concepts of modern budget theory, in which the pursuit of management efficiency was the watchword. Frederick Taylor, the founder of scientific management, is said to have "deplored the traditional post-mortem uses of accounting" and encouraged his followers to think along different, more

---

*Parts of this chapter are adapted and revised from chapter 6 of Lohmann (1980) and chapter 26 of Lohmann & Lohmann (2002).

future-oriented lines (Wren, 1994, p. 199). What was needed, Taylor mused, were ways to look ahead at the future. Thus was born the essential management timeline: Financial statements report past monetary positions and activity up to the present, whereas budgets project similar information into the future. Conventional budgets showing itemized income and expense projections are typically future-oriented versions of statements of financial activity, such as the one in Table 5.4.

James O. McKinsey was one of the pioneers in the development of budgets as planning and control aids (Wren, 1994, p. 199). In 1903, Henry Hess developed what he called a "crossover chart" showing the connections among volume of production, fixed costs, variable costs, sales, and profits. At about the same time, John R. Williams first proposed the *flexible budget*, in which expenditures are shown to vary with activity. These notions are all important precursors of contemporary budgeting and break-even analysis as discussed here and in chapter 9. Walter Rautenstrauch is thought to have first used the term *break-even point* in 1922 for the beginning point of financial surplus: the unique combination of income and expenses where total costs and variable income are equal and a particular level of output is anticipated. This is completely in line with but a somewhat broader understanding than the conventional HSE notion that budgets must be in balance, where income and expenses are equal without reference to an explicit level of output. By the 1930s, budgets were already in common use in a variety of human services settings, although construction and terminology varied widely. Lohmann (1976) was the first to apply Hess's and Williams's concepts of breaking even to human services. Others have since advanced the methodology (Martin, 2001; Mayers, 2004; D. R. Meyer & Sherraden, 1985; Vinter & Kish, 1985). Linkage of income, expenses, and service levels in budget planning has since become standard practice, at least in the financial management literature of social work. It is not clear whether this notion has gained acceptance in actual practice.

THE ENTERPRISE BUDGET FRAMEWORK

Figure 6.1 shows a schematic of the conventional human services budget system. Budget making, like social research, cost studies, and accounting, is built around a shared focal point. In research, that focal point is termed the "unit of analysis." In cost studies, it is conventionally termed the "cost center" or "cost object" and, in accounting, the "entity" or "accounting entity." Something similar to the shift from fund to enterprise accounting may currently be underway in human services budgeting. The *budget entity*—the unit for which the primary, or all-funds, budget is prepared—is undergoing two sequential changes. The first is the long-term development of *program budgeting*—in which the income and expense categories of a budget conform to the basic program structure of the enterprise. Martin (2001, pp. 10–16), Feit and Li (1998, pp. 67–76), Mayers (2004, p. 60), and Lohmann (1980) all examined aspects of the role of programs in budgeting. It is clear from these discussions that significant differences remain in the role and function of public (governmental) nonprofit and for-profit budgets. Yet, it is equally clear that there have also been important convergences.

Figure 6.1: A Budget Systems Model of Human Service

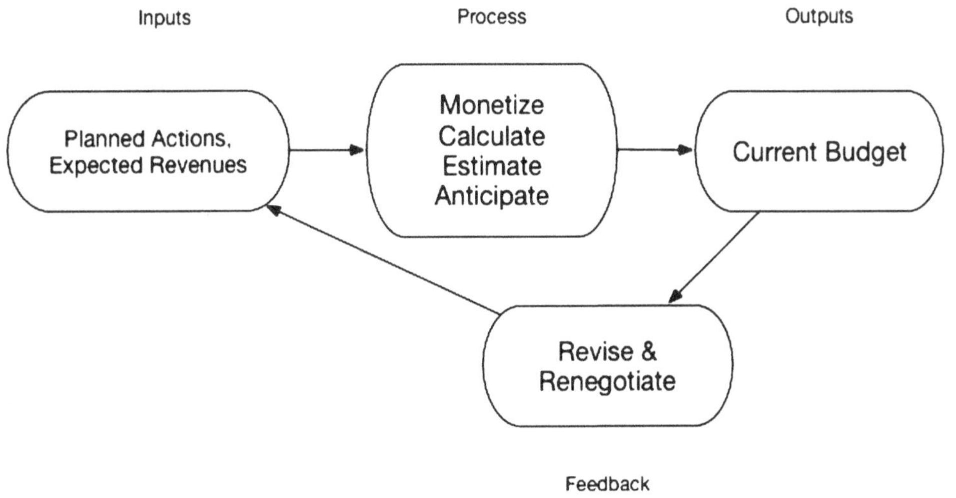

Inputs	Process	Outputs

Planned Actions, Expected Revenues → Monetize Calculate Estimate Anticipate → Current Budget

Current Budget → Revise & Renegotiate → Planned Actions, Expected Revenues

Feedback

Doing a budget for a single program, as in a grant proposal or a targeted fundraising task, is a relatively straightforward exercise. Doing a program budget for an entire HSE with several programs is not nearly as clear-cut, and in cost analysis, where various direct and indirect costs must be teased apart, or in break-even analysis, where fixed and variable costs must be distinguished, things can get more complicated. Regardless, program structures are currently the backbone of HSE budget making, whether defining the entire budget entity in a single-program HSE or outlining the main components of that entity in a multiprogram HSE.

The second development is the model of an enterprise budget (or all-funds budget) for the organization as a whole, intended to take account of all relevant income and expenses of the enterprise.* Keeping track of all income and expenses of an organization used to be an erratic, hit-and-miss proposition, but the enterprise assumption in accounting has provided a framework for a similar approach in budgeting. In general, the enterprise budget entity will be the same as the enterprise accounting entity. With multiple possible sources of income, multiple programs, and both enterprisewide and program-specific expenditures governed by a single management, a complete budget picture is necessary for board members, top managers, and other stakeholders to understand what the enterprise as a whole should be doing. Linking an enterprise budget with the tools of financial analysis also offers an HSE unprecedented levels of integration between the financial and nonfinancial aspects of planning. Just as it is the role of enterprise financial statements to provide an entitywide portrait of past performance and current position, so it is also the role of an enterprise budget—usually in combination with one or more subentity budgets—to summarize an integrated view of future expectations for the HSE.

---

*With the replacement of fund accounting in the FASB accounting standards of HSEs discussed in the previous chapter, the term "funds" and phrases such as "all-funds" have become, technically speaking, anachronisms. However, their use in government accounting is widespread and the meaning of available resources is usually clear.

Base and Increment

One of the oldest and most universal of budget practices is derived from the budget expectations known as base and increment. Despite decades of efforts by academics and management theorists to overturn or minimize them, most budget practices take place against a background of these two important ideas. First, the concept of *base* and the *base budget*, refer to a normative notion distantly related to the legal idea of property rights: What has been ours in the past should remain ours in the future, and efforts to change that must be explained and justified.

Thus, funding at a particular level in a given fiscal year, and even more so if the funding occurs at that level over a period of years, frequently becomes a base (or baseline) expectation for future funding decisions. This expectation can be seen in operation in most United Way systems, public allocations systems, and elsewhere. When asked what they expect in this year's funding, those involved routinely respond with answers such as, "Well, last year we got . . ." Among the most remarkable yet unrecognized achievements of the program grant public distribution systems in both government and foundations has been the weakening of this expectation.

The related idea of a positive increment, or gain, and its negation, the decrement or decrease, reports the degree of year-to-year change in budgets (see, for example, Angelica & Hyman, 1997; Mason, Wodarski, Parham, & Lindsey, 1985; Wineburg, Spakes, & Finn, 1983). It is easily expressed as a percentage. Any budget can incorporate the increment directly by adding two columns, one showing comparable figures for the previous year and the other showing the percentage change.

Varieties of Budgets

Another result of the silent revolution has been consideration by management scholars in social work of a number of different systems and approaches to budgeting and a range of proposals for changes in budget practice. A single budget system—line-item budgeting—has been the norm for HSEs since the 1920s (see Table 6.1 for a typical line-item format).

This arrangement dates to a time when community-level federated financing operations in most major cities mandated such budgeting for the agencies they supported. Table 6.2 shows a reproduction of an actual budget report for Hull House in 1935. There are numerous points of note about this report: It was submitted in the height of the Great Depression. It is titled a "budget report," but the information is presented in the format of a balance sheet. It shows an HSE with relatively large assets but one that is quite poor in cash and liquid assets. Less than 1 percent of the total assets shown are in the form of ready cash, and another 1 percent is deferred income. It appears that the vast majority of Hull House assets were tied up in its endowment (presumably the book values of investments that, given the time, may have been overvalued) and its capital (presumably the real estate holdings of the Hull House campus and summer camp property in Wisconsin). The value of such holdings could only be realized if they were sold. Prior to

Table 6.1: A Conventional Line-Item Budget Format

Item No.	Line Item	Last Year Budget	Last Year Actual	This Year Budget
	Public Support and Income, All Sources			
1	Allocation from United Way or other campaigns			
2	Contributions			
3	Special events			
4	Legacies and bequests			
5	Contributed by associated organizations			
6	Allocated by other (for example, community foundation) funds			
7	Fees and grants from government agencies			
8	Membership dues			
9	Program services fees and net incidental income			
10	Sales of materials			
11	Sales of non-mission-related services			
12	Investment income			
13	Miscellaneous income			
	Expenses			
14	Salaries			
15	Employee benefits			
16	Payroll taxes, etc.			
17	Professional fees			
18	Supplies			
19	Telephone			
20	Postage and shipping			
21	Occupancy			
22	Repair and maintenance of equipment			
23	Printing and publications			
24	Travel			
25	Conferences, conventions, and meetings			
26	Specific assistance to individuals			
27	Membership dues			
28	Awards and grants			
29	Miscellaneous contributions			
30	Total expenses (add items 14–29)			
31	Payments to affiliated organizations			
32	Board designations for specific activities for future years			
33	Total expenses for budget period for all activities			
34	Total expenses for activities financed by restricted funds			
35	Total expenses for activities financed by unrestricted funds			
36	Excess (deficit) of total support and income over expenses			
37	Depreciation of buildings and equipment			
38	Major property and equipment acquisition			

Note: A column of assigned line numbers like those in the United Way chart of accounts or some other standard source might also be included. Columns for additional prior or future years can also be added without disrupting the basic logic of the budget.

Table 6.2: Hull House Budget Report (1933–1935)

Community Fund of Chicago
Budget Report of Hull House Association

Category	Amount ($) by Fiscal Period		
	12/31/33	12/31/34	6/30/35
Assets			
1. Cash on deposit, operating funds	3,123.93	2,591.75	2,730.23
2. Cash on deposit, special funds	14,000.00		15,880.75
3. Petty cash	239.41	248.90	235.00
4. Accounts receivable	6,599.97	2,922.25	2,656.59
5. Notes receivable			
6. Investments	615,927.25	573,750.00	571,450.00
7. Inventories, fuel and supplies	285.75	226.74	226.74
8. Real estate and buildings (institutional)	756,391.87	756,391.87	756,391.87
9. Furniture and equipment	84,715.90	84,715.90	84,715.90
10. Unexpired insurance	2,533.02	3,449.23	3,515.56
11. Automobiles			
12. Cash in closed bank	257.25		
13. (blank)			
14. Total assets	1,484,074.35	1,424,296.64	1,437,802.64
Liabilities and Surplus			
15. Accounts payable	7,828.18	4,965.06	7,633.72
16. Notes payable			
17. Loans and contracts			
18. Mortgages payable			
19. Contracts, residential homes for older adults			
20. Trust funds			
21. Deferred income		1,500.00	
22. Endowments for operating income	535,027.25	475,438.13	473,183.05
23. Capital	846,314.92	844,081.58	851,810.65
24. Endowments for special purposes	94,900.00	98,311.87	105,175.22
25. Total liabilities and surplus	1,484,070.35	1,424,296.64	1,437,802.64

Note: Line 13 is blank in the original. I assume that someone at Hull House or the Chicago Community Fund must have been superstitious!

the current enterprise assumptions, there was no way of determining the extent to which this statement was a full or partial reflection of the actual financial position of Hull House. Given the nature of fund accounting and the budget technology of the time, there could easily have been other funds (for example, rental income from the Jane Club, electricity sales for the electrical generator, and income from the lunchroom) that are not reflected here. It cannot be known from this statement whether (a) the report was normal practice at the time; (b) it may reflect a special set of information the community fund had requested; or (c) it was a substitute for a more normal budget report worked up by the Hull House financial staff out of necessity, along the lines of, "We have no significant income to report, but we do have assets!" Finally, note the use of the term "surplus" in the balance sheet format. This may have been before the heyday of fund accounting, when the proper term would become "fund balance," and definitely preceded usage of the current term, "net income." The strategic use of the term "capital" (the resources to produce services) and its distinction from the investments of the endowment is the basis for a hypothesis that this statement reflects some estimate of the value of Hull House real estate (buildings and grounds): Those buildings and grounds (unlike the endowment) functioned as operating capital used to produce the services of Hull House. Much useful information of this type is encoded in financial statements and reports.

LINE-ITEM BUDGETS

Lohmann (1980) embraced aspects of the line-item approach—and, in particular, the historical, partial, and sequential decision-making style of incrementalism, albeit within a program budget framework. Other, more recent academic contributors to the social work literature on budgeting have been less enthusiastic. Feit and Li (1998), Martin (2001), and Mayers (2004) all raised important questions about the limitations of the incremental approach to budgeting and make proposals for various program and performance budget reforms. These objections mostly relate to the scope of change rather than the style of decision. In support of this conclusion, Jones, True, and Baumgartner (1997) concluded that in the public sector, "volatility (in budget results) indicates dissensus and that budgeting was more volatile and probably less consensual in the past than in the supposedly rancorous present" (p. 1337). A large portion of the human services practice community remains firmly entrenched in whatever version of line-item incrementalism their particular HSE has inherited from its own past. Meanwhile, the ongoing academic dialogue over the best budget system for use in HSEs has continued, powerless to affect the traditional incrementalism of the budget practice community. One of the sources of ambiguity in the academic and research debates has been confusion between incrementalism, or satisficing, as a decision style—how people actually make budget decisions—and incrementalism as a theory of program or operational change. As a result, differing perspectives on how to make decisions and the nature of change often talk past one another. Despite this ambiguity, however, real progress has been made on ways to improve budgeting in HSEs. The key question is how to get more of those insights adopted in practice.

Figure 6.2 shows the general types of budget system that have been proposed relative to HSEs in the past few decades in a two-by-two table differentiating decision style on the horizontal axis from the theory of change on the vertical. Probably the most utopian proposal for budgeting ever developed is the planning, programming, and budgeting system (PPBS), which was adopted with great fanfare and

Figure 6.2: General Types of Budget Systems

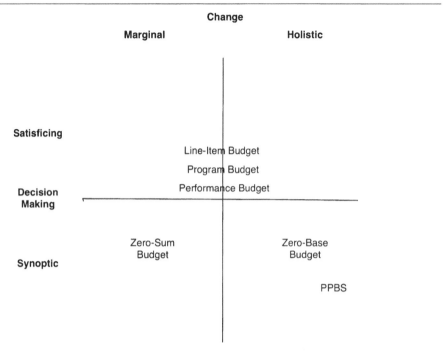

Note: PPBS = planning, programming, and budgeting system.

later quietly abandoned by the U.S. Defense Department in the late 1960s. This system posed, among other things, a highly rationalistic decision style, a program of zero-based budget decisions, and an extensive system of rigorous economic analysis that placed heavy emphasis on the careful and detailed examination of outputs and outcomes (Buttrick & Miller, 1978; Clynch, 1979; Otten, 1977). Despite its failure as a system, the model was brimming with interesting and worthy ideas and proposals and has been the departure point for understanding connections between budgeting and planning ever since. Although the PPBS as a formal system is long gone, a good bit of its terminology has survived, for example, in United Way's naming of its "program planning and budgeting system" (United Way of America, 1975). That system was not much more than a graft of program budgeting formats onto a fundamentally incrementalist, line-item design, but it has also been responsible for widespread adoption of at least limited forms of program budgeting in practice.* In more recent decades, a variety of state governments embraced various forms of zero-base and zero-sum budget systems. A usable idea that emerged from these experiments is the formatting of HSE decision packages. Martin's (2001) discussion of program and performance budgets, for example, is framed around such decision packages, and several of those ideas are included here and in chapter 13.

---

*This comment is intended as a description and not a criticism of the United Way approach, which has held its own as an important part of the quiet revolution, as a number of the following tables and figures show.

ENTERPRISE (ALL-FUNDS) BUDGET

Table 6.3 shows a conventional line-item enterprise budget for a small public HSE, which receives most of its funding from a legislative appropriation, supplemented by fees and a small grant. This is a standard budget format and, except for the appropriation line item, would probably be pretty much the same for any HSE, a social work department in a nonprofit housing agency, or even a for-profit HSE (such as a nursing home, rehabilitation hospital, home health agency, or hospice). This budget shows income from several sources and expenses categorized by line item.

Note that whereas the expense items in Table 6.3 are similar to those shown in other line-item budgets, there is an additional revenue item for legislative appropriations that one would expect to see only in public agency budgets. The income items with zero balances (contracts and donations) are not necessary to this budget and ordinarily would not be included in presentation copies. Table 6.3 is an example of a straightforward line-item budget and also serves as a fixed reference point for several of the discussions that follow in this chapter.

BALANCED BUDGETS

In the nonprofit and public human services budget paradigm, decision makers have little reason to anticipate profits, and even budgeting for a surplus is usually treated as a special circumstance. Ordinarily, HSE budgeting only requires

Table 6.3: Enterprise Budget for a Public Agency

Category	Amount ($)
Income	
Appropriations	1,198,753
Fees	250,000
Grants	20,000
Contracts	0
Donations	0
Total income	1,468,753
Expenditures	
Wages and salaries	1,233,134
Office rental	37,483
Communications	21,428
Travel	137,240
Equipment	32,284
Supplies	7,184
Total expenditures	1,468,753

identifying sufficient resources to achieve the stated purposes of the program, that is, to balance the budget. This is the fundamental anchor of the break-even assumption that characterizes most human services budgeting (see Lohmann, 1980, chapter 1) and is well established in both practice and theory. All of the sample budgets shown in this chapter and elsewhere in this book are shown in balance. However, not all budgets used in practice will necessarily be in balance. Where an unbalanced budget is presented, it would be a good practice to include an additional line item at the end indicating an "anticipated surplus income" or "anticipated deficit" along with an explanatory note, simply because most readers of the budget will be expecting it to balance. The assumption with the enterprise budget system as a whole, as it is in the accounting system, is that things will be in balance: Total anticipated income should equal anticipated expenses plus any planned surpluses or less any planned deficits.

In presenting budgets, it is always a good idea to find and note explicit pathways, thus leaving a trail of breadcrumbs back to the original budget baseline. Within the scope of an enterprise budget, there may be a wide variety of associated sub-budgets. Each funded grant, each distinct program, every separate department, and each special project may have its own budget, and presumably each of these will have links to the enterprise budget. Table 4.1, for example, shows an enterprisewide subentity budget for the wages and salaries, personnel, or human capital expenses budget.

Three essential characteristics define every HSE budget, including sub-budgets:

1. A defined or established objective, purpose, or mission (for example, a program, service, department, formal organization, or work program of a single worker). This can be referred to as the "budget object" or "entity."
2. A plan for expending the resources necessary to achieve that objective (anticipated expenditures or costs and some indication of where the resources will come from).
3. A coordinated plan estimating the resources to be obtained on behalf of the same object (anticipated income).

There may or may not be accompanying memos, reports, or proposals detailing the spending and income plans. The packages of most grant applications illustrate this symbiosis clearly. The underlying assumptions for budgeting are that resources for any given purpose are limited, that no worthwhile objective or purpose can be achieved without some expenditure of resources, and that one cannot expend what one does not have (or cannot obtain).

THE BUDGET PROCESS

The following list shows the steps involved in a conventional budget process formulation as visualized by United Way of America's program planning and budgeting cycle.

Preplanning: Establish the timetable and notify everyone concerned. Schedule meetings. Make room reservations and so forth.

Kickoff: Make any necessary formal announcements, informal notifications, or public notice required.

Data collection: Pull together last two years' budgets, with one or two of the most recent statements of functional expenditures.

Prepare draft budget: Develop a complete mock-up of the new budget, plugging in estimates as needed. *Limit circulation!*

Present to finance committee: Be prepared for a candid and thorough examination. Be analytical, not defensive! Understand which changes are agreed to and which were just ideas batted around. Make sure you leave the meeting clear on who is to do what and by when.

Revise draft: Make necessary and agreed-upon changes.

Present to board for approval.

Publish "final" budget.

Repeat as many of these steps as necessary to revise the budget and keep it up to date (for example, can the finance committee approve changes, or do all changes go back to the board?).

The process begins with a preplanning (or planning to plan) stage and continues through adoption of the budget. Although this discussion projects a linear, step-by-step progression from start to completion, everyone recognizes that budgeting is anything but straightforward. Typically, there are fits and starts, delays, and interruptions, and sometimes there is more than a little backtracking. This process is often presented as a circle (see Mayers, 2004, p. 50), which represents its cyclical (annual) nature without misstating its fundamentally linear character.

Budgeting is usually a multiperson social process, with a complex division of labor and room for numerous activities to be occurring simultaneously. However it is constructed, budgeting is typically a year-round task, with different activities and responsibilities arising at different times of the year.

FIXED, FLEXIBLE, AND ACTIVE BUDGETS

One important distinction that has become increasingly clear over the years arises because of circumstances dictated by the source and characteristics of the income being budgeted. For example, there are budgets where the total funds available for expenditure are known from the start. In addition, the plan and actual expenditures are in line with the express wishes (or restrictions) of a donor or grant maker. In such cases, we are dealing with a classic fixed budget (McCready & Rahn, 1986). Table 6.4 shows a common form of line-item fixed budget, in this case, a grant or project budget.

The only real questions with such budgets are, how quickly or slowly will funds actually be expended, and is it necessary to seek modifications at some point? Customarily, fixed budgets are also line-item budgets. Such a budget may constrain its recipient to spending only within the limits set by the individual line

Table 6.4: Grant or Project Budget

Category	Amount ($)
Salaries and fringe benefits	
Professional	285,000
Support staff	59,680
Fringe benefits (at 28%)	96,510
Office space	19,487
Travel	38,238
Communications	4,240
Equipment	6,338
Supplies	1,840
Total project expenditures	511,333

items, and major deviations within categories may necessitate renegotiation of the budget. The biggest problem is that such categories seldom make much sense in programmatic terms: If what is paid in rent goes up or the phone bill goes down, what are the implications for clients or program goals? Typically, these are unclear. Yet, protracted discussion and even conflict may arise over the size of these individual line items, to the chagrin of program budget advocates.

More flexible budgets can ordinarily be achieved in one of two ways: by reducing the number of line items or by explicitly granting the budget administrators greater leeway to shift funds between categories. Tables 6.5, 6.6, 6.7, and 6.8 show several different forms of radically simplified line-item budgets. In Table 6.6, all line items are lumped into the tripartite AICPA headings of administration, fundraising, and program. Presumably, there would be back-up documents used to arrive at these numbers, such as Table 6.5, but the normal expectation would be that once the budget was approved, spending would be bound by Table 6.6, not by the details in Table 6.5, and the administrators of this budget would have the flexibility to spend within these three broad categories. Another alternative, shown in Tables 6.7, 12.1, and 13.5, was initially developed by the National Association of College and University Business Officers (NACUBO) and has already been in use for several decades in some colleges and universities. Again, a preliminary detailed line-item budget (not shown) may be necessary to arrive at this budget. And again, the point is to enhance flexibility in budget administration. In the budgets in Tables 6.7 and 6.8, there are only two line items: *human capital*, also known as *human resources* or *personnel*, a category that includes all fringe benefits and human capital-related expenses such as training, and *current expenses*, a residual category including everything that is not personnel related. Note also that there is a possible third category sometimes used and labeled *capital expenses* that comes into play only when there are large, permanent expenses involved, such as buildings and

Table 6.5: Grant or Project Budget with AICPA Breakout

| Category | Budget ($) | Type of Expenditures | | |
		Mgt. and General ($)	Fundraising ($)	Program ($)
Salaries and fringe benefits	285,000	42,750.00	14,250	228,000
Professional	59,680	8,952.00	2,984	47,744
Support staff	96,510	14,476.50	4,826	77,208
Fringe benefits (at 28%)	19,487	2,923.05	974	15,590
Office space	38,238	5,735.70	1,912	30,590
Travel	4,240	636.00	212	3,392
Communications	6,338	950.75	317	5,070
Equipment	1,840	276.00	92	1,472
Supplies	0	0.00	0	0.00
Total project expenditures	511,333	76,700	25,567	409,066

Note: AICPA = American Institute of Certified Public Accountants.

infrastructure (Hatry, Millar, & Evans, 1985). Particularly given the high proportion of personnel-related expenses—sometimes up to 80 percent or more of the total—this approach holds considerable appeal for human services. In a typical line-item budget, as in Table 6.4, anywhere from 60 percent to 90 percent of all line items are used to allocate what is often only a small percentage (10 percent to 40 percent) of the total budget, whereas a few personnel items allocate the majority of funds. In cases where professional budget managers have the respect and trust of those approving the budget, the increased flexibility offered by simplified budgets, such as those in Tables 6.5 through 6.9, may constitute a net improvement in budget efficiency and effectiveness. It would also be possible to combine the AICPA and NACUBO formats into another matrix budget, such as the budget in Table 13.5.

Table 6.6: Grant or Project Budget Using AICPA Summaries Category Amount ($)

Management and general	76,700
Fundraising	25,567
Program	409,066
Total project expenditures	511,333

Note: AICPA = American Institute of Certified Public Accountants.

Table 6.7: Grant or Project Budget with NACUBO-Type Headings

| Category | Type of Expenditures | | |
	Budget ($)	Human Capital ($)	Current Expense ($)
Salaries and fringe benefits			
Professional	285,000	285,000	
Support staff	59,680	59,680	
Fringe benefits (at 28%)	96,510	96,510	
Office space	19,487	19,487	
Travel	38,238		38,238
Communications	4,240		4,240
Equipment	6,338		6,338
Supplies	1,840		1,840
Total project expenditures	511,333	460,677	50,656

Note: NACUBO = National Association of College and University Business Officers.

By contrast, in the variable budget situation of all fee-based services, whether or not they are supported by third-party contracts and multifunded agencies, the very act of delivering service can provoke the expenditure of resources and also generate income, thus modifying the total available resources. In such cases, the conventional fixed budget is seldom more than an approximation. Variable budgeting is concerned with three items: income, expenses, and levels of service output. Thus, some calculation protocols may be needed, as in microeconomics in those rare cases when service supplies are known and demand can be predicted or break-even analysis where they cannot. Furthermore, although cash flow considerations can be important in both fixed and variable budgets, they are much more important in the variable budget, as funds are constantly coming in as well as going out, and the concern for cash flow and accounts receivable (monies earned but not yet received) becomes a major consideration in solving the budget problem.

Table 6.8: Grant or Project Budget with NACUBO-Style Summarized Format

Category	Amount ($)
Human capital	460,677
Current expenses	50,656
Capital expenses	0
Total budget	511,333

Note: NACUBO = National Association of College and University Business Officers.

Table 6.9: Enterprise Budget, Year 2

Category	Amount ($)
Income	
Donations	120,000
Fees	150,000
Grants	511,333
Contracts	687,420
Total income	1,468,753
Expenses	
Wages and salaries	1,233,134
Office rental	37,483
Communications	21,428
Travel	137,240
Equipment	32,284
Supplies	7,184
Total expenses	1,468,753

Another key difference of variable and fixed budgets is that whereas the *budget reserve* in any grant-funded operation is merely the amount remaining or unexpended at any given time, the budget reserve of a variable budget is a complex, dynamic, and ever-changing quantity that takes into account not only what is collected and expended but also what has been earned but not yet received (accounts receivable) as well as what everyone involved is doing. All of these factors can fluctuate with the passage of time. In such cases, calculating a variable budget is a very complex task indeed!

DUAL SETS OF SKILLS OF BUDGET MAKING

Effective budgeting involves both analytical and behavioral skills (see Figure 6.3).* From this vantage point, budgeting consists of two discrete sets of skills: (a) those involved in analysis, including the mental, arithmetic, and notational skills necessary to solve the puzzle and the rhetorical skill to present a clear, coherent case; and (b) the kinds of interpersonal skills involved in conducting negotiations, carrying on discussions, and making group decisions to convert budget documents into legitimate authoritative plans capable of governing staff behavior. Ordinarily, in HSEs, preparation of budgets involves combinations of analysis and negotiation. In the smallest HSEs, the same people may perform each set of tasks jointly and serially. In large settings, these tasks may be part of complex divisions of labor, with entire units or departments responsible for each. In all cases, it is important

---

*Part of the remainder of this chapter is adapted from Lohmann, 1980, chapter 6.

Figure 6.3: Analysis by Budget Behavior

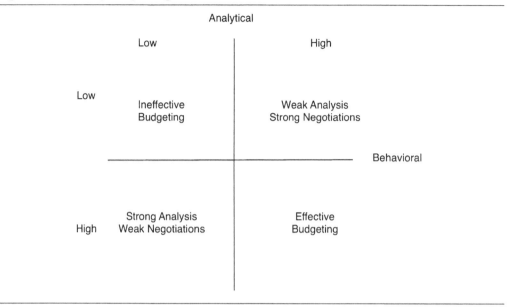

to remember the symbiotic relationship that exists between the analytic and inter-actional dimensions of budgets. The most perfect technical solutions are of little value if they are also unacceptable to those concerned. Budget making and plan-ning are problem solving. Budget decisions are ordinarily made in light of some problem analysis, for example, whether it is the kind of economic analysis favored by proponents of the PPBS or the explicitly political analysis of a vote-counting congressional representative deciding whether to support a particular federal grant proposal. Likewise, if it is to have any impact, even the most sophisticated budget analysis is subject to the expectation that it must be understood by those whose decisions it is intended to influence (Fitzsimmons, Schwab, & Sullivan, 1979). Although they are often treated as separate dimensions or even as separate approaches to the realities of budget making, the analytic and the interactional dimensions are both necessary for an understanding of the allocation of resources in human services.

BUDGET SYSTEMS

The term *budget system* is used here to refer to a wide range of standard situations, from the allocation activities of a local United Way organization to the appropria-tions activities of a state legislative committee or the grant-related decision-making of a community foundation. The reference, in each instance, is to the systematic and interrelated character of certain events and activities that occur under the heading of budgeting. That systematic character usually consists of a mixture of rules (for example, the limits on percentage increases in a particular year) and institutions (for example, announced requests for proposals, budget hearings, and formal decision meetings).

Among the principal elements in many budget systems is a *summary* or *consolidated budget document*, which is an authoritative statement by the principal decision-making authority of the results of their efforts. The enterprise budget of an HSE serves this purpose. The printed federal budget also serves this purpose, as do comparable state budgets.

Because of the aggregate (or lumped) nature of such a final budget statement, it is perhaps inevitable that the full import of budgetary actions cannot be found in the final budget but must be gleaned from these other intermediate sources and directly from participants as well. The question "What really happened in there?" is a frequently heard one in budget settings, for good reason. In a very real sense, budgeting at the working level is often a veritable subculture of understandings, reactions, and agreements, as well as formal decisions. Gaining a sophisticated understanding of this level of budgeting activity and its implications for administrative action is often the single greatest challenge facing the human services administrator.

Budget systems of greatest interest in the human services can be classified in three different ways. First, there are the larger arenas: those organized situations or contexts in which presenters and their proposals compete with other organizations and interests for portions of a distribution of funds. There are four general types of such arenas in contemporary human services organizations: (1) public appropriations in Congress, state legislatures, and city councils; (2) public distributions in hundreds of federal and state agencies engaged in the distribution of public funds through grants review and contracting procedures and thousands of private foundations; (3) federated distributions such as United Way contributions or Combined Federal Campaigns, in which citizen decision makers divide income raised in a consolidated fundraising campaign among groups of member agencies; and (4) internal allocation systems, in which internal HSE decisions must allocate income generated by donations and fees.

Second, human services budget systems can be classified on the basis of how budget decision making is conceived and carried out. Five conceptions of budget making are most relevant: the incremental model, performance budgeting, program budgeting, program planning and budgeting, and zero-based budgeting. Because a good deal has been written on each of these topics yet much of it fails to make clear distinctions between what such systems actually accomplish and what their designers hope for them to accomplish, discussion of each of these is of an evaluative character.

The third dimension—the degree of change—shown in Figure 6.2, is the domain of John Friedmann's (1973) innovative planning, but there is actually very little professional literature on the use of budgets to bring about major social change. Whether there is a focus on maintaining the status or on massive social change will, in most instances, depend on some combination of the personal motives and skills of budget negotiators, HSE missions, available resources, and the larger context. As far as I am aware, there are no instances or examples in which dedicated reformers highly committed to bringing about major social change first set out to modify or transform a budget system!

PUBLIC APPROPRIATIONS

Significant progress in understanding the management of finances in the public sector has been a fairly recent development (Schick, 2007). Because of the system of funding of human services that has developed since the 1960s, public appropriations budgeting has primarily had indirect effects for most human services agencies except for the highest-level state agencies. Unfortunately, the significance of state-level funding is still not fully appreciated by many social work professionals, and research in this area remains woefully inadequate.

Detailed understanding of state budgetary processes is typically limited to a few key insiders employed by large public bureaucracies; members of legislative liaison committees; and the political action committees of professional associations, public interest groups, trade associations, and private interest groups (Karski & Barth, 2000).

The majority of human services professionals today operate with an understanding of state budgeting at or below the level of sixth grade civics textbooks. Just as important, the published literature in this area is very limited and seldom focuses directly on systematic analysis of budgetary practices and concerns. Thus, about the only way for a human services professional to gain a sophisticated understanding of state-level public appropriations is to become directly involved in the process in a given state.

For the most part, budget practices in the public appropriations context are likely to remain a highly specialized domain of greatest interest to federal and state government employees, public administration researchers, NASW political action committee members, and others whose job assignments or volunteer civic activities bring them into this context.

DISCRETIONARY GRANTS

Since the Great Society era in the 1960s, another type of budget system has emerged in and around governments at all levels, as well as in the system of the nearly 100,000 foundations that have sprung up in the United States. Its importance to HSE rivals or surpasses that of public appropriations. It is a distribution system built around the distinction between the constitutive acts of legislative bodies and foundation founders and the distributive acts of administrative and professional decision makers, whose actions are shaped by many factors. This system is termed *discretionary* because of the high levels of choice involved in the distribution of funding. The growth of discretionary grant funding of human services programs has meant the emergence of an entirely new level of budgeting activity largely in the form of transactions between professionals in administrative settings. This class of activity, from the vantage point of those seeking, is called "grantsmanship"; from the supply side, it's called "grant making" (Carlson, 2002; Coley & Scheinberg, 2008; M. S. Davis, 1999; Lauffer, 1997; Ward & Hale, 2006).

Although some of the public aspects of the appropriations system, such as public notification requirements, have been carried over to the public discretionary grant system, other requirements, such as the publication of guidelines governing the distribution of funds, have grown up on their own. This distribution system as it operates within federal government agencies in the U.S. Department of Health and Human Services, the U.S. Department of Housing and Urban Development, and other federal and state agencies gives relatively large and nontransparent discretionary opportunities to relatively unaccountable public officials. Despite numerous claims that foundation grants involve private action for the public good, whether these grants are in the public interest is hard to determine. The reality is that discretionary grants made by foundations involve even higher levels of discretionary decisions about what is in the public good and even less transparency, with accountability generally only to the governing trustees of the foundation.

This system is a quasi-market one; the characteristics of the distribution system make centralized control and planning virtually impossible (Lowi, 1969, 1995). Furthermore, general legislative oversight of grant distribution systems has been limited to nonexistent. One important formal difference for HSEs between the public appropriations and discretionary grant systems involves the question of continuity and change. One of the key characteristics of both governmental and foundation grant distribution systems is that they typically do not make any assumptions about baseline or ongoing funding. Often, quite the opposite is true. HSEs funded through the public distributions context usually have no assurance of continued support, either legally or formally. At the same time, many foundation grants operate with elaborate rationales to justify short-term funding: seed money, demonstration grants, and model programs. Most discretionary grants are, by default, provided only for short periods of time (for example, a three-year support window) with no commitments for ongoing support. With good reason, such funding is often said to be soft money. This formal difference may be more apparent than real, however, for experience has shown time and again that agencies already receiving funding are likely to receive future support from a funding agency.

Foundations are often highly selective in awarding grants, and some public agencies publicize the percentages of grant applications funded to support claims of high selectivity, discriminating judgment, quality, and high standards. Claims that 90 percent of all applications received are rejected are not unheard of. What is seldom reported, however, is the percentage of funded projects and programs that are more or less continuous. A kind of closed membership of agencies and programs that are, in effect, first in line for funding feature most public distribution systems in both government and foundations. In the case of federal funding, the most concentrated example of this is the case of the *beltway bandits*, the growing number of nonprofits and consulting firms funded over and over again by federal authorities (Ghani, Carnahan, & Lockhart, 2006; Sharkansky, 1980).

Realistically, it is hard to imagine how public distribution systems could operate any other way: Funding agencies accountable for their performance to Congress or legislative bodies can ill afford to pursue high-risk funding strategies or fund high-risk grantees. It is reassuring to fund an agency previously funded that is currently performing acceptably. Likewise, from the standpoint of the HSE, the circumstances of funding may be largely a matter of indifference, provided that some degree of certainty and continuity is assured. It is frustrating to jettison programs because grant support is lost, and it is difficult to seek out new sources of grant money each year.

Thus, there are good reasons on both sides for the public distribution system that has emerged. Yet, many questions remaining concerning its efficiency. Might it not be more efficient simply to openly acknowledge funding continuity in grant-in-aid programs? Yet, such acknowledgment would fly in the face of the current interest in fiscal accountability, particularly at the political level, where concerns with waste, fraud, and abuse of public trust continue to carry great weight (McNeal & Michelman, 2006; Zack, 2003).

Although grants continue to be an important source of income for human services, the long-term future of public distribution budgeting remains unclear. Conservative movements have been attempting to completely eliminate public discretionary grants for decades, with limited success. There is little doubt that anti-welfare-state politics still carry great appeal, and complete elimination of all federal and state discretionary grants for human services is one possible eventuality. Nevertheless, the system of public grant funding that has evolved also shows a great many signs of vitality, and most human services agencies will continue to rely at least partially on grant funding as long as possible.

VOLUNTARY FEDERATED DISTRIBUTIONS

Perhaps the other most significant type of budget system affecting human services agencies today are the federated distribution systems, in which recognized member agencies receive shares of income generated by annual federated or consolidated fundraising campaigns. Most widely known among such campaigns are the 4,000 local affiliates worldwide of United Way International. Less well known but equally relevant in this category are the Combined Federal Campaign directed at federal employees, assorted combined campaigns of state employees, several Black United Funds, Red Feather, and a host of other similar systems. These fundraising enterprises can be distinguished from single-agency and cause-specific fund drives, such as those conducted by the American Heart Association or the American Cancer Society, and from national agencies with local affiliates (many of whom participate in United Way) by the allocative mechanisms through which decisions on resources are made.

The range and diversity of federated distribution systems makes generalizing about their budgetary practices difficult. In some communities, for example, the United Way operates like a public utility, with public budget hearings, newspaper accounts of transactions, and a generally public posture. In other communities, allocation of funds to agencies is handled by community leaders serving on budget committees in a manner once described by one of them as "discrete but appropriate." A few tentative generalizations about voluntary federated distribution systems can be made. First, distribution decisions are typically handled as community trusts by committees of local citizens (as opposed to the relatively unaccountable professionals of the public grant and foundation worlds), ideally, a board or committee of deciders not directly involved with the HSEs or others receiving funding. This condition alone should ensure the presence of at least minimal levels of community accountability in federated distribution systems.

Second, there is a tradition among the larger urban federated funding entities of engagement in social or program planning, priority studies, and need determination studies to create a knowledge base for more effective allocation decisions (Brilliant, 1990; Cnaan & Milofsky, 2007; Kettner, Moroney, & Martin, 1990; Tropman, 1972; Weil, Reisch, & Ohmer, 2013). As a result, funding decisions are likely to take into account factors other than the pattern of demands expressed by the member agencies. Third, although it is still not widely recognized, federated operations such as United Way of America along with the Urban Institute's Center for Charitable Statistics, the Foundation Center, and Guidestar have become significant forces for improving the financial management capacities of agencies in the voluntary sector (Palmer & Randall, 2001; United Way of America, 1974, 1975; see also J. S. Glaser, 1994).

As an important contribution to the American model of fundraising, United Way and the various combined government campaigns pioneered the model of workplace giving, in which pledges are solicited not by contacting potential donors at home but by reaching donors at their job sites. The future of this aspect of federated ventures and their unique budgetary systems is currently uncertain (Manser, 1960; Smith, 2014). Voluntary contributions to human services agencies are a relatively paltry source of income compared with other sources, notably public funds. In addition, many human services may have largely opted out of the initial burst of renewed private philanthropy that began in the 1990s, and many voluntary human services agencies once supported entirely through donated funds are now largely supported by public distributions.

One feature of the human services budget system first developed by private foundations and later adopted by federal agencies is the use of expert review committees to advise in decision making. For whatever reasons, federal scientific agencies today routinely use expert reviewer panels to assist in grant decisions, whereas human services funders do not. Whereas peer review is nearly universal in social work professional journals, comparable application of expertise in the funding process at all levels of human services budgeting has not been nearly as common.

INTERNAL SYSTEMS

One of the essential features of the quiet revolution in human services financial management is a transformation of meanings of *inside* and *outside* the organization. In the budget systems discussed above, a key feature is that human services request income from external sources, whether those sources are higher in a hierarchy or external grant makers. This situation means that HSEs are often in direct competition with other agencies for funds. A budget system with competition of an entirely different sort arises when an HSE generates significant amounts of its own income from donations and program services income. In this context, the individual enterprise is not a player in some larger budget system where competition is centered around competing proposals for funding. In donation- and fee-based systems, human services budgeting corresponds more closely to the capitalization of small businesses and competition that is product centered rather than proposal centered. Rather than negotiating a contract between two parties—the outside funder and the funded HSE—a primary feature of this type of budget involves predicting income and developing expenditure patterns in light of those predictions. We might call this kind of budgeting an "internal budget system."

Internal budget systems have the advantage of maximizing discretionary decision making within the enterprise and not requiring extensive negotiations outside of it, but they also introduce new elements of uncertainty. It is the need to deal with that uncertainty that has given new importance to financial analysis, especially cost analysis, break-even analysis, and cash flow analysis. Any number of contingencies during the budget period may upset the delicate balance of predicted income and expenses. If these contingencies result in greater income, the enterprise will be in a happy place and experience a budget surplus. However, if they result in less income, a budget deficit may result. Such a situation can be particularly problematic for the HSE that has few cash reserves, investments, or other financial resources to fall back on. Borrowing to cover such income shortfalls will probably be short-term and unsecured (unless the agency owns a building or other valuable assets). In this context, the critical dimension in internal budgeting is how HSEs can make the most accurate income predictions possible.

Program service income has numerous advantages, particularly in tying income generation directly to service delivery (a link often termed *metering*). Even when fees are only a part of the total income package, with other funds coming from earmarked or designated program funds, an HSE may have an important element of flexibility. Except where fees are tied to specific program operations by grant agreement, board of directors' action, or some other arrangement, it should be possible to use such income as flexible problem-solving tools. In one budget year, funds may support a defunded program until different grant funding arrangements can be made and at another time provide matching moneys for a grant, or *risk capital*, to start a new research program or training activity. Even when amounts are quite small, the careful administrator can get considerable use out of such discretionary funds. An ever-present problem in such instances, however, results from the habits formed by decades of grant and contract funding. Without realizing it, administrators can easily tie discretionary program service income to existing external commitment and voluntarily surrender their most precious feature. This is particularly true of fee income committed to matching grant funds. Matching money linked to a grant this year will not be free for some other use next year if the grant is to be continued. With such funds, the management challenge is to keep enough financial capital free to allow some flexibility while making effective use of funds.

Another key feature of internal budget systems used to allocate program service income and donations is their continuous nature. While most externally contracted budget agreements result in fixed or at least semi-fixed budgets, internal budgets are nearly always flexible budgets subject to regular, often continuous adjustment as circumstances (in particular, predicted and realized income and expenses) change.

BUDGET CYCLES

Making a budget is not akin to solving a scientific problem or mathematical puzzle. It is an intensely human encounter in which competing interests seek to capture scarce resources for their own ends. Authoritative decisions must be made, and some measure of conflict is an inevitable element in all budgeting in both external and internal systems. Typically, there are a number of regular events that define the full cycle of any given budget system. Wildavsky (1967, pp. 241–250; 1973) was the first to outline the federal budget cycle. In the ensuing decades, research has borne out that similar cyclical dynamics apply to most other budget systems as well. (Recall the United Way budget process mentioned above.) Most HSE budget cycles are nominally annual, although, as we have seen, taking a longer view is always helpful. The budget cycle usually coincides with or is synchronized with accounting and tax reporting cycles. During the typical budget cycle, several standard benchmarks can usually be observed, such as requests from funding authorities for preliminary proposals, requests for proposals, and final decisions. This may be accompanied in some instances by guidelines, targets, or criteria to be used in creating budgets. Another element in most budget cycles is a deadline for submitting a specific (and documented) budget request to the staff of the budget authority. That proposal may be treated as preliminary to be reviewed and modified by the staff (with or without entity participation) or as final to be presented directly to the formal decision-making authority for consideration without preliminary review. It may be accompanied by an opportunity for a hearing or formal presentation by the applicant and be followed by a decision from the authority, the various stages of implementation of that decision (notifying the recipient, drafting a legal contract or agreement as needed, and actually distributing the money), and the follow-up of the pattern of utilization of the funds by the recipient. These steps appear to be fairly universal and represent a mix of common sense, collective experience, and lack of plausible alternative ways of doing things.

Another of the principal characteristics of budget cycles in human services is that different activities may be occurring simultaneously, and programs or agencies receiving funds from more than one funding source may be involved with several budget systems at the same time. As discussed in more depth in chapter 12, Figures 12.1 through 12.4 and Table 12.2 capture some of that simultaneity in translation of the United Way budget wheel into program evaluation and review technique (PERT) charts. In some cases, the events and activities of a budget cycle are spread out so widely that budget making is a more or less continuous, year-round concern, giving rise to flexible budgets. In other cases, the budget process may be telescoped into brief and intensive periods of activity. In HSEs with multiple sources of income, minor differences in the phasing of different budget cycles or overlapping or simultaneous events in different systems can present major management headaches unless these differences can be synchronized and integrated in agency routines.

SUMMARY OF BUDGET SYSTEMS AND CYCLES

HSEs will be involved in at least one of these budget systems and may be involved in several simultaneously. Public appropriations systems assume ongoing operations. Negotiations therein tend to be concentrated around increments of increase or decrease. Participation in public distribution systems is not assured and the potential for a zero-sum mode of operations always exists. Federated appropriations systems, by contrast, possess restricted memberships and operate like public appropriations systems, with negotiations focused largely on the increments. The fortunes of agencies in such arrangements have an additional degree of uncertainty, however, which is tied to the success of the annual fundraising campaign. In some years, state and local agencies may face similar uncertainties in tax collections. Budgeting in agencies and programs supported by donations and fees takes on a substantially different character, for the entire budget operation must be focused on income projections rather than negotiations with a funding source.

PROGRAM BUDGETS

Program budgets for particular programs, such as those in Tables 6.4 through 6.8, and all-funds or enterprise budgets, such as that in Table 6.9, each have their uses, but it is sometimes useful to reconcile the two and combine them into a single document. Table 6.10 shows such a budget, breaking out the enterprise budget shown in Table 6.3 into three separate programs, with corresponding line items for each program. Although the total budget is in balance, note that Programs B and C are subsidizing Program A, which has $57,014 more in expenses than income. Making such cross-program redistributions is ordinarily a simple matter when dealing with donations and program service income but can get quite complex when grants and contracts are involved (Rosentraub, Harlow, & Harris, 1992). The particular transfers shown here involve discretionary funds, would be more apparent than real, and would not have existed if the original allocation of donations as income to Programs B and C in Table 6.10 had been made differently. In such cases, it is simply a minor adjustment to revise an initial faulty assumption. If any of these funds were restricted, such budget adjustments could become quite complex. In order to show all programs in balance, if that were desirable, this imbalance could be easily resolved by shifting donations to make the Program A donations item $97,014 and reducing the donation items for Programs B and C correspondingly. Then all three programs would be in balance.

Tables 6.11 and 6.12 show a simple analysis of the proportionate contributions of each type of income to each program in Table 6.10. (Each column in Table 6.11 totals 100 percent.) Table 6.12 shows the same basic categories as Table 6.11, but the proportions are computed horizontally in this case, showing how each form of income is allocated among the three programs. (In Table 6.12, each row totals 100 percent.) Note that the cells with zero income are the same in both directions. Figure 6.4 shows a portion of the same information in pie chart form. Creating such

Table 6.10: Line Item and Program Matrix Budget

Category	Program A ($)	Program B ($)	Program C ($)	Total ($)
Income				
Donations	40,000	40,000	40,000	120,000
Fees	50,000	50,000	50,000	150,000
Grants	511,333	0	0	511,333
Contracts	0	287,000	400,420	687,420
Total income	601,333	377,000	490,420	1,468,753
Expenses				
Wages and salaries	569,040	268,320	395,744	1,233,104
Office rental	12,483	12,000	13,000	37,483
Communications	7,000	7,428	7,000	21,428
Travel	57,840	37,380	42,020	137,240
Equipment	9,800	11,284	11,200	32,284
Supplies	2,184	2,500	2,500	7,184
Total expenses	658,347	338,912	471,464	1,468,723

Table 6.11: Income Proportions Table, Simplified

Income	Program A (%)	Program B (%)	Program C (%)
Donations	6.6	10.6	8.1
Fees	8.3	13.3	10.3
Grants	85.1	0	0
Contracts	0	76.1	81.6

Table 6.12: Distribution of Program Income, by Type

Income	Program A (%)	Program B (%)	Program C (%)
Donations	33.3	33.3	33.3
Fees	33.3	33.3	33.3
Grants	100	0	0
Contracts	0	41.8	58.2

Figure 6.4: Pie Chart of Program A Income

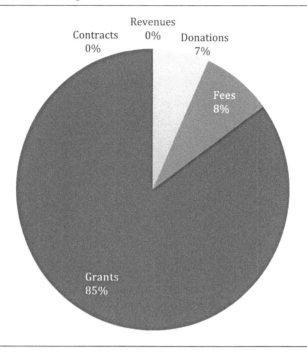

Figure 6.5: Pie Chart of Current Monthly Spending (Month)

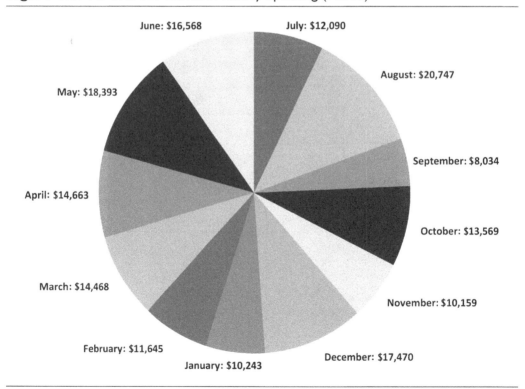

Table 6.13: Expanded Budget Matrix

Category	Total Budget ($)	Management and General ($)	Fundraising ($)	Programs, Total ($)	Program A ($)	Program B ($)
Income						
Donations	120,000		120,000		48,000	72,000
Fees	150,000			150,000	150,000	
Grants	511,333			511,333	511,333	
Contracts	687,420			687,420		687,420
Total income	1,468,753			1,468,753	709,333	759,420
Expenses						
Wages and salaries	1,233,134	135,645	98,651	998,839	449,477	549,361
Office rental	37,483	7,497	7,497	22,490	10,120	12,369
Communications	21,428	8,571	4,286	8,571	3,857	4,714
Travel	137,240	68,620	41,172	27,448	12,352	15,096
Equipment	32,284	2,155	6,457	23,672	10,652	13,020
Supplies	7,184	2,371	2,874	1,940	873	1,067
Total expenses	1,468,753	224,858	160,935	1,082,959	487,332	595,628

Note: Row and column totals may not match exactly, because of errors due to rounding.

tables and graphics in advance of decisions can serve to clarify important features of a budget to various stakeholders.

Table 6.10 shows a matrix budget combining the line-item budget shown in Tables 6.9 and 6.3 with the AICPA differentiation of management and general fundraising and program expenses. Rather than the customary consolidation of all program expenses in the AICPA categorization, Table 6.13 breaks out two separate programs. It is also the basis for the reassignment of indirect costs shown in Tables 8.1 and 8.2. In column 2 of Table 8.1, the proportion of total expenses that each line item represents is listed. In column 3, those proportions are used to divide management and general costs among fundraising and the two programs.

CONCLUSION

For much of the history of social work involvement in human services, the problem of budgeting went largely unrecognized in the professional literature and received an unspecified range of practical solutions in practice. When it was finally recognized in the professional literature in the second half of the 20th century, the principal problem was diagnosed as that of allocating proposed expenses. The quiet revolution and, in particular, the growth of program service income as a factor in the total income package of human services, brought subtle but important changes to the nature of the key budget problem. Now, both income and expenses are in play. The essence of the issue is that unlike donations, which vary independent of levels of service output, program service income (fees) vary in proportion to the volume of services produced. Thus, makers of budgets heavy with program service income generally should expect to be less engaged in negotiations with external funders and more concerned with financial analysis to determine the combined effects of the proposed budget on income, expenses, and service output. Those making HSE budgets allocating grants, contracts, donations, and program service income must be concerned with both negotiations and analysis. In the following five chapters, we examine the rising usefulness of several types of financial analysis for their ability to resolve aspects of this new reality.

Budgeting is the second major system of financial management in human services and has long been the central focus of social work writing and theorizing about financial management. There is something close to universal agreement that budgeting is a planning process, an insight that has been the basis for numerous proposals for movement away from the more trivial aspects of line-item budgeting and toward more systematic program, performance, zero-base, and zero-sum budgets. At the same time, information and database technologies have reduced the salience of many of these questions to mere differences in preferred output formats. Furthermore, such variations as the categorization of administrative, fundraising, and program expenses and the distinction of human resources and current expenses raise the additional prospect of simplified and more flexible line-item budgets. These various threads will be gathered together into an integrated model of budgeting and financial analysis termed *syncretic financial management* in chapter 13.

7

Financial Analysis

Most social workers are familiar with the term *analysis* as a descriptor for various professional methods of investigation of the individual psyche or family and other relationships. Financial analysis, as detailed in the next six chapters, is the third major component of the financial system of HSEs, and embodies a somewhat similar notion of the idea of analysis, albeit in a dramatically different context. All analysis involves seeking improved understanding of something—an object or analysand—by taking it apart (figuratively, cognitively, or mentally) and examining the various parts. Analysis is often contrasted with the companion process of synthesis, which involves putting things back together again, sometimes in new and different ways. Financial analysis, as it is detailed in these chapters, entails important elements of synthesis as well.

Analysis is an element of financial problem solving in general. It involves identifying, defining, and profiling costs and determining balanced budgets with break-even points that imply particular levels of service under diverse conditions. It also involves determining financial ratios useful in profiling problems and measuring the impact of problem-solving efforts, monitoring financial inflows and outflows, and tracking the impact of shifting financial conditions on cash flows. Analysis may be necessary to define financial problems, in identifying and sorting through alternative solutions, in investigating and profiling the preferred solution, and in determining whether that solution is working (Hodges, 1982). This obviously involves dealing with a great deal of complexity and variability. Financial problem solving in an HSE with numerous sources of resources, including significant amounts of program service income, is even more complex because such problem solving has elements of what some call "wicked problems," that is, complex problems characterized by difficult-to-recognize requirements and incomplete or contradictory information. Under such conditions, the incremental methods of "muddling through" (Lindblom's original phrase to characterize marginal analysis) have proved over time to hold great appeal for financial management practitioners, so much so that they form the basis for an emerging third system of HSE financial management.

This chapter and the five that follow explore what has been coalescing into this third major financial system consisting of a variety of financial analyses. This chapter introduces this concept, as well as a variety of general, orienting, and theoretical perspectives of financial planning, the uses of financial analysis, and financial evaluation techniques. Each of the short chapters that follow is focused on a single approach or perspective on financial analysis.

Financial analysis is defined as the selective, targeted scrutiny and processing of information provided in budgets and financial statements and supporting data from the accounts and other management information systems. Calculations of various monetized measures are conducted to assess different aspects or dimensions of financial performance and the financial condition of the enterprise. Such indicators can inform managers about various features of the ongoing operation of the HSE. These chapters focus on five major modes of financial analysis: cost analysis, break-even analysis (also known as cost–value–revenue analysis), ratio analysis, social accounting, and financial scorecards. Additional modes of financial analysis—accounts receivable analysis, accounts payable analysis, and cash flow analysis—are introduced and discussed in chapter 12 in the context of assessing financial operations.

ENTERPRISE PLANNING

In the social enterprise context, social planning is nearly always program planning (A. J. Kahn, 1969a, 1969b; Morris, Binstock, & Rein, 1966). John Friedmann, a planning theorist, suggested that there are two general types of planning, which he termed "allocative planning" and "innovative planning" (Friedmann, 1973). The first of these is typically the most relevant to financial management. Allocative planning involves *planning*, or the deliberate preparation of a set of decisions for action in the future, with particular attention to *allocation*, or the assignment of resources to various purposes and tasks. Typically, allocation involves or is accompanied by some mode of financial analysis directed toward such general questions as "What are our priorities?" "What are we trying to do?" and "What will it cost to do it?" Budgeting in the social enterprises is one of two principal loci for organization-level allocative planning. The other is program planning, which is also nearly always associated with some budget activity at some level (for example, in grant writing). As terms such as United Way's PPBS suggest, program budgeting involves efforts to bring budgetary and program planning into what might be termed "maximum feasible convergence."

Program planning is an activity in which problems are identified and defined, alternative strategies of problem solving are analyzed and implemented, and recommendations for action are made. Program planning consists of the strategies that typically lend their name and function to the activity also known as "strategic planning" (Gummer, 1992). *Strategic planning* thus refers to forms of allocative planning with attention to setting priorities; allocating resources; strengthening operations; and ensuring that employees and other stakeholders are addressing common goals, working toward agreement on intended outcomes, and realigning the HSE with its constantly changing environment.

At one time, the thinking was that program planning in human services should be closely aligned with community organization practice and social policy and viewed as a community-level function identified as "social planning" (Johns & De Marche, 1951). Separate and distinct community-level organizations responsible for strategic planning were considered necessary and appropriate next steps in the evolution of human services, and social planning was seen as an evolving career line for social workers (A. J. Kahn, 1969a, 1969b; Morris et al., 1966). Since then, one of the important dynamics of the quiet revolution has been the extensive devolution of social planning from a community-level to an enterprise-based activity. This forms another dimension of being more businesslike. Program planning in the HSE has become the primary locus of social planning for human services in many communities today. In some cases, a large HSE may have a separate planning department, committee, or program. In most instances, however, allocative and strategic questions arise principally in and around HSE budget systems. It is this dynamic that gives the model of budgeting discussed in the previous chapter its unique character. When planned change occurs in many communities today, it is only through enterprise-based planning focused heavily on budget processes, including grant writing; contract negotiations; fundraising; and, when appropriate, program service income. The major exceptions to this trend arise on the less frequent occasions when government agencies or general purpose or community foundations introduce initiatives for social change. These are often framed as occasions for what Friedmann called "innovative planning." Thus, most genuine program innovation and change today arises at the HSE level, and there is often no feasible alternative to pursuing change through the budget process. Reframing this new reality is one of the primary reasons for envisioning a coherent HSE-based financial analysis system, as sketched in Figure 7.1.

FINANCIAL PLANNING AND ANALYSIS

In the previous chapter, we looked at the organization of various budget systems. To pursue the connection with allocative planning further, we now examine two distinct models of choice in budget planning that have emerged over the years. Another management planning theorist, J. B. Quinn, labeled these the "power behavioral approach" and the "formal systems planning approach" (Quinn, 1980). Others have referred to them as the political and rational approaches to program planning and budgeting. Whereas it might at first appear that the difference is one of unthinking power plays versus a well-thought-out but strategically inept approach, in reality, the differences are typically matters of what is analyzed, together with how deep and thorough the analysis may be and the role of conflict and disagreement. The critical question, which is seldom far from the center of focus in this discussion, is how appropriate planning choices are to be made.

Figure 7.1: General Financial Analysis System

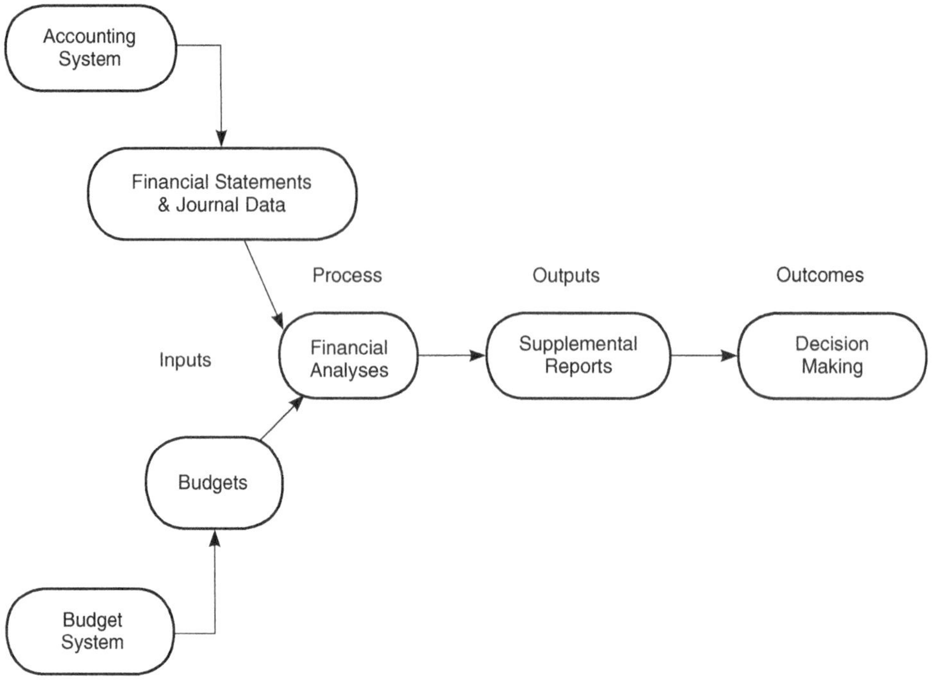

INCREMENTAL PLANNING AND ANALYSIS

One approach to allocative planning involves the development of a strategic or business plan, which provides answers to a wide variety of practical questions. Like many approaches to rational planning, the business plan is often a highly contingent document where the answers are never fully certain and often changing (see Appendix C). The particular approach to allocative planning and financial analysis called "incrementalism" is closely associated with an interdisciplinary group of political, economic, and management scientists and philosophers. Aaron Wildavsky was a political scientist who closely studied the development of the U.S. budget in research on the U.S. Bureau of the Budget (now the OMB). Charles Lindblom, an interdisciplinary social scientist; David Braybrooke, a philosopher; and Robert Dahl, another political scientist, developed a formidable theoretical base for incrementalism as a general theory of decision making and planning (Braybrooke & Lindblom, 1963; Dahl & Lindblom, 1992; Lindblom, 1990). Also important are three economists with very different views: Herbert Simon (1997), Frederick Hayek, and Ludwig von Mises. Hayek and von Mises were major (although uncited) influences on Lindblom and Braybrooke.* Their concepts of satisficing, spontaneous

---

*Hayek and von Mises also influenced the commons theory of Elinor and Vincent Ostrom, but that tangent is not relevant here.

order, and bounded rationality take the issue of rational decision making out of the lone Cartesian mind and into the context of interpersonal relations. Finally, to this volatile mix can be added one important proviso from the political philosopher Benjamin R. Barber (1988).

The resulting perspective is termed *marginal analysis*, a multidisciplinary (sociological, psychological, economic, and political) perspective on how allocative decisions are and should be made. It assumes a perspective that Frederick Hayek called "intellectual modesty" and acknowledges forthrightly that knowledge of the anticipated outcomes, impacts, and consequences of future actions of allocative planners and budget decision makers is always partial and incomplete. Moreover, it acknowledges that no single plan or budget should ever be expected to totally transform or change an existing situation, except perhaps through a sequence of smaller steps, none of which may seem all that transformative. Just as important, those involved in budgeting who seek to make big changes also need to be attuned to opportunities for change that may arise only infrequently and to be ready to act when opportunities present themselves.

The choice here is not between two comparable approaches to practice but between actuality and an idealized version of that practice. The philosopher of science Abraham Kaplan (1964) characterized this distinction as "logic in use" verses "reconstructed logic." This is, in other terms, the oft-noted distinction between actual practice and theory, beloved by most practitioners. Marginal analysis and incremental budgeting are examples of actual practice. Systems such as PPBS are examples of reconstructed logic.

In Wildavsky's original (1967) argument, budgets in the public sector are less significant as management instruments for public operations than as occasions for working out political agreements and bargains. Much the same might be said for the HSE budget and planning processes, with allowances for important differences in the overtly political (as opposed to simply interpersonal) dynamics of the process. Wildavsky stressed the calculating political perspective over the rational economic one. Others see the issue quite differently. Martin (2001, p. 76), for example, distinguished between political and financial management (that is, presumably professional and technical) perspectives on budgeting. Martin's dismissal is, as much as anything, a matter of differing perspectives talking past one another. This is not just a matter of a reasoned choice between political and rational or professional views. It runs far deeper than that. At some level, "politics"—that is, interpersonal dynamics, including disagreements, conflict, manipulating and maneuvering, the exercise of interpersonal influence, power, authority, and all else conjured up by that word—may overtake reasoned discussion and become inevitable in budgeting and planning. This is because of something the political philosopher Benjamin Barber termed "the sovereignty of the political": "To speak of the autonomy of the political is in fact to speak of the sovereignty of the political" (B. R. Barber, 1988, p. 14). With that esoteric-sounding phrase, Barber explained why—under what conditions and within what limits—we ought to take seriously Wildavsky's view of the political erupting into otherwise seemingly rational or scientific settings, including planning and budgeting. In those cases where two conditions arise, Barber argued, politics will necessarily prevail over reason, science, religious certainty, and rational approaches. This must include those logic models that make planning and budgeting fully comprehensible, predictable processes, not subject to whim, caprice, or chance. The two conditions are (a) there is a collective choice to be made that affects others not involved in the actual choice and (b) uncertainty exists about what is to be done. Although he has no apparent connection with them, Barber's assessment is consistent with the whole body of interactionist thinking about planning, budgeting, and policy making. In Lindblom's (1990) terms, in such cases, persuasion and interpersonal dynamics will prevail over abstract reasoning, especially reasoning seeking the one right answer. Instead of abstract analysis, rationality becomes the giving of persuasive reasons. It is the actual workings of the sovereignty of the political in real budget and allocative planning situations and not an informed, rational choice by theorists and writers between political and rational explanations of budgeting and planning that is at work here. This is also why, much as we might prefer to choose one or the other, both political and rational perspectives on planning and budgeting are necessary in the incrementalist view referred to here as marginal analysis.

One of the most compelling arguments for this view is that it offers a description and justification of the way people actually do things. Regardless of whether it can be said to be the right way, everyone is pretty much in agreement that most planning and budget decisions are made marginally, sequentially, and in successive steps. As U.S. Senator Everett Dirksen allegedly said of the federal budget, "A billion here, a billion there, and the next thing you know you're talking real money!"* Only infrequently in an HSE budget process can one expect to see the most profound and searching questions of purpose faced squarely and forthrightly, with a willingness to reason the matter through to a definitive answer, no matter what. Such an approach to decisions may be suitable for philosophers, some economists, and zealots of abstract reasoning, but it is seriously out of touch with the fluid context of day-to-day agency and program administration. Instead, Lindblom and Simon both have suggested that budget makers tend to *satisfice*—that is, to consider those factors and alternatives of which they are aware, by habit or choice, and those that they cannot avoid (Simon, 1997, pp. 240–244). Sometimes this even means seizing upon and accepting the first plausible solution to present itself. Indeed, this is one of the main reasons for combining planning and the tools of financial analysis in the HSE financial picture. Together they offer ways of introducing elements of careful, dispassionate reasoning and evidence-based analysis into situations that can otherwise consist primarily of *logrolling, horse trading,* and some of the other colorful terms for political choice.

Such behavior is often seen by advocates of various forms of rationalism (for example, the developers of PPBS in the 1960s and their fellows today) as flaws in the system or plain irrationality. It is often tied to various critiques and satires of

---

*The Web page of the Dirksen Center (n.d.) details the provenance of this famous quote and reports that there is no hard evidence that Senator Dirksen ever actually said this. As the site notes, several people recall Dirksen making the statement on the Johnny Carson show, but there is no surviving video of the episode in question to confirm their recollections.

bureaucratic actors who are seen as flawed people incapable of full rationality. Far from being a deficit, however, Braybrooke and Lindblom (1963) argued, it is the peculiar strength of this most conventional approach that it provides maximum opportunity for reconciling the claims of the future with the legitimate claims of the past. As they have for the past half-century, adherents of marginal analysis in the current world still find it to be both realistic and normative, consistent with extensive research data on social change from sociology, social psychology, and American history (Rogers, 2003, pp. 320–346).

The main implication of this perspective for HSE financial management is clear: Those engaged in financial planning and budget practice do not need to radically alter their behavior, seek to transform their thinking, or radically redesign any processes in order to be more effective. Effectiveness is not to be found in adopting the right logic model of planning or budgeting but comes about when those in situ decide to be more effective and are not blocked or hindered in their efforts to do so. A logic model is "a framework that attempts to identify and clarify the links between [planned or projected] outcomes sought by an organization, the outputs [actually] created by the organization's activities that are designed to achieve [those] outcomes and the inputs of resources needed to support [those] activities" (Murray, 2005, p. 346). Meanwhile, Barber's approach alerts us that financial planning and decision making can never be always and only political, that their political nature is, itself, highly contingent. Where there is certainty—whether by explicit agreement or mere indifference—there typically will be none of the jostling, pushing, and shoving associated with organizational politics. In the financial planning context, this approach suggests that when a convincing rational analysis is offered and all those involved accept (or merely tolerate) the correctness and the adequacy of the analysis, reason will prevail and choices will be made rationally. There is plenty of room for the various forms of financial analysis discussed in the following chapters, but rational problem solving may, at times, also be supplemented, augmented, and sometimes even completely overturned by overtly political tactics and strategies. This is not so much a matter of strategic choice as it is one of contingent responses to differing situations.

In financial planning, rational consensus is always contingent and subject to change, even at a moment's notice. If even one unconvinced dissenter is not party to such a rational consensus, any of the participants may at any time resort to politicizing the issue through persuasion, propaganda, influence, power plays, threats, intimidation, and the full arsenal of political responses. A lone dissenting actor may simply be overruled, which is a democratic political solution, or may be capable of politicizing the issue for everyone, forestalling action or even overturning the result. B. R. Barber's (1988) approach suggests a very contingent answer to the question of whether budgeting is rational or political: It is, his approach suggests, rational until reason breaks down and then it becomes political, but politics too may be reasonable. Partisans of more technocratic, neutral, professional, and rationalist views of budgeting may not be convinced by Barber's analysis, but their objections demonstrate at another level exactly the point that marginal analysis has always proclaimed.

STATISTICS

It should be noted also that the incremental model of marginal analysis recognizes not only a contingent role for politics in rational planning and analysis but also an important, if not yet fully realized, place for statistics in financial analysis. In a superficial sense, *statistics* is the science of gathering and organizing data, but in a more important sense it is the study of prediction and the science of error. With tools such as probability theory, statistical analysis offers the means for examining the characteristics of a sample and estimating how likely it is that the population from which the sample was drawn will share the same characteristics.

For the most part, the analytical methods examined in the next few chapters deal with situations in which the samples being examined are relatively small and identical to their populations. That is, they are 100 percent samples of the population. Even in such cases, certain tools of descriptive statistics such as means, modes, medians, ranges, variances, and contingency tables for formulating hypotheses may be useful. In a few instances (for example, a study of travel costs or client service episodes), financial analysts may be dealing with large enough populations (numbers of transactions) that genuine statistical sampling may be necessary, and the use of tools like regression analysis may be appropriate.

While it is relatively straightforward to note the potential usefulness of descriptive and inferential statistics in financial analysis in human services, it is also necessary to note the absolute paucity of discussion of this matter in the social work literature. Martin's (2001) chapter 9 on forecasting may be the only published attempt to address a statistical topic in the published financial management literature of human services. Surely, this is a topic that ought to receive greater attention in the future.

LOCI OF CHANGE

It is fairly easy to predict that financial planning and budgeting practitioners will probably continue doing things in the near future pretty much the way they have been doing them in the past. Incrementalists will continue to be fairly comfortable with the status quo, whereas operations researchers and other rationalists will not. It is important to note, however, that the discomfited may in the future continue to do what they have done in the past, that is, serve as an important source of proposed innovations and reforms in financial planning and reform. Indeed, it may be the case that rationalism is a necessary or sufficient condition for constructing the logic models. The key question, then as now, will be whether and which proposed reforms actually make their way into practice.

In this view, one of the principal avenues to change will continue to be adoption of new ways by students and new professionals. Convincing experienced and battle-hardened professionals to change the ways they do financial planning and budgeting is always going to be an uphill fight—one that is too overwhelming for the small cadre of researchers, teachers, and reform-oriented professionals concentrating on these problems. There are, however, other avenues yet to be pursued (not including asking busy professionals to change the way they think). More is said on this in the final chapter.

A FIVE-YEAR HORIZON

When adopting a planning perspective on financial management, success depends at least in part on some alteration in the usual limited budget time horizon of the single fiscal year. Planning is concerned with the future, and effective planning also requires a good, thorough understanding of the past. Thus, one of the simplest and most prosaic but useful and versatile tools available for financial planning and analysis is to adopt a five-year timeline or horizon incorporating past, present, and future perspectives together in a single sweep. The five-year timeline—two years past, the present year, and two future years—is an arbitrary choice. A three-year horizon will be more workable in some cases, and there are cases to be made also for seven-, nine-, or even 10-year horizons under appropriate circumstances. The point is that there was consensus that the five-year time horizon model can easily be applied to longer and shorter periods.

This is usually reflected in the presentation of documents bracketing the present year between one or more past and future years. One can obtain remarkably improved insight into the financial position of an HSE simply by asking what has happened in recent years, what is happening currently, and what is expected to happen in the next year or two? It is sometimes sufficient to look at a three-year horizon—last year, this year, and next year—but, in other cases, an additional two or more years will even better enable the analyst to spot a wider variety of trends as well as flukes. This is a well-understood point in financial analysis. For example, the technique of fiscal distress analysis as introduced in chapter 10 follows a standard three-year time frame—this year and the past two years—to discover whether there is already a trend toward ongoing problems. (Projecting a year or more into the future would add little to such an analysis.)

Arrays of three, five, and seven years can typically be shown in either vertical or horizontal fashion, as in Tables 7.1 and 7.2.

Table 7.1 shows the five-year projection of known and anticipated income and expenses in a vertical array. Table 7.2 shows the same information in a seven-year horizontal alignment. (Note that past numbers are real and shown in boldface in both tables, whereas future numbers are estimates and not presented in boldface. Also, the real past numbers for income and expenses are different, whereas the future estimates of income and expenses are shown in balance.) One of the additional advantages of multiyear perspectives is that there is great potential for visual or graphic representation of multiyear data in a timeline or a bar graph, as

Table 7.1: Five-Year Timetable of Income and Expenses

Category	Two Years Past ($)	Last Year ($)	This Year ($)	Next Year ($)	Two Years Out ($)
Income	**74,283**	**81,912**	**83,000**	88,000	94,000
Expenditures	**72,799**	**82,427**	83,000	88,000	94,000

Note: Numerals in **boldface** represent actual income and expenditures. Nonboldface items are future projections.

Table 7.2: Seven-Year Timetable of Income and Expenses

Time Point	Income	Expenditures
−3 years	**77,251**	**74,468**
−2 years	**74,283**	**72,799**
Last year	**81,912**	**82,427**
This year	83,000	83,000
Next year	88,000	88,000
+2 years	94,000	94,000
+3 years	100,000	100,000

Note: Numerals in **boldface** represent actual income and expenditures. Nonboldface items are future projections.

in Figure 7.2. Visual learners among an organization's stakeholders who consider a data table impenetrable may immediately grasp the significance of such a graph (J. A. Meyer, 1997). Figure 7.2 shows the information from Table 7.1 as a bar graph, visualizing the relative differences from year to year. Showing the same information as a line graph would tend to emphasize the continuities (or lack thereof). There are many other possible permutations of this same basic approach that are

Figure 7.2: Five Years of Income and Expenses

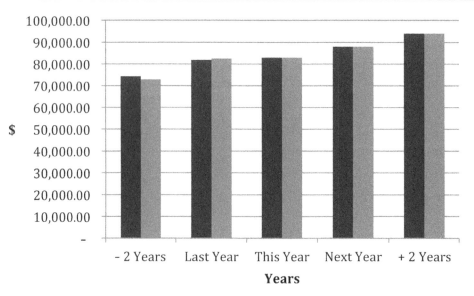

Note: Income is represented by the lefthand (darker) columns and expenses by the righthand (lighter) columns.

not shown here, including three-year (last year, this year, next year), nine-year, and 10-year projections (adding one or four additional years to each end of the timeline, or three at one end) focusing on specific items, such as rent, UBIT taxes owed, or any other item of interest.

It is, of course, possible to extend timeline imagery by delving further into data about the past or future or more deeply into quarterly or monthly changes. In most cases, however, taking more detailed views of quarterly or even monthly data may be a more useful approach. Figures 12.5 and 12.6, for example, show month-to-month breakouts of the 30-month data series shown in Table 12.4. As a general framework, the multiyear time frame rivals, and in many ways surpasses, the single fiscal year as the basic planning perspective on what is happening in an HSE.

BALANCE

Another important general concept in planning and analysis is the idea of balance as expressed in the trial balance, the balance sheet, the balanced budget, and elsewhere. In financial analysis, meaning frequently arises and is clarified from the comparison of two quantities to one another. One may be equal to the other, in which case they are said to be "in balance."

Some of the most basic of these questions of balance involve balancing costs against various other variables, for example, cost–benefit analysis and ratio analysis. When one is seeking to balance costs, the question is often less one of numerical equality per se than one pertaining to the quantitative relation of two variables to one another (or their ratio). In the timelines introduced in the previous section, for example, the question of changes in the ratio of income to expenses—the income–expense ratio—may reveal important clues about what is happening or expected to happen. A particularly useful application of this is presented in the discussion of fiscal distress ratios in chapter 10. Chapter 6 demonstrated the importance of balancing the budget. In chapter 9, more complex versions of balance are discussed that involve the proximity of three, four, or even five quantities—fixed and variable income, fixed and variable costs, and service output levels.

The technique of break-even analysis, or what Mayers (2004, p. 158) termed *cost–volume–revenue analysis*, extends the traditional budgetary notion of the balance between income and expenses into a three-dimensional relation between income, costs (as measured by expenses), and service outputs. The underlying insight is a fundamentally important one: A given level of income and a matching level of spending imply a certain, finite level of service that can be delivered with those resources. Associated with this is a perspective on wasted effort. The general assumption is important, if somewhat vague, specifically, that it is unfortunate (wasteful) not to attempt to fully utilize all of the resources that are available.*

---

*This is an assumption that can be criticized or faulted in a number of ways, but the point remains that in the context of financial management of HSEs, it has been a guiding ideal for more than a century, dating back to the days of the charity organization societies. It is an important part of what many people mean when they refer to the efficient use of resources.

This is a question of balancing needs and resources, as earlier generations of social workers well knew. In chapter 9, a variety of ways to estimate or predict the future relationships among all three of these variables are outlined and discussed.

In chapter 10, some of the preliminary comments made in chapter 5 are examined in further detail in the discussion of various financial ratios that can be built from the data in a standard set of financial statements. All of these financial ratios are closely associated with the particular form of balance built into accounting systems: Assets must always equal liabilities and net income. The culmination of this chapter is the introduction of a set of ratios for identifying when an HSE is in fiscal distress.

Chapters 11 and 12 take up subjects that may well put the reader slightly off-balance, simply because they deal with subject matter that is novel in the context of financial analysis in HSEs. We noted some of the implications of the limits of the monetized perspective of financial management in chapter 1. While most people have been long aware of the imbalance between quantitative, monetized measures and qualitative observations, only a few investigators have tried to do anything about it. Chapters 11 and 12 deal with some of the farther reaches of contemporary research and practice concerned with some of those limits.

Yet another notion of balance is involved in the relatively novel approach of the balanced scorecard and the scorecard proposal in chapter 11. The scorecard approach, in general, seeks to systematically identify and integrate ways to extend the fundamental insights of budget balance and the balance between income, expenditures, and service levels even further into the enterprise. Although developed initially for business enterprises by faculty at the Harvard Business School, it became clear over time that balance scorecard techniques have at least as much applicability—and perhaps more—to nonprofit and governmental enterprises (Niven, 2003). Even so, practitioners and researchers in human services have been slow to adopt this novel approach; in at least one case, a formative evaluation rejected this approach outright (Kong, 2007). It is uncertain at present whether conventional balanced scorecards will be useful to financial management in HSEs. It seems clear, however, that a related approach using a financial scorecard (discussed in chapter 13) may suggest a rationale for an integrated format to bring together the results of various financial analysis techniques in a single source.

CONCLUSION

The entire emerging system of financial analysis is, by comparison with accounting or budgeting, relatively underdeveloped and involves a multitude of tricky questions regarding the cost of services, the definition of outcomes, and the like. A broad range of these issues and questions can be approached by the analytic techniques discussed in the following chapters. In this environment, many of the research methods developed in social work education, particularly those related to evaluation research and descriptive statistics, can be usefully applied and even invaluable. It remains to be seen whether these assorted techniques will be considered a single analytic system or as multiple semirelated but still largely independent systems. On the assumption that it would be a positive development to move toward the former, chapter 13 takes up, under the label of a "syncretic system" of budgeting and analysis, questions of next steps and how to move in those directions.

8

Cost Analysis

The cost analysis method is relatively simple to describe and usually straightforward to apply once basic terminology is clear (see Figure 8.1). The measurement of cost is not only important in its own right (Tinkelman, 1998, 2005) but also fundamental to a variety of other forms of analysis introduced in the chapters that follow. Despite some early and controversial* studies of the cost of casework and the relative cost of case recording by Hill and associates in the 1950s, cost measurement approaches did not really get established in the social administration literature until the 1980s (Doelker, 1979; Feit & Li, 1998, p. 174; Grundy, 1996; Hairston, 1985a; M. D. Hall, 1981; J. G. Hill, 1960a, 1960b; J. G. Hill & Ormsby, 1953; Keener & Sebestyen, 1981; Kirwin & Kaye, 1993; Lohmann, 1980, p. 311; Lohmann & Lohmann, 2008; Martin, 2001, pp. 92–115; Mayers, 2004, pp. 72–78).

COST DEFINED

Much of the theory of cost derives from a single economics journal article by Ronald Coase (1937) that introduced the concept of *transaction cost*, which is the cost of actually doing or performing something. Thus, as J. G. Hill's studies in the 1950s found, one of the most enduring of controversial cost questions throughout the human services is what constitutes appropriate levels of administrative cost (J. G. Hill, 1960a, 1960b; J. G. Hill & Ormsby, 1953). Human services do not administer themselves. Delivering services in large organized settings necessarily implies not just direct service delivery but also supervision, overhead, and management (and other so-called indirect services). Indirect services in this sense are transaction costs, and the distinction of direct and indirect services stems from cost studies and Coase's concept of transaction costs. Knowing this, however, has done little

---

*Controversy was focused principally on J. G. Hill's findings about the indirect cost of casework. Too little time, it was argued, was spent with clients, and too much in supervision and other activities not of any direct benefit to clients.

Figure 8.1: Subsystems Model of Cost Analysis

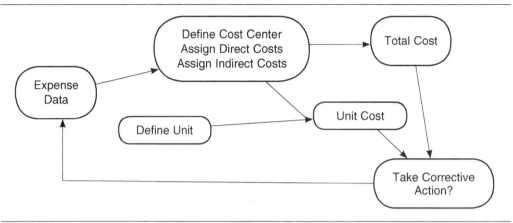

to resolve the question of appropriate levels of administrative costs in HSEs. In the same sense, imposing percentage limits, such as the 8 percent administrative cost limit included in titles of the Older Americans Act (1965), has not resolved the issue, either. The tripartite AICPA distinction of administrative, fundraising, and programs costs has at least helped to clarify the issue, and research by Richard Steinberg, Dennis R. Young, and others has done much to point the way toward possible solutions (Hairston, 1985a; Steinberg, 2004, 2008; D. R. Young, 2007).

Applications of cost concepts to the HSE setting are subject to two different but related definitions of the key term "cost." These differing approaches are in some sense a clash between theoretical and practice concepts; they reflect both theoretical and practical differences in the approaches of the accounting and economics professions. Coase's (1937) original economic approach is usually identified as *opportunity cost*, an approach that can involve considerable effort to monetize some components of cost, while the accounting approach usually relies on using only existing expense information and is known as *outlay cost*.* The accounting approach to cost is closest to the intuitive sense of the term. It arose organically in practice over many decades and measures costs in terms of expenditures, or "outlays," of cash and other fungible resources. It is thus a narrowly monetized approach. As a general rule, if an outlay cannot be measured in money terms, it cannot be reckoned as an outlay cost. This monetized approach sometimes results in confusion between the concept of cost and the price paid by a consumer, but this difference is relatively easy to sort out in most instances by considering a simple example:

> An advertisement in the newspaper for the grocery store where Becky regularly shops reads, "Today only—all six-packs of soft drinks—$2." That

---

*An extreme example of the opportunity cost approach can be seen in studies by Gary Becker (1976) and others of the economic value of human life, which among other things, costed out the average market prices of the chemical elements in a human corpse. This was before widespread awareness of black markets in the sale of body parts and provoked great controversy and more than a little derision among noneconomic social scientists.

sounds great and Becky would like to get at least five six-packs of her favorite root beer, but the grocery store is 10 miles from her office and will be closed by the time she finishes work this evening, so she will have to go during her lunch hour. The regular price of that same root beer is $3.50. Her HSE has done careful cost studies and found that the average (and reimbursed) cost of mileage in her (and everyone else's) car is $.50 a mile. Becky wonders if it would be worth it to give up her lunch break to get the root beer at such a good price.

　　Analysis: What is the cost to Becky of the root beer? $2 \times 5 = \$10$. Assuming that there are no other costs beside her mileage—perhaps a dubious assumption—what would be the full cost of Becky's root beer? ($10 + [\$.50 \times 10 \times 2 = \$10]) = \$20/5 = \$4/$ six pack.

　　That is outlay cost. It does not attempt to take into account the opportunity cost to Becky of giving up her lunch break. So Becky decides it wasn't such a good bargain after all, and she will walk to her regular store after she gets home and buy her usual six-pack at the regular price of $3.50.

OPPORTUNITY COST

The economists' model of cost (opportunity cost) can be thought of as a more robust model of "full cost" or "total cost." (Note that full cost can also be dealt with strictly in terms of outlays and in HSE cost studies usually is.) Opportunity cost is based on the economic principle of scarcity and choice: Not all goals can be achieved simultaneously and not everything can be done at once, and thus some opportunities must be foregone or given up in order to achieve any particular result. Those alternatives not selected—in particular, the second-best ones—offer a basis for determining the cost of choosing the first, or preferred, alternative. Ideally, such costs measured in terms of alternatives foregone must be monetized, but sometimes opportunity costs cannot be and must be reckoned only qualitatively.* In such cases, the market value of items that can be priced, or the nearest equivalent prices in other cases, becomes very important.

　　The opportunity cost of Becky's trip to the grocery store would also have to take into account the opportunity costs for her of missing lunch. At least part of this would be quantifiable in a case where Becky ordinarily ate lunch for free in the cafeteria as an employee benefit, but on her 20-mile round trip to the grocery store, she stopped at a fast food place to pick up a quick sandwich. More complex would be the situation where Becky routinely ate lunch at her desk while reviewing the next day's case records. Not only does this involve something difficult to monetize, it also involves an indirect cost—not to Becky but to her HSE of the lost time in processing case records. An additional unquantifiable effect would be Becky

---

*This is the basis of the distinction between cost–benefit analysis, where both terms can be monetized, and cost–effectiveness analysis, where only costs can be monetized and benefits must be dealt with in terms of nonmonetary measurements or even just nominal variables.

foregoing her usual quiet lunch hour to relax, shut her office door, and prepare for the afternoon's adventures.

It should be clear from this example that many possible cost elements enter into a full reckoning of the opportunity cost of anything. An interesting example of this in the opportunity cost approach to valuing volunteer contributions is presented in chapter 11. For now, it is important to remember that in most HSE cost studies, full cost typically implies not all possible costs including opportunity costs as in the economy model but only those that are previously monetized in the HSE accounting records. One of the major reasons for this is recursive, determined by turning the cost analysis model on itself: The opportunity cost of studying opportunity costs is usually much higher than the cost of studying outlay costs, which usually can be done through an examination of available information from the accounting system and financial statements.

COST OBJECTS

In conducting any cost analysis, it is essential to remember also that cost is never a freestanding variable. Cost is always a characteristic or dimension of something else, the completion of the phrase "the cost of _____." It is this relational quality that distinguishes costs from expenses. Thus, one of the most important steps of all forms of cost measurement is the definition of a cost center or cost object, which is the magnet to which a series of related expenses are attached; the answer to the question, the cost of what? In cost theory, a cost object may be many different kinds of things, from an entire enterprise or program to a discrete event or activity or set of similar events or activities; tangible objects (for example, cars or buildings); or many other possible objects, whether material, symbolic, or temporal. Martin (2001, pp. 92–113) drew an interesting parallel between cost centers and programs, but it is important to remember that programs represent just one important type of cost object. There can be many others as well. Programs and other types of cost objects can also be described by the relation between the financial inflows and outflows associated with them: Thus, an income center (for example, contributions) would be one defined primarily in terms of the importance of its income, or inflows, and an expense center (that is, transportation or personnel costs) would be one defined in terms of outflows, with no important or distinguishable income inflows. Travel of social workers to visit clients and operation of a parking lot may both be cost objects, but in the former there is typically no offsetting income, thus making it an expense object, whereas the latter may involve the collection of parking fees, making the question of whether it is an expense or income center (that is, does income offset expenses?) an important issue.

There are no fixed definitions or rules in cost measurement. Thus, explicitly noting the definitions (of a cost center) and assumptions is very important. Everything depends on the policy context and management intent. There are several reasons one might wish to define a particular type of income, for example, contributions as a cost center: It may be a necessary preliminary step to determine the cost to the agency of generating greater future contributions. This would be a common approach to take, for example, in determining either the outlay cost or the opportunity cost of developing a grant. (In most cases, the costs of grant development are considerable but are usually not tracked or measured.)

Programs and other cost centers may sometimes generate more in associated income than the total of the costs involved. In such cases, they are sometimes termed "profit centers," but in following the principle outlined in chapter 1, they are identified here as "surplus centers." The opposite of a surplus center would be an expense center—any cost object that fails to take in income to match its total costs. It is customary in many colleges and universities to have designated surplus centers, such as bookstores and cafeterias and sometimes residence halls. The administrators of such units have a consistent instruction: We expect you to generate surpluses. By contrast, graduate programs, and especially doctoral programs, are usually expense centers, where the associated income is insufficient to cover the full cost of the program.

It is probably also a widespread result in HSEs that some programs generate surpluses, whereas others operate at losses, and that various means of informal redistribution within the budget system balance out the differences. Programs for low-income clients are nearly always expense centers, but it is not at all clear which human services programs might consistently be surplus centers. Indeed, it is even plausible to suggest that one of the distinctive characteristics of human services financial management is that all service programs are expense centers. It is usually a good idea not to draw such distinctions, however, without seeking to fully understand the consequences they imply. If, for example, it were true that, all other things being equal, all human services are expense centers, this would have important implications for financial planning and budgeting. It would suggest, among other things, a strong division of labor between income-generating centers (for example, grant writing and fundraising) and service delivery, with an important redistributive role for budgeting and financial planning. Note that there are always important principles of equity, fairness, and just treatment associated with identifying surplus and expense centers and the transfers between them. Stakeholders involved will usually find interesting ways of raising these issues. Ultimately, attempting to fully balance all income and expenses in all cost objects is impossible, and it would be foolish to even try. It is far better to establish informed policies regarding expectations: What cost objects are expected to be income centers, which are expected to be expense centers, and which are expected to break even?

RECURRENT COST PROBLEMS

One of the most consistent errors associated with the application of base and increment in budgeting is failure to take into account the recurring nature of some costs. For example, adding a new permanent staff position will not only incur an increment in additional expenses for the next budget cycle, but that additional cost will henceforth be part of all future budgets. The nonrecurrent cost fallacy arises often in social agency budgeting, as a one-time provision (such as grant funds or a one-time gift) is made for what will be an ongoing added cost to the base budget without consideration of the ongoing future obligations this represents. Without sufficient attention to this problem, social agency budgets can quickly become unmanageable.

A GENERAL APPROACH

Cost analysis is one of the methods of financial analysis to be introduced into human services in recent decades. Some might say it has been reintroduced because of a long hiatus following the Philadelphia Cost Studies of social work in the 1950s (see J. G. Hill, 1960a, 1960b; J. G. Hill & Ormsby, 1953). In this chapter, the term "cost analysis" is used in a more general sense than that used by other authors speaking to the social work audience. Martin (2001), for example, limited his treatment of cost analysis to determinations of total program cost in public settings. "Cost analysis or cost determination," he noted, "are the names historically given to the actual process involved in determining a program's total cost," and he remarked that "cost analysis will be used to compute the full cost of a human service program and to develop both a performance budget and a program budget" (Martin, 2001, p. 92). In a similar vein, Mayers (2004) stated, "Direct costs are roughly equivalent to program costs" (p. 75). Such construction of cost analysis as a technique applicable only to the financial evaluation of programs is unnecessarily limited. Although both of these statements are true, they tend to suggest unnecessarily narrow limits on cost analysis.

The cost analysis methods listed below can be applied to any cost question that can be stated in the form, "What is the cost of _____?" Cost analysis should be seen as a general research methodology akin in important respects to survey research, behavioral analysis, or historical case studies. The same cost measurement methods can be used for determining the cost of just about anything, not only total program costs but also the cost of program components, such as administrative or fundraising cost, or freestanding cost centers, for example, client transportation, staff travel, meal services, pillows and blankets for homeless shelters, needle exchange programs, protest marches, and a host of other cost questions. Furthermore, essentially the same cost study method and approach applies whether one is using outlay or opportunity costs.

COST DEFINITIONS

Cost analysis can be distinguished from *cost accounting*, which is a specialized form of accounting in which ongoing determinations of the cost of a unit of output directly from transactions is built into the accounting process itself and reflected in an array of financial statements beyond those already discussed (see Finkler,

2013). Anyone who has recently had a hospital stay or seen a detailed hospital bill detailing such cost items as injections, IV bags used, and meals served is familiar with one such product of cost accounting. Cost accounting tends to be of two general types, depending on how the principal cost object categories are organized: process cost, focusing on such things as the cost of various types of surgery, and job cost, focused on the cost of treating a particular patient, although some blending of the two types often occurs. With the role of individualization in human services, it seems safe to predict that any future cost accounting systems in the field are likely to focus on job cost systems. Full-fledged cost accounting, as is done in hospitals today, requires a high level of definition and close articulation with the program structure, well beyond that envisioned by contemporary performance management models in human services (Martin, 2001, pp. 65–75). Until HSEs reach this level of accounting, if ever, there is likely to be a continuing reliance on cost analysis studies.

Cost analysis is a methodology for determining after the fact or estimating before the fact the cost of various items (or defined cost centers) by specialized study of financial statements and sometimes by recovering additional accounting data directly from the transactions recorded in journals and ledgers. Conducting a cost study is ordinarily a seven-step methodology:

1. Define a relevant cost center or cost object.
2. Define the period for the cost study.
3. Identify all of the expenses directly relevant to the cost center during that study period.
4. Identify all of the relevant indirect costs for the same period.
5. Establish a basis for apportioning appropriate (a fair share of) indirect costs to the cost center.
6. Combine the direct and indirect costs to establish the full cost of the center or object.
7. If the cost study is concerned with average (mean) unit costs, determine the number of units of output or production. Division of the full cost by the number of units of output will produce a unit cost.

One of the most fundamental characteristics of cost studies over time is comparability, and consistent definition is basic to establish comparability. If a series of studies of transportation costs sometimes include maintenance costs for vehicles and sometimes exclude them, the results may be consistently precise, predicting costs to the penny, and yet completely useless for establishing any trend.

There is no standardized format for reporting cost studies in human services. For most purposes, the kinds of formats used in research reports (and discussed in most research textbooks) will be useful, because the same kinds of questions and considerations are involved: background statements of the context and issues, discussion of the key definitions and assumptions, listing of the procedures involved, statement of the findings, and discussion of the implications.

COST AND OTHER CENTERS

Some cost centers are best defined in programmatic terms, in which case expense is joined with purposes or objectives to form explicit accountabilities called *responsibility centers*. As Martin (2001) noted, "All programs should be treated as responsibility centers" (p. 13). In the Kettner–Martin performance management approach, responsibility centers can be expense, income, surplus, or investment centers, so named because of their designated functions—primarily defined by outlays; primarily defined by resource inflows; defined by a mix of income and expenses, with income exceeding expenses; or defined by "a program that manages the endowment, investments and other assets" of the HSE (Martin, 2001, pp. 14–15), respectively. To this list, I would add one additional special kind of expense center termed the "loss center." Unlike a simple *expense center*, where typically only the expenses (and no associated income) are tracked, the *loss center* is a special type of expense center in which both income and expenses may be known or understood and, as a matter of policy, income is either nonexistent or fails to cover expenses, but the activity is designated to continue anyway. Perhaps the foremost example in human services is training.

Financially speaking, responsibility for training is nearly always defined as a loss center—a target for sunk costs with little or no hope of offsetting income, except in those rare cases when training grants may be available. Yet, social administrators in human services continue to fund training activities to the extent they are able to because they recognize that this is a clear case where monetized costs are usually more than offset by nonmonetized benefits—to the employees who are trained but also to the HSE and ultimately to the clients who receive better services as a result.

A final type of responsibility center or object to note here is the *innovation center*, which is a center designated as a target for the allocation of resources by management decision for the specific purpose of generating change. Responsibility for change can be handled in any of a number of different ways. A staff person, program unit, or department may be informally recognized, for example, as the "technology guru" of the HSE, or a person may be formally designated as the "vice president for innovation," for example. The costs involved may be formally tracked through a series of cost studies or they may be just informally noted. In any case, it is important to note that responsibilities of many types nearly always have burdens and costs associated with them, and it is important to find ways to recognize those costs and take them into account.

Administrative, Fundraising, and Program Costs

Three important types of costs that we have already seen as important categories of expenses in the chapter on budgeting were defined several decades ago by the AICPA and have been incorporated into GAAPs for nonprofit organizations, as well as captured by IRS Form 990. Thus, for accounting purposes, administrative, fundraising, and program expenses are defined in such a way that the first definitions directly implicate the set of such expenses as cost centers, as outlined in this chapter. The third category, program expenses, implies a program structure of the type discussed in detail in the Kettner–Martin performance management approach (Kettner & Martin, 1993a, 1995, 1996; Martin & Kettner, 1997, 2010) and in Martin (2001, pp. 10–17).

Administrative costs (also sometimes called *management and general expenses*) are defined as those costs incurred for the overall direction of the organization, general record keeping, management, budgeting, board-related activities, and related efforts. In most cases, these would include direct supervision, education, and training expenses. Overall direction usually includes the salaries of the CEO of the enterprise and his or her support staff (secretaries, administrative assistants, and so forth). If the CEO spends significant amounts of time directly supervising fundraising or program personnel, it may be appropriate to apportion a reasonable amount of related expenses to those functions.

Usually also charged as administrative costs are expenses incurred in marketing or public relations for the enterprise, such as promoting favorable impressions of the enterprise's program, name, image, or logo in public, and the costs of information dissemination such as annual reports. *Fundraising costs* usually involve more than just the cost of soliciting and collecting donations. Such expenses include the cost of salaries connected with ongoing fundraising efforts or special events or campaigns, expenses of transmitting appeals to the public (such as postage) and maintaining mailing lists, record keeping, and time spent issuing receipts and depositing funds. The expenses of fundraising consultants, contractors, or affiliates engaged in fundraising for the enterprise should also be included.

The third category, *program service cost*, is likely to be the most meaningful for most social workers, but in the AICPA financial model, it is purely a residual category for all other types of expenses. This is the category that Martin (2001) and Mayers (2004) have been most concerned with in the discussion above, as approached from an accounting perspective. Program expenses include everything that is not otherwise classifiable as an administrative or fundraising expense. The reason for this, in the words of the original AICPA formulation of this concept, is simply that "program services will vary from one organization to another depending on the services rendered" (Lohmann, 1980, p. 42). In the example discussed below, program costs are defined as direct costs (consistent with OMB Circular A-122 [U.S. Government Printing Office, 2012]), whereas fundraising and administrative expenses are treated as indirect costs to be allocated across programs and fundraising.

FIXED AND VARIABLE COSTS

Another way to look at costs in the assignment of expenses to cost centers, which may be particularly useful in the following chapter on break-even analysis, is to distinguish the actions associated with expenditures and to specify whether the expenses involved are fixed, that is, remain constant over the study period, or variable, rising or falling with fluctuations in the level of outputs. Note the important qualifier "varying with level of output." Fluctuations in expenses that cannot be linked to fluctuating levels of output are best treated as random in cost studies. For some types of cost study, it will be necessary to classify the expenses involved as either fixed or variable, depending on the behavior of the expense over time. The annual salary of a full-time salaried fundraising professional will ordinarily be a fixed cost of fundraising, because the salary remains the same month after month, whereas a group of part-time employees hired for short periods during a fundraising campaign will ordinarily represent variable costs, as will printing, the expenses of fundraising luncheons, and a variety of other expenses (Clark & Jordan, 2001).

Note that fixed and variable are really only the poles between which there are several other possibilities. Another type is *step-variable costs*, which change only in increments; they remain fixed for periods of time and then change. A midyear salary increase for the fundraising professional profiled in the preceding example is an example of a step-variable cost. A fourth type is *mixed costs*, which contain an identifiable fixed cost element and a variable cost element. Thus, certain types of equipment rental, for example, may include both a fixed monthly charge and a variable per-use charge. Cost accountants have devised several highly specialized methods for sorting out the fixed and variable elements in mixed costs, including the high–low, scattergram, and least squares methods.

THE STUDY PERIOD

It is also necessary in doing cost study analyses to establish an explicit period of time to be studied. This is one place where the previously discussed five-year timeline can be usefully applied. Thus, time studies may determine the allocation of workers' time over a two-week period. (Anything more may be deemed unnecessarily disruptive or repetitive.) But a study of transportation costs, in which all the relevant data can be retrieved from the accounting records, may look at much longer periods (monthly, quarterly, or yearly expenses) depending on the volume of data involved and the cost of data collection and analysis. Generally speaking, in cost studies, longer study periods are preferable to shorter ones in most instances.

Another important consideration in the study period is what cost analysts call the *relevant range*, or the time period in which the definitions and assumptions are expected to hold true. The clearest case of this occurs with fixed costs: If the relevant time point for salary changes occurs once per year with the budget, salaries can ordinarily be treated as fully fixed costs, whereas midyear salary increases, as noted, may require treating salaries as step-variable costs.

COMBINING DIRECT AND INDIRECT COSTS

The *total cost*, or *full cost*, of any cost center is the sum of its direct and indirect costs. *Direct costs* are simply those expenses that can be readily assigned to the cost object without a problem. *Indirect costs* are those assigned to some other cost center, often a support center, some portion of which must also be recognized in order to determine the full cost of an object. The point is made clearly with the example of administrative, fundraising, and program costs. In assessment of program performance, program expenses can be defined as direct costs, with administrative and fundraising costs apportioned to each program on some reasonable basis. (More on the basis for this follows.) Both Martin (2001) and Mayers (2004) relied heavily on the definitions of direct and indirect costs in OMB Circular A-122 (U.S. Government Printing Office, 2012).*

Step 6 in the cost study methodology listed above says to "combine the direct and indirect costs" to determine the full cost of a cost object or center. Martin (2001, pp. 92–117) offers a number of interesting insights and comments on the assignment of direct costs in a program context. But the same ideas apply in other settings. Thus, for example, without the need to refer to the program structure, Alice, the executive director of a small HSE, developed the budget shown in Table 6.3 with total projected income of $1,468,753 and expenses of the same amount. After the budget was accepted by her board, Alice began to wonder about the full cost of her two programs, so she set out to do a cost analysis. Table 6.13 shows how she first split the total budget into the categories of administrative, fundraising, and program expenses and further divided the budget between the two programs, here named Program A and Program B. Although she began by simply splitting expenses across these five categories, she decided that income split out in an interesting manner as well. The $120,000 amount budgeted for donation income, for example, was assigned to the newly created fundraising function, which had yet to generate much income. She further split this amount as income for the two programs on a 40 percent and 60 percent basis. Fees are generated exclusively by Program A, which also received the grant noted in Table 6.4. Program B was solely responsible for the contract income of $687,420. Expenses were divided on a seemingly proportionate basis, with the result that the total budget of $1,468,753 was first divided into $224,858 for management and general (or administrative) costs, $160,935 in fundraising costs, and $1,083,959 in program costs. Alice then divided the $487,332 assigned to Program A and $595,628 assigned to Program B by that latter amount. So much for the direct cost assignments, Alice thought. Now what do I do with the indirect costs? After a bit of thought, she decided to first allocate management and general costs to fundraising and the two programs on a proportionate basis, as in Table 8.1. She knew that not everyone would handle it in this way, but she wanted the fundraisers to know the full extent of what was expected of them. Then, in a second step, she rolled the revised fundraising costs into the two programs. Thus, while her budget showed expenses of $487,332 for Program A and $595,528 for Program B, the full cost of these two programs was actually $660,938 and $807,815, as shown in Table 8.2.

---

*OMB Circular A-122 defines direct and indirect costs in the specific context of federal funds, but this approach does not differ markedly from other uses of these same terms.

Table 8.1: Step 1. Reassignment of Management and General Expenses as Indirect Costs

Area of Expenditure	Direct Cost ($)	Proportion (%)	Reassigned Management and General ($)	Revised Total Cost ($)
Fundraising	160,936	12.94	29,092	190,028
Program A	487,332	39.18	88,095	575,427
Program B	595,628	47.88	107,671	703,299
Total		100.00	224,858	1,468,753

Note: Row and column totals may not match exactly, because of errors due to rounding.

UNIT COST

One of the principal uses of this kind of cost data is to determine unit costs, which are generally defined as

$$\frac{\text{Full Cost of a Program}}{\text{Number of Units of Program Output}}$$

Unit cost information almost always combines a monetized measurement such as total cost with one or more nonmonetary measures such as the number of clients served, the number of hours of service provided, or some comparable measure. Unit cost measures are both interesting and necessary information for a variety of purposes, most important for determination of fees, establishment of contract rates for third-party contracts, and other similar income determinations. The general rule that applies across the board is that fees and charges should be set at rates equal to or exceeding average unit costs.

Table 8.2: Step 2. Reassignment of Fundraising to Program Costs

Program	Revised Total Cost	Proportion	Reassigned Fundraising	Full Cost
Program A	575,427	.45	85,513	660,938
Program B	703,299	.55	104,515	807,815
Total			190,028	1,468,753

Note: Row and column totals may not match exactly, because of errors due to rounding.

COST REDUCTION AND ELIMINATION

One of the more discouraging aspects of contemporary financial management practice in human services is all the nonsense and falderal associated with public policy–related efforts at cost reduction. For more than 40 years and despite the complete absence of any credible data justifying such a conclusion, one of the political articles of faith regarding publicly subsidized human services is that whatever their current costs may be, they are inefficient and too high. Although this has proved to be a very serviceable political ideology, it makes little administrative sense and has little or no evidence to support it. Along with his many positive accomplishments, the aforementioned management guru Peter Drucker has to be reckoned as one of those most responsible for perpetrating this view, which has now taken on a life of its own (Drucker, 1954, 1969). Despite any evidence that this is so—indeed, in the absence of any agreed-upon measures of efficiency—human services are typically deemed to be inefficient and ineffective in principle, and the best course of action short of elimination is said to be some program of cost reduction. It is important to realize that this is 99 percent political ideology and that in attempting to make the opposite case, those responsible for human services have often mounted only very weak defenses.

COSTING SOCIAL PROBLEMS

One of the standard features of a certain type of social problem and social policy analysis is the inclusion of one or more allegedly authoritative estimates of the cost that the particular social problem represents to society as a whole. The underlying logic of this particular exercise is to transform social problems from moral and political issues into technical, economic ones. As an example, a few years ago, a Reuters news service headline trumpeted, "The Massive Cost of Underemployment," which a table in the article estimated to be $148 billion per year (Salmon, 2010). Generally, such estimates of the cost of social problems serve an important purpose in highlighting that the problem in question is a real and serious one. One is inclined to think, "$148 billion! That's a very big number! Underemployment must be a very serious problem." (It is!) Aside from that, however, such estimates of the social cost of a particular problem have very little meaning or significance, except for macroeconomists who attempt to track such matters. The basic problem is that for most of the population, although it can be argued that all share in the problem, there is no real experience or perception of any actual cost associated with it.

COST EFFICIENCY?

One of the pseudoconcepts that one hears periodically is the completely misguided and ill-informed notion of cost efficiency, an idea that has no place in financial management of HSEs. The concept does show up in the professional literature in connection with the evaluation of banks, but it is carefully defined there in a way that has no particular applicability to the HSE setting. In the human services field, talk of cost efficiency usually turns out to be a nonsense statement, a conflation of two otherwise unrelated qualities or ratios. It makes approximately as much sense to talk of cost efficiency as it does to talk about outcome outputs or efficiency quality. Cost is one dimension of measurement, specifically, the measure of outlays or opportunities forgone, and efficiency, the ratio of inputs to outputs, is another. Unless operationally defined in a careful manner that modifies at least one of these definitions, cost efficiency will remain just a silly pseudoconcept with no significant applications in financial management.

CONCLUSION

Since its introduction many decades ago, the concept of cost has become a central, universally accepted parameter for describing and evaluating human services. This has proved true to a far greater extent than for other parameters such as efficiency, effectiveness, or quality. Although there are two distinct ways of approaching costs—the accountants' model of outlays and the economists' model of opportunity cost—the outlay cost model, defined as a selection of expenses linked to a cost center, object, or magnet, is very much the norm in human services management. A thorough understanding of the basic outlay cost model is also fundamental to other modes of financial analysis in HSE. In particular, the ability to distinguish direct and indirect costs, as well as fixed and variable costs, is fundamental to applications of the break-even analysis model discussed in chapter 9.

9

Break-Even Analysis

It should be relatively clear to most readers that there may be a range of predictable relations or connections among costs, the income needed to offset those costs, and the volume of human services that can be produced under a particular set of circumstances. This can be expressed as "the more services you produce, the greater the total cost and the more income you will have to generate (all other things being equal)." Taking advantage of this intuitive insight is the domain of a range of techniques known as *break-even analysis* (Lohmann, 1976, 1980), which is a type of cost–volume–revenue analysis (Mayers, 2004, p. 158).* It is also related to a conceptual approach in for-profit managerial economics examining what is known as the cost–volume–profit relationship (Brewer, Garrison, & Noreen, 2016). Social administration studies of HSE have only begun to examine these connections.

This chapter introduces the basic terminology, graphics, and formulas of break-even analysis and cost–volume–revenue analysis and discusses several applications. The basic terminology of break-even analysis that students should master includes the previously discussed concepts of income, expenditure, total income, fixed cost, variable cost, and fee (or price). In addition, new terms to be discussed include the break-even point, contribution, total contribution, contribution margin, and a set of related formulas.

Break-even analysis and cost–volume–revenue analysis are initially useful for students of financial management in social work as ways of understanding, mapping, and measuring in dynamic fashion the complex and subtle connections between income, expenditures, and service outputs. It may be true that when you have more, you can spend more and therefore produce more services, but is it ever possible to say how much more? Over and beyond this orienting purpose, however, break-even analysis also offers a range of useful tools for the working

---

*As noted in chapter 6, the management historian Daniel Wren in effect attributes key connections between break-even analysis and the crossover chart to the scientific management specialists Henry Hess and John R. Williams, who proposed the flexible budget at about the same time.

financial manager in an HSE to conduct various forms of sensitivity analysis, to understand and predict differing likely outcomes under different conditions, and to better formulate programs and policy for the organization. Figure 9.1 is a preliminary sketch of break-even analysis as an independent analytical subsystem.

As the diagram shows, the outputs of break-even analysis are most likely to be fed back into the budget system—in most cases, in the form of support for various budget revisions. What does not show in Figure 9.1 is that much of this feedback from the results of break-even analysis can take place in the preliminary, formative states of budget preparation and serve as evidence for at least some of the proposals built into the formal budget. The accounting system is, by comparison, largely impervious to this and other forms of feedback from financial analysis. Accounting data are what they are and, for the most part, present outputs that serve as the data for various forms of financial analysis but do not input any results.

BREAK-EVEN ANALYSIS

Formally speaking, break-even analysis is, as the associated "cost–volume–revenue" term suggests, any examination or investigation of the relations between a set of fixed and variable costs, the real or projected volumes of service activity, and a range of possible variable income they might produce. Figure 9.2 shows a graphic representation of a set of break-even relations, including the break-even point, which is also the beginning point of surplus income (in dollars shown on the vertical axis). At that point, income matches expenditures and a certain level of possible service output is implied (and shown in units of service on the horizontal axis).

From that point on, as the volume of service output increases, income will continue to outpace expenses, and the financial surplus will continue to grow. The principal limit at that point will be the total volume of service that it is possible to produce with the present resources and cost configuration. The challenge taken

Figure 9.1: Break-Even Analysis Subsystem

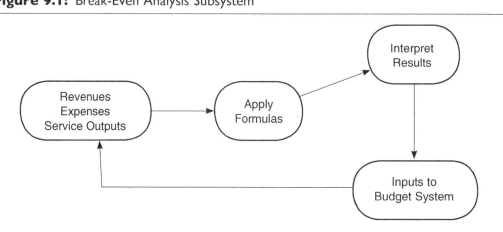

Figure 9.2: Break-Even Graph of Fixed and Variable Income and Expenses

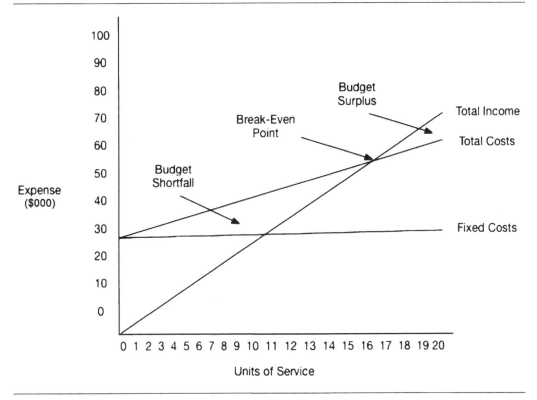

on by the break-even analysis technique is to ensure that that point (and the corresponding income) is greater than the level of anticipated expenses. It should not automatically be assumed that there will always be a break-even point, however. As Figure 9.3 illustrates, under some conditions (for example, when fees are set unnecessarily high), expenses never rise to the level of breaking even with income (or vice versa). Note that if the opposite is true—if income never catches up with expenses—it is nothing less than the operational definition of a failed or impossible program. If there is no circumstance under which anticipated income can match anticipated expenses, it is time to return to the planning table and find ways to cut expenses or locate more income.

As with any mathematical problem in which we are solving for one unknown, break-even analysis allows us to readily determine a value for any one of those variables (income, cost, or volume) if we know the value of the other two. It also provides limited ways to estimate all three simultaneously. For the present purposes, budgets such as those discussed in chapter 6 can be thought of as portraits of special (and limited) instances of cost–volume–revenue analyses in which fixed and variable costs are not separated and service volume is not identified. Most line-item budgets are computed for only one particular balanced set of income, expense, and output levels. Conducting break-even analysis enables us to extend that approach and see the effects—in either graphic or tabular form—of numerous

Figure 9.3: Situation with No Break-Even Point

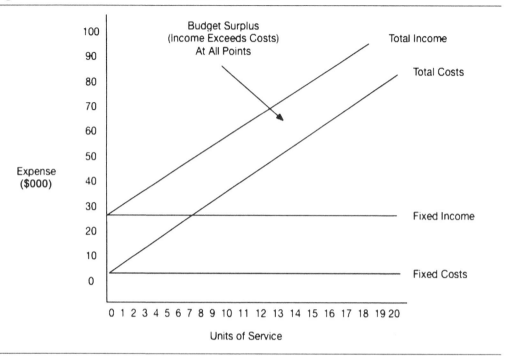

different combinations. In some cases, notably some grant and contract budgets, assumptions about the volume or level of services to be provided are detailed, but whether or not they are explicit, we can assume that any particular budget with a quantity of anticipated income and anticipated expenditures also implies a particular level of services.

Lohmann (1976, 1980) introduced break-even analysis to social administration as a graphic tool for service planning in multifunded agencies. D. R. Meyer and Sherraden (1985) introduced a mathematical version. Mayers (2004, p. 158) identified a useful list of several possible specific uses for this approach:

- to determine appropriate service levels for grants and contracts
- to predict how changes in service levels will impact income
- to plan fundraising functions in which donations exceed costs
- to set fees for services
- to identify adequate income levels to support service delivery

These are just some of the most useful things that can be done with the break-even approach applied to HSE budgets. In the context of applying break-even analysis to budgeting, there is one crucial definition that must be accepted and recognized: It is that costs (*C*; a break-even analysis term) equal expenses (*E*; a budget term):

$$C = E$$

In addition, the term *income* is used here for all financial inflows, just as it is in budgeting and throughout the book. On the basis of these two terms—income (R) and cost or expense (C)—the first and most essential definition involves defining the break-even point (B) itself:

$$B = (R_T - C_T)$$

This is the fundamental idea of a balanced budget, as previously discussed, expressed as a mathematical equation. A second important definition is the following:

$$C_T = C_F + C_V$$

It says that total costs (C_T) are the sum of total fixed costs (C_F) and total variable costs (C_V). This is another standard definition, taken from conventional business use of the break-even methodology that has the effect of tying break-even analysis directly to the budget. For nonprofit settings, a slight variation of the business approach is sometimes warranted—one that comes in handy when budgeting a mix of fixed and variable income. Certain fixed budget items, such as grants and donations (which for purposes of break-even analysis do not vary with service output levels and therefore are assumed to be fixed income), can sometimes be usefully distinguished from variable income items and fees (which do vary with service levels). It simply applies the same logic of the previous definition to income:

$$R_T = R_F + R_V$$

Here, R_T is total income, R_F is fixed income (from grants, donations, and other income that does not vary with the level of services delivered), and R_V is variable income (direct client fees, third-party fees, and any other income pegged or metered to the delivery of services). Note that to make this distinction work, all income must be assigned to one of a standard set of income categories.

So far, however, we have not gotten beyond expressing the basic ideas of a balanced budget in mathematical terms. Moving into the distinctive realm of break-even analysis requires a third term, the idea of service outputs, and a critically important assumption. The assumption is that every balanced budget expresses or implies an assumed level of service that can be delivered on the basis of that budget. The basic idea is simple enough: If the budget includes funding for a single worker, then the volume of service to be produced cannot exceed what that one worker is capable of doing during the budget period. In fixed income situations, this is a relatively simple matter of how accurate the prediction of output is: Will it turn out that the worker can do more (or less) than expected? We simply cannot know in advance. However, when working with variable income, which not only cannot be known in advance but also rises or falls with the level of service actually delivered, the problem becomes much more interesting.

Figure 9.2 shows a graphic version of the grant/project budget developed by and shown in tabular form in Table 6.4. Note that this graph plots a straight linear prediction of the relation between spending and service outputs. It is also possible to present step-variable or mixed-cost projections in either graphic or tabular form. Betsy's budget showed total anticipated expenditures of $511,333, which were to be matched by income from the grant. No explicit assumptions of levels of service to be provided have been mentioned so far, although the grant would likely have contained some mention of this. Assume, for purposes of the example, that dollar volumes on the vertical axis in Figure 9.4 are plotted in hundred thousand dollar increments and service units on the horizontal axis are in hundreds of hours. Note that the income line in Figure 9.4 is a flat line perpendicular to the base of the graph to indicate that (a) the total amount of the grant remains the same under all circumstances and (b) it represents the upper limit of possible spending under the grant. If the grant were the only income for this program or project, this would not be very interesting, and break-even analysis would be of no particular use. However, in the event that the grant provided only partial support for Betsy's program and the program was also going to charge fees to some clients, then we would be dealing with both fixed income (from the grant) and variable income (from program service fees) as well as both fixed and variable expenses. This is the real domain of break-even analysis. At this point in the history of financial analysis in human services, no other budget-related analysis is capable of handling this particular problem. The curvilinear supply and demand curves of economic analysis might be applied, but we clearly are not dealing with either supply or demand in the usual sense here, and the mathematics involved

Figure 9.4: Break-Even Graph of Grant

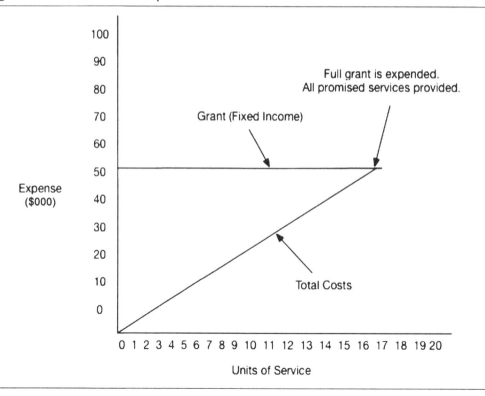

in such scenarios are much more complex (Jegers, 2008; B. Keating & Keating, 2009; D. R. Young, 2007).

The expenditure/cost line rises diagonally from the $0 point at the lower left to the point where it intersects with the horizontal line (the break-even point) at the upper right. The break-even point is the point where the budget balances. In this case, the budget balances on the assumption that all of the funds will be spent. Figure 9.4 is a simple graphical expression of what have long been the standard assumptions of existing budget balancing techniques. Yet, an interesting added value comes into focus when Betsy looks at the bottom line, which shows the service levels (measured as total hours of services to clients provided) anticipated in the grant, rising from the zero point (no services) at left. Whether the ratio between total expenses and the level of services would actually remain constant at all levels of service (probably not!) need not concern us at the moment. Regardless of a more complex reality lurking underneath, that assumption is implicit in most grant budgets as prepared and submitted: If 50 percent of the grant is expended, then 50 percent of the promised service should have been delivered. If no services were provided, then no funds should have been spent. That is Grant Writing 101, except that both of those assumptions are highly unrealistic.

One question remains: How did Betsy come up with the estimate of 1,000 service hours to be delivered by the grant? The conventional answer provided in budgets that do not follow a systematic break-even analysis approach might well be a seat of the pants guesstimate or practice wisdom. She might guesstimate, for example, that this grant will allow each of the five social workers she hopes to partially support with the grant to provide roughly 200 hours of grant-related services each during the annual grant period. They might do so, for example, by offering an average of four hours per week for 50 weeks.

$$\frac{1,000}{50 \text{ weeks} \times (4 \text{ hours} \times 5 \text{ workers} = 20 \text{ hours/week})}$$

The traditional fixed budget approach locks Betsy into this single set of assumptions: Her $511,333 budget will support five workers for a total of 20 hours of service per week. But her five workers actually work 40 hours per week; what happens if they spend more or less time on the grant? In addition, in that case, the presumed unit cost of services provided under the grant would be $511.33 per hour. But what if the hours per worker estimates are wrong? Or a worker quits? Or for some other reason this whole folder of assumptions cannot hold? Under conventional grant budget practices, we would simply be befuddled at that point and would need to begin again with a different set of assumptions to pursue another singular solution. Break-even analysis offers several ways to begin to approach multiple answers to such questions, including the possibility of a specified range.

$$511,333 \div 1,000 = 511.33$$

To pursue this point further, in the example presented here, Betsy will rely on the following set of standard definitions and notations:

R_T = Total Income
E_T = Total Expenditures
C_T = Total Cost
F_T = Total Fixed Cost
U_T = Units of Service
P = Unit Price
U_{TC} = Total Unit Cost
V_{CU} = Variable Cost/Unit
V_{TC} = Total Variable Cost*

This amount introduces a slight discrepancy, because an independent cost analysis by Betsy of the services was the basis for tentatively pricing services at $500 per hour, which is the amount that the HSE could be charging fee-paying clients for the same services. Ordinarily a small (2.26 percent) variance such as the difference between $500 and $511.33 might be simply dismissed or swept under the rug as an unavoidable error of estimation. If the grant makers were to learn of such a discrepancy, however, they very well might ask Betsy to explain why it is that they are being charged over 2 percent more than fee-paying clients. Does this not mean that grant funds are indirectly supporting private pay clients who may not be eligible for services under the grant's terms? (It does, indeed, mean that!)

With the simple spreadsheet shown in Table 9.1, Betsy can also tease apart several options, provided that she can begin with three data items: total fixed costs, variable cost per unit, and fee or charge per unit. From those three numbers, using the standard break-even formula, she can determine the quantity of units of services necessary for total income to equal total expenditures. Betsy already knows that under the assumption that her budget is in balance, both total income and total expenditures are $511,333. Following the full cost and break-even assumptions, she will assume this same amount as the total cost and total income of the grant-funded project. She must, at this point, analyze the grant budget shown as Table 6.4, separating out the anticipated total fixed costs and total variable costs.

Betsy can also determine the exact combinations of all these variables at different points. In this example, where fixed costs are $281,233.30, variable costs are $45 per hour, and the fee charged is $100, the program would break even at 5,113 hours of services provided. That is less than one-fifth of the fee but five times the number of hours required. As Table 9.1 shows, at this point, the budget will balance at $511,333.27, total income and total expenses (fixed cost plus total variable cost) will be equal, and the total cost per hour will equal the anticipated fee

---

*The main break-even formula used to compute the examples in this chapter is $U_T = \dfrac{F_T}{P - V_{CU}}$ (that is, the total number of units of service necessary to break even can be determined by dividing total fixed costs by the difference between the unit price and the variable cost per unit, or what is often identified as the contribution margin).

Table 9.1: Simple Break-Even Analysis

Category	Amount ($)
Fixed costs	281,233.30
Variable cost/unit	45.00
Fee/unit	100.00
Break-even quantity	5,113.33
Total variable costs	230,099.97
Total income	511,333.27
Total costs	511.333.27
Cost/unit	100.00

of $100 per unit of service. In this case, break-even analysis offers a richer, more amplified portrait of a balanced budget.

Break-even analysis also allows Betsy to tease apart and examine more closely the assumptions built into her budget, as well as to engage in various forms of "what if" analysis. What if, for example, only three-quarters of the hours of services are provided during the grant period? Does this mean that exactly three-quarters of the money should be expended? In this case, that could be true under certain assumptions, as Betsy can see in Table 9.2. She assumes spending about three-quarters of the total budget (in the example shown as Option B, a balanced budget of $388,175 is 75.9 percent of the original budget of $511,333). In that case, if she

Table 9.2: Break-Even Options

Category	Option A: Original ($)	Option B: 75% ($)	Option C ($)	Option D ($)
Fixed costs	281,233	281,233	210,925	281,233
Variable cost/unit	45	27.55	27.55	53
Fee/unit	100	100	100	100
Break-even quantity	5,113	3,882	2,911	5,983
Total variable expenses	230,100	106,942	80,206	317,135
Total income	511,333	388,175	291,131	598,368
Total expenses	511,333	388,175	291,131	598,368
Cost/unit	100	100	100	100

assumes that fixed costs and the fee of $100 per unit remain unchanged, the variable cost per unit would drop from $45.00 to $27.55 (61.2 percent), whereas the number of anticipated units of service produced would, indeed, also be 75.9 percent. The major problem with this alternative is that fixed costs remaining unchanged might suggest a considerable measure of underutilized capacity. If Betsy were to also reduce fixed costs to 75 percent of the original (as in Option C) and keep the other assumptions of Option B the same, she would have a whole new set of figures to deal with: total fixed expenses of $210,925, a break-even quantity that drops to 2,911 units (56.9 percent of the original estimate), total variable expenses of $80,206 (34.9 percent of the original), and a budget that balances at $291,131 (56.9 percent of the original estimated budget).

And what if her workers are actually able to provide more than 5,000 hours of service under the terms of the original grant? What would this do to her initial assumptions? In the conventional budget situation, it shreds them entirely, and she must start all over. With break-even analysis, that is just one more plausible scenario, as in Column D. If, for example, they were able to deliver approximately an additional 1,000 hours of service with fixed costs remaining constant, the variable expense per unit would rise to $53, total variable expenses would rise to $317,135, and the budget would balance at $598,368 (due primarily to the increased fee income from the approximately 1,000 additional hours of service provided).

Moreover, using this same set of assumptions, Betsy is able to examine several other possibilities. What if, for example, the grant gets off to a very slow start, and in the period available, the HSE is only able to deliver 75 percent of the service hours anticipated? How much money would actually be expended? Or what if the average length of a unit of service (one hour) is too limited, and the five workers together are actually able to deliver 8,000 hours of service in the grant period? What would this do to the cost per unit of service? These two assumptions can easily be followed out. We can see that delivery of 75 percent of the number of service units (3,750) would result in an expenditure of only 73.4 percent of the grant (because of the effect of the variable costs).

$$5,000 \times .75 = 3,750$$

$$\$375,363 \div \$511,333 = 73.4\%$$

Likewise, as the righthand column of Table 9.2 shows, working with the present total fixed and variable costs would reduce the unit cost from $100 to $53 and hypothetically could generate roughly $600,000 in total income. (In this case, the grant total would not change, but there might be a good bit of necessary explaining and negotiating with the grant makers over the question of why the grant-related project was generating a large surplus over the original amount of the grant and what was to be done with that surplus.)

There is an important red flag here, however: For all of these assumptions to work together at 8,000 hours, the variable cost per unit would hypothetically fluctuate between a high of $53 per hour and a low of $27.55 per hour. If Betsy's original assumptions about variable costs were solid, that is extremely unlikely to prove viable. As she is no doubt aware, there is little basis for believing that such substantial scale economies are lurking in these estimates. This may be purely a mathematical fluke of the way we are approaching the problem (in reverse order). It is more likely that although the various numbers of hours might be accommodated within the original fixed cost estimates, the variable costs would, in all likelihood, continue at something close to the same $45 per hour rate, thus affecting the total variable cost estimates. In other words, taking full costs into consideration, it is unlikely that the plan to deliver a large number of additional hours of service within the grant budget would prove viable without some additional close scrutiny.

Break-even analysis can also accommodate the close comparison of the difference between fees and variable costs per unit, or what is called the *contribution margin* (see Table 9.3). Such calculations are shown in Tables 9.4–9.7. Table 9.4 is a simple design, easily created on a spreadsheet, that shows various combinations of fixed costs ($50,000) and variable costs at various service levels that must be balanced against the projected revenues to be generated by those same service levels. As the righthand column of the table shows, income and expenses break even in this particular set of assumptions (that is, the program) at around 2,400 hours of service. The righthand column of Table 9.5 translates the same set of data into a set of financial ratios, building on the standard income–expense ratio discussed previously. Table 9.6 introduces the idea of step-variable costs (such as might occur when it becomes necessary at a particular service level to add an additional part- or full-time worker to increase the number of hours any further). Note that at 2,000 hours and again at 3,000 hours, in the present example, total fixed costs take a sudden and dramatic step upward ($16,800 in each case). Note also that this causes our program, which was running surpluses up to that point, to suddenly be in a deficit position. Table 9.6 contains a fixed budget assumption (as from a grant). Clearly, if the plan is to increase the number of service units beyond 2,000 or, even more ambitiously, beyond 3,000, additional grant income must be located somewhere, because the current cost structure would not support such a move! Finally, Table 9.7 introduces a variable budget assumption (from additional donations or fee income?) that would allow us to get the budget back in balance at higher service levels. Note, however, that with the new assumption, the budget holds at the 2,000-unit level, but at 3,000 units, the budget once again is in deficit.

These are just some of the many ways in which the simple assumptions of the break-even model can be applied.

Table 9.3: Unit Contribution Margin

Rate	Cost ($)
Fee charged per unit of service	100
Variable cost per unit	45
Contribution margin	55

Table 9.4: A Range of Break-Even Points

Units	Total Variable Cost ($)	Total Expenditures ($)	Budget ($)	Surplus or Deficit ($)
1,000	10,000	60,000	74,000	14,000
1,200	12,000	62,000	74,000	12,000
1,400	14,000	64,000	74,000	10,000
1,600	16,000	66,000	74,000	8,000
1,800	18,000	68,000	74,000	6,000
2,000	20,000	70,000	74,000	4,000
2,200	22,000	72,000	74,000	2,000
2,400	24,000	74,000	74,000	0
2,600	26,000	76,000	74,000	−2,000
2,800	28,000	78,000	74,000	−4,000
3,000	30,000	80,000	74,000	−6,000

Note: Total fixed cost in this table is assumed to be $50,000.

Table 9.5: Break-Even Analysis Options with Associated Income–Expense Ratios

Number of Units	Total Variable Cost ($)	Total Expenditures ($)	Budget ($)	Income– Expense Ratio
1,000	10,000	60,000	74,000	0.81
1,200	12,000	62,000	74,000	0.84
1,400	14,000	64,000	74,000	0.86
1,600	16,000	66,000	74,000	0.89
1,800	18,000	68,000	74,000	0.92
2,000	20,000	70,000	74,000	0.95
2,200	22,000	72,000	74,000	0.97
2,400	24,000	74,000	74,000	1.00
2,600	26,000	76,000	74,000	1.03
2,800	28,000	78,000	74,000	1.05
3,000	30,000	80,000	74,000	1.08

Note: Total fixed cost in this table is assumed to be $50,000.

Table 9.6: Break-Even Analysis with Step-Variable Fixed or Semi-Fixed Cost

Fixed Cost ($)	Number of Units	Total Variable Cost ($)	Total Expenses ($)	Budget ($)	Surplus or Deficit	Revenue–Expense Ratio
50,000	1,000	10,000	60,000	74,000	14,000	0.81
50,000	1,200	12,000	62,000	74,000	12,000	0.84
50,000	1,400	14,000	64,000	74,000	10,000	0.86
50,000	1,600	16,000	66,000	74,000	8,000	0.89
50,000	1,800	18,000	68,000	74,000	6,000	0.92
66,500	2,000	20,000	86,500	74,000	−12,500	1.17
66,500	2,200	22,000	88,500	74,000	−14,500	1.20
66,500	2,400	24,000	90,500	74,000	−16,500	1.22
66,500	2,600	26,000	92,500	74,000	−18,500	1.25
66,500	2,800	28,000	94,500	74,000	−20,500	1.28
83,000	3,000	30,000	113,000	74,000	−39,000	1.53

Note: Fixed costs in this table are really only semi-fixed. They are adjusted upward at 2,000 and 3,000 units of service.

Table 9.7: Break-Even Analysis with Step-Variable Fixed or Semi-Fixed Cost and Variable Income

Fixed Cost ($)	Number of Units	Total Variable Cost ($)	Total Expenses ($)	Budget ($)	Surplus or Deficit ($)	Revenue–Expense Ratio
50,000	1,000	10,000	60,000	84,000	24,000	0.71
50,000	1,200	12,000	62,000	86,000	24,000	0.72
50,000	1,400	14,000	64,000	88,000	24,000	0.73
50,000	1,600	16,000	66,000	90,000	24,000	0.73
50,000	1,800	18,000	68,000	92,000	24,000	0.74
66,500	2,000	20,000	86,500	94,000	$7,500	0.92
66,500	2,200	22,000	88,500	96,000	$7,500	0.92
66,500	2,400	24,000	90,500	98,000	$7,500	0.92
66,500	2,600	26,000	92,500	100,000	$7,500	0.93
66,500	2,800	28,000	94,500	102,000	$7,500	0.93
83,000	3,000	30,000	113,000	104,000	−$9,000	1.09

Note: In this table, fixed costs are semi-fixed, and the total budget (anticipated income) is adjusted upward with levels of service.

LIMITATIONS OF BREAK-EVEN OR
COST–VOLUME–REVENUE ANALYSIS

As part of her investigation, Betsy also found that there are a number of limitations to the break-even model that are worth noting:

- Break-even analysis assumes that the relative proportions of fixed and variable costs of each unit of production remain constant over the period of the analysis. In enterprisewide applications, where several service products are produced or outputted and, to a lesser degree, in any case where human services are produced in the relationship between social worker and client, this can, at times, be a serious distortion.
- The break-even analysis model tends to work best for short-term analyses (for example, within a given fiscal year). The longer the period of analysis, the less certain the projections. The reasons for this are as follows:
  - The model assumes that fixed costs will remain fixed. Although this is generally true in the short run, major changes in the scale of production are likely to cause fixed costs to rise (or fall), as in the examples cited in Tables 9.6 and 9.7 and elsewhere. It may be possible to track these changes with break-even analysis, or it may not be.
  - The model also assumes the linearity of average variable costs, that is, that variable costs will remain constant over the range of possible outputs produced. In some cases, this can be controlled for to some extent by using step-variable costs.
- The break-even analysis model also assumes that the quantity of goods produced is equal to the quantity of goods sold. Although this can be a problem in manufacturing, for example, it is not ordinarily a problem in HSEs because the very act of producing a service is inherently also the act of delivering (or selling) the service to the client and automatically generates a sale or billing opportunity, as the case may be.
- Of greatest concern to economists is that break-even analysis/cost–volume–revenue analysis is only a supply-side perspective, whereas microeconomic models focus on the seemingly more realistic interplay of supply and demand. This is usually not a major problem for HSE applications, however (unless the budget analyst has economic training), because human services typically do not have fixed, advertised, or publicized prices, and the circumstantial urgency of client need (a psychosocial notion that tends to drive economists slightly berserk!) rather than the rational choice of consumer demand is typically the guiding consideration.

These limits are all worth noting and keeping in mind any time a break-even analysis or cost–volume–revenue analysis is undertaken. Together, they do not make a strong case against use of this set of techniques. However, they do suggest the importance of avoiding undue reliance on the results of an analysis.

SOME APPLICATIONS OF THE BREAK-EVEN ANALYSIS MODEL

In this section, we explore a number of additional uses of the basic break-even formulas, starting with Table 9.4 showing a fixed (grant-funded) budget of $74,000, a range of units of service from 1,000 to 3,000 at intervals of 200 units, total fixed costs of $50,000, and total variable costs of $10/unit. Table 9.6, Table 9.7, and Table 13.9 show the systematic introduction, one at a time, of possible alternatives to these assumptions. Table 9.6, for example, not only shows the dollar amounts of projected surpluses or deficits but also calculates the income–expense ratio (see Martin, 2001, p. 57). Table 9.6 modifies the assumption of the original model that costs are fixed across all possibilities and introduces a step-variable fixed cost that increases with every additional 1,000 units of service. Requirements for additional supervision at fixed increments, for example, might have an effect like this. As the example shows, this change moves the break-even point downward rather dramatically. In Table 9.7, the step-variable fixed cost assumption is retained and a rolling budget is implemented with the introduction of a $10 per unit copayment assumption. As the example shows, this change moves the break-even point back to where the budget balances upward to just below 3,000 units of service.

Finally, we might combine all of these and show the further implications of the various permutations with a complex spreadsheet that can simultaneously model and take into account donations, grants, and fee income and even estimate the impact of sliding scale fees. Such a spreadsheet (Table 13.9) is part of the discussion in the final chapter.

Sliding scale fees can be treated in break-even analyses in a manner analogous to the business practice of discounting: If one knows the sliding scale and can estimate the proportion of total units of service offered at the reduced fees (or discounted prices) and the amounts of the discounts (or fee reductions), it is relatively easy to calculate the impact on total income.

Total Income (Total Units of Service × Full Fee) − Reduced Fee ×
Units of Service Offered at Reduced Rate

The range of 10 possible configurations of costs, budgeted income, and service levels shown in Table 9.4 predict that the budget will be in balance at $74,000 with a service level of 2,400 units. The model in Table 9.5 translates the dollar amounts of surplus or deficit shown in Table 9.4 to the income–expense ratio, which predicts, for example, that production of 83 percent of the units of service (2,000 of 2,400) would result in expenditure of 95 percent of the budgeted income, whereas production of half of the budgeted units (1,200) would still result in expenditure of 84 percent of the budget. Inexperienced analysts might be inclined to assume that delivering half the services during the grant period would result in expenditure of half of the funds, but this is not so: Such an assumption, in this case, fails to take into account the effects of fixed costs, which can be expected to remain fixed regardless of levels of actual service provided. The fixed cost per unit decreases as the number of units increase (from $50 per unit at 1,000 units produced to $25 per unit at 2,000 units and $16.67 at 3,000 units). Meanwhile, Table 9.4 and Table

9.5 both assume that the variable cost per unit remains the same at all levels of production. Table 9.6 and Table 9.7 introduce step-variable fixed costs in which the assumption is that because of some known factor (for example, additional supervision due to accreditation requirements), fixed cost increases by one-third at every additional 1,000 units of service. Note that this has no effect on total variable costs, which remain the same in Table 9.6 and Table 9.7, but that it increases total anticipated expenditures, shifting the break-even point downward from our previous prediction of 2,400 to somewhere between 1,800 and 2,000 units. In our hypothetical example, Jane and her budget team plan to compensate for this and seek to balance their budget at somewhere near the original figure of 2,400 units of service by introducing a $10 copayment requirement for all clients. Concerned that some clients would be unable to afford such a copay, Jane and her budget team were able to secure pledges from several board members to cover the copays for the estimated percentage of clients unable to pay. Table 9.7 shows the result of these assumptions. This variable (or rolling) budget amount represents the combination of the original $74,000 budget from the grant plus the $10 copay multiplied by the estimated units of service. Jane and the team were delighted to discover that introducing the copay shifts the break-even point back to and even well above the original 2,400 units of service level (somewhere between 2,800 and 3,000 units of service).

It would be possible at any time, of course, to use the original break-even formulas noted above to determine the exact break-even point, but Table 9.6 and Table 9.7 reflect the assumption that Jane and her team have decided that for planning purposes, these estimates are close enough. Note also that they are aware that a smaller copay would bring the break-even point back down somewhat. Thus, a fee of $6.88, for example, would balance the budget at 2,400 units (actually, with a $12 surplus!). However, making change for that amount could be a management nightmare, and once the idea was introduced, the board members agreed to cover lower-income clients, and the agreement of the grant makers was secured, Jane and her team decided to stick with the $10 figure for the copay.

CONCLUSION

Anecdotal evidence seems to confirm that although the tools of graphic and formulary break-even analysis and cost–volume–revenue analysis have been available for a very long time, they have yet to gain acceptance among HSEs. Alternatively, if they have gained footholds in human services budgeting, the published literature has yet to acknowledge that new reality. Rather, it appears that standard practice is still seeking to accommodate the realities of variable income sources such as program service income and donations with the tried-and-true practices of fixed income budgeting. To the extent that this is the case, it is a clear instance of a partially obsolete and inappropriate management technology rendering the challenges of budget planning even more difficult and daunting than they need to be.* Despite

---

*Formative documents on the management technology perspective in social administration on which this work is based include Sarri and Vinter (1970) and Turem (1986).

its well-known limitations, the break-even model offers a wide range of possible ways to analyze information on fixed and variable costs, anticipated service levels, and projected income under many different circumstances. Combined with the innovative approaches of abbreviated line-item budgeting and cost analysis, discussed in the two previous chapters, and ratio analysis and social accounting, discussed in the next two chapters, break-even analysis is a key component of an emerging analytical system for financial management in human services.

10

Ratio Analysis

Ratio analysis is the process of using quantities from financial statements to calculate decimal fractions, termed *ratios*, in order to assess various financial conditions and circumstances of human services agencies. A ratio in this sense is simply a fraction derived from division of a numerator (derived from one item on a financial statement) by a denominator (derived from another item on the same or a different financial statement). Although the methodology is relatively simple and easily generalized to other measures and indicators, in its original pure form, the term refers to ratios derived from financial statements only. Ratio analysis is only one of the major forms of financial analysis, but it is an increasingly important one for HSEs (Chabotar, 1989). In this chapter, we look at a variety of different ratios and proposed regimens of ratio analysis.

In general, there are four kinds of ratios:

1. "seat of the pants" judgments based on practice wisdom in specific situations
2. standard measures with no particular grounding other than convention
3. practice wisdom validated by empirical research, particularly research addressing issues of reliability, validity, and generalizability
4. industry standards (widely accepted definitions combined with research testing)

The process of defining financial ratios closely resembles the operational definition of variables in research: The numbers in themselves have no apparent meaning, but when they are associated with empirical realities, procedures for defining them, and organizational processes for which they serve as proxies or indices, they can provide a great deal of useful information about the operations to which they refer. In addition, a number of ratios are widely recognized and have standard interpretations.

Thus, for example, one of the most general ratios used in all commercial and nonprofit settings is the ratio of assets, or owned resources, to debt, or liabilities:

$$\frac{\text{Liabilities}}{\text{Assets}} \quad \text{or} \quad \frac{\text{Assets}}{\text{Liabilities}}$$

This ratio can be constructed with either figure as the denominator and the opposite figure as the numerator, although the analyst must be careful to note which way it is done because they require slightly different interpretations. With liabilities as the numerator, healthy financial statements will ordinarily produce a decimal fraction of less than 1, and any ratio greater than 1 will reveal an enterprise whose obligations (liabilities) exceed its capacity to satisfy them. This is one of several possible definitions of bankruptcy, and when it occurs, there is legitimate cause for concern. This ratio provides useful data to view in historical perspective also, as examination of the same data for a series of periods (six quarters or five years, for example) may (or may not) reveal a consistent trend. A pattern like that displayed in Figure 10.1 is cause for concern. The ratio shows that in each successive fiscal year over a five-year period, the proportion of liabilities is increasing, with no variation in the pattern.

These data suggest an organization is headed for trouble, as total liabilities are steadily increasing, perhaps even accelerating, relative to the total assets required to satisfy them. Note that this could be for any of a number of reasons: slowly increasing assets and more rapidly increasing liabilities, for example, or decreasing assets and more slowly decreasing liabilities. This is an instance of ratio analysis.

Figure 10.1: Bar Graph of Historical Current Ratios

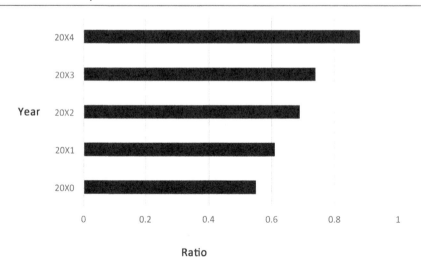

Note: These are data of a fictional organization in which the ratio of liabilities to assets has been growing consistently every year. The five-year pattern indicates that the organization may be slowly sliding into a financial situation from which it may not recover. Unless this trend is reversed, severe fiscal distress or bankruptcy looms.

Another more recent ratio with interesting possibilities is the one adapted from Thomas Piketty (2014). More detailed examples are provided in chapter 11.

The initial advocate of contemporary approaches to ratio analysis in human services was Robert Elkin, a CPA with a national accounting firm who conducted several important consulting studies for, among others, the Child Welfare League of America, Family Service Association, and Travelers Aid before beginning a second career as a social work administration faculty member at the University of Maryland (Elkin, 1967; 1985; Elkin & Molitor, 1984, 1985). Creasie Hairston, who has more recently been a leader of the Network for Social Work Management, also published an important early article on the topic of ratio analysis (Hairston, 1985b). Accountant Ralph Drtina (1982) offered the earliest complete proposal for a set of management indicators in the *New England Journal of Human Services*. These publications, as well as a number of more recent works discussed below, are indicative of a very important cross-pollination between social administration and the accounting profession that began decades ago with a few individuals and has produced some very interesting work on ratios for financial management (Chabotar, 1989). The most important of these to date are the fiscal distress ratios discussed below.

Several assumptions are fundamental to the application of ratio analysis to human services (Lohmann, 1980, pp. 249–250):

- Ratios will be most meaningful in those areas where the financial structure of the enterprise (accounting and budgets) matches or mirrors the program structure. (Note: This assumption is also basic to the Kettner–Martin performance management approach [Kettner & Martin, 1993a, 1995, 1996; Martin & Kettner, 1997, 2010].)
- Critical decision points can be identified at which the observation and measurement of performance and results may be especially insightful.
- In those instances, numerical ratios offer special insight into performance.
- Ratios lack inherent meaning. They can be expected to gain meaning from two long-term strategies:
  1. *trend analysis*, in which sequential comparisons are made of current ratios with previous ratios to detect changes
  2. *unit comparisons*, in which ratios for one service or program unit are compared with similar or comparable units in other enterprises, standard guidelines, or published national norms

A SYSTEM OF STANDARD RATIOS

Martin (2001) focused exclusively on six of the most common ratios from the business world to define the generally accepted practices of financial management practice in the area of ratio analysis. Any HSE (and there are many!) that does not regularly and routinely compute these six ratios from its financial statements is purposely and willfully choosing to keep itself in the dark regarding its own financial performance! Financial malpractice may be an (only slight) overstatement, but, at the very least, failure to compute and use these ratios is a case of the absence of due diligence.

Although Martin (2001) does not note this, each of the eight ratios introduced below, like the Piketty assets/net income ratio, has an interesting feature: They all produce decimal fractions that can be interpreted in dollar terms.

Current (or Liquidity) Ratio

The current ratio is defined by the following equation:

$$\text{Current Ratio} = \frac{\text{Current Assets}}{\text{Current Liabilities}}$$

Interpreting this equation in dollar terms, we can assume that a ratio of .23 in the current equation means that for every dollar of current assets, the enterprise has 23 cents in liabilities. (Also see Table 10.1.)

Long-Term Solvency Ratio

The long-term solvency ratio is computed as follows:

$$\text{Long-Term Solvency Ratio} = \frac{\text{Assets}}{\text{Liabilities}}$$

It is generally assumed that organizations with low ratios of liabilities to assets will be in a stronger position, all other things being equal, than those with high ratios. A primary reason for this is that in the event of a solvency crisis of some sort, the HSE with a low ratio would have greater resources left after its liabilities were resolved. A ratio of .8 or higher, on the other hand, would suggest that 80 cents or more out of every dollar would need to be committed to satisfying those liabilities.

Table 10.1: Historical Current Ratios

<Name of Enterprise>
(Past Five Years)

Year	Ratio
20X0	.55
20X1	.61
20X2	.69
20X3	.74
20X4	.88

Contribution Ratio

The computation of the contribution ratio is as follows:

$$\text{Contribution Ratio} = \frac{\text{Largest Income Source}}{\text{Total Income}}$$

In this case, a contribution ratio of .73, for example, would tell us that for every dollar in income coming into this HSE, 73 cents come from the single largest income source (whether a grant, program service revenues, or other source), whereas the remaining 27 cents come from all other income sources combined. That would suggest a very heavy reliance on a single source of income.

Note that traditional emphasis in the contribution ratio is only on the single largest income source for the reasons discussed above. It can also be worthwhile, however, to occasionally compute a comparable ratio for each of the additional income sources (perhaps in descending size) as well, as indicators of their relative positioning in the "pecking order" of the enterprise. Thus, to know, for example, that the contribution ratio for the largest source is 25 percent and the ratio for the second-largest income source is 9 percent suggests not only a significant gap between the first and second income sources but also that there would have to be a significant number of additional income sources (<9 percent each) to account for the remaining 66 percent of the total—10 or more.

Income–Expense Ratio

The income–expense ratio is a historical measure, as opposed to the future-oriented measures discussed in the earlier break-even analysis chapter. This ratio makes it possible to determine whether or not the enterprise broke even—covered all of its expenses—during the period indicated in the statement of cash flows from which it is computed. As a general rule, a ratio of 1.0 or greater would indicate evidence of some surplus for the period, whereas a ratio of less than 1.0 would indicate that expenses exceeded income for the period. Reminder: As noted previously, it is usually a mistake in human services to consider such surpluses to be profits, except in those cases of private practice where they are to be distributed to owners or shareholders. Surpluses are simply the excess of income less expenditures. Profits are the portion of such surpluses designated for or actually distributed to owners or shareholders. Even in commercial, for-profit ventures, this distinction is utilized and worth keeping in mind. Apple Inc., for example, is one of many companies with a long record of accumulating huge undistributed surpluses—many billions of dollars in total cash on hand—nearly every year. Although shareholders would, of course, have legal claims to their proportionate share of those surpluses in the event that the company were liquidated, to refer to those surpluses as "profits" misstates both their position and their function. Apple, like many other companies, uses portions of its surplus, among other things, to avoid borrowing and to purchase other, smaller computer companies. There is a valuable lesson—alas, too often not learned—for human services in such examples.

Table 10.2: Sustainability Ratios

<Name of Enterprise>
<Date>

Year	Ratio
−2 years	.97
Last year	.94
This year, budget	1.00
This year, actual	.84
Next year	.75
+2 years	.48

$$\text{Income–Expense (Break-Even) Ratio} = \frac{\text{Total Income}}{\text{Total Expenditures}}$$

In interpreting the income–expense ratio, we enter into one of many areas of controversy in managing the finances of human services. Apple and other corporations could theoretically break even every year if they distributed all of their surpluses, but as experience has shown, to do so would be a grievous (and entirely self-inflicted) wound. Yet, this is precisely the standard that many "experts," politicians, and lay people have tried to apply to human services for many years. In keeping surpluses to an absolute minimum or just breaking even, the HSE, whether an organization, a program, a department, a special project, an association, an educational enterprise, or a community organizing project, is forced to seriously inhibit its own ability to deal with unforeseen or unexpected circumstances. It is simply reality that people quit jobs, equipment wears out, supplies are exhausted, donations unexpectedly decline, grants go unfunded, and contracts get cancelled. The enterprise that hews closely to the standard of maintaining no surplus funds by expending all of its income has very limited capacity to deal with any of these contingencies. Thus, experts such as Herzlinger (1979), who really understand this situation, have long encouraged nonprofits and other human services to strive for break-even ratios above 1.0. Exactly how high to push this ratio is an open question. There are important trade-offs here: Push it too high and the ability to deliver services is impeded.

Thus, this is not simply a case of the higher the ratio, the better. In general terms, having a break-even ratio above 2.0, for example, would, in an environment of unmet needs and the absence of some reasonable explanation for such a great surplus, merely suggest to many that the agency has excess resources it could make more effective use of. This would mean that for every dollar spent

Figure 10.2: Bar Graph of Sustainability Ratios

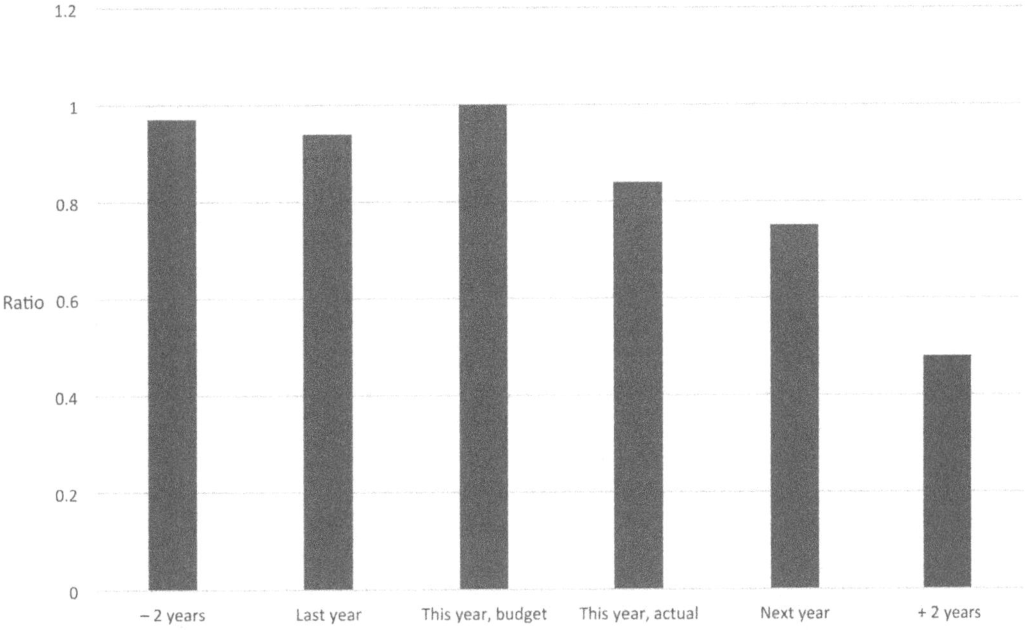

on service, the HSE had two dollars coming in. Note also that continued examination of this ratio over a period of time is essential: For example, under some circumstances, a consistent ratio of 2.0 at the end of the fiscal year over multiple years might merely reflect a time lag in reporting or programming circumstances. At the end of each fiscal year, the HSE might have a large but temporary surplus, perhaps the result of seasonal programming, and the surplus might effectively be used up—producing a ratio of, say, 1.3—six months later, only to see the cycle repeat itself once again in the fourth quarter of that year as another large surplus is again accumulated.

Programs–Expense Ratio

The last three ratios to be discussed here all relate to the previously discussed AICPA cost distinctions of management and general expense, fundraising, and program costs, which constitute one of the most profound developments in the long history of financial management. Each of these three ratios can be derived by working from the detailing of these costs in the version of the statement of functional expenditures outlined in FASB Standard 117 and using the following formula:

$$\text{Program Expense Ratio} = \frac{\text{Program Expenditures}}{\text{Total Expenditures}}$$

Management and General Expense Ratio

The phrase "management and general expense" is used more or less interchangeably with "administrative expense." This ratio is computed with the following formula:

$$\text{Administration Ratio} = \frac{\text{Administrative Expenditures}}{\text{Total Expenditures}}$$

This is one of several financial standards adopted by the National Charities Information Bureau since 1998 (Martin, 2001, p. 57). It is also one of the most highly controversial ratios in the HSE setting, with many believing that the lower the administrative expense ratio, the better, with no exceptions. A provision in the Older Americans Act (1965), for example, limits administrative costs to 8 percent (a ratio of .08 or lower), with no exceptions.

Such a view is highly prejudicial against small organizations, of which there are many in human services. It fails, among several subtleties, to take into account the economies of scale and scope associated with administrative costs. This should be evident with a simple comparison: A low administration ratio of .1 in an organization with total expenses of $10 million leaves $1 million for administration, whereas the same ratio for an organization with total expenses of $100,000 leaves $10,000, barely enough to pay a fraction of one full-time salary. Since there are a number of standard administrative requirements—including doing a budget—that must be handled regardless of the size of the organization or its total budget, it might be necessary for the latter organization to have a ratio of .4 or higher just to cover the basic necessities. A ratio of .1 for the larger organization could, in some circumstances, provide high salaries, plush offices, and other accoutrements. Thus, excessive focus on percentages in administrative cost ratios may be detrimental to smaller HSEs.

Fundraising Ratios

The final pair of ratios discussed in this section are derived from data on the statement of activities. The first was originally devised by the AICPA for use with tax-exempt/tax-deductible nonprofit 501(c)(3) organizations and is now incorporated into the standard financial statements endorsed by FASB. It measures the effectiveness of fundraising expenses as a percentage of total expenses and yields what can be thought of as a measure of the scale of fundraising activities. Thus, an organization with a very high ratio (actually, anything above .5) can legitimately be thought of as doing primarily fundraising rather than spending most of its money on service provision. At the same time, very low ratios (<.1) may give rise to questions about whether greater fundraising efforts might enhance the service mission.

$$\text{Fundraising Expense Ratio} = \frac{\text{Fundraising Expenditures}}{\text{Total Expenditures}}$$

Although this comparison of one part of expenses with the whole is interesting, probably the most useful fundraising ratio can be termed the "fundraising effectiveness ratio." This is the ratio of fundraising outlays to income raised from fundraising. It has an interesting interpretation: In general, the higher the ratio, the more effective the effort, but any ratio higher than .5 is evidence that the fundraising effort is getting results. A ratio of .51, for example, means that for every $50 spent on fundraising, $51 is raised.* Although that may not be a very impressive result, it is at least a positive one. In the first couple of years after a fundraising program has been established by an HSE, one might anticipate that this ratio would initially be at or close to that point or even below it. With an established program, however, it might be expected that this ratio will always be above 1.0 and ideally well above it. A fundraising effort that spent $25,000, for example, and generated $500,000 would have a ratio of 20.

$$\text{Fundraising Effects Ratio} = \frac{\text{Fundraising Income}}{\text{Fundraising Expenditures}}$$

EFFICIENCY INDEXES

Perhaps the single greatest shibboleth in ratio analysis is the efficiency ratio. There have been many proposals over at least a century calling for the measurement of efficiency and far more accounts that proceed on the (false) assumption that efficiency is already a well-known, well-understood, and routinely measured ratio that is based on generally accepted principles of financial management practice. This is far from the case. Going back to the 19th century, efficiency was seen as a cultural and moral idea, not an analytical one (see, for example, Gruber, 1991; Lee, 1937; Leiby, 1991; Rimer, 1991; Stern, 1991; Wildavsky, 1991). Actual definitions and measurement of efficiency in financial management have been few and far between; even after more than a century of concern, no proposals have reached the status of generally accepted principles of financial management practice. Perhaps the most common practice is to attempt to define efficiency in a highly abstract way—most commonly as the ratio of inputs to outputs—and not pursue the matter further.

Efficiency most likely began its long trajectory far from human services as an engineering ratio, proposed by someone in scientific management during the machine age. The ratio of input to output is, in fact, a standard measure of the efficiency of energy use in machinery. From there, it may only have been a short leap into the moral world of "scientific charity." Efficiency, as the ratio of inputs to outputs, is part of the previously discussed systems model of performance management spelled out by Kettner and Martin (Kettner & Martin, 1993a, 1995, 1996; Martin & Kettner, 1997, 2010). (Note: Effective use of this model requires careful

---

*I am grateful to Richard Steinberg, nonprofit economist at Indiana University, for first pointing this out.

and explicit attention to the precise definitions they offer.) From there, one would expect it to be a simple matter of operationalizing suitable measures of input and output and converting them into a ratio. Yet, the effort is seldom quite that clear-cut. In this section, a few other approaches to measuring efficient performance are considered.

At least four entire issues of the journal *Administration in Social Work* have been devoted to efforts to define and measure efficiency and effectiveness. In 1987, Patti, Poertner, and Rapp edited a special double issue on effectiveness that touches (mostly indirectly) on many of the issues involved in constructing efficiency ratios. In 1991, Pruger and Miller (1991a, 1991b) edited another double issue devoted to efficiency. In that issue, W. Johnson and Clancy (1991) observed that publicly funded behavior-changing programs in both the nonprofit and the public sectors are widely perceived by politicians and the public as inefficient. These authors found that it is necessary to know what efficiency is to determine whether such conclusions are warranted. They further observed that to take steps to improve efficiency requires knowing how to measure it, what knowledge is needed to improve program efficiency, and how to overcome organizational obstacles.

Perhaps Murray Gruber (1991) captured the essence of the matter when he noted that "to enter the world of efficiency prescriptions is to leap down the rabbit hole into an Alice in Wonderland world where everything becomes very curious" (p. 175). He commented that efficiency often disguises unacknowledged values and consequences behind a screen of seeming rationality and empiricism. Heffernan (1991) proposed moving efficiency entirely out of the realm of monetized measurement (where, some might argue, it never has been). As a substitute, a behavioral methodology called "data envelopment analysis" to observe and compare the actual performances of actors in similar situations was suggested. None of this or any of the other articles in these two special issues move very far in the direction of monetized measurement of efficiency. Thus, we have a history of more than a century of interest, a widely accepted dictionary definition of "efficiency," and a great deal of attention in the journal literature. What we do not appear to have is a body of research findings on HSE that can be examined, critiqued, and improved upon. What we have never had at any time in the past century is a single published finding of an actual case of unambiguously efficient (or for that matter, inefficient) human services output. There are no standard measures; no norms like the .51 fundraising effectiveness ratio; and, above all, no evidence supporting the claim that human services are inefficient. As noted above, much of the recent literature on the subject is still struggling to define "efficiency" in measurable terms. There is, however, one recent article that seeks to do just that.

Tinkelman and Donabedian (2007) offered a fascinating ratio analysis approach to the measurement of efficiency. They identified four related ratios and a methodology for combining them into an index of what they term "an accounting measure of overall efficiency" (p. 5). The four ratios are as follows:

1. proportion of total income actually expended in current year
2. proportion of total expenditures devoted to programs

3. units of output that result from that expenditure
4. the (dollar) value of the total units produced, expressed as an index

When combined into an index using the procedure described in the article, these four factors are said to measure the value of units produced per dollar of income received, which defines, Tinkelman and Donabedian (2007) claimed, an accounting measure of overall efficiency. This approach yields an actual, operationally defined, measurable variable that deserves to be called "efficiency." After more than a century of political hot air on the subject, applying this actual measurement, perhaps within the context of the Kettner–Martin performance management model, shows promise toward yielding the first-ever actual measurement of this much-abused notion (Kettner & Martin, 1993a, 1995, 1996; Martin & Kettner, 1997, 2010).

FINANCIAL VULNERABILITY MODEL(S)

Whereas the actual measurement of efficiency remains in its infancy, significant progress has been made in the ratio measurement of another variable, labeled "fiscal distress" or "financial vulnerability."* The overall idea is to identify conditions or danger signals indicating that an HSE is in a weakened condition or vulnerable to financial stress or crisis. The initial question is whether prediction of fiscal distress or financial vulnerability in HSEs is possible. Even a few years ago, one might have been tempted to say no. However, in recent years, a small group of accounting researchers has been working on this problem, and, at this point, it is plausible to offer a tentative yes to that question. Although the early work on financial vulnerability was done in commercial settings, the issue has turned out to have as great or greater applicability to nonprofit settings. In both cases, the prediction of financial vulnerability begins with a ratio analysis approach.

The earliest studies defined *financial vulnerability* as the likelihood that a firm would file for bankruptcy (Beaver, 1966, as cited in Tuckman & Chang, 1991). Such a conception was not applicable to nonprofit and public settings in human services, as nonprofit organizations seldom file for bankruptcy and public human services agencies almost never do. Instead, they just quietly close up shop, give away their few remaining assets (or let the courts do that), and disappear. Two later studies found that many vulnerable private companies also never filed for bankruptcy and that some companies that did file did so for other reasons (Frank & Torous, 1989; Gilbert et al., 1990; both as cited in Tuckman & Chang, 1991). This led to a complete reconceptualization of financial vulnerability in the for-profit sector. The term was redefined as the (in)ability to recover from financial shock, a conceptualization that is more applicable to HSEs across the board. In the case of

---

*In general, the term "fiscal" is avoided in this volume except in reference to the public treasury, which is its real meaning. The root "fisc" originally referred to the treasury of ancient Rome or to the emperor's purse—a link to the original meaning of "budget" as explained at the start of chapter 6. In this case, however, the term "fiscal distress" is used as that is the term adopted by the developers of this technique.

HSEs, such shocks might include sudden and unexpected losses of income; sudden, dramatic, and unexpected increases in spending; loss of a major grant; loss of a large proportion of current clients; major disasters; or other similar unexpected events. Along with filing for bankruptcy, researchers identified at least two other important and objective measures of financial vulnerability: (a) three consecutive years of net losses and (b) sudden and dramatic decreases in expenditures.

An important dependent variable that is especially relevant for human services also quickly entered the research picture: reduction in programs or services. Tuckman and Chang (1991) studied completed IRS Form 990s of nearly 4,800 non-profit organizations and found a high likelihood that 501(c)(3) public charities would reduce their program services following a financial shock. In their study, they examined a number of variables and were able to identify four ratios as predictors of financial vulnerability:

- inadequate equity balances
- revenue concentration
- low administrative cost
- low operating margin

Tuckman and Chang (1991) defined *equity balances* as the ratio of total equity to total expenses. A lower ratio, they reasoned, means lessened ability to replace lost income after a financial shock. Thus, lower ratios mean greater vulnerability. The authors defined *revenue concentration* along the lines of the contribution ratio discussed above, except that their ratio measure was the sum of all income sources divided by total income squared. Organizations with fewer revenue sources, the authors further reasoned, are more vulnerable than those with a broader array of funding.

Tuckman and Chang's (1991) third measure, low administrative costs, is usually seen as the most controversial of all of the ratios discussed in this chapter or anywhere else, as their finding (confirmed since then several times) runs directly counter to what has long been conventional wisdom in human services. Lower administrative cost rates, they found, are almost always associated with greater financial vulnerability. (The reader is advised to reread this sentence as many times as necessary!) The reason for this is relatively straightforward: Lower spending on administration results in diminished capacity for management problem solving, thus limiting the ability of an HSE to adapt to or respond to financial shocks. The fourth measure found by Tuckman and Chang to be associated with financial vulnerability is *lower operating margins*, a ratio constructed as the difference of total income less total expenses divided by total income. Lower operating margins were found to be associated with greater financial vulnerability.

Tuckman and Chang's (1991) sample consisted of nearly 4,800 nonprofit organizations—including religious organizations, educational institutions, health and human services agencies, foundations, and other public charities—which they divided into five categories, or *quintiles*, on the basis of their data analysis. The analysis showed that those in the second quintile on the four measures combined were at risk of financial vulnerability, and those in the lowest quintile were severely at risk. Use of these four indicators might, however, prove problematic for an HSE to determine its vulnerability, as it would be impossible to locate the HSE relative to the quintiles. It might still be useful, however, to evaluate the HSE on these three measures—the possibility of filing for bankruptcy, three continuous years of losses, or sudden drops in expenditures—as indications of potential problems. First, high ratios on one measure, combined with low ratios on all the others, would be less cause for concern, whereas high ratios on three or four would be cause for greater concern. One difficulty, however, is that what is considered a "high ratio" and what is considered a "low ratio" is still a subjective judgment. Some help might come from a historical analysis using a five-year timeline, as discussed previously. As with certain medical tests, any ratio that remains constant for a period of time and then suddenly changes would be a cause for concern.

The challenges of measuring financial vulnerability were taken further by Greenlee and Trussel (2000), who defined a *financially vulnerable public charity* as an entity that reduces the proportion of program-to-total spending in three consecutive years. This introduces another simple-to-administer measure: Has this proportion been reduced in an HSE? If so, the Greenlee–Trussel research suggests there is cause for concern. These authors developed a prediction equation to determine the probability of financial vulnerability using modifications of the four variables identified by Tuckman and Chang (1991). Probabilities greater than 10 percent, they concluded, were indicative of a strong likelihood of financial vulnerability, whereas those below 7 percent were indicative of no vulnerability, and those between 7 percent and 10 percent were "indeterminate." This research on financial vulnerability was extended even further in more refined, technical approaches by Trussel (2002); Hodge and Piccolo (2005); and E. K. Keating, Fischer, Gordon, and Greenlee (2005).

Readers who may wish to use the Greenlee–Trussel prediction equation should consult the original research article and a subsequent article by E. K. Keating et al. (2005) for operational definitions and other details. Others may prefer to use a simplified approach (an approach that should work in modified form with each of the other ratios discussed in this chapter as well):

- Using data from a set of financial statements, construct each of the four ratios. Where possible, construct each ratio for multiple (three to five) years.
- Using the discussion and your own common sense, rate each of the ratios in terms of risk of vulnerability: 5 (high risk), 3 (moderate risk), or 1 (low risk).
- Combine your ratings for the four ratios. (The higher the combined rating scores, the greater the risk of vulnerability.)
- Identify the trends that you observe. Are there differences in the ratios in different years? What patterns do you observe? Are vulnerabilities increasing, decreasing, or simply fluctuating randomly?

Most important, feed the information derived from these ratings as feedback back into the financial planning system. If financial vulnerability exists, what steps need to be taken to deal with it?

COST–BENEFIT ANALYSIS AND COST-EFFECTIVENESS ANALYSIS

Two economic techniques related to ratio analysis that once appeared very promising for constructive examination of the positive impact of human services are cost–benefit analysis and cost-effectiveness analysis (Cowger, 1979; Cox, Keith, Otten, & Raymond, 1980; Sherraden, 1986; Yates, 1995; D. W. Young & Allen, 1977). The former involves construction of a ratio of benefit, such that it can be said that for every dollar invested in a program or service, there is a benefit of some additional dollar value. Thus a cost–benefit ratio of 1.00 : 2.40, for example, would indicate that for every dollar input into a program, there was a return of $2.40. Although there are numerous published methodological discussions of cost–benefit methods, the technique itself is not actually used that often. The principal reason appears to be the difficulty of constructing meaningful monetized measures of the value of benefits for most types of services. The primary exception has been employment training programs, where it is possible to specify benefits in terms of increased future earnings and to compare these with training costs.

As a result, the more commonly used technique is termed *cost-effectiveness analysis*, which involves combining a monetized measure of cost with a nonmonetized but quantitative measure of impact or effectiveness. Thus, many types of outcome measures and virtually all types of performance management indicators used in human services fall within the cost-effectiveness rubric.

CONCLUSION

This chapter has presented and examined a broad selection of financial ratios that should be of interest to every HSE. The basic set of eight ratios proposed by Martin (2001), together with an assets/net income ratio adapted from the work of Thomas Piketty (2014) and the fundraising effectiveness ratio, are readily available for use by officials of any HSE willing to simply extract the necessary information from existing financial statements. The assets/net income ratio is interesting in large part because it lends meaning to an otherwise useless piece of financial information. A ratio measurement of efficiency proposed by Tinkelman and Donabedian (2007) may be the first actual practical measure of efficiency published and has promise of yielding some real evidence in a domain long caught in an endless cycle of argument over definitions and factional propaganda. Finally, the published work of Tuckman and Chang (1991; also see Chang & Tuckman, 1994), Greenlee and Trussel (2000), and others (Keating et al., 2005) on the prediction of financial distress has yielded a variety of highly usable ratios and measurements that enable the leadership of an HSE to monitor vulnerability to threats in the financial milieu.

Perhaps the most interesting feature of these assorted financial ratio measurements is that they can be applied—or easily adapted—for use in all types of HSEs: public, nonprofit, commercial, third sector, fourth sector, incorporated, unincorporated, and so forth.

11

Social Economy

SOCIAL ACCOUNTING

In this chapter, we delve into another new and interesting domain with a variety of potential applications to use in the HSE financial situation. The field of social accounting and the concept of the social economy may be new to many readers, but a number of investigators have been working in this area for many years and at least a portion of their labors are ready for use in HSE practice. From a conceptual or theoretical standpoint, the *social economy* is a label applicable to the kind of situations introduced in chapter 1—the social and economic space where mixtures of monetized, nonmonetary quantities (for example, outputs) and qualities (for example, community, empowerment, development, and justice) come together. Social accounting represents, in a purely technical sense, a radical extension of the methodology of ratio analysis discussed in the previous chapter. Yet, there may be a great deal more at work here as well. In a fundamental sense, contemporary efforts in social accounting link up in important ways with the core of the social work mission, namely, the focus on "social change and development, and the empowerment and liberation of people" (International Association of Schools of Social Work, n.d.). It might even be said that "principles of social justice, human rights, collective responsibility and respect for diversities are central" not only to social work but also to social accounting and social economy.

This chapter is intended, among other things, to introduce several important—and dramatically different—approaches to what might be referred to as the *social accounting problem*, that is, the need to account more systematically for human capital resources in HSEs and other nonprofit entities, with an eye toward issues of social justice, human rights, collective responsibilities, and respect for diversities. This leads into exploration of emerging perspectives on the third sector, fourth sector, commons, and social economy. Taken together, this represents some of the most interesting work occurring today in ongoing efforts to link financial management concerns not simply with the technical management side of social administration but with the main body of social work thought.

A good place to begin this journey is with an examination of three periods of social accounting, based on the historical analysis and reconstruction of Laurie Mook (2013). After a brief introduction to the three periods, we examine two quite different responses: the social indicators movement of the late 1960s and 1970s and the efforts to measure volunteer contributions. We then move on to a closer look at the third period, beginning with an examination of a body of work by Kettner and Martin in performance management. After this, we look at a number of contributions by Laurie Mook and her associates at the School of Education at the University of Toronto and, more recently, Arizona State University. We conclude this examination of social capital with a brief discussion of the Canadian model of social economy outlined and recently extended to the United States by Mook; her colleague and mentor, Jack Quarter; and others (Mook et al., 2015; Quarter et al., 2010).

THREE WAVES OF SOCIAL ACCOUNTING

This chapter begins with a definition. Mook (2013) stated that "social accounting expands the range of criteria taken into consideration when measuring performance in the context of an organization's environment, both social and natural" (p. 18). Academic critics of traditional financial accounting practice in the 1960s and 1970s converged around an approach termed "critical accounting." This was before accountants paid much attention to HSEs and was a part of social constructionist and new social problem perspectives that emerged in this same period (see, for example, Berger & Luckmann, 1966; Kitsuse & Spector, 1973). In a vein that would be recognized by many social workers, critical accountants argued, among other things, that the act of counting certain things and not other things shapes a particular interpretation of reality. The constructivism of critical accounting was combined with a strong interventionism. Mook (2013) stated, "At its best, critical accounting seeks not only to understand the world but also to change it" (p. 19). Yet, as she noted, the early critical accounting approach to change remained largely theoretical, with few practical proposals or consequences. Critical accounting offered few alternative models to address issues of justice and no tools or strategies to guide actual accounting practice. Thus, despite the proximity of critical accounting, the actual accounting practices and GAAPs that began to emerge in the 1970s did so without any discernible impact or influence from critical accounting.

SOCIAL ACCOUNTING

The kind of social accounting that Mook advocated largely shares the critical accounting critique but places greater emphasis on a working framework suitable for use in, for example, expanded, value-added environmental and sustainability accounting. "While accountants have the option of continuing with the current accounting systems that sustain the status quo, they also have the ability to create more democratic, transparent and participatory accounting practices in the context of a broader strategy for social change" (Mook, 2013, p. 20). This statement strikes directly at the core reason that social workers should be interested in developments in social accounting: They are entirely consistent with where leading figures in social work see the profession going.

Social accounting projects fall into two basic categories. In *supplemental social accounting*, qualitative data and descriptive statistics are used "to assess the extent to which an organization is meeting the expectations of stakeholders in executing its mission" (Mook, 2013). By contrast, in *integrative social accounting*, social, environmental, and economic data are integrated into the actual accounts of the enterprise (Mook, 2013). As the placement of this chapter suggests, most of the social accounting projects that should be of greatest immediate interest to HSEs currently are of the supplemental type. Yet, interesting work on integrative social accounting may, at some point in the future, influence the accounting practices and GAAPs discussed in chapter 5 as well.

According to Mook (2013), there have been three waves of integrative social accounting since the 1970s. The first was a period of bold experimentation with alternative accounting models for for-profit organizations that effectively burned out in the 1980s. Among its products, Mook noted, were a proposed social and financial income statement developed at the consulting firm of Apt Associates, a socioeconomic impact statement developed by David Linowes, a statement of fund flows for socially relevant activities developed by Dilley and Weygandt (1973), a social impact statement suggested by Estes (1976), and a goal-oriented profit-and-loss statement by Gröjer and Stark (1977).

A second wave emerged in the 1990s, with a more realistic approach about what could be measured and a much stronger emphasis on sustainability. Mook divided the efforts of this second wave into two categories: those applying primarily to for-profit organizations and those applying to others—notably, nonprofit organizations, foundations, and cooperatives. One of the best-known of the for-profit category is Elkington's (1998) triple bottom line approach. Following the groundbreaking definition of sustainable development by the United Nations' Brundtland Commission in 1987, Elkington (1998) proposed investing for the "three p's"(people, profit, and planet) and a corresponding triple mode of accounting (social, financial, and environmental). Among the ideas applying to other organizations, Mook noted, are a social impact statement by Land, a cooperative social balance sheet, and B. J. Richmond's (1999) concept of community social return on investment. Mook's own contributions on this topic include expanded value (Mook et al., 2015), market value of volunteer activity, community social return on investment (Mook, 2013; Quarter, Mook, & Richmond, 2007), and "expanded value added" statements (see Tables 11.3–11.4).

The third wave of integrative social accounting began in the new millennium and continues today to "incorporate both qualitative and quantitative measures while integrating financial, social and environmental factors" (Mook, 2013, p. 21). Products include the balanced scorecard (see the format in Table 11.1) and the nongovernmental organizations supplement of the Global Reporting Initiative (2010). Although she did not include Tinkelman and Donabedian's (2007) treatment of

Table 11.1: Balanced Scorecard Format

Category	Objectives	Measures	Targets	Incentives
Financial				
Customers				
Internal operations				
Learning and growth				

The balanced scorecard format shown is adapted from R. S. Kaplan & D. P. Norton, 2001, *The strategy-focused organization: How balanced scorecard companies thrive in the new business environment.* Boston, MA: Harvard Business School Press.

efficiency, as noted in previous chapter, this should perhaps be included here as well. Readers interested in more details on these models should consult Mook (2013, pp. 21–30) for additional information and citations on these various sources.*

VALUATION OF VOLUNTEERS

One of the earliest developments in social accounting relates to assorted efforts to operationally define and measure volunteer activities. Karst (1960) may have been the first to set forth a plausible scheme for measurement of the contribution of volunteers. This remains an important social accounting dimension for those HSEs that use volunteers (Pearce, 1993; Rosentraub et al., 1992). See Table 11.2 for a contemporary version of this approach that emphasizes labor market comparability. Tables 11.3 and 11.4 also incorporate volunteer valuations into their respective calculations.

PERFORMANCE MEASUREMENT

Performance measurement offers another way to approach the integrative social accounting perspective (Carnochan, Samples, Myers, & Austin, 2014; Martin & Kettner, 2010; Ritchie & Eastwood, 2006). If one were needed, Tinkelman and Donabedian's (2007) focus on the measurement of efficiency provides one of many possible links between these two ideas: Performance management is a notion that arose in the specific context of public management. It has been defined as "the regular collection and reporting of information about the efficiency, quality and effectiveness of government programs" (Martin & Kettner, 1997, p. 17). The Government

---

*The treatment of Mook and colleagues' ideas about social accounting here is by necessity highly selective and incomplete. Interested readers would be well served to dig more deeply into the works cited here. A good place to begin your reading on social accounting is Quarter, Mook, and Richmond (2007), but for the larger perspective of the social economy, see also Mook, Quarter, Armstrong, and Whitman (2015) and Quarter, Mook, and Ryan (2010) for discussions in the U.S. and Canadian contexts.

Table 11.2: Market Value of Volunteer Activities

Fiscal Year 20XX

Activities	Hours	Hourly Rate ($)	Total ($)
Board	2,048	28.38	58,143
Committees	45,990	22.47	1,033,395
Volunteers	1,750	19.08	33,390
Subtotal	49,788		1,124,928
Program 1	69,400	25.85	1,793,990
Program 2	23,645	19.08	451,147
Program 3	685	19.08	13,070
Program 4	9,125	25.85	235,881
Subtotal program activities	102,855		2,494,088
Total			3,619,016

Table 11.3: Community Social Return on Investment

Fiscal Year 20XX

Resource Inputs ($)		Benefit Outputs ($)	
Income	648,647	Expenses	642,051
Volunteer labor	78,321	Volunteer labor	78,321
		Outcomes	
		Primary benefits	
		New salaries acquired	587,274
		Promotions	189,649
		Secondary benefits	
		Unemployment benefits	14,721
		Disability benefits	17,641
		Food stamps	32,248
		Other related services	6,412
Total	726,968	Total	1,568,317

Ratio of return on community investment: 1:2.16

Table adapted from L. Mook, J. Quarter, & B. J. Richmond, 2007, *What counts: Social accounting for nonprofits and cooperatives* (p. 149). Medina, OH: Sigel Press.

Table 11.4: Expanded Value-Added Statement (Partial)

December 31, 20XX

Item	Description	Financial ($)	Social ($)	Combined ($)
Outputs		447,019	132,635	579,654
External purchases		192,655		192,655
Value added		254,364	132,635	386,999
Stakeholders				
Employees	Wages and benefits	254,364		254,364
Volunteers	Volunteer labor		1,100	1,100
Clients	Skill development		4,950	4,950
	Donations		1,100	1,100
	Mentorships		36,885	36,885
	Volunteer speakers		34,500	34,500
	Gratis consultations		18,900	18,900
Monetized social capital			35,200	35,200
Total value added		254,364	132,635	386,999

Table adapted from J. Quarter, L. Mook, and A. Armstrong, 2009, Social accounting and accountability. In *Understanding the social economy: A Canadian perspective* (p. 312). Toronto, Ontario, Canada: University of Toronto Press.

Table 11.5: Performance Budget

20XX Fiscal Year
After-School Adventures

Measure	Result
Total budgeted program cost	$45,472
Outcome performance measure	One latchkey kid kept off the streets and socially involved for one hour
Number of outcomes	10,800[a]
Cost per outcome	$4.21 per child per hour

[a]An average of 24 children are involved for an average of 2.5 hours per day, five days a week, for the 180 days of the school year (24 × 180 × 2.5 = 10,800 outcome units).

Table adapted from L. L. Martin, 2001, *Financial management for human service administrators* (p. 88). Boston: Allyn & Bacon.

Performance and Results Act of 1993, amended in 2010, and the ongoing GASB Service Efforts and Accomplishments initiative together establish at least a beginning framework for consistent performance measurement in HSEs (Gerrish, 2015; Meezan & McBeath, 2011; Moynihan & Kroll, 2015). Note that a good bit of work remains to be done in this area before anything that can be called a performance measurement system is in place throughout the domain of HSEs. A number of states—prematurely, perhaps—have already mandated performance management systems for human services (Martin, 2001, p. 66). Kettner and Martin (1995) have done yeoman work on defining performance measurement for human services, framed within the general problem of organizational performance in human services organizations. In their work, they have identified a number of characteristics of good performance measures (Kettner & Martin, as summarized in Martin, 2001, p. x) and have taken some of the first steps toward monetizing performance accounting.

CHARACTERISTICS OF MONETARY PERFORMANCE INDICATORS

A good performance indicator should have the following:

Quantifiability: The indicator has a numeric value as a real number. Procedures exist to express the indicator either as a monetized value (for example, cost data) or as a ratio, one of the terms of which is a monetary value (for example, cost–benefit or cost-effectiveness data).

Clarity: The indicator is clearly defined, both semantically and operationally, and, if possible, has a supportive body of knowledge (concepts and theory) supporting its use.

Reliability: The indicator measures what it claims to measure. There is available data on its reliability.

Feasibility: The cost of measurement is low in proportion to the monetary value of what is being measured.

Validity: There is a broad consensus among a clear reference group of both researchers and practitioners that this is a good measure.

As noted in chapter 6, Martin (2001) has made a strong case for the importance of performance management in HSE financial management. That case is built around two important budget innovations: the program budget and the performance budget, which link outcome and performance measures to total expense estimates. In Martin's handling, both of those innovative formats take on the characteristics of decision packages. This is a highly promising approach. A logical next step would be to explore more fully what a complete enterprise budget composed of such decision packages would look like, how it would function, and how it might relate to the financial statements. Since these questions appear to go above and beyond the immediate concerns of the Government Performance and Results Act of 1993, amended 2010, and the GASB Service Efforts and Accomplishments, which served as Martin's presenting problem, an integrative social accounting perspective may offer a suitable conceptual frame for approaching them.

The focus in this chapter on the various devices and approaches of social accounting and performance management also connects with a variety of social economy perspectives. One of the most important of these is the revival of the 19th century cooperative ideal that has emerged, largely on and surrounding the Internet in recent years in what is usually called the "sharing economy." Cooperatives loomed large in earlier perspectives on the social economy, but as noted in chapter 3, today they are one of a rapidly growing number of alternative forms of enterprise available to human services. Meanwhile, the sharing economy idea is taking off in a variety of new and unexpected directions.

SHARING ECONOMIES

It may be unclear to some contemporary readers, but there is a substantial philosophical tradition behind cooperative enterprises, as discussed in chapter 3, summed up by the centrally important concept of economic cooperation. Under the heading of social enterprise and sharing economies, an entirely new form of economic cooperation has surfaced in the present in some highly interesting ways that have been largely ignored by social work but are very relevant to the discussion of HSEs. Originally associated with varieties of Christian and community socialism, much of the original 19th century idealism and enthusiasm for economic cooperation was swamped in the 20th century waves of reaction against all possible variants of the word "socialism," a term now routinely equated with state socialism and Leninist and Maoist totalitarianism. If economic cooperation is a socialist idea and socialism is equated with the gulag, the thinking goes, it too must be a very bad thing indeed! In this way of thinking, it seems at times as if all forms of human cooperation not devoted to life as an unending competitive struggle for survival and "red in tooth and claw" must be viewed with great suspicion or rejected outright. In this way, a great many worthwhile activities and possibilities have been needlessly cast aside.

At the same time, new versions of the old cooperative ideal have recently resurfaced in a bewildering variety of places, particular in online settings and discussions, many of them ironically at the forefront of contemporary business thinking. For example, the decidedly individualistic and profit-focused cofounder of Zipcar, Robin Chase (2015), wrote in a blog post, "We are witnessing the end of capitalism as we know it." She goes on to explain that "The old model of unwieldy [corporate] behemoths is giving way to a new one of collaboration. Welcome to the world of peers." Two modal ideas shape this economic change, according to Chase: harnessing excess capacity and discovering new forms of economic cooperation. "More minds working together will always be exponentially smarter, more experienced, and more well equipped than fewer ones who work inside a single company or government." Ideological capitalists, Chase argued, will claim that we are driven by self-interest and incapable of sharing, but "it could be that our own self-interest may be driving us to share everything—provided we get more than we give." In a society characterized in large part by its abundance, the range and scope of such economic sharing of excess capacity is truly amazing—cars, bicycles, apartments, vacation homes rented out by their owners—and a great deal more (Chase, 2015; see also Korten, 1999).

Chase is by no means the only one suggesting a redrawing of the once-fixed line between for-profit and nonprofit and public activities. Edwin Frank, editorial director of New York Review of Books, a small niche publishing venture that is a division of the commercial literary newspaper the *New York Review of Books*, summed up the emerging social enterprise philosophy when he said, "This is not a nonprofit—it should make money, yes, so that's certainly a consideration. But the imperative is to publish good books. That comes first" (Rohter, 2015). This trend toward social enterprise, which began with such revolutionary activities as Ben & Jerry's ice cream and Paul Newman's salad dressings, has continued to gather steam and currently poses the possibility of an entirely new fourth sector. David Billis (2010) is among the leading voices foreseeing a blended social economy combining entirely new forms of public, nonprofit, and for-profit activities, and although social work and human services have attracted little attention in this regard, the profession and the field have long been in the thick of things.

The sharing ideal and the sharing economy, for example, have already had significant impacts on a variety of human services. Over and beyond traditional ideas of charity that influence donations of money, goods, and services and traditional human services cooperatives in childcare and elsewhere, a variety of human services programs—including Salvation Army and Goodwill stores, food banks, pantries and soup kitchens, housing repair services, and housing construction programs such as Habitat for Humanity—are all built on sharing economy models, as are those health and human services programs built around donated volunteer professional time. As Chase (2015) noted, a common theme tying all of these sharing economy programs together is the fuller utilization of excess capacity. This ties in to a theme almost as pervasive as the search for efficiency and that is the elimination of waste. More is said on this subject in chapter 13. And, as Frank suggested, in the new social economy, profit is not always seen as diametrically opposed to the pursuit of lofty social purposes (including justice).

COMMONS

An interesting variant on the sharing economy and social economy themes is captured by some recent work on the subject of commons. From within conventional economics, the late Elinor Ostrom was awarded a Nobel Prize for a monumental body of work on common pool economics (Ostrom, 1990, 2002). One of the most interesting recent tangents of the Ostrom approach was the focus on knowledge commons (Hess & Ostrom, 2007). Within nonprofit and third-sector studies, Lohmann (1992, 2015, 2016) recast the economic rationalism of commons theory into an award-winning theory of voluntary action with emphasis on the associations engaged in common goods production. Yet, there has been another massive but somewhat inchoate approach to commons that has gone largely unnoticed in the social work literature, one that is related to developments in the sharing economy, fourth sector, and social economy perspectives as well as the Ostrom and Lohmann approaches to commons. Perhaps it came about in response to the striking individualism, social Darwinism, and anti-welfare-state sentiments of neoliberal social policy initiatives in recent decades. Whatever the reasons, a striking variety of practitioners, social media users, and others, including many in social work, have gravitated to the commons perspective in a variety of ways. There is, for example, the Creative Commons copyright regime (http://creativecommons.org), the nascent front yard commons movement (http://www.onthecommons.org/magazine/create-commons-your-own-front-yard), the shared resources of the Wikipedia Commons (https://commons.wikimedia.org/wiki/Main_Page), the Flickr Commons (https://www.flickr.com/commons), and an almost endless chain of open-source software (http://sourceforge.net/home.html) and urban practice-oriented sites (http://www.onthecommons.org/). This is truly an international movement. In the British newspaper *The Guardian*, Justin McGuirk (2015) asked, "Can the city be reimagined as a commons, or is commoning (only) the realm of tiny acts of autarchy and resistance?" At this point, the principal conceptual bridges between commons and HSEs are the sharing economy and social economy perspectives. If the international commons movement is influencing the practice of human services finance, those influences have yet to manifest themselves in the published literature of the field.

KEEPING SCORE?

As fans of sports such as baseball, basketball, and tennis are aware, a scorecard can be a convenient way to tabulate certain information in highly condensed form in order to follow the progress of the game or match. In baseball, for example, noting hits, runs, and errors in each inning is common, and in basketball, records are kept of two-point and three-point shots and free throws attempted and made, as well as points scored by each player. Scores, games, and sets are all duly recorded in tennis, whereas scoring in cricket is a mystery to all but the cognoscenti of the game. In soccer, with its notoriously low-scoring game structure, shots on goal, corner kicks, and penalty kicks are among the statistics tabulated.

The balanced scorecard approach to management is something like this and involves identifying a variety of quantitative indicators in areas of strategic concern. The publications of R. S. Kaplan and Norton, Niven, and others have advanced the balanced scorecard approach as viable not only for businesses but perhaps even more for mission- and strategy-driven governmental organizations and nonprofit enterprises (Banker, Janakiraman, & Konstans, 2001; Best Practices, 2001; R. S. Kaplan, 1996; R. S. Kaplan & Norton, 1993, 1996, 2001; M. W. Meyer, 2002; Niven, 2002, 2003; Olve, Roy, & Wetter, 1999; Whittaker, 2001). In the balanced scorecard approach, various variables and measures are organized under a set of standard headings (see, for example, Tables 11.1 and 11.7).

In the earliest of several iterations of the balanced scorecard approach, the focus was on efforts to identify a standard list or balanced categorization of areas or topics for which indicators were to be identified. Kaplan and Norton (R. S. Kaplan, 1996; R. S. Kaplan & Norton, 1993) generally focused on a scorecard of four standard headings: (a) financial, (b) customers, (c) internal operations, and (d) learning and growth. Apparently, consensus among users often pointed toward an optimum of about 20 indicators or measures selected by the individual analyst, which would mean something like four to six indicators under each heading.

Beginning in the mid-1990s, a second approach to the design of balanced scorecards emerged. This approach was intended to overcome the seemingly arbitrary nature of indicator selection that had arisen in the first iterations of balanced scorecards. Particularly important in this newer approach were efforts to link specific indicators to strategic objectives of the enterprise. The design and adoption of "strategy maps" became a widespread practice. These strategy maps are graphic visual aids showing a limited number of objectives as text blocks within bands corresponding to the indicator categories shown above.

By the first years of the new millennium, the balanced scorecard approach evolved further with the addition of vision and destination statements. Thus, for example, an HSE might state its mission as follows: "The mission of Community Services Associates, Inc., is to offer a comprehensive range of individual, family, group, and community services to residents of our community."

Independent of a more comprehensive balanced scorecard approach, about this same time, the use of vision ("Where do we see ourselves going?") statements became a widespread practice in some HSEs, although the use of destination statements ("Where do we want to end up?") may still be somewhat less common. For example, that same agency might envision something like this: "It is the vision of Community Service Associates, Inc., that we will be able in the future to fully serve all clients who have need of our services, without the necessity of needless delays or triaging choices."

Table 11.6: Program or Performance Budget

20XX Fiscal Year
After-School Adventures
June 20XX

Measure	Planned	This Month	Year to Date	Variance
Program cost	$45,472	$3,790	$24,791	Over
Number of outcomes	10,800	875	5,240	Under
Cost per outcome	$4.21	$4.33	$4.73	Over

Note: Outcome performance measure = one kid kept off the streets and socially involved for one hour.

Table adapted from L. L. Martin, 2001, *Financial management for human service administrators* (p. 90). Boston: Allyn & Bacon.

Table 11.7: Part of a Balanced Scorecard

Indicator	Objectives	Measures	Targets	Incentives
Financial budget system	Balance budget	Income–expense ratio	Break even	
Accounting system	Adopt enterprise accounting	GAAPs	This fiscal year	Reduce audit exceptions and problems
Financial analysis system	Adopt some social accounting	Community value-added statement	This fiscal year	Improved community accountability
Clients	Adopt some client outcome measures			
Internal operations	Decrease short-term liabilities	Cash flow analysis	Maintain two-month cash reserve	Avoid late fees and interest charges
Human capital: staff expertise	Upgrade hiring of new employees	Ratio of staff-to-graduate degrees	40% of staff with MSWs in five years	Improved accreditation profile
	Offer staff training	Staff certifications	50% of staff certified in their areas in five years	Salary increases

Note: GAAPs = generally accepted accounting principles.

One of the additional features the balance scorecard approach introduced were more detailed vision (or direction) statements. For example, the financial section of a vision statement might read something like this:

> Since its founding in 1967, Community Service Associates, Inc., has been strongly tied to pursuit of federal and state grants and state purchase of service contracts, with no support from United Way, only a limited number of private pay clients, and only those few donations that came in sponta- neously. In December, 21XX, the board of directors voted to pursue some new directions in an effort to shore up the increasingly dire financial situ- ation in which the organization found itself. These new directions can be summed up as an effort to pursue a more syncretic financial system, includ- ing a newly revitalized fundraising operation and a stronger emphasis on financial analysis.

The question of what value balanced scorecard approaches may hold for HSEs and, in particular, for financial management is still largely unanswered. In a pub- lished analysis available online, Eric Kong (2007) adopted a rather categorical no- holds-barred approach to the analysis of various analytical approaches to human services management. He concluded without any nuance or qualifiers that SWOT (strengths, weaknesses, opportunities, and threats) analysis, industrial organiza- tion, a resource-based view, the core competency or knowledge-based view, and balanced scorecards "are inapplicable in the social service nonprofit sector" (Kong, 2007, p. 297). Kong's view is clearly a strongly felt one; only something he terms an "intellectual capital approach," he suggested, is applicable to nonprofit social ser- vices. It hardly seems necessary at this point to refute or revise Kong's categorical (and not entirely convincing) null hypothesis, much less to follow his advice and dismiss the balanced scorecard approach entirely. Instead, in the final chapter, a modified scorecard approach that is indebted to the balanced scorecard is outlined, an approach focused primarily on financial issues and concerns.

CONCLUSION

In purely intellectual terms, the developments of social accounting and the model of the social economy should be of considerable interest to HSE financial manage- ment, particularly as they relate to social enterprise and the emerging fourth sector. Yet, developments in social accounting may be among the least known and used features of the system of financial analysis introduced in these chapters. However, when viewed in the context of the other analytical techniques discussed in previ- ous chapters, it is not at all difficult to see where these pieces can fit in. For any HSE using volunteers, the methods of monetizing the value of volunteer efforts can be usefully employed. Furthermore, the community social return on invest- ment and value-added statements offer additional useful information, particularly on the economic impact of human services. These social accounting approaches integrate well with developments in monetizing outcome measurement, program budgets, and performance budgets. Despite some published skepticism about the potential applicability of the balanced scorecard approach, it also seems likely that some form of scorecard may be useful as an integrative framework reaching beyond the required financial statements and presenting an integrated set of data on the current financial condition and performance of an HSE. Social accounting approaches and techniques thus should have important roles to play in the HSE financial analysis systems of the future.

12

Monitoring Financial Operations

The final piece in the puzzle of enterprise financial management—typically not really a system but merely bits and pieces of one—is called here the "financial operating system," previously dealt with as "implementation" (Lohmann, 1980). It is concerned with oversight, monitoring of ongoing operations, and the daily grind of service delivery. This is a vital piece of enterprise financial management. It is where the spending decisions and transactions recorded as accounting entries originate, as well as the space occupied during the interim periods between budget negotiations and the locus of the practice problems that point to the need for financial analysis. This chapter will investigate a variety of themes and issues, the bits and pieces of an effort to formulate something relatively systematic.

ESTABLISHING A FINANCIAL OPERATING SYSTEM

Human services budgets and accounting are, for the most part, in place; financial analysis with the methods noted in the preceding chapters can be conducted as needed. What more needs to be done? The biggest answer to that question typically involves assigning responsibilities and putting in place organizations, institutions, and structures to assure ongoing monitoring and oversight of financial operations. Establishing and periodically reviewing and updating adequate systems of record keeping are important parts of this challenge. Another large part of this task involves periodically comparing budget projections with actual performance. In addition, accounts receivable, accounts payable, and cash flows may all need to be monitored on an ongoing basis. One additional step, discussed in the final chapter, involves establishment of a regime for monitoring operating capacity. A key issue for all of this is identifying who in the HSE should be responsible and held accountable for seeing that these assorted operating concerns are taken care of. In the following discussion, that responsibility is assigned primarily to the finance committee, but the comments hold for whomever is given those assignments.

BOARD AND STAFF RESPONSIBILITIES

One of the continuing challenges in this area involves the assignment of responsibilities to board and staff members and, in some cases, other stakeholders as well. The two most basic questions here are, Who should make the assignments? and What is the best way of doing things? In the case of corporations, in general, the formal legal answer could not be more clear: These are self-governing entities in which the board of directors is the ultimate authority and bears full responsibility for managing the affairs of the corporation. Executive directors, CEOs, and officers (presidents, secretaries, treasurers) acting on behalf of the organization are legal agents of the board and other staff are employees of the board. Regardless of how clear-cut the law is on that point, however, reality in financial decision making can often be quite murky. The actual allocation of responsibilities between board and staff within a particular financial management regimen will vary by type of enterprise, HSE history, and individual circumstances. Many human services, like many business corporations and more than a few other nonprofits, are, in the present era, enamored of the myth of the CEO as the autocrat in charge (Anheier & Themudo, 2005). Regardless of what the law or principles of self-governance may dictate, the director may, in fact, call all the shots. Other HSEs strive to maintain somewhat more democratic governance where finances are concerned, and some actually succeed. A major problem with laissez-faire approaches to financial leadership is that they can easily devolve into what might be called the tyranny of the second administrative assistant: a situation where a lower-level bureaucrat makes all of the critical financial decisions without the benefit of the big picture. It needs to be recognized that in any system where everyone is allowed to do their own thing, for some people, that will mean controlling others and manipulating the system.

MANAGEMENT BY WALKING AROUND

One highly useful management strategy for spotting potential problems and troubleshooting goes by the colorful but descriptive name of "management by walking around." A very good use of a financial manager's time is simply moving about the enterprise, asking general questions like "How's it going?" and "What kind of problems are you having at present?" In many cases, this may be a useful way to uncover financial issues and problems early, before they become major crises: "I was going to put this in a memo, but as long as you're here . . ." is the kind of prefatory comment to watch for. Walking-around management, however, is not something to try once and then discard. Usually, the first time the boss is seen outside her office is more an occasion for nervousness and anxiety than anything else. In addition to management by walking around, there are other, more systematic approaches. One of these is the standing finance committee.

THE FINANCE COMMITTEE RE-ENVISIONED

Two of the stock features of the traditional model of financial management in voluntary associations that has been around for hundreds of years are the treasurer, who handles the actual financial management, and the finance committee, to which the treasurer is accountable. This model is long-standing for good reason. It is a wise and sensible practice to establish and use a formal finance committee—whether it consists of board members, staff members, or some combination—for advice, planning, and decisions and in myriad other ways. In the broadest terms, institutional advancement of the HSE should be the mission of such a committee, and each of its separate tasks should be seen as part of that larger whole. Perhaps the biggest mistake most novice social work financial managers make is to assume that they can do everything related to institutional advancement themselves, whether this involves fundraising, interpreting financial statements, managing the budget, conducting financial analyses, or providing oversight of the process. This is more likely to be a case of the more, the merrier: When making financial decisions, two heads are better than one, and three are better still, a logic that may hold to, perhaps, six or eight committee members. The real criterion here should be having a working committee of sufficient size and interest but one that is also small enough that everyone can have a say without meetings going on endlessly.

Consultants and trainers often hear the complaint from executives along the lines of "I'd love to have a finance committee I can call on, but I can't get anyone on my board interested." Usually in such cases, there is something going on just below the surface: Those directors may actually be communicating the message that they want the appearance of involvement and transparency without the reality of genuine participation, or they may subtly be communicating the message that there is only one right decision or that the decision has already been made.

Effectively functioning finance committees can be an important part of the efficient operation of a successful financial management regime. The responsibilities of such a committee should be clear from the preceding discussion:

- management and oversight of the accounting process and especially the production of financial statements
- management and oversight of the budget process, including the need for periodic revisions of the budget
- commissioning, management, and oversight of special financial studies
- management and oversight of the dissemination of financial information
- oversight of the production and maintenance of an up-to-date financial policy and procedures manual
- management and oversight of the enterprise's portfolio of investments, although in those cases where there are sizeable sums involved, the committee's role may be primarily one of oversight, with day-to-day management of the investments left to others (see, for example, Fry, 1998)

ANNUAL MEETINGS AND REPORTS

A working finance committee might, as noted, assume responsibility for developing and overseeing plans for the dissemination of financial information, including through holding annual meetings and the regular publication of financial items in newsletters and annual reports. Among the traditional practices of voluntary agencies and membership associations that have fallen into disuse are the production of an annual report (containing audited financial statements and current budget information) and the convening of an annual meeting at which the annual report is presented and discussed and information about other upcoming financial developments is offered. In some areas, annual reports and meetings are legally required for corporations, although enforcement for human services is very lax. That is not the primary reason for reviving their use, however. The well-done annual meeting and report together can be a highly effective way for various groups of stakeholders to get together, get to know one another, discuss their common and unique concerns, and reaffirm their commitments to the enterprise of which they are a part. During periods of change, these venues can also serve as ways to share information about new directions, as well as to renew the social compact and offer reassurance about ongoing enterprise commitments.

POLICY AND PRACTICES MANUAL

Another responsibility that might be undertaken by a working finance committee is that of establishing a financial policy and practices manual, which lays out in appropriate detail the necessary rules and expectations for a workable financial management strategy, lists established financial policies, notes the repertory of procedures and practices, and documents ways of doing things in a manner or form that falls short of serving as a formal policy statement (Bernstein, 2000; R. G. Glaser, 2014; McMillan, 1999). Under the direction of the financial committee, one very workable way to deal with all of this is to keep things together in a physical or electronic notebook on the order of a policy and procedures manual (or handbook). Any one of a broad range of software programs such as Evernote and Microsoft One Note can simplify this task and make it more manageable.

READING FINANCIAL STATEMENTS

One of the challenges for a vigorous financial committee is to expect the members to actually look at and read financial statements, budget documents, and reports of financial analyses. In part, the incorporation of financial statement data and ratios in the balanced scorecard proposed in the preceding chapter is directed toward making that information more palatable to various stakeholders, including finance committee members. There may be an important training mission here. There is a long tradition of largely meaningless nonprofit financial statements that is yet to be overcome. Board and committee members and other stakeholders may be unaware of how to read these statements, not realize that such statements contain useful information, or not understand the ways in which financial ratios can considerably extend their understanding of what is actually going on. Some targeted training sessions directed to this issue might be needed.

PROGRAM EVALUATION AND REVIEW TECHNIQUE AND PERT COST

Another major task for the finance committee would be to commission a series of PERT studies, and later *PERT cost studies* (those that determine the cost of each step in a process as well as the sequence), to be included in the financial policy and practices manual. This process might begin with Gantt charts as a way to identify all of the appropriate steps involved in various processes; then proceed to PERT charts, identifying the complex pathways and timings involved; and finally, after a suitable cost study capability has been created, move to develop PERT studies as a way of monitoring the transaction costs of all of this activity and keeping them in line.

A number of figures shown here illustrate aspects of this process. In this example, let us assume that after she became CEO of a small nonprofit HSE, Brook negotiated a $25,000 planning grant to study, refine, and improve the budget process. The HSE that Brook directs is a United Way member organization, so in the preplanning stage, the decision is made to develop the plan using the United Way planning wheel (see Mayers, 2004, p. 50). Table 12.1 shows a simplified project budget for the $25,000 grant.

Figure 12.1 shows a Gantt chart detailing the HSE's budget process and time estimates (in days) of each segment of the process. Note that the total equals approximately 15 months but the project can actually be completed in less than a year because certain activities will be occurring simultaneously. Note also that the separate bars of what is essentially a bar graph are drawn to scale, with the 45-day bars 1.5 times longer than the 30-day bars.

Table 12.1: Project Budget, NACUBO Format

Category	This Year ($)	Next Year ($)
Human capital	6,740	10,720
Current expenses	3,260	4,280
Capital expenses	0	0
Total	10,000	15,000

Note: NACUBO = National Association of College and University Business Officers.

Figure 12.1: Gantt Chart of a Budget Process

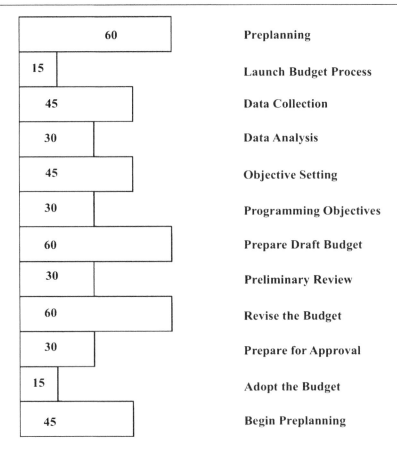

Note: Numbers represent time estimates (in days) of each segment of the process. This diagram is based on a planning wheel diagram published by United Way of America: See R. S. Mayers, 2004, *Financial management for nonprofit human service organizations* (2nd ed.; p. 50). Springfield, IL: Charles C Thomas.

Figure 12.2 shows the information from the Gantt chart in standard PERT syntax, where a line indicates an activity and the nodes at the ends indicate the beginning and ending events of that activity. Note that the lines are also drawn to scale, with the 60-day lines exactly twice as long as the 30-day lines.

Figures 12.3 and 12.4 and Table 12.2 develop the Gantt chart further by splitting each step in the process into two or more steps following the United Way planning wheel, assigning costs to each step, and connecting the steps as PERT charts. Note that for the purposes of this example, the anticipated times and planned costs are developed separately. In addition, all three have two added steps at Level 9 that are not on the original United Way wheel, dealing with dissemination of the approved budget. HSEs can inadvertently appear less than transparent by not taking into account the need to notify and publicize major decisions, as in the approval of a budget.

Figure 12.2: Translating Gantt Bars into Pert Syntax: Circles (Events) and Lines (Activities)

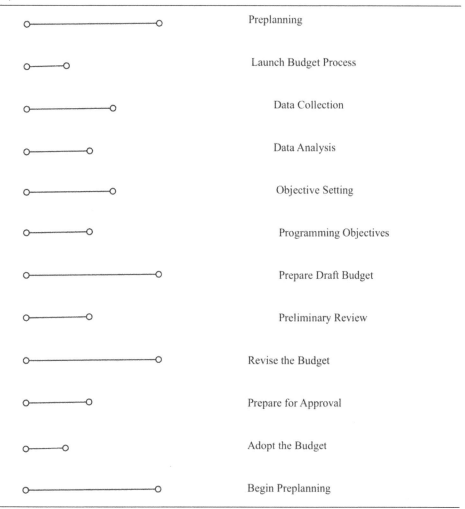

Table 12.2 shows the detailed listing of the time and cost estimates of each step in the process.

Figure 12.4 shows one important application of this process: a graphic representation of the data from Table 12.2 as a PERT chart. The first estimate is the estimated cost of each component of the budget process, using the previously mentioned $25,000 grant available for budgeting.

MANAGEMENT BY EXCEPTION

In a policy-defined environment also characterized by explicit legal conditions (for example, incorporation, filing an IRS Form 990 exempt entities tax return, and the nondistribution constraint), managed by a finance committee, with formal

Figure 12.3: PERT Budget Process

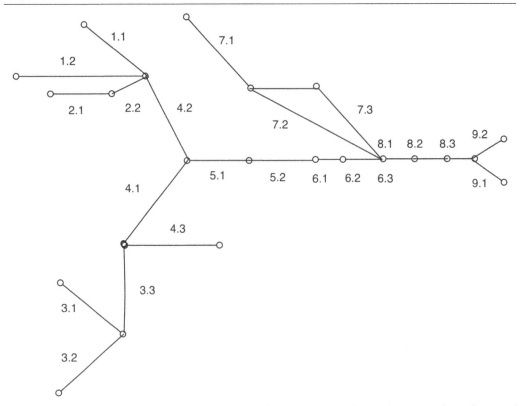

Note: PERT = program evaluation and review technique. See text for explanation of numbers and configuration.

accounting and budget systems, and at least some regular procedures outlined in a policy and procedures manual, it becomes relatively straightforward to practice a financial management strategy termed "management by exception." In a functioning management by exception environment, the assumption is that major matters will be governed by established policy and procedures most of the time and that, therefore, management attention can focus on those issues and concerns that deviate from policy and established practice—that is, the exceptions.

One important class of such exceptions are those cases where the routine administration of existing policy would create costs, hardships, negative or adverse consequences, or even the precise opposite results of those intended by the policy. Another important group of exceptions requiring attention is those issues or problems not presently covered by existing policy or procedures. Thus, for example, when an entirely new set of social problems comes along, this may be a time of many exceptions for an enterprise and its management. Homelessness; HIV/AIDS; and gay, lesbian, bisexual, and transgender issues were all in this position within recent memory, as were changes in IRS Form 990 and, before that, the newly formulated general accounting principles of FASB and GASB. Management by exception

Table 12.2: PERT Cost Estimates of a Budget Process

Planning Step	Number of Units	Cost ($)
1.1 Design budget structure	45	1,000
1.2 Collect preliminary data	45	1,000
2.1 Define broad goals and mission	15	300
2.2 Decide on tentative objectives	15	300
3.1 Gather needs and problems data	60	1,500
3.2 Gather resource availability data	60	1,500
3.3 Identify assumptions and constraints data	15	500
4.1 Set specific, time-limited objectives	30	500
4.2 Prioritize the objectives	15	500
4.3 Design self-evaluation system	60	3,000
5.1 Design specific tasks	45	1,000
5.2 Deploy staff, plant, and equipment	60	4,000
5.3 Design staff assessment system	60	4,000
6.1 Estimate expenses and outlays	30	500
6.2 Estimate public support and income	15	500
6.3 Process the budget with funders	15	500
7.1 Explore new funding	45	1,000
7.2 Eliminate part or whole program	15	500
7.3 Adjust service level	15	500
7.4 Introduced needed austerity	15	500
8.1 Vote on modified budget	15	300
8.2 Obtain board approval	15	300
8.3 Adopt balanced budget	15	300
9.1 Notify staff	15	500
9.2 Publish and distribute budget	15	500

Note: PERT = program evaluation and review technique.

Figure 12.4: PERT Cost Chart

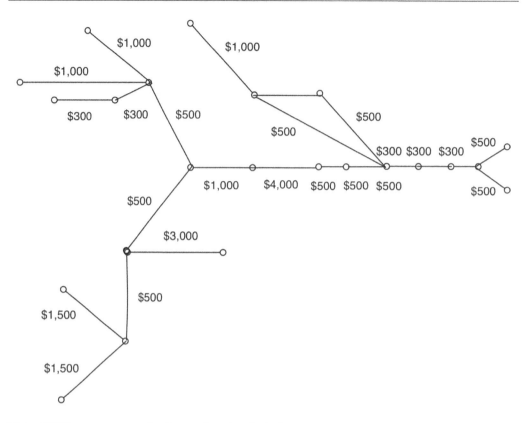

Note: PERT = program evaluation and review technique.

is often a particularly appealing approach to those managers who are attracted to problem-solving situations.

ACCOUNTS RECEIVABLE MANAGEMENT

Accounts receivable, as discussed in chapter 5, are one of the major categories of assets (Michalski, 2012). When they appear as a single line on the balance sheet, they can appear neat and tidy, summarizing all of the various sums that others owe to the enterprise. Managing receivables, however, often involves activities that go beyond simple bookkeeping.

Types of Receivables

There are as many different types of accounts receivable as there are types of assets, and each may require different handling: By their very nature, unsolicited contributions usually will not provoke accounts receivable. Because there is no way to identify in advance who will make such contributions, it is futile to spend time thinking about how to collect them. Past-due memberships and unpaid pledges may both require periodic gentle reminders to individual members or donors that they have not yet fulfilled their obligations. Diplomacy is often a good idea. Many will respond to the first notice, but at least a few will require further action. Both timely and targeted information are essential here. Remember how annoying it can be to receive general notices sent to everyone that urge you to pay your dues after your dues have already been paid! Thus, the time between developing a list of such unpaid obligations and the action taken to collect should be as short as possible. All things considered, the single largest area of concern with accounts receivable is likely to be unpaid program service fees, although in some circumstances, grant makers and contractors may also be problematic.

Billing and Floats

A key provision of accounts receivable planning is the set of arrangements for billing private pay clients, insurance companies, state contractors, and others for services rendered. The *float,* or the time period between actual provision of the service and payment of the fee, is an important consideration here as well as with accounts payable. It has become fairly standard practice for health and human services providers to post signs near the reception desk indicating that "Payment is due at the time of receipt of services" or some other such sentiment, and most clients will recognize the message and respond accordingly. Such policies certainly simplify the process of billing and collecting accounts receivable and serve to shorten the typical float from months to minutes.

Reviews, Aging, and Write-Offs

Enterprises with a large number of receivables may, from time to time, also find it necessary to review current accounts receivable and make determinations about whether there is any realistic hope of actually collecting the amounts due. One fairly common practice is to *age* receivables, that is, to classify them by the length of time they have been past due. One common practice is to follow the *30–60–90 day rule* used to categorize receivables that were billed one month, two months, and three months in the past, perhaps with different actions implied with each group. The older the account due, naturally the more seriously collection efforts are usually viewed. At some point, a determination may be made that there is no hope of collecting a particular amount due and that the sensible thing to do is to *write it off,* that is, to discontinue listing it among the set of accounts receivable. Remember, however, that at least some of your clients will talk with one another, and if word gets out that it is your policy to routinely just write off accounts 90 days past due, some clients may choose to wait out this period. Assorted for-profit businesses, cooperatives, and other tax-paying entities may be able to count such write-offs as expenses in determining their tax liability. However, for most tax-exempt nonprofit entities, write-offs of accounts receivable are ordinarily just that: recognition that a particular obligation to the enterprise is so unlikely to be recovered that there is no point in continuing to list it as an expected income. The actual accounting steps to handle such write-offs are not central to the current discussion. Accounting practices in this case are universal enough that any competent bookkeeper will know what to do. In any case, the principal financial management concern is with establishing the strategy, policy, and grounds for possible exceptions associated with writing off these assets.

Another step prior to writing off uncollectable accounts worth mentioning is the possibility of turning such accounts over to collection agencies or attorneys for action.* The proper action to take needs to fit with the facts of the situation: Enterprises dealing with fee payments from poor clients, for example, or those perceived as newcomers in the neighborhood will want to think very carefully of the overall implications before taking any action. The presence of sliding scale fees may be an important indicator, for example.

ACCOUNTS PAYABLE MANAGEMENT

Managing accounts payable is ordinarily a far simpler process for the HSE, with one major qualifier. As long as there are sufficient funds available to pay all the bills, the main management consideration in the typical HSE is to establish and maintain a routine payment schedule. (This is a good subject for a page in the policy and procedures handbook, so that everyone in the HSE understands the ground rules.) Managers can ordinarily assume that those to whom payments are due will also operate with the 30–60–90 day rule. In some cases, vendors will expect payment upon receipt of services, so the HSE may need to have procedures in place for the immediate issuance of payments by check or electronic funds transfer. This can be problematic for the HSE where the treasurer or another board officer must sign all payments. But even in the most tightly board-controlled payment systems, this may involve nothing more complicated than having a mechanism for activating the system (for example, notifying the treasurer) or some other form of preapproval when an appointment for service is made (for example, for air conditioner service or a plumber). In other cases, when a bill for goods or services arrives, it is usually safe to assume that payment of the obligation within the first 30 days (or 25 days, if assuming exceptionally slow mail service) following receipt will be satisfactory from the biller's standpoint. It is usually a good idea to note the billing date, so if use of the float is needed, the bill can still be paid and the payment received by the vendor before the next billing date.

In the current era of low interest rates, processing accounts payable is ordinarily a simple matter. In some cases, enterprises with lots of cash in the bank may

---

*Note the proper use of the term "agency" here: The collection bureau, firm, or attorney seeking to collect an uncollected account receivable on behalf of your enterprise is, indeed, functioning as your agent in the full legal and theoretical meaning of the term.

simply wish to issue checks or pay by electronic funds transfer immediately upon receipt of services or (somewhat later) mailed invoices. In such cases, accounts payable (especially smaller amounts) may never even make it into the accounting records as liabilities; they may simply show up as expenses, cutting out one entire round of recording. It is safe to assume that future time periods will not always involve such low interest rates. In periods of higher interest (that is, whenever credit card and bank accounts charge high fees), the float on accounts payable may be an important consideration.

BUDGET MONITORING

Another important task is the regular monitoring of the budget, a task that includes comparison of actual income and expense performance against the predictions of the budget. Table 12.3 shows a standard monthly report for a line-item budget that presents the current budget figures, spending for the month, spending for the year to date, and remaining balances. There are several other possible variations that might be used in this report instead, such as percentages of remaining funds in each category or by program, aggregated summaries of total income and expenses only, or any of the simplified budget formats such as the AICPA or NACUBO formats shown in chapter 6. The main point is to determine the profile of remaining, or unspent, funds. It is equally important that this information be shared with all of those responsible for original budget decisions.

Table 12.3: Monthly Financial Report

Category	Budget ($)	This Month ($)	Year to Date ($)	Remainder ($)
Income				
Donations	120,000	15,400	94,724	25,143
Fees	150,000	12,500	128,571	21,429
Grants	511,333	42,611	438,285	73,048
Contracts	687,420	57,285	589,217	98,203
Total income	1,468,753	127,796	1,250,797	217,823
Expenses				
Wages and salaries	1,233,134	102,761	1,056,972	176,162
Office rental	37,483	3,124	32,128	5,355
Communications	21,428	1,786	18,367	3,061
Travel	137,240	11,437	117,634	19,606
Equipment	32,284	2,690	27,672	4,612
Supplies	7,184	599	6,158	1,026
Total expenses	1,468,753	122,397	1,258,931	209,822

CASH FLOW MANAGEMENT

Careful tracking of accounts receivable and accounts payable is one of the ways to avoid embarrassments and misunderstandings. It is also one of the first steps in good cash flow management (Dropkin & Hayden, 2001; Hairston, 1981; Linzer & Linzer, 2007, 2008; Reider & Heyler, 2003). Careful management with an eye on cash on hand can also avoid unnecessary costs and losses. One of the biggest accounts payable for many HSEs will be the quarterly payment of FICA and employee income tax withholdings; sometimes financial managers may feel the pinch of available cash needed to make such payments. One of the most grievous mistakes in this area is failing to submit quarterly employee withholdings to the IRS on time and in full, which can subject the HSE to significant additional costs with fines and penalties. The IRS does not accept insufficient cash on hand as a reason for withholding quarterly payments, which are typically a percentage of total payroll for the quarter. This reality all by itself can be a reason to focus on cash flows and the availability of ready cash when payments are due.

It may not yet be clear to the reader why the FASB would mandate a statement of cash flows (for an example of such a statement, see Table 5.3) as one of the four primary financial statements for nonprofits. Similarly, it may not be evident why the list of ratios recommended in chapter 10 includes the current ratio. The answer to both questions is to be found in the concept of *liquidity*, a financial idea that refers to the ability of an enterprise to pay off its debts. (The current ratio is a measure of short-term debt.) It is equally as possible for an HSE as it is for an individual to be asset rich and yet cash poor, unable to meet current obligations. And although this all sounds arcane and esoteric, in reality, liquidity problems can be quite distressing, a threat to survival for the HSE, and a considerable challenge for managers and leaders.

Kayla learned this when she was faced with the situation in the third week of December of not having enough cash on hand to pay the salaries of the 24 part-time homemaker/home health aides employed by her program.* These workers were mostly undereducated, low-income women whose households survived from paycheck to paycheck and who were expecting their mid-December checks to buy holiday presents for their kids and special food items they had on layaway. The problem arose for a clear, if not particularly simple, reason: State government was having financial problems that year and the state treasurer, who was not a big supporter of social service contracts, had ordered state agencies to delay payments on state contracts. The agencies were not to default on the contracts; he insisted on just delaying payments. In the past, state contracts had always paid off in an average of about 45 days after invoices were submitted, and Kayla and her board had managed to avoid problems in the past by keeping at least a 60-day cash reserve on hand, just in case. But suddenly, with the state treasurer's announcement, the anticipated delay in payments ballooned from an average of 45 days to 180 days, meaning that for the rest of December and possibly the first five months of the

---

*This is a fictionalized account of an actual incident. As they say, the names have been changed to protect the innocent.

new year, Kayla was facing the prospect of no cash coming in. Kayla and her board had gotten word of this possibility from informants in the state agency several months before, and they had been able to build their cash reserves from an average 60 days to just over 90 days. Even so, if the problem persisted for six months, the agency would simply have to shut down. Someone alerted statewide news media and they picked up the story (particularly the "no Christmas presents for poor kids" angle, which the governor's political opponents relished!). The public response was strong. Under pressure from the governor and leaders of the state legislature, which opened its annual session in mid-January, the state treasurer backed off from the controversial policy, found the money somewhere, and paid off the contracts at the normal 45-day pace. The usual state payment was received on December 23 and, thanks to Kayla and her bookkeeper working late that day, workers' checks were issued that same evening. All of the workers picked them up later that night or the following morning.

But what if that had not happened? What if Kayla's program really would have had to attempt to go for five to six months without cash from its principal contract? The answer in this case is, unfortunately, quite simple: Despite the fact that her HSE was in a relatively strong cash position, the sudden loss of liquidity for that long a period would have forced them to close and lay off all workers. This is one of the most disturbing aspects of the silent revolution and, in particular, the spread of public service contracting. It has transformed social agencies into enterprises and made them more businesslike, including in their new levels of vulnerability to short-term liquidity problems. Any small business faced with a comparable situation would be similarly threatened.

Table 12.4 is based on the actual 30-month income, expenses, and cash balances of a small, nonprofit HSE. It was developed after an experience not unlike Kayla's. All of the numbers are real. The table is an extract of an ongoing monthly record that shows fluctuations in income and expenses over an extended period. The third column shows the percentage increase or decrease in income, and the fifth column shows the comparable increase or decrease in expenditures. In both cases, deficits are shown in parentheses (for even easier spotting of trends, they might also be shown in red). Adding a line at the end of each month may be the simplest way possible to keep track of cash flow. Although Table 12.4 does not track daily or weekly fluctuations within each month, the same logic would apply, and during critical periods, cash flow could be monitored each day or week as well.

Monitoring *cash flow*—the money moving into and out of the bank accounts of an HSE and the effects on the balance of cash on hand—is one of the routine but absolutely necessary aspects of enterprise financial management. There are at least four essential elements needed to do this. The first is up-to-date copies of the previously mentioned statement of cash flows (or the daily or weekly equivalents). The second is a cash flow plan following the logic of opening balance, plus cash in, less cash out to determine the closing balance. See Tables 12.5 through 12.8 for examples. Depending on the fluctuations in cash flow for the enterprise, the cash flow plan may show quarterly (as in Table 12.5); monthly; or, in some cases, even weekly fluctuations in cash position and activity. Table 12.6 shows a simplified quarterly cash flow plan, and Table 12.7 shows estimated average daily cash flows.

Table 12.4: Month-by-Month Record of Income and Expenses

<Name of Enterprise>
Monthly from June 20X4 through January 20X7

Month	Income Actual ($)	± %	Expenses Actual ($)	± %	Cash Balance ($)	Difference
June 20X4					8,854	
July 20X4	13,743		12,090		10,507	1,653
August 20X4	13,975	1.017	20,747	1.716	3,736	(6,771)
September 20X4	10,719	0.767	8,034	0.387	6,421	2,685
October 20X4	13,546	1.264	13,569	1.689	6,398	(23)
November 20X4	12,370	0.913	10,159	0.749	8,609	2,211
December 20X4	13,391	1.083	17,470	1.720	4,531	(4,078)
January 20X5	12,494	0.933	10,243	0.586	6,782	2,251
February 20X5	14,100	1.129	17,300	1.689	3,582	(3,200)
March 20X5	14,560	1.033	13,851	0.801	4,291	710
April 20X5	16,181	1.111	14,347	1.036	6,125	1,834
May 20X5	16,525	1.021	17,812	1.242	4,838	(1,287)
June 20X5	14,756	0.893	15,983	0.897	3,612	(1,227)
July 20X5	13,291	0.901	13,286	0.831	3,617	5
August 20X5	16,562	1.246	15,994	1.204	4,186	568
September 20X5	16,950	1.023	11,645	0.728	9,491	5,305
October 20X5	24,114	1.423	25,104	2.137	8,501	(990)
November 20X5	19,955	0.828	19,617	0.781	8,839	338
December 20X5	17,176	0.861	15,956	0.813	10,059	1,220
January 20X6	17,950	1.045	17,453	1.094	10,556	497
February 20X6	15,193	0.846	24,224	1.388	1,525	(9,031)
March 20X6	26,447	1.741	20,902	0.863	7,070	5,545
April 20X6	18,165	0.687	18,307	0.876	6,928	(142)

(continued)

Table 12.4: Month-by-Month Record of Income and Expenses (*Continued*)

<Name of Enterprise>
Monthly from June 20X4 through January 20X7

Month	Income Actual ($)	Income ± %	Expenses Actual ($)	Expenses ± %	Cash Balance ($)	Difference
May 20X6	18,068	0.995	18,670	1.020	6,326	(602)
June 20X7	16,794	0.929	11,531	0.618	11,589	5,263
July 20X7	21,852	1.301	28,874	2.504	4,567	(7,022)
August 20X7	25,306	1.158	29,935	1.037	(62)	(4,629)
September 20X7	21,339	0.843	24,821	0.829	(3,544)	(3,482)
October 20X7	29,674	1.391	15,741	0.634	10,389	13,933
November 20X7	20,845	0.702	21,653	1.376	9,581	(808)
December 20X7	19,859	0.953	17,562	0.811	11,878	2,297
January 20X7	19,299	0.972	21,837	1.243	9,340	(2,538)

Note: Row and column totals may not match exactly, because of errors due to rounding. Figures in parentheses represent negative values.

Figure 12.5: Five-Year Bar Graph of Monthly Expenditures

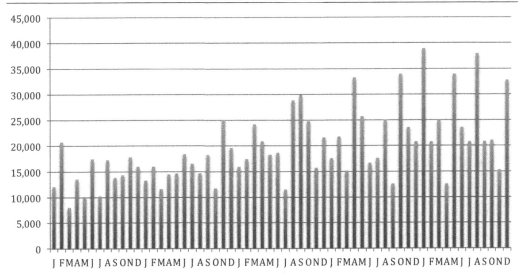

Note: Months are labeled in repeating pattern: J is for January, F is for February, and so on, through December.

Table 12.5: Quarterly Cash Flow Plan

Category	First Quarter ($)	Second Quarter ($)	Third Quarter ($)	Fourth Quarter ($)
Available cash, previous period	159,720	20,100	21,940	(180,120)
Cash receipts, source				
Clients	50,000	50,000	50,000	50,000
Grants	250,000	250,000	250,000	250,000
Contracts	290,500	320,500	290,000	290,000
Insurance				
Investments				
Donations	30,000	50,000	40,000	120,000
Total cash receipts	620,500	670,500	630,000	710,000
Cash paid to employees	434,000	402,000	409,500	390,500
Cash paid for employees	121,520	112,560	114,660	109,340
Additions to endowment taxes paid (UBITs)			100,000	
All other cash paid	204,600	154,100	207,900	234,300
Total cash disbursements	760,120	668,660	832,060	734,140
Available cash, next period	20,100	21,940	(180,120)	(204,260)

Note: UBITs = unrelated business income taxes.

Table 12.6: Quarterly Cash Flow Plan, Simplified

Category	First Quarter ($)	Second Quarter ($)	Third Quarter ($)	Fourth Quarter ($)
Starting cash balance	159,720	19,600	20,940	181,120
Income, all sources	620,000	670,000	630,000	710,000
All disbursements	760,120	668,660	832,060	734,140
Ending cash balance	19,600	20,940	(181,120)	(205,260)

Table 12.7: Estimated Daily Cash Flow

Cash Flow	First Quarter ($)	Second Quarter ($)	Third Quarter ($)	Fourth Quarter ($)
Average daily inflow	6,889	7,444	7,000	7,889
Average daily outflow	8,446	7,430	9,245	8,157
Average daily difference	−1,557	14	−2,245	−268

Note: Average daily difference was derived by simple subtraction.

Table 12.8: Cash Flows by Program

	Program 1 ($)	Program 2 ($)	Program 3 ($)	Total ($)
Cash receipts				
From clients	12,600	8,400	5,500	26,500
From grants	31,500	29,000	0	60,500
From contracts	125,500	74,500	95,000	295,000
From donations	120,000	90,000	80,000	290,000
From insurance	4,000	2,000	3,000	9,000
From investments	24,000	24,000	24,000	72,000
Total cash receipts	317,600	227,900	207,500	753,000
Cash disbursements				
Cash paid to employees	183,600	145,830	141,270	470,700
Cash paid for employees[a]	31,776	23,334	30,605	85,715
Taxes paid	0	0	0	0
Additions to endowment	20,000	0	0	20,000
Other cash paid out	54,400	37,280	41,757	133,437
Total cash disbursements	289,776	206,444	213,632	709,852
Additions to cash	27,824	21,456	(6,132)	43,148

[a]This item should include all cash flows associated with payments made by the employer on behalf of employees, including the employer's share of social security and Medicare taxes, health insurance premiums, and retirement contributions.

The last two elements in a sound monitoring scheme for cash flows are a set of guidelines or targets for average daily cash on hand and the related figure of the number of days that available cash is expected to last (see Table 12.7). In situations where there are major differences in cash flow, it is even feasible to break down cash flow planning by program, as in Table 12.8.

CONTINGENCY FUNDS

Another important question to be addressed in cash flow planning is the matter of how much cash should be kept on hand at any given time. In the example above, Kayla and the board routinely kept a 60-day supply and, anticipating problems, tried to bump this up to a 90-day supply. Situations will vary widely. Under most circumstances, it would be impractical for any HSE to maintain more than a three-month cash reserve, and, for many, even two months may seem overly ambitious. The discussion of financial distress in chapter 10 noted how unjustified concerns over keeping administrative cost rates low can actually hamper the ability of HSEs to respond to financial crisis situations when they arise. Many of these same concerns arise, with much the same effects, in the case of cash management, where similar misunderstandings can have similar effects. There is a sort of unwritten (but very powerful) rule among some public charities that might be expressed as, "If we didn't spend all the funds we have, how can we possibly ask for more?" It is worth noting that the question itself reflects a sort of confusion. This is a misapplication of the break-even principle also discussed previously, as well as a classic example of the confusion between the general asset position and cash flow. Many HSEs in the past have tied themselves in knots and seriously hampered their responsiveness by not keeping enough ready cash on hand. The likelihood for the typical HSE is that having too little cash on hand is a much more serious and threatening problem than having too much.

Opinions differ widely, however, about how much is enough: How much ready cash (or liquid assets) should an HSE seek to have on hand at any given time? Some believe that a one-month reserve is sufficient; others may counsel two or even three months. It depends on a number of different things, including staff willingness and ability to occasionally defer paychecks. One thing is fairly certain, and that is that all HSEs have a limit beyond which they cannot go. In the example above, there was no chance that Kayla's HSE could go for five or more months of cash drought. However, it does not necessarily follow that every agency should strive to have the maximum possible ready cash on hand. There is a trade-off here between cash on hand and the *opportunity cost* involved, specifically, the other uses to which that cash can be put in the meantime. So, the answer to "How much cash to keep on hand?" is always "Just enough!" however maddeningly vague that may be. Historical experience is usually a very useful guide here. If the HSE is constantly running low on cash or unable to make payments (or pay employees) without delay, then it may be prudent to increase the cash reserve. Conversely, if there are never any cash flow problems and there is always a very healthy checkbook balance, it may be prudent to at least ask, "Are we keeping too much ready cash on hand?" Particularly in times of low interest yields on checking accounts, it may be a wise decision to retire additional funds from the checking account into other, interest-bearing investments, for example, or at least to seek additional guidance (Fry, 1998).

MONITORING THE BUDGET

Another of the ongoing responsibilities in the period between budget approvals and revisions is the task of monitoring the budget and comparing it against expenditures. In most cases, this will involve shared responsibilities and a division of labor, with the CEO and the budget committee concerned with the overall budget and an assortment of departmental and program leaders, grant managers, and others keeping an eye on their particular parts of the budget. It might be a good idea to include some understanding of these various expectations in the policy and procedures manual, for example, in a list beginning with "Grant managers are responsible for . . ." Part of this overall monitoring task should involve keeping a weather eye on the long-term trends, not only changes in the absolute amounts as in Figure 12.6 but also changes in the relative proportions of income and expenses as in Figure 12.7. As these figures demonstrate, this is often done quite effectively through the use of diagrams.

One ever-present, important question is how to handle overspending of budgets and spending outside the bounds of the budget. In most cases, this will be dealt with best on a case-by-case basis (or management by exception). In cases where inappropriate spending not covered in the budget or overspending is common or otherwise uncontrollable, specific language in the policy and procedures manual aimed at preventing overspending may be necessary. In some cases, those employees (including chief executives, department heads, and others) who simply fail to pay attention to overspending concerns, red flags, or warnings, particularly those who clearly and deliberately overspend the budget, may be subject to disciplinary action, sanctions, or even dismissal for their actions. In extreme cases involving misuse of funds, even civil and criminal proceedings may be pursued.

RECORD KEEPING

The interim period between budget revisions is also an important time for record keeping. The accounting system is in place to track formal financial transactions,

Figure 12.6: Third-Quarter Income for Five Years

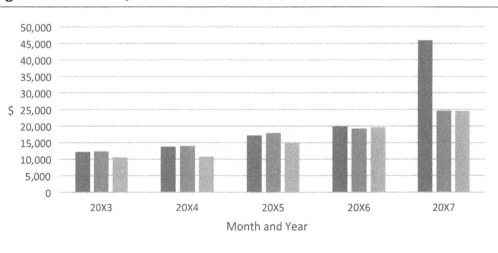

Month and Year

■ July   ■ August   ■ September

Note: The values in this table are based in part on the Actual Income column of Table 12.4 (with additional data before and after).

Figure 12.7: Third-Quarter Income and Expenses for Three Years

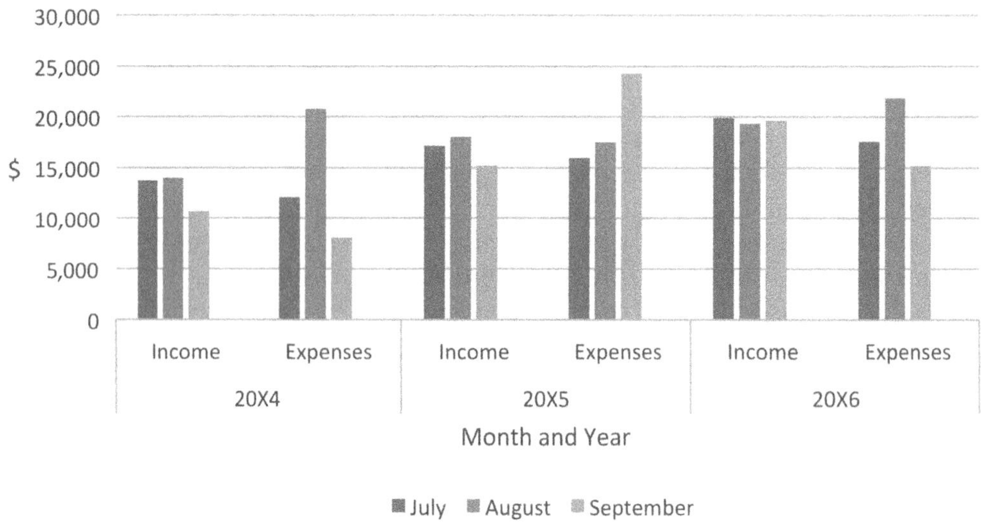

Note: The values in this table are based in part on Actual Income and Actual Expenses columns of Table 12.4.

but there is usually a variety of additional information needed to support and document the appropriateness of those transactions. These may include time cards or other records of when people arrive at work and leave, travel records, and so forth.

EMPLOYMENT AND COMPENSATION RECORDS

Every enterprise that employs people is required by a mix of local, state, and federal law to maintain a variety of records. It would take another volume the size of this book or longer to attempt to deal with all of them.

SALARY SCHEDULE

In an HSE of any size, there will be a wide variety of rates of reimbursements of employees (wages and salaries). It is sometimes useful to try to codify these into a single salary schedule. It may be possible to do some codification and systematization of these differences. Electronic spreadsheets are ideal for this purpose. Such salary schedules have a variety of uses, such as informing department and program heads of expectations for new employees and for salary increase recommendations. Particularly when first introduced, salary schedules can also be the source of a great deal of trouble. Before releasing such a document, careful thought should be given to how to respond to all of the employees who determine they are below the salary they ought to be receiving and ask for a raise!

The salary schedule shown in Table 12.9, for example, is computed from four variables (hours worked, base hourly rate, grade increment, and level increment).

Table 12.9: Salary Schedule

Level	Salary ($)				
	Grade 1	Grade 2	Grade 3	Grade 4	Grade 5
1	400.00	440.00	484.00	532.40	585.64
2	440.00	484.00	532.40	585.64	644.20
3	484.00	532.40	585.64	644.20	708.62
4	532.40	585.64	644.20	708.62	779.49
5	585.64	644.20	708.62	779.49	857.44
6	644.20	708.62	779.49	857.44	943.18
7	708.62	779.49	857.44	943.18	1,037.50
8	779.49	857.44	943.18	1,037.50	1,141.25
9	857.44	943.18	1,037.50	1,141.25	1,255.37
10	943.18	1,037.50	1,141.25	1,255.37	1,380.91

Note: Formula information input in Excel spreadsheet: hours per week = 40; base rate = $10 per hour; grade increment = 0.1; level increment = 0.1.

For clarity in presentation, these values are set at 40 hours per week at a base rate of $10 per hour and grade and level increments of 10 percent. This was set up in an Excel spreadsheet with the values corresponding to the four variables as named cells. The cell at the upper left (moved to the table note for display purposes) has the formula Base_Rate × Hours (per day, week, month, or year). All of the rest of the cells in the top row of numbers carry variations of the formula $RC - 1 +$ ($RC - 1 \times$ Grade_Increment), and the remaining cells in the lefthand column have the formula $R - 1C + (R - 1C \times$ Level_Increment), where R = the row number and C = the column number. Once the row and column are fleshed out, the "Fill Down" feature will complete the table. Using "Fill Right" should produce the same result. After the basic table is established and the values shown in the table note are entered, the values in the salary schedule should be the same as those shown here. At that point, locking the basic table while leaving the four named cells unlocked should allow unlimited adjustment of the table. Changing the value of any of the four basic variables should produce an entirely different set of results. For example, to see annual salary figures, change "40" in the hours cell to "2,000" (50 weeks at 40 hours per week) or 2,080 (52 weeks at 40 hours per week).

CONCLUSION

The burdens of financial management are too much to load upon a single individual, even the harried but heroic director of a small-budget nonprofit organization.

In a nutshell, this is the case for the use of a working treasurer and a finance committee—to oversee not only ongoing accounting and budgeting responsibility but also the development of a system of financial analysis, day-to-day operations, and the flow of income and expenses. A closely related consideration is the development and periodic updating of a policy and procedures manual to literally keep everyone on the same page regarding operations. Gantt, PERT, and PERT cost charts together with scheduling software are useful tools both for sketching the big picture for a year or more at a time and in planning day-to-day (even hour-by-hour) events and activities. For the HSE with program services income or an active fundraising program, some oversight of accounts receivable is in order. For every HSE, at least minimal attention to accounts payable is needed. One other important consideration for any HSE with multiple sources of income is ongoing attention to the matter of cash flow planning.

13

Toward Syncretic Financial Management

At this point, the reader might well ask, "Do all of the changes and transformations of the quiet revolution in financial management add up to a genuine paradigm shift in HSE financial management? Do they constitute an entirely new way of looking at the task of managing human services finances, akin to the 16th century Copernican revolution, as the paradigm shift language would suggest?" The best available answer is "Well, almost, but not quite." Despite rather massive changes in financial accounting, improved understanding of budgeting, and the continuing accumulation of tools for financial analysis, there has not quite been a radical transformation in financial management practice—yet. One principal reason that the quiet revolution has remained limited in its transformational effects is the seeming hesitancy of the practice community to embrace the full range of these changes. In fact, in the absence of outright coercion—such as that applied by the combined forces of the IRS, the FASB, the GASB, and several other national accounting authorities—much of the available technology of budgeting, financial analysis, and operations management is being applied in practice on a hit-and-miss basis currently. When federal, foundation, or federated funding sources, for example, mandate the development and adoption of outcome measures or when accrediting bodies get behind such guidelines, the response from much of the practice community is still likely to be, "You can make us develop these indicators, but you can't make us pay any attention to them!" Before there will be anything like a genuine paradigm shift away from the Ptolemaic model of budgeting and financial analysis as it emerged and evolved slowly over the last century, it will be necessary to find more effective strategies to encourage the adoption of these new practices. Until that happens, the potential for improved financial management practice in the available technologies will remain enormous but as largely just potential. The remaining discussion in this chapter addresses some additional aspects of that potential.

SYNCRETIC SYSTEMS?

The adjective *syncretic* refers to the combination of different beliefs or philosophies. The term is often used in religious contexts, but it also applies in other circumstances. Here, the term describes the intent of this final chapter, which seeks to combine different, even divergent, elements of financial practice theories, philosophies, and theoretical positions regarding how human services finances should be managed, as a contribution to furthering the future paradigm shift in HSE financial management. As has been detailed step by step throughout the previous chapters, the past few decades have been a time of building a substantial repertory of financial management tools for use in human services settings. These developments have shored up the enterprise accounting system; have elaborated program and performance budget systems; and have unveiled a broad range of output and outcome measurements and costs, such as break-even, ratio, and cash flow analyses, and interesting related developments in law and social accounting.

Change in accounting required a major shift in thinking, movement away from the use of fund accounting in nonprofit systems and partly away from the same scheme in government accounting, toward more enterprise-based approaches that emphasize the continuity with private practice. Changes in budget thinking have been more fragmentary, partial, and less complete but include the detailing of program and performance budgets, decision packages, break-even analysis, and a host of other innovations. Meanwhile, on a wide variety of fronts, refinements and applications of cost, ratio, cost–benefit, and other forms of analysis as well as developments in outcome measurement and social accounting have proceeded apace. Taken together, these diverse developments all point toward the emergence of a single, unified, syncretic financial management system for human services, capable of integrating accounting, budgeting, analysis, and operations into something very much like an integrated whole perspective and perhaps even eventually a single unified system. In this chapter, a number of ideas for continued development and further synthesis of these base systems are introduced and discussed.

With respect to budgeting, Lawrence Martin (2001) advanced the field several steps forward with the introduction of the theory of performance management into financial management and the use of program budget and performance budget packages in the financial context. Unfortunately, a reader might still get the impression that program and performance budgets are only usable in the public sector and that budgeting involves an either–or choice between conventional incremental and line-item budgeting and the novel use of program and performance packages. A closer reading of the full range of Martin and Kettner's work, however, along with that of Mook and others in social accounting, reveals essential parts of the underlying syncretic possibilities. In this chapter, that approach is pursued a step or two further, with the exploration of additional pathways for integrating elements of program and performance budgeting with cost analysis, break-even analysis, ratio analysis, social accounting, cash flow management, financial scorecards, and assorted other innovations from the base of enterprise accounting and the implementation perspectives of both conventional operating systems and recent thinking about operation capacity analysis.

The essence of the syncretic position presented here can be summarized as follows: Analytical thinking in budgeting practice as well as actual decision making are well captured by the incremental model of marginal analysis and conventional line-item budgets as presented in chapter 6. Together, these constitute a sufficiently solid, reliable baseline for evidence-based practice, and there is no need to encourage practitioners to abandon them. There is, however, ample reason to encourage practitioners to supplement and extend existing budget practices with a wide range of the tools already available. Furthermore, improved rationality and other, more synoptic approaches to budget decisions and greater emphasis on budgeting for social change may actually be possible in the future through more refined and sophisticated uses of information technology and computer programming. Although present practice is still heavily dependent on line-item budgets and narrowly incremental decision making that focuses primarily on minor, year-to-year adjustments, this may not always be the case. At least some of the past controversies over the incremental model have arisen not from close comparison of two viable budget models (sometimes called the political and the rational) but from comparison of the actual status quo with a variety of hypothetical proposals by rationalist reformers who—for good reasons—thought things ought to be done or thought about differently. Nearly all of the reforms discussed above (including line-item budgeting at one time) began as rational reform proposals that appeared impractical and overly rationalistic. Accounting reformers with the AICPA, FASB, and GASB may have only been interested in easing the burden on financial auditors by making the fundamentals of business, nonprofit, and government accounting more homogeneous—making uniform accounting principles truly more generally accepted. If so, that was—and is—a lofty and worthwhile objective.

Some budget reformers, on the other hand, seem to have been convinced that people who were doing budget and financial analysis were acting improperly and needed to acquire new ways of thinking about what they had been doing (J. Kahn, 1993). In retrospect, at least some such disagreements appear to have hinged largely on confusion between budget decision making and budget presentation formats—a difference, perhaps, of logic in use versus reconstructed logic, as noted previously (A. Kaplan, 1964).* At any rate, it now appears likely that many of the transformations in budget practices might be accomplished—at least in HSE—without any significant changes in how people doing budgets go about thinking about the problems or making decisions. Contemporary information technology and, in particular, understanding that the same databases of budget information can be presented in a wide variety of different output formats (or printouts) has opened vast new vistas of possibility. We have only begun to explore some of them here. Database technology and a variety of spreadsheets and data matrices offer a

---

*The real choice here is not between two comparable approaches to practice but between actual practice and an idealized version of that practice. This is, in other terms, the oft-noted distinction between actual practice and theory beloved by many practitioners. Marginal analysis and incremental budgeting are examples of actual practice, whereas systems such as PPBS are best seen as examples of reconstructed budget logic.

pathway to reconciling differences between line item, program, performance, and other budgets, which turns out to be mostly a matter of designing of formats and data algorithms to achieve the desired results.

PATHWAYS TO CHANGE

One of the questions raised by these possibilities is how to accelerate the rate of adoption of new financial management technologies by existing human services. There are at least three ways that the rate of change might be accelerated, which are not mutually exclusive.

First, in a top-down approach, a national body of practitioners, such as NASW, the Network of Social Work Managers, or a national coalition of such groups, could take the lead in an effort toward increasing the rate of adoption of financial management improvements. (The ECFA and the UWASIS efforts a few decades ago both offer good models.)

Second, in a bottom-up approach, students with some financial management experience or coursework on the subject could assume similar leadership roles in their respective practice communities, using social media to initiate and coordinate a grassroots movement for financial management improvement. In an extension of this approach, interested social work faculty might seek to recruit students and enlist HSEs in their communities in such efforts.

Third, the least desirable alternative would be for national governmental and accrediting bodies such as the federal OMB or the IRS to seek to impose improvements in budgeting, financial analysis, and operations in the way that these federal offices and GASB and FASB have mandated the current financial accounting regime.

Figure 13.1 shows the budget systems chart introduced earlier (see Figure 6.2) with an added layer termed the "zone of feasibility." The basic idea is first that there is widespread agreement (even among the most zealous rationalists) that fully synoptic (or complete rationality in) decision making (the lowest zone on the figure) and complete social change (ironically, the farthest right on the chart) are probably impossible ideals. Three perpetual questions can be posed: (a) How rational can decision makers train themselves to be? (b) How much social change can be made through a medium like budgeting? and (c) Is there any connection between the degree of rationality and the level of change? Whether one adheres to the rationalist position, the incrementalist one, or some other more syncretic view, it may be equally foolhardy to suggest that current approaches to budget decisions are somehow ideal and that no further improvements in the scope, comprehensiveness, or effectiveness of decisions in practice are possible.

Much the same perspective applies to the issue of change: Thus, the zone of feasibility extends to some indefinite border to include both a greater degree of synoptic rationality and a larger scope of social change. In particular, computer programs better able to track the interaction effects of particular marginal budget decisions might enable substantial improvements, but there is currently no available evidence that anyone is working directly on that problem as it relates to human

Figure 13.1: The Zone of Feasibility

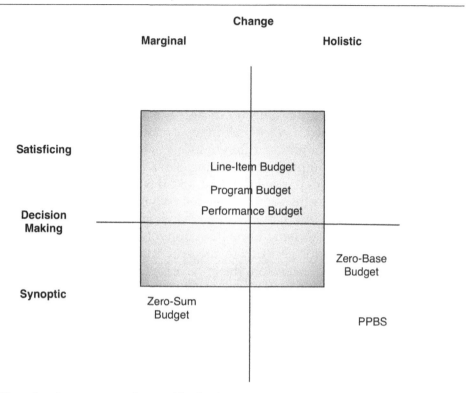

Note: PPBS = planning, programming, and budgeting system.

services and only a little evidence of indirect approaches to it. (See the discussion of operational capacity analysis later in this chapter.)

Even more important, if there are to be future advances in the direction of improved rational decision making, they will almost certainly involve better, more effective use of available data-processing capabilities. All things considered, the likelihood of a new and improved form of the human thought process or even major modifications in how social workers go about thinking about allocative decisions in human services seems remote. Information technology might facilitate better linking of financial statements to budgets and to reconciling enterprise, or all-funds, budgets with a wide variety of subenterprise budget breakouts for program, departmental, and special project budgets. This is fundamental for understanding the ways in which the various forms of financial analysis discussed earlier can be systematically introduced into the budget system.

LUMPING AND SPLITTING REDUX

The secret to accommodating line-item, program, performance, and other budgets is currently available in the previously mentioned process of lumping and splitting. *Lumping* in this case consists of nothing more complex than adding together a row or column of figures and presenting them as a single sum, whereas *splitting* involves identifying and breaking out the constituents of a single sum and showing them as separate items. For those who prefer their terminology more sedate, esoteric, or pedantic, Wassily Leontief, the economist who developed economic input–output analysis, used the terms "aggregation" and "disaggregation" for the same operations (Leontief, 1986, p. 41). Thus, any full enterprise budget is a lumped (or aggregated) document, whereas departmental, program, and grant budgets all represent specific, partial splits (or disaggregations). Likewise, a full enterprise budget can be presented in various lumped or split versions to present the same information while highlighting different facets of it.

Viewed from a lumping and splitting perspective, line-item, program, performance, enterprise, departmental, and all other budgets are not qualitatively different documents in the same sense that two novels, for example, are different. For example, the link between the backward-facing statement of financial activity and the future-oriented line-item budgets is clear. At the same time, we have a second reference point from the enterprise assumption in accounting and its future-oriented extension, the enterprise (or all-funds) budget. Together, these documents and their associated construction processes offer the core of an integrated web of financial documents into which it is easy and straightforward to weave additional methods of financial analysis and operations management. From this vantage point, line-item, program, performance, departmental, and other budgets fit together neatly like the pieces of a jigsaw puzzle. They also point toward an unfinished agenda of challenges and tasks that can be brought together and elaborated for each HSE by using available integrating tools such as strategic plans, business plans, and scorecards.

A NOTE ON COMPOSITE CLASSIFICATION

The discussion of classification of income sources in chapter 4 requires one more comment here in the context of syncretic financial management. In an age of electronic information systems, it should not be difficult (in fact, merely a matter akin to assigning a few flags or one-digit fields in the accounting database) to develop a composite classification system to classify each individual income item received and recorded by all of the approaches discussed in chapter 4. Each flag would correspond with a different classification scheme and would be coded in binary fashion (for example, blank or 1). In this way, a check received on a certain date could be flagged as program service income, specifically, a restricted donation (solicited or unsolicited) from a client in payment of a fee charged, and in any other ways deemed appropriate.

Advantages of Line-Item Budgeting

According to Martin (2001, p. 83), there are four noteworthy advantages to line-item budgets. The advantages are simplicity and ease of understanding, detailed listings of the sources and amounts of income items, the categorized listings of proposed

Table 13.1: Three Decision Packages

**20XX Fiscal Year
After-School Adventures**

Decision 1	Result
Total budget	$45,472
Outcome performance measure	One latchkey kid kept off the streets and socially involved for one hour
Total number of outcomes	10,800 hours of supervised care[a]
Cost per outcome	$4.21 per child per hour

Decision 2	Result
Total budget	$12,483
Outcome performance measure	Average one grade level improvement in reading scores
Total number of outcomes	1,728 hours of assisted reading[b]
Cost per outcome	$7.22 per child per reading hour

Decision 3	Result
Total budget	$2,413
Outcome performance measures	Each enrolled child will learn to play three board games: chess, checkers, and backgammon
Total number of outcomes	72 learned games[c]
Cost per outcome	$33.51 per child per game

[a]An average of 24 children are involved for an average of 2.5 hours per day, five days a week for the 180 days of the school year ($24 \times 180 \times 2.5 = 10,800$ outcome units).
[b]An average of 12 children and 12 community volunteers are involved for an average of one hour per day, four days a week for the 36 weeks of the school year ($12 \times 4 \times 36 \times 1 = 1,728$ outcome units).
[c]An average of 24 children learn to play each of the three games ($24 \times 3 = 72$ outcome units).

expenses, and the assumed condition of balance. To this might be added the presumed intuitiveness and universality of line-item budgets: Just about anyone can pick them up anywhere and get a pretty good notion of what is expected to occur, although it may not be clear when, where, why, or how it is expected to happen or what difference it is expected to make. What is proposed here is to combine those advantages with some of the less clear advantages of other approaches to budget formats.

PERFORMANCE BUDGETING

One element of syncretic financial management that seems yet to be fully realized anywhere in human services is "performance budgeting," a precursor to Martin and Kettner's performance management. The idea first arose at the federal level in the period after World War II. Although the nuances separating performance budgeting from other approaches to budget making may be subtle, the central issue from an HSE standpoint is whether the performance of agencies should be evaluated by funding sources as part of the ongoing budget review process. Martin (2001, p. 77) stated that performance budgets relate program outputs to resource inputs in ways that measure the efficiency of agency programs, but no evidence of this is offered. As noted in an earlier discussion, efficiency is a concept much talked about but seldom convincingly measured. As part of the proposed syncretic system outlined here, the Tinkelman and Donabedian (2007) proposals for the actual measurement of efficiency, in combination with measures such as the fiscal distress measurement package and the Piketty-inspired asset–net income ratio, show promise of realizing the frequently expressed hopes for measurement of the tricky variable efficiency. This alone would be a major step forward in the development of HSE performance budgeting for all settings, whether public, private, or in the third or fourth sectors.

The initial formulations of public performance budgeting decades ago came from public economists, who measured outputs in terms of productivity. That is, they sought to measure outputs as a ratio of resource inputs measured in dollar terms, an approach closely related to cost–benefit approaches. More recent output measurement efforts in the human services have sought to take advantage of improvements in noneconomic social science measurement techniques and measure social and psychological variables, for example, cost per ordinal unit of output counted but not further quantified. Aspects of both the performance management paradigm and the social accounting paradigm suggest distinct acceleration of movement toward integration of this long-sought element of performance budgeting with the conventional line-item budget model (for budget models, see Verheyen, 1998). Again, the integrated format ideas grounded in enterprise accounting and enterprise budgets as discussed above tie these various bits and pieces together nicely.

Another piece of the performance budgeting puzzle often alluded to but never fully resolved is the incorporation of genuine quality elements into the financial systems model. We are, in reality, still only at the beginning stages of adequate incorporation of quality measurement into performance management in human services. For example, the definition of quality as "the amount (#) or proportion (%) of the product produced or the service provided . . . that meets a specified quality standard" is interesting but circular (Martin, 2001, p. 66). To say that "quality is what meets a quality standard" fails to answer the more fundamental question: What is it about quality that makes something a "quality standard"? We know, of course, that quality is a characteristic, an essential property, or a condition of excellence, but what are the particular characteristics, properties, or conditions of human services that constitute quality services in that sense?

In human services, the word "quality" is probably used most often in the phrase "the quality of life," in which it has connotations of well-being, viability, and meaningfulness. The next most common usage might be in open-ended survey questions and equated with client satisfaction: "How satisfied are you with the quality of the service you received?" The primary significance of a quality approach, however, has not been the successful resolution of budget decision problems. This is not intended as a criticism of any existing approaches to quality but as a signpost of future work that remains to be done. At least a few instances of quality can be identified using the quality standards approach, but there are many areas in which no such standards currently exist. The International Organization for Standardization has established the standards of ISO 9000, but no one seems to have examined them for their relevance for human services. There was a brief flurry of interest in total quality management and quality circles some years ago when Japanese management was all the rage, but that faded without noticeable result (Berman, 1995; DeCock & Hipkin, 1997; Gummer, 1996; Gunther & Hawkins, 1996, 1999; Hwang & Aspinwall, 1996; Kearns, Krasman, & Meyer, 1994; Martin, 1993a, 1993b; Reed, Lemak, & Montgomery, 1996). Human services scholars have yet to discover Six Sigma, a more recent favorite approach to quality in the general management context. Overall, much hard work in this area remains to be done. The Kettner–Martin incorporation of quality into the systems model for performance management and Martin's (2001) examples point us toward the next steps in defining output quality in HSE. Unfortunately, in the decade or more since those publications, there is scant evidence that the human services management or research communities have taken up the challenge.

One possible approach consistent with marginal analysis might be open-ended attempts to identify one or more of those qualities piecemeal—the characteristics, attributes, properties, or conditions of human services that present themselves as inherently or intrinsically desirable—and to integrate them a piece at a time into the budget performance paradigm without reference to inputs, outputs, outcomes, efficiency, effectiveness, or any of the other elements of comprehensive rational–deductive models. Themes arising in the social capital literature, such as trust, and many of the notions associated with cultural or spiritual capital spring to mind as currently low-hanging fruit in this regard. A more prosaic approach might be to seek to define at least some aspects of quality in the context of reduced risk of harm or danger.

Advantages and Disadvantages of Performance Budgeting

The major advantage of performance budgets, according to Martin (2001, p. 86), is that they provide information on the volume of service provided by an HSE program, the associated costs, and unit costs. In addition, it is important to note that performance budgets shift the level of budget debate from line items to programs and the associated program costs, outputs, and efficiency (and quality?). For anyone who has ever participated in hours-long discussion of the pros and cons of a particular line item such as office supplies, the importance of those points cannot be overstated! The major disadvantage cited by Martin is one the proposed syncretic approach is intended to overcome: the seemingly esoteric nature and resulting underutilization of cost analysis techniques.

On balance, the advantages of performance budgeting appear to vastly out-weigh the disadvantages, particularly if practical approaches to the widespread dissemination of cost analysis methodology among HSEs can be worked out. The principal obstacle to full implementation of performance budgets within a syncretic budget system bringing together line-item, program, and performance output formats in any given HSE would appear to be the absence of a complete listing of appropriate performance measures. As things presently stand, there is nothing in the published literature detailing anything more extensive than isolated examples like those included here, and nothing to suggest that any existing HSE has rolled out an actual, operational performance budget system design. A listing of performance measures intended for use in a real HSE setting would be a good start.

PROGRAM BUDGETING

Performance budgeting also raises questions: What is the performance? What is it that is being performed (or, in service delivery parlance, "delivered")? The consensus answer to that question specifically is service provision, and, in general, services occur through programs. Thus, it is only a small step from the concept of performance budgeting to the concept of program budgeting (Lohmann, 1980; Martin, 2001). The identification of a suitable program structure is an essential prelude to identifying outputs in the performance model. The current NTEE and UWASIS models have started this process, but each is a committee product that leaves much to be desired. In my experience, one of the benefits of the popularity of the management by objectives model of management and the development and use of taxonomies such as UWASIS, NTEE, and the philanthropy tree is that most HSEs today are able to see their services in program terms due to standardized national classification schemes. More important, perhaps the various stakeholders of these organizations (donors, volunteers, board members, and community leaders) are able to understand the HSE as the sum of its programs rather than its line items. For those who do not already have a clear understanding of what programs are and how they are structured, chapter 2 in Martin (2001, pp. 10–16) outlines the steps involved in developing a program structure. In any event, common sense suggests that performance budget and program budget approaches—where budget decisions are made by grouping expenditures for similar sets of (in PERT terminology) events and activities, or performances—are compatible developments. This is an important point of the syncretism called for here. The development of a performance-based program structure in HSEs, like the attachment of a fundraising program to the existing income generation system, might best be viewed as an evolutionary task undertaken in a series of discrete steps over a period of time. In recognizing that there still may be a ways to go for a particular HSE, however, it is important also to appreciate the progress made thus far.

Under the watchful eye of its finance committee, an HSE might over a five-year period plan to develop a full and complete program structure, with as many output and outcome measures as possible, and begin laying plans for a comprehensive set of program budget formats. It might then move toward a composite budget information system capable of generating line-item, performance, and program budgets for all appropriate units. As the preceding discussion suggests, such an integrated system should also be capable of producing break-even data where program service income and donations are involved. This would seem especially important in the case of those designated surplus centers or programs expected to produce budgeted surpluses and those loss centers whose budget deficits must be made up elsewhere within the enterprise budget. A truly syncretic system would also routinely produce a designated set of ratios, such as the standard ratios and the all-important financial distress measures discussed in chapter 10. The analysis system might also routinely estimate the value added by volunteers (see Table 11.2), as well as assorted measurements of the community social returns on investment (see Table 11.3) and expanded value added (see Table 11.4) of the various major programs of the HSE. Note that one long-term future element of Table 11.4 might be the addition of tertiary benefits measurement with monetary estimates of the value added by social, cultural, and political capital generated by programs. Table 11.5 shows a performance budget combining many of these ideas and modeled on the approach of Martin (2001). Table 11.6 shows a performance report associated with performance budgeting.

There may be some accounting systems available today with budget capabilities able to incorporate all of this into a single, automated system. If so, I am not familiar with them. In all likelihood, a fully syncretic system of the type described here would have to be pieced together from existing technology. All of the tables, budgets, figures, and graphs shown in this book were prepared with Microsoft Excel. Quicken for Nonprofits and other accounting systems have some limited capabilities for this task. Nevertheless, with the present state of the art, it is more likely that for most HSEs, this would involve feeding accounting information into a series of prepared spreadsheets to produce the desired results. In line with the scorecard idea, perhaps such spreadsheets might all be enclosed as multiple sheets of a single Excel workbook. The problem of organizing such a system, however, is not insurmountable. The biggest challenge involved is setting up the spreadsheets to be as calculative as possible and making (and testing!) the proper connections. Much of the hardest work remaining to be done is in the definition and setup. Once this setup is completed, the typical bookkeeper or accountant for an HSE should be able to prepare and distribute the various reports on a regular basis. The astute reader will note that the recommendation here is that building such a comprehensive system be approached piecemeal, in the well-known incremental manner.

POTENTIAL PROBLEMS

A variety of problems may occur in the course of implementing a syncretic approach to financial management in human services. For example, the logic of program budgeting by itself could be conducive to a breakdown of the integrity of organizational units in the budget document; some programs are not neatly or easily contained within a single department or unit. This alone may be a major reason why matrix organizations and matrix budgets never really caught on in human services despite some very intriguing proposals (Ryan & Washington, 1977). When proposed expenditures for similar activities from an objective standpoint are linked under a common heading (for example, "income maintenance"), regardless of the organizational units in which they are to be performed, all kinds of issues of organizational territoriality (or "turf"), duplication of efforts, and other questions begin to arise. Although program budget information provides more accurate perspectives for decision makers on the overall performance patterns within the budget system, its value to the administrator of a particular department is clearly limited when the program is scattered across several departments. Likewise, at each programmatic level, one is likely to find a similar situation—the information, in effect, is clear principally to those at the next highest level at which expenditure is to occur.

Discussion of performance budgeting, like performance management, has been limited almost exclusively to public settings (see Martin, 2001, pp. 65–75). In contrast, program budgeting has been a popular reform idea with grant makers and others interested in public distributions and federated allocations systems such as United Way for decades. Yet, as noted in chapter 6, elements of programming, planning, and budgeting and zero-based budgeting, like decision support packaging, represent important potential variations on some of the essential notions of program budgeting models. The problem, as always, is going to be how to get the main line of budget practitioners to embrace and adopt them.

On the one hand, there are very real potential benefits of program budgets in management, but on the other hand, there are also very real difficulties facing those who seek to implement a program budget scheme within existing budget arenas. It is not likely, for example, that program budgets alone will take the politics out of budgeting, although it might redirect them somewhat. Political decision makers are almost certain to continue to make their calculations on the "pork barrel" potentials of public expenditures, for example, even if program budgeting were to completely replace line-item budgeting. Even so, the incremental gains in budget control and planning enabled by program budgeting would represent a substantial improvement to administrators over existing practices. In sum, the past debates over program budgets have largely failed to sort out the different legitimate uses of budget information. No budget system per se should be expected to exercise a controlling influence on the way decisions are made. However, the critical step, from an enterprise standpoint, is to link budget decisions and implementation. For this purpose, program budget approaches offer enormous possibilities for extending the capabilities of management control and planning. Furthermore, the integration of program budget and program accounting schemes, like the management–fundraising–program typology, have created unique opportunities for direct feedback from the accounting system to agency decision making, even though most HSEs have yet to realize this potential.

More than three decades ago, Lohmann (1980) wrote that the "jury is still out on the question of the utility of program budgeting in human services" (p. 143). Although that may still be true in terms of widespread adoption of program budgeting formats and even more so in terms of performance budgeting, the burden of proof in terms of budget theory and expert opinion has shifted heavily in their favor. The examples cited in this chapter are intended to further add to that evidence base (Goodman, 1969; Gross, 1985; Stretch, 1980; Vinter & Kish, 1985). It is one of the tenets of the syncretic approach outlined here that incorporating elements of program and performance budgeting into existing budget practice can offer important advantages to most HSEs.

One of the interesting yet curious episodes in the history of public budget reform in the United States was the rise and fall of PPBSs in the 1960s. These systems represented a radical alternative to budget practice, combining uncompromising notions of program budgeting with extensive use of cost-effectiveness techniques and a synoptically rational model of budget arenas as scientific problem-solving bodies. The PPBS approach was at one time mandated for the entire federal government (an unwise action that was later quietly rescinded).

Nevertheless, establishing program structures linking cost measurement to budgeting, synoptic rationality, and zero-based and zero-sum choices has continued to influence budget theory in subsequent decades. The PPBS approach was perhaps the ultimate rational model of budget making. Nothing quite as rational, comprehensive, and complete has appeared since then. The idea that each major budget choice should be subject to thorough reconsideration each year continues to appeal to some and appall others. Ultimately, however, the comprehensive rationality of this model proved too unrealistic and difficult to implement in the federal budget context and too clearly conducive to increasing the political power of "neutral" economists (whose cost-effectiveness determinations become the only real decisions in this budgeting approach) to warrant sustained commitment.

Even so, one should not conclude that the PPBS misadventure was entirely meaningless. In the human services, for example, it is largely because of this model that we are aware of the tremendous stock of analytical tools that can be applied to financial issues and problems. Additionally, both the current awareness of a linkage between planning and budgeting and the articulation of the political theory of budgeting may be credited to PPBS. It was largely in reaction to this model that Wildavsky first wrote of the politics of the budgetary process, and program structures such as UWASIS, the NTEE, and McCully's philanthropy tree are founded on models of comprehensive program structures derived from this system. These are substantial accomplishments for a reform that failed.

Advantages and Disadvantages of Program Budgeting

Martin (2001) introduced a particular non-line-item budget (like the ones portrayed in Table 13.1) and identified a number of advantages and disadvantages of program budgeting. Program budgets, he says, provide information on the "amount of (client) outcomes" and the attendant program costs. On balance, the advantages of program budgeting appear to outweigh the disadvantages. It would thus be advantageous for an HSE to embrace program budgeting fully, particularly if it can be fully integrated with existing line-item budgets as the syncretic approach advocates. As Figure 13.1 shows, this mode of program budgeting can also be used to pose and cost different dimensions of a single program separately, or even to detail decision alternatives.

Tables 13.1–13.7 and 13.9 present a proposed partial set of integrated syncretic budget documents. In Table 13.2, the program budget target of $45,472 is shown together with monthly and year-to-date performance data. In the far-right column,

Table 13.2: Program or Performance Budget

20XX Fiscal Year
After-School Adventures
June 20XX

Measure	Planned	This Month	Year to Date	Variance
Program cost ($)	45,472	3,790	24,791	Over
Number of favorable outcomes	10,800	875	5,240	Under
Cost per outcome ($)	4.21	4.33	4.73	Over

Note: Outcome performance measure: one latchkey kid kept off the streets and socially involved for one hour. Cost per outcome = $4.21 per child per hour.

Table adapted from L. L. Martin, 2001, *Financial management for human service administrators* (p. 90). Boston: Allyn & Bacon.

labeled "variance," is a declaration by the budget analyst of whether the budget is over- or underperforming on each item in the current period.

Primarily for orientation purposes, Table 13.3 presents a conventional line-item budget of the same information, and Table 13.4 situates the same set of program information within a break-even analysis showing the basis for determining the total number of anticipated outcomes (10,800 service hours) and the cost per outcome ($4.21). Table 13.5 presents a full matrix budget for the program budget first laid out in Table 6.4, except using the simplified AICPA × NACUBO formats. It is purposely presented in this manner to illustrate the inability of that document

Table 13.3: Line-Item Budget

After-School Adventures
Fiscal Year 20XX

Category	Amount ($)
Salaries and fringe benefits	
Professional	29,711
Support staff	5,680
Fringe benefits (at 18%)	6,370
Office space	0
Travel	1,470
Communications	1,424
Equipment	633
Supplies	184
Total project expenditures	45,472

Table 13.4: Break-Even Analysis

After-School Adventures
Fiscal Year 20XX

Measure	Amount ($)
Fixed costs	22,044.48
Variable cost per outcome	2.18
Fee per outcome	4.21
Break-even analysis	
Number of outcomes	10,800
Total variable costs	23,427.52
Total income	45,472
Total costs	45,472
Cost per outcome	4.21

to locate the $45,472 detailed in Tables 13.2–13.4. There is an easy fix for this: Splitting the "program" column into either two columns (labeled "after-school adventures" and "other programs") or multiple columns that list each program separately would be straightforward.

Table 13.6 brings the social accounting document known as the "community social return on investment" into the same budget frame as Tables 13.2–13.5 by projecting the impact on the community of the investment represented by the $45,472. We see, for example, that that amount of anticipated expense is accompanied by a budgeted amount of $8,225 for volunteer effort (based on an analysis like that seen in Table 11.2 but not shown here). On the expense (or credit) side of Table 13.6, we also show the primary and secondary outcomes, like those discussed previously in Table 11.3. The primary benefit is said to be cost savings to parents from other

Table 13.5: Matrix Budget, AICPA × NACUBO

Category	Management and General ($)	Fundraising ($)	Program ($)	Total ($)
Human capital	69,100	20,000	371,577	460,677
Current expenses	7,600	5,567	37,489	50,656
Capital expenses	0	0	0	0
Total	76,700	25,567	409,066	511,333

Note: AICPA = American Institute of Certified Public Accountants; NACUBO = National Association of College and University Business Officers.

Table 13.6: Community Social Return on Investment

After-School Adventures
Fiscal Year 20XX

Resource Inputs ($)		Benefit Outputs ($)	
Income	45,472	Expenses	45,472
Volunteer labor	8,225	Volunteer labor	8,225
		Outcomes	
		Primary benefits	
		Savings on daycare	21,200
		Secondary benefits	
		Prevent repeating grades	141,721
		Tertiary benefits	
		Parent networking	26,740
		Reading readiness	42,600
Total	53,697	Total	285,958

Ratio of return on community investment: $1.00 : $5.33

Table adapted from L. Mook, J. Quarter, & B. J. Richmond, 2007, *What counts: Social accounting for nonprofits and cooperatives* (p. 149). Medina, OH: Sigel Press.

forms of day care, whereas the considerably larger secondary benefits to the community are the anticipated savings resulting from prevention of repeating grades for students enrolled in the program. An additional estimate of monetized tertiary outcomes of parent networking and reading readiness resulting from the program are also offered. Data and rationales forming the basis of these primary, secondary, and tertiary benefits are not presented here but would ordinarily be part of the full syncretic budget presentation.

Development of a comprehensive program structure for the HSE would be a major obstacle to full implementation of program budgets within a syncretic budget system bringing together line-item, program, and performance output formats and various modes of financial analysis in any given HSE. Relying on available tools already in use—such as the AICPA classification of management and general, fundraising, and program costs—and distinguishing direct and indirect costs, such a model could probably take into account not only direct service programs but also indirect programs, for example, management, fundraising, marketing, and so forth. Again, using the enterprise budget as "the whole" offers a key reference point for identifying when all of the various parts, or *components*, have been included in such a program model. Table 13.7 lays out one possible approach to a syncretic enterprise budget, albeit without detailing a full program structure to go with it.

Table 13.7: Syncretic Budget

Human Services Enterprise
Fiscal Year 20XX

Category	Outcomes	Financial[a] ($)	Social ($)	Total ($)
Projects				
Fundraising initiative	>$4.80:$1.00	25,000		25,000
Volunteer initiative[b]	>$5.30:$1.00		285,958	285,958
Total projects		25,000	285,958	310,958
Program budgets				
After-School Adventures[c]	10,000 hours child work	45,472		45,472
Human capital, training[d]		254,364	132,635	386,999
Crisis intervention	2,654 hours crisis work	186,817	155,220	342,037
Total program budgets		486,653	287,855	774,508
Performance budgets[d]				
Home visit program	7,000 hour patient contact	492,678		492,678
Homemaker program	32,500 hour	246,019		246,019
Home-delivered meals	32,500 meals	218,403		218,403
Total performance budgets		957,100		957,100
Total budget		1,468,753	573,813	2,042,566

Note: This table is based on the budget data presented in Table 6.3.

[a]Performance budget data from L. L. Martin, 2001, *Financial management for human service administrators* (p. 90). Boston: Allyn & Bacon.
[b]Budgeted $120,000 income.
[c]Based on Table 13.3.
[d]Based on Table 11.4.

ZERO-BASED BUDGETING

One is tempted initially to dismiss zero-based budgeting as simply another unrealistic effort by technocrats to depoliticize the budgetary process. Closer examination, however, reveals a critical distinction to be made between the unrealistic zero-sum assumption of PPBS that every expenditure should be completely justified every year and the zero-based budgeting assumption that every expenditure should be subject to periodic reexamination and justification although not necessarily every year.

Zero-based budgeting also incorporates a more realistic approach to program structures than that found in the PPBS model in the "decision packages" approach (Pyhrr, 1970, 1973). The essence of the zero-based innovation is a combination of the linkage of planning and budget decisions found in PPBS (decision packages) with an essentially incremental decision model that serially and marginally makes decisions selectively on decision packages. At each level in an organizational hierarchy, a manager is seen to work with discrete sets of decision packages (essentially work programs) of proposed objectives and sets of alternatives for attaining objectives, each costed with a proposed budget. Yet, this is not the synoptic "take no prisoners" PPBS approach. In the best marginal manner, no effort is made to list and analyze all possible alternatives; rather, attention is concentrated on a small set of the most likely options.

Pyhrr (1977, p. 2) noted four common steps in the zero-based budgeting approach:

1. identification of decision units
2. analysis of each decision unit within a package
3. evaluation and ranking of all decision packages to prepare a single enterprise request (a top management activity)
4. preparation of a detailed operating budget reflecting those decision packages approved in the budget appropriations

Pyhrr's packaged approach to decision making has survived well beyond the zero-based budgeting approach—which for HSEs is now little more than a historical footnote. As Martin (2001) first showed, in the context of program and performance budgeting, the decision package approach can be adapted to all types of human service settings. Table 13.1, for example, shows the degree to which a performance budget can function as a decision package (in this case, showing several decision options, dimensions, or alternatives), with backup line-item and program budget information, relevant cost studies, break-even analysis, and ratios as needed by the decision makers involved. Table 13.8 shows a simple Likert-type scale that might be used for ranking such decision packages.

Table 13.8: Likert-Type Scale for Ranking Decision Packages

Scale Item	Score
Recommend for full funding	5
Recommend for full funding with reservations	4
Recommend for partial funding	3
Recommend for partial funding with reservations	2
This package is not ready for decision	1
Reject	0

Table 13.9: Break-Even Analysis with Multiple Sources of Income

1	2	3	4	5	6	7
Category	Inputs	Service Level (#)	Fixed Cost Per Unit ($)	Total Income ($)	Total Cost ($)	Surplus or (Deficit)
Fixed income	**25,000**	1,000	46.19	34,000	52,847	(18,847)
Fee	**9.00**	2,000	23.09	43,000	59,507	(16,507)
		3,000	15.40	52,000	66,167	(14,167)
		4,000	11.55	61,000	72,827	(11,827)
Unit increment	**1000**	5,000	9.24	70,000	79,487	(9,487)
		6,000	7.70	79,000	86,147	(7,147)
Total fixed cost	**46,187**	7,000	6.60	88,000	92,807	(4,807)
Human capital cost	**38,987**	8,000	5.77	97,000	99,467	(2,467)
Other fixed cost	**7,200**	9,000	5.13	106,000	106,127	(127)
		10,000	4.62	115,000	112,787	2,213
		11,000	4.20	124,000	119,447	4,553
Total variable costs	**6.66**	12,000	3.85	133,000	126,107	6,893
Variable human capital cost	**5.61**	13,000	3.55	142,000	132,767	9,233
Variable current expenses	**1.05**	14,000	3.30	151,000	139,427	11,573
		15,000	3.08	160,000	146,087	13,913
		16,000	2.89	169,000	152,747	16,253
		17,000	2.72	178,000	159,407	18,593
		18,000	2.57	187,000	166,067	20,933
		19,000	2.43	196,000	172,727	23,273
		20,000	2.31	205,000	179,387	25,613

Note: Column numbers are retained in this table only to facilitate the discussion in the text. They serve no other purpose. The values in the Inputs column are boldfaced to indicate that they are the only values to be supplied by the analyst. Everything else in the table is constructed by formula.

It is truly one of the ironic aspects of the quiet revolution in financial management that although the larger contexts that spawned them have gone by the wayside, both the program structures model of PPBS and the decision packages model of zero-based budgeting have survived and merit continuing attention as components of a syncretic approach. The first two steps of Pyhrr's list are already accommodated in the performance budgeting approach. The last two could also be included with the development of a detailed, enterprise-level budget built on these program packages, such as the one shown in Table 13.7.

BREAK EVEN WITH MULTIPLE SOURCES OF INCOME

Another set of possible avenues suggested by the syncretic model is for the enhanced use of even more sophisticated spreadsheets in financial analysis. Table 13.9, for example, shows a spreadsheet in which a break-even analysis showing a range of possible solutions established by using a standard increment (1,000) in the number of units of service is combined with a fixed source of income (in this case, $25,000, but it could be any combination of a known quantity of grants, contributions, or allocations). In addition, it is also possible to add sliding scale fee calculations into such a table, treating them as discounts. The spreadsheet is set up so that the figures shown in boldface are all the original entries needed and supplied by the analyst, while the rest of the table is computed by formulas in the spreadsheet.

The values in column 1 of Table 13.9 are labels only for the user-supplied values in column 2. They do not apply to the right of the empty column between columns 2 and 3. In an electronic spreadsheet, the values in column 2 are meant to be supplied by the analyst, based on budget and program planning data. To be maximally useful, the spreadsheet should be constructed so that all of the values in columns 3 through 7 are calculated by standard break-even formulas. The values in column 4 represent total fixed cost divided by the unit increment values in column 3. The values in column 5 represent the fixed income estimate (grants plus donations) plus the fee multiplied by each unit increment in column 3. The values in column 6 combine total fixed cost plus total variable cost per unit multiplied by the number of units in column 3. Column 7 is the difference between column 5 and column 6. Thus, any change in the data in column 2 will recalculate the values in columns 3 through 7. Note that the values in column 4 diminish from a high of 46.19 to a low of 2.31. This is typical behavior for fixed costs per unit and is due to a constant amount ($46,187) being divided by incrementally larger numbers from 1,000 to 20,000. It is the exact opposite of variable cost, where total variable cost increases (or decreases) with increases (or decreases) in the number of units of service, whereas the variable cost per unit remains constant. The figures in column 7 show that the break-even point for this set of assumptions occurs between 9,000 and 10,000 units of service and that at 11,000 units, there is a projected surplus of $4,553.

Such a spreadsheet could further be created to show almost any combination of line-item or simplified budgets itemization, however lumped or split. In this case, the fixed cost listing uses one set of categories and the variable cost per unit section uses another. Note that with the fixed cost per unit calculation of the total income produced by various levels of service in this table, calculation of total income is a matter of adding fixed income (in this case, $25,000) and various variable income from a fee of $9/unit times the number of units of service. We might also adjust for estimates of various amounts of services offered at each reduced rate of the sliding scale in this calculation. Total cost is also easily computed as fixed cost per unit plus variable cost per unit to produce a total cost per unit figure that is then multiplied by the total number of units. Efforts to recreate these exact numbers by these formulas will not produce exactly the same results in this case because two calculations of sliding scale fees are built into the formulas (not shown). One reduced fee is applied to 20 percent of units produced at each level and a second fee is applied to another 20 percent. Note that in column 7, this approach does not yield an exact break-even point but rather a range of surpluses or deficits within which breaking even occurs.

HUMAN CAPITAL AND THE SYNCRETIC APPROACH

The inclusion of financial capital in a syncretic approach to financial management is simple; straightforward; and, one might even suggest, self-evident. The inclusion of human capital is considerably less so, although the work of Mook and her colleagues (Mook, 2013; Mook et al., 2007) offers a range of interesting approaches. Even so, readers of a more practical bent may be wondering why there is an emphasis in this volume on human capital. The first and most immediate answer—as in the case of the social accounting chapter—is that it provides a convenient linguistic shorthand for beginning to connect traditional social work concern with the knowledge, skills, and values resources of practice to the dollars and cents perspectives of financial management. This has the potential to be a much stronger and deeper connection than it currently is. A second important reason is that progress in outcome and quality measurement may be approaching the natural limits of the kind of common sense ad hoc approach that has been dominant for the past 40 years. In the future, answers to questions of outcome and quality may be fruitfully pursued using social and economic theory in more systematic ways. Of all of the conceptual and theoretical perspectives currently available, human capital and associated ideas of social, cultural, political, and even spiritual capital possess the greatest potential for forging closer linkages with meaning in the financial management context.

The concept of human capital as it is used here is the most general of the forms of nonfinancial capital to be discussed in this chapter. It can be seen to consist of three dimensions: *cognitive capital* (attitudes, values, competencies, experience, skills, tacit knowledge, innovativeness, and talents, together with the capacity to learn), *structural capital* (the valuable insights embedded in the organizational culture, policies, and established practices and competencies of the enterprise), and *relational capital* (the networks of formal and informal relations with staff, clients, and other stakeholders insofar as these have resource-generating capabilities) (Wimpfheimer, 2004). Relational capital is sometimes mistakenly called social capital, although that idea has broader connotations that also include important dimensions of cognitive and structural capital. Human capital is general in focus in that a number of other terms used for nonmonetized capital are treated here as types of human capital. These include social capital, political capital, cultural capital, symbolic capital, and spiritual capital. Human capital, in this sense, is also highly specific as it is used here. We are not, in general, concerned with these various forms of human capital as they occur in society, culture, or polity, but only as factors in the production of human services by enterprising individuals, groups, and communities. In the specific context of human services organization and delivery by social workers, we may also define human capital as the knowledge, skills, and values possessed by the social workers who make up the HSE to the extent that they serve as resources for the production of human services.

Social Capital

Although the term originated with L. J. Hanifan, whose book *The Rural School Community Center,* originally published in 1916, included an entire chapter on the subject (Putnam, 2000, p. 19), modern usage of the term "social capital" can be traced to Robert Putnam's (2000) book *Bowling Alone: The Collapse and Revival of American Community.* Also important in the history of social capital but far less known to the general reader is the work of Jane Jacobs, the urban reformer whose ideas about urban scale, streets, and other notions have important cognitive, structural, and relational dimensions (Jacobs, 1985, 2002, 2004). The sociologist James Coleman (1988) articulated the key insight that made the concept of social capital relevant to financial management more than a decade earlier. Social capital, Coleman argued, offers a way to reconcile key theoretical dimensions of sociology and economics. Coleman's insight (like David M. Austin's political economy writings in social work) is key to the contribution of human capital to financial management. One important set of pathways for this are the social accounting perspectives pioneered by Laurie Mook and her associates (especially Mook, Sousa, Elgie, & Quarter, 2005). The general thrust of all of this work is clear: It provides an antidote to the extreme individualism of the vast body of economic approaches to rational action. This is where the real value of social capital is to be found for financial management in human services. It is not at all certain, for example, that progress in developing measures of outputs, outcomes, service quality, and community impacts will progress any further and faster in the near-term future than the minimal accomplishments and glacial pace of the past 50 years. However, if it does, it will most likely be because of closer and more systematic links to concepts of human capital.

In Coleman's (1988) reckoning, social capital is a nonmonetized resource for action to be found in the obligations, expectations, information channels, and social norms of individual and collective social actors (for example, groups, organizations, and communities), with important implications for monetized resources. A great many analyses of social capital followed Putnam (2000) in zeroing in on trust as a key source of obligations, expectations, and norms; networks as informal information channels; and the distinction between bridging and bonding social capital. Bridging capital fosters the building of new relationships between individuals, groups, and communities, whereas bonding capital addresses the reinforcement and strengthening of social relationships. Other discussions have also connected the idea of social capital to Granovetter's (1973) distinction of "thick" and "thin" social ties and Clifford Geertz's identification of culture with "thick" description (J. C. Alexander, Smith, Norton, & Brooks, 2011, p. 14; see also Granovetter, 2005). The long-term question for financial management in human services is whether any of these interesting notions or ideas derived from them can be monetized. Can they be transformed into measures of performance? Do they lend themselves to ratio measurement? Do they suggest new ways of looking at or defining service outcomes?

Perhaps the oldest form of attempting to consider social capital as a monetized resource is through what accountants have traditionally called "goodwill." Closely related to this might be economists' attempts to measure such things as the "warm glow" associated with acts of philanthropy and to determine the extent of "crowding out" of one set of resources, notably individual donations, by others, especially foundation grants and government grants and contracts (Andreoni, 1990, 1993). Economists have long been concerned with the ideologically loaded question of whether the provision of human services by government crowds out (that is, discourages or eliminates) charitable contributions and private philanthropy. Close study of ideas like these in a context such as that of social accounting might yield new and additional measures for monetizing outcomes (as goodwill), impacts (as warm glow), or the scarcity of resources (due to crowding out). At this point, however, those are all highly speculative, researchable ideas whose effect on financial management practice is still far in the future.

Cultural Capital

For management purposes, the concept of structural capital has often been tied closely to the internal structure of organizations, to organizational culture. Meanwhile, for at least 50 years, social workers have understood the importance of looking outside. The concept of cultural capital as a form of structural capital offers a means to bridge the connections between inside and outside. The term "cultural capital" was first introduced by Bourdieu and Passeron (1990) to explain how observed differences in children's lives promote social mobility, over and beyond economic resources. It generally refers to education levels, intelligence, language skills, speech styles (for example, quoting poetry or statistics), manner of dress, "coolness," and a wealth of other such matters, in some cases including occupation or residency. Thus, a social worker trained and certified in the very latest therapeutic techniques may have a measure of cultural capital with certain client groups (for example, those who value expertise), whereas another who is less well trained may have an equal measure of cultural capital with other groups (for example, adolescents) solely based on her style of dress or mastery of the vernacular language of the neighborhood. Connections such as these have major potential for the development of more meaningful measures of service output, outcomes, and measures of quality. Moreover, the Bourdieu–Passeron research and work on cultural capital since then articulate ideas that fit well with other research on children and culture, which opens vast horizons for future connections to the immediate concerns of financial management.

Intellectual Capital

Eric Kong (2007) interpreted Stewart (1997) as defining intellectual capital in organizational terms as the resources for wealth creation (a fine nonprofit idea!). Kong cited Edvinsson and Malone's (1997) definition of intellectual capital as "the possession of knowledge, applied experience, organizational relationships, customer relations, and professional skills that provide . . . a competitive edge in the market" (p. 44). In the contemporary context of communities of HSE that are often in competition with one another for scarce resources, the relevance of what Edvinsson and Malone have stated can be rendered clearer simply by dropping (or reinterpreting) the last three words "in the market" and changing the word "customers" to "clients." Intellectual capital, in this sense, overlaps substantially with social capital (relationships and relations) and with cultural capital (knowledge, experience, and skills). If there have ever been efforts to measure in financial (social accounting) terms the knowledge, applied experience, organizational relationships, client relations, and professional skills of specific human services, those efforts are not evident in the published literature. Do more knowing workers with more and wider experience, better networks, and higher levels of professional skill provide better, more effective services and do so more efficiently? The honest answer is we simply do not know at this point. Until we begin to ask such questions more pointedly and effectively, measuring the purported efficiency and effectiveness of services will have important elements of fiction and mystery attached to them, and measurements of the cost of services will remain largely unanchored.

Political Capital

The idea of political capital as a metaphor for levels of political support has been around for a long time, and there is an enormous published literature spanning several disciplines on the subject. Even so, the prospect of turning it into anything like a monetized variable useful in the financial management of HSEs remain quite limited, in part because of the nature of the concept itself. If an enterprise has the kind of political advantage connoted by the idea of political capital, just about the last thing in the world one would want to do is advertise the fact by transforming it into a public indicator. Even so, the strategies of building, saving, and spending political capital are useful ways of approaching certain questions in financial management. Issues of relationships with donors, constituencies, grant makers, and other stakeholders are readily approached from a political capital standpoint. Even if you cannot count your political capital, it can be useful to know when it is there and when it is not.

Symbolic Capital

Another interesting dimension of human capital is the idea of symbolic capital. Studies of symbolic capital have tended to be conducted predominantly in anthropology (and some parts of sociology) and to focus on matters of prestige, honor, and recognition. The connection to issues in social work and human services is often a negative or inverse one, as human services clients often don't receive enough of that. Thus, for example, the awarding of (or receiving) an honor or recognition can be seen to be a grant of a certain measure of symbolic capital. Attention to branding in nonprofit management represents one attempt to capitalize on symbolic capital (Laidler-Kylander, Quelch, & Simonin, 2007). Institutions, cities, buildings, and neighborhoods can all be vested with symbolic capital. Think, for example, of what symbolic values are conjured up by New York City, Hollywood, Silicon Valley, or Nashville.

Perhaps the most important expressions of symbolic capital in financial management are those associated with the fiduciary duties and related ethical and legal constraints discussed in chapter 1. Periodically, national-level controversies arise when human services such as the American Red Cross, United Way, or other iconic HSEs are criticized for their activities, and huge amounts of the symbolic capital of these enterprises are consumed in the unfolding events (see, for example, J. S. Glaser, 1994). Social capital concerns in this area also arise around issues of trust. The notion of symbolic capital intersects with notions of intellectual capital in the area of knowledge for practice and with the related notion of spiritual capital. Some in social work will even find sustenance in assorted proposals for spiritual capital (Finke, 2003; Zohar & Marshall, 2004). It remains to be seen whether positive connections important for financial management can be drawn from notions of prestige, honor, and recognition to the central concerns of financial management with accounting, budgeting, and financial analysis.

Summary

The notion of the various forms of capital has been an exceeding popular one in the noneconomic social sciences, as observed by the number of adjectives that the term has acquired. It is quite easy from the vantage point of a "hard-nosed" and monetized financial management perspective to reject all of these approaches. The conceptual and theoretical perspectives of human capital and those in the forms of social, cultural, political, intellectual, and even spiritual capital possess great potential for forging closer linkages with meaning in the financial management context. However, as long as we continue to pursue the idea that humanistic social work practice takes place in one isolated arena and hard, cold financial realities (which are just as human) are hashed out in another, there is no likelihood that this potential will ever be realized, except perhaps by accident. To reject this nexus outright, however, would be to overlook potentially useful ways of viewing the problems and issues of financial management. In many cases, the "soft and squishy" humanist issues of relationships, power, networking, prestige, and the like may come across as more practical, commonsense, and businesslike when posed in the language of these various forms of capital. Such forms of human capital may serve to introduce new possibilities for solving some of the unresolved questions of service outcomes, impacts, and quality. Furthermore, they may help resolve some of the issues of operating capacity raised in the next section.

OPERATION CAPACITY ANALYSIS

Among the newest analytical techniques available to those managing the finances of HSEs is operating capacity analysis (OCA), an idea directly in tune with the syncretic model introduced in this chapter. OCA is concerned with better understanding in quantitative terms the ratio between actual output and output capacity. In the OCA approach, capacity utilization is defined as the extent to which the HSE actually uses the available installed capacity that it has. As an example, a nationally certified family therapist who primarily does intake eligibility determinations for an HSE might be a case of underutilizing a valuable (and possibly very expensive) resource. In general, this notion of identifying and (where possible) measuring organizational capacity fits in well with three of the ideas. The first is the long-standing concern with efficiency, an issue that dates back to the late 19th century days of the charity organization societies, when one of the major concerns was more efficient organization of the delivery of services. The second is Robin Chase's (2015) comments about the discovery of underutilization of resources. The third is the central focus in the commons literature on the "tragedy of the commons," the problem of overharvesting and overutilization of resources. For example, the focus on burnout in the social work literature can, from an OCA perspective, be seen revealing as an issue of overutilization, an attempt to do too much with too few resources. A good bit of the OCA discussion has been carried on in macroeconomic circles, whereas much of the management-level discussion of measuring the unused capacity of particular organizations involves a mix of rather esoteric quantitative economic and engineering techniques in manufacturing.

These considerations, however, should not obscure the reality that "waste and abuse" have been powerful political weapons used against some HSAs and social workers over a long period. OCA—whether quantitative or qualitative—offers a straightforward way to begin to think about and address those issues. It would be a relatively simple and direct matter, for example, to construct a survey questionnaire to periodically allow stakeholders to identify issues of underutilization (waste) of existing resources—both financial and human.

Waste may be defined for purposes of financial management in the HSE simply as unutilized capacity. Setting aside the political problems of wasted monetary resources and the multiple judgment calls they entail, this discussion concentrates only on the human capital aspects of the matter. One of the most interesting attempts to deal with this problem was the development of a capacity audit to quantify key inpatient delays in an acute care tertiary hospital setting in Australia (Zeitz & Tucker, 2010). The general idea of a capacity audit represents a solid insight and could, without too much difficulty, be translated to the HSE context in the United States. Several developments along these lines are underway.

The Marguerite Casey Foundation has developed the Organizational Capacity Assessment Tool that offers clues to what kinds of concerns are actually involved in OCA. It was adapted from an earlier instrument known as the McKinsey Capacity Assessment Grid (McKinsey & Company, n.d.). The grid examines four dimensions: (a) leadership capacity, (b) adaptive capacity, (c) management capacity, and (d) operational capacity. In the Casey Foundation approach, *leadership capacity* is defined as the ability of leaders to inspire, prioritize, make decisions, provide direction, and innovate. *Adaptive capacity* is the ability of the HSE to monitor, assess, and respond to changes. *Management capacity* is the ability of managers to ensure effective and efficient use of resources, and *operational capacity* is defined as the ability of the organization's operations to implement key organizational and programmatic functions (Weiss, 2005). Additional information on the basic design of the McKinsey Capacity Assessment Grid can be found online at http://www .vppartners.org/sites/default/files/reports/assessment.pdf. The McKinsey grid is organized around seven dimensions: (a) aspirations, (b) strategy, (c) organizational skills, (d) human resources, (e) systems, (f) infrastructure, (g) organizational culture, and (h) culture with numerous subcategories. Both the McKinsey grid and the Casey Foundation adaptation are structured as variants of the scorecard approach, although the McKinsey grid was clearly a first draft that includes everything but the kitchen sink, and the Casey modification offers more coherent organization, more consistent with the scorecard approach. Each of the 58 total items is assigned to one of four categories: (a) clear need for increased capacity, (b) basic capacity in place, (c) moderate level of capacity in place, and (d) high level of capacity in place.

CONCLUSION

A great deal has come together already in the quiet revolution in the financial management of human services. Nonprofit and for-profit accounting systems are fundamentally complete and compatible, and under the guidance of GASB, the public accounting regime is farther along than it has ever been. Public officials have used the guidance of GASB, the amended GPRA, and a constant stream of innovations in grant making from federal officials and other sources to transform public HSE budgeting. In the process, they have introduced major innovations in program and performance budgets, while other forms of matrix budgets and simplified line-item budgeting have emerged in a variety of contexts. Combined with the various analytical and operations management techniques discussed in previous chapters, these developments offer a rich stew of possibilities for improved financial management in the HSEs of tomorrow. Yet, the many possibilities may have already gone beyond what an HSE's management has the capacity to absorb and, while still modest (in comparison, for example, with the rate of change in information technology), the rate of innovation in this area shows no signs of slacking. After many years of relative inactivity, in the past three decades, higher education faculty and researchers in accounting, business management, public administration, social work, and other fields have begun to work on various solutions to practical and theoretical problems in this area. Yet, few have taken up the challenge of implementation and adoption of workable innovations. The proposal here for syncretic financial management systems is, in part, an effort to call attention to this important gap in the action. Even the most impressive analytical and operational systems fully integrated with accounting and budget systems will do no good if they are not used.

Appendix A

McCully's Case for a Paradigm Shift in Philanthropy

Figure AA.1: Paradigm Shift in Philanthropy

Philanthropy's Current Paradigm-Shift

OLD PARADIGM — 20TH CENTURY	NEW PARADIGM — 21ST CENTURY
Technology:	**Technology:**
• Telephone • Snail-mail • Printing on paper	• Information and communications revolution with computers and Internet • Global, universally accessible, telecommunications • All charities become visible and accessible by everyone • Multimedia, hand-held devices, social networks, crowd-fundraising • Widgets enable frictionless, instantaneous one-click grants and donations • Unlimited, low-cost, databases and spreadsheets enable "Big Data"
Economy:	**Economy:**
• National, post-World War II manufacturing, stable, steady-growth, large national corporations, local community oriented	• Global, high-technology, service economy • Rapidly expansive, innovative, generating huge new wealth • Old companies merging to take advantage of global markets • Corporations less local-community oriented
Institutions:	**Institutions:**
• Large private foundations lead and professionalize the field • Community foundations multiply • Large national corporate charities, some federated, industrialize fundraising by direct mail and telemarketing • National professional associations created for grant-makers, fundraisers, and charities, dividing philanthropic community into separate constituencies • IRS-based data conflates and confuses charities with "non-profits" — hugely inflates numbers • National Taxonomy of Exempt Entities (NTEE) sorts into smaller interest groups named idiosyncratically, not logically or systematically	• New mega-foundations, with new styles, bring new leadership • Donor-advised funds rapidly grow and multiply • Innovations abound; Internet speeds-up communications and eliminates geographic impediments, reducing need for national top-down associations and conventions, and creating new online professional networks (e.g. LinkedIn) • Decentralized virtual philanthropic communities emerge in cyberspace • Internet promotes systematization — e.g., of data systems, taxonomy of fields, searches for and direct access to all charities • Leading national donor-advised funds (NDAFs) develop virtually complete, donor-based, charities datasets, systematically taxonomized for donor education, liberating philanthropy from IRS-based conflation and confusion with "nonprofits" • NDAF donor datasets enable new depth and breadth in statistical analyses of donor behavior
People:	**People:**
• Professionalization makes philanthropy highly technical, dominated by social science-trained professionals and technical, procedural lingo	• New wealth-creators emerge as risk-taking donor-investors, and explore unconventional modes of giving and volunteering • Major donors are younger, systematic, data-driven, quantifiers. They reject the negative vocabulary, conceptualization, and rhetoric of the Old Paradigm • Want constructively to improve the human condition, more like the classical concept of philanthropy
Practices:	**Practices:**
• Industrialized mass fundraising by telemarketing and direct mail • Donors not represented by national institution. Independent Sector formed to represent everybody, but actually composed of national foundations • Grant seeking and fundraising become sales transactions, increasingly competitive and adversarial, pitting fundraisers against grant makers and donors	• Promoting increased giving and philanthropy itself • Donor education; venture philanthropy; giving circles; e-philanthropy • Social network systems; collaborations in and among constituencies and sectors • Professional community broadens to include philanthropic advisors, scholars, and media
Culture:	**Culture:**
• Social scientific; social engineering, purporting to attack roots of problems; vocabulary is technical • The word and concept of "philanthropy" falls into disuse	• Humanistic and social-scientific self-development for both donors and beneficiaries; social scientific tools for explicitly humanistic ends • Use of the word and concept of "philanthropy" is revived • Classical humanistic culture of philanthropy seen as quintessentially American — informed building Colonial society, the Revolution, the Constitution, anti-slavery, and women's suffrage movements
Rhetoric:	**Rhetoric:**
• Inadvertently negative and moralistic "Giving back", "Giving away", through "non-profits", or "tax-exempt entities" in the "third sector" to the "disadvantaged" and "needy." • Generosity = how much one gives.	• Constructive appeal; "Donor-Investors", "Making a difference," quantifiable impacts, "social change," and "charities" • Generosity = relation of giving to wealth
Results:	**Results:**
• Giving = < 2% Gross Domestic Product and Adjusted Gross Income • Only 25% of taxpayers Itemize Charitable Deductions • Less than 20% of estates over $650,000 make charitable bequests • 5% of largest charities get 80% grant dollars	• Too soon to tell — combined factors above will drive significant increase The paradigm-shift depicted above is in progress. The "New Paradigm" column is, therefore, a projection — not just of certainties, but also of what seem to be probabilities. This chart's purpose is to encourage and assist future planning.
Glossary: Philanthropy: Private initiatives for public good. Paradigm-shift: Total transformation of a mature field.	How will this historic shift affect your institution and practice? George McCully – *Catalogue for Philanthropy* - © 2015 [For more information: gmccully@cfp-ma.org]

Received from G. McCully, 2015. Reprinted with permission of the author. A version appears in "On the Unity of Philanthropy, the Humanities, and Liberal Education," *Catalogue for Philanthropy*, http://www.philanthropicdirectory.org/blog/gmccully/unity-philanthropy-humanities-and-liberal-education

Appendix B
Sample Fiscal Distress Report

Note: In this example, each set of equity balances is presented in a table that is preceded by a description of the situation and followed by a conclusion. This is followed by a general conclusion at the end.

Bobtown Family Service, Inc., is a nonprofit corporation established in 1952. It currently has a 501(c)(3) classification and receives approximately 40 percent of its income from sponsorships. The remaining 60 percent comes from ticket sales to its regular quarterly productions. At the end of the 2005 fiscal year, it had assets of $340,000 and no appreciable debt ($2,100 in outstanding accounts payable).

Bobtown Educational Collaborative, established in 2009, is also a nonprofit corporation, classified as a social welfare organization or 501(c)(4), which means that the enterprise is exempt from federal and state taxes but contributions to it cannot be deducted from the taxes of donors. The financial statements of the organization, not surprisingly, show no such donations. All income to the collaborative comes from training and educational services offered by collaborative members. The collaborative has no permanent assets and had $49,000 cash on hand at the end of the last fiscal year.

EQUITY BALANCES

The *equity balances ratio* is seen as a measure of the capacity of an organization to withstand sudden financial shocks: The lower the ratio, the lower the ability to deal with financial distress; the higher the ratio, the greater that ability. The equity balances for the two organizations profiled here, as based on information included in their respective IRS Form 990s, are presented in Table AB.1.

Although the difference in the size of these two organizations is considerable, it is apparent that even though Bobtown Family Services is considerably larger, Bobtown Educational Collaborative is in a considerably stronger position with

Table AB.1

Organization	Equity Balance
Bobtown Family Services	.031
Bobtown Service Collaborative	.570

respect to equity balances. This means that in the event of a sudden financial shock, Bobtown Family Services would be considerably more vulnerable, because it has proportionately far fewer financial resources to call upon.

INCOME CONCENTRATION

The *income concentration ratio* is a measure of the capacity of a nonprofit organization to withstand financial distress resulting from the sudden loss or drastic reduction of a single financial source.

In the current examples, from this ratio (which purposely was determined using a formula with made-up numbers from the Greenlee–Trussel ratio, so the numbers the user obtains may be quite different from these), it is evident that because both organizations are largely dependent on ticket sales, the likelihood of the loss of any one customer is fairly remote, and neither has a grant or donation large enough to represent a significant percentage of total income, both organizations are in similarly strong positions (see Table AB.2).

ADMINISTRATIVE EXPENSE RATIO

The *administrative expense ratio* is a measure of the management capacity of a nonprofit organization to respond to fiscal distress. In this case, Bobtown Family Services is an all-volunteer operation, giving it an extremely low administrative expense ratio (administrative expenses are actually less than 1 percent of total income, whereas Bobtown Educational Collaborative has a relatively high ratio of nearly 35 percent, owing largely to the fact that it is, by the nature of its mission, fully staffed with a highly professional team of educational and marketing professionals).

Table AB.2

Organization	Income Concentration
Bobtown Family Services	.0084
Bobtown Service Collaborative	.0045

Table AB.3

Organization	Administrative Expense
Bobtown Family Services	.009
Bobtown Service Collaborative	.346

There can be little doubt, in the case of this ratio, that Bobtown Educational Collaborative is in a far stronger position than Bobtown Family Services on this indicator. Although donors or grantors would undoubtedly be highly critical of the collaborative of its extremely high administrative expense ratio, and some might be foolish enough to praise the family services agency for its extremely low ratio, the conclusion seems obvious that in the event of actual fiscal distress, the team of professionals working with the collaborative are much better positioned to recognize and deal with financial problems than the volunteers for the other social agency, who would likely have to work largely with extremely limited resources.

OPERATING MARGINS RATIO

The *operating margins ratio* is a measure of flexibility and the ability to adapt to sudden changes in environment. Somewhat surprisingly, given the other indicators, these two organizations score almost identically on this indicator.

Both scores are close enough to the midpoint to make any conclusion about their flexibility and adaptability very difficult to support. Because the scores are not very high, we cannot conclude that either organization would be well positioned for a flexible response to sudden changes in its funding, but they also are not low enough that we can conclude that there is little likelihood that they could cope.

CONCLUSION

Comparison of these two organizations on the four indicators suggests a somewhat mixed picture. Despite its smaller size, Bobtown Educational Collaborative currently has a considerably stronger equity balance and a far stronger administrative expense ratio. Both organizations are well positioned relative to other nonprofits

Table AB.4

Organization	Operating Margins
Bobtown Family Services	.56
Bobtown Service Collaborative	.57

with respect to the diversification of their funding sources. Neither is likely to be at great risk from the loss of a single funding source. In addition, they are very similarly matched with respect to operating margins, although it is difficult to draw any significant conclusions about either. On the basis of these ratios, it seems clear that Bobtown Educational Collaborative has a strong advantage over Bobtown Family Services on two of these four indicators, suggesting that it would be more able to cope with fiscal distress in those areas.

Appendix C
Outline for Business Plan

1. Mission, Objectives, and Vision
   a. What is the mission of the HSE?
   b. What are the main goals and objectives?
   c. What is the guiding vision of the HSE?

2. HSE History
   a. When was the HSE founded?
   b. What are other points about its history relevant to understanding its present position?

3. Office Locations and Facilities
   a. Where are the offices located?
   b. Characterize the facilities (Owned? Rented? Special features?).

4. Services
   a. Characterize the range of services offered.
   b. What are the principal outcomes of those services?

5. Environmental Analysis
   a. Describe or characterize the client population(s) served.
   b. Describe any competitive advantages of HSE staff in skills and training.
   c. Describe the community needs.
   d. Describe the community trends.
   e. List the suppliers, institutional consumers, and competitors.

6. Strategy and Implementation
   a. Describe the HSE's strategic position(s), as well as their relative advantages and disadvantages.
   b. Describe the strengths and weaknesses of the HSE's strategy and implementation plans.

    c. Describe the marketing approach.

    d. What strategic alliances have been formed?

7. Management Summary
    a. Describe the organization and governance structures.
    b. Describe the management and leadership.
    c. Describe the human capital plan.

8. Financial Plan
    a. What are the sources of income?
    b. What are the financial "soft spots"?
    c. Provide a break-even analysis.
    d. Provide a cash flow plan.
    e. What are the financial ratios?

Glossary

account A term with a dual meaning for managing finances in human services. In a psychosocial sense, it is the narrative or story of a related set of events or activities offered by a particular person or from a particular point of view. In accounting, it is a set of related records recording or summarizing a particular set or type of monetized financial transactions

accountability In the financial context, specifically being accountable for what is done with resources. This is usually a matter of tracking income and detailing and explaining expenditures.

accounting Systematic capture, recording, summary, reporting, and analysis of financial activity.

accounting cycle The regular, periodic accounting events and activities occurring between the opening of a fiscal year and the activities associated with closing.

accounts payable A set of related accounting records detailing monetized amounts and sums owed by the entity to others. A liability.

accounts receivable A set of related accounts detailing monetized amounts and sums owed to the entity and expected to be received at some point in the future. An asset.

accrual basis The current standard for all forms of human services accounting. Financial transactions are recorded as they occur, which creates a distinction between expenses and disbursements, the problem of cash flow, and the category of liabilities known as "accounts payable."

administrative cost A standard category of total or full cost summarizing the costs incurred for the overall direction of the enterprise, general record keeping, general management, accounting, budgeting, financial analysis, and related costs.

administrative ethics The decisions and choices made by administrators, managers, and supervisors viewed from a moral perspective.

age of grants   The historical period (beginning in approximately 1963) when the U.S. government began awarding categorical or program grants for human services.

agency   A term with related dual meanings. In principal-agent theory (a part of rational choice theory in economics, sociology, philosophy, and management), it refers to the power or capacity of acting. It is particularly interesting in action representing someone else. (For example, "She is our agent in these negotiations.") In ordinary social work practice, the term most often refers to a group or organization delivering human services. In financial management, the term "enterprise" is also used in that latter sense.

AICPA   The American Institute of Certified Public Accountants, the official accrediting body for certifying CPAs in the United States.

all-funds budget   Financial document summarizing the full or complete budget for a human services organization or entity.

allocation   Financial planning process designating or assigning anticipated expenses or costs to one or more cost centers.

annual reports   Periodic reports issued once every 52 weeks, 12 months, four quarters, or 365 days, sometimes in conjunction with a designated annual meeting, conference, or celebration. Annual reports may consist solely of a set of financial statements or also include descriptive or narrative information on programs and services.

appreciation   The increase in value of an asset over time.

appropriation   The allocation of income to specific purposes by a congressional or legislative body.

ask   A widely used term in fundraising for a strategic occasion or event at which a major donor is asked for a particularly large gift; the term may also refer to the gift request itself (for example, "We invited the donor to lunch at the country club for the ask. . . . Our ask was for $2 million").

asset   Anything of monetary value owned by an agency, organization, or entity. One of the five basic accounting categories for summarizing or categorizing accounts.

audit   A periodic (usually annual) investigation of the financial statements of an HSE to determine their accuracy and fidelity with law and policy.

audit exception   An item identified in an audit report as an exception to the general opinion stated by the auditor. This is usually a technical problem, but it may also be evidence of a violation of the generally accepted accounting principles (GAAPs), malfeasance, or illegal activity.

audit report   A signed, written report by a qualified accountant indicating the completion of examination of a set of financial records and a statement of whether or not they conform to GAAPs and whether the financial statements attached are accurate.

auditor   Someone who conducts an audit. Certified financial audits in the United States are conducted by CPAs using GAAPs. In Great Britain, Canada, and other Commonwealth countries, certified audits based on GAAPs are conducted by chartered public accountants (also CPAs).

balance   In general, the numerical value of an account or set of accounts after appropriate additions and subtractions. In budgeting, the preferred or desired condition when anticipated income and anticipated expenditures are exactly equal.

balance sheet   A universally recognized accounting report in which the state of the entire financial entity at a particular moment in time is summarized by listing total assets (A), total liabilities (L), and net income (N) according to the formula $N = A - L$.

balanced budget   A budget in which total anticipated income equals total expected expenses.

balanced scorecard   A social accounting (scorecard) approach to evaluation and accountability attributed to Robert S. Kaplan and David P. Norton.

base   A fundamental concept of budget theory. The theoretical beginning point of budget analysis and calculation summarizing both the amount of last year's budget and the figure to which the enterprise presumably has some implicit moral claim (or entitlement) and the amount necessary to continue operations at the current level.

base budget   Any budget used as a starting point or a baseline for further development. A reference.

basic accounts   The fundamental categories of a system of financial accounts. There are five basic accounts or accounting categories: assets, liabilities, net income, income, and expenses.

billing   Issuing or sending out bills or invoices for amounts due for services delivered. A key step in processing accounts receivable.

block grant   A creation of fiscal federalism characterized by the lumping of a variety of legislative objectives and programs and devolution of discretionary authority from federal administrative agencies to the states.

board of directors   The governing group of an entity, especially a corporation. In the case of a 501(c)(3) nonprofit corporation, the nominal owners of the assets who are prohibited by law from receiving surpluses.

bonding capital   Forms of social capital for maintaining and strengthening the ties between members and participants within groups.

bookkeeping   The task of actually making entries in the financial records (or "books") to record transactions.

break-even analysis   A planning technique and presentation format for examination of the relationships between income, expenditures, and service levels.

break-even point   The monetized value at which budget assumptions regarding income, expenses, and service levels are consistent with one another.

breaking even   The condition or circumstance where income equal expenditures; also widely known as "balancing the budget."

bridging capital   Forms of social capital for maintaining and strengthening the ties between groups, organizations, and other social structures. For example, federated financing requires high levels of bridging capital.

budget   A financial plan detailing planned expenditures and usually also anticipated income in the form of a table. By convention, budgets are usually shown as balanced, meaning that total income equals total expenditures.

budget analysis   Process of scrutinizing items in a budget and drawing conclusions about their implications for the HSE.

budget categories   The highest-level categories in an accounting typology, or chart of accounts. Under GAAPs, these are assets, liabilities, net income, income, and expenses.

budget cycle   A sequence of events incorporating such activities as a request, publication, or circulation of criteria or guidelines, deadlines, formal presentations, and acceptance or approval decisions.

budget entity   The financial or economic unit for which a budget is prepared or that a budget describes. May be an enterprise, department, program, or some other unity.

budget format   A standardized form or template used as the normal or expected format within a particular budget system. Examples include the budget formats used by United Way of America and the U.S. government grants systems.

budget increment   The increase (increment) or decrease (decrement) marking the difference between the current and the previous budgets.

budget system   An integrated arrangement of rules, policies, organizations, and procedures governing how budgets are to be formulated, approved, revised, and evaluated.

budgeting   The financial activity concerned with preparing a detailed plan for the future obtaining of income and expenses in a manner designed to coordinate efforts, maximize efficient use of resources, and attain desired goals.

business concept   A key feature of a business plan; the "big idea" of the enterprise or service (for example, to provide shelter for abused and neglected children or to provide lodging for people who are homeless).

business plan   A planning document prepared in any of a number of standard formats and addressing a range of important business decisions or issues.

capital   Goods functioning as the means of production. Types of capital most commonly used in human services include financial (monetized) capital and human capital (for example, the skills, abilities, and knowledge of people, including social capital).

capital budget   A monetized plan detailing future capital expenditures and capital improvements.

capital expenditures   Monetized outlays for the purchase of durable goods, including real estate, equipment, and supplies expected to be long-lasting.

capital improvement   An improvement of a durable, long-standing, or permanent nature (for example, a new or renovated building).

capitalization   A term sometimes used loosely in human services settings for any process of acquiring assets to begin an enterprise or program. (See also "seed money" and "upfront money.")

capitation   An approach to budgeting and contracting used in some managed care systems and intended to design, establish, or encourage incentives for efficient, effective, and high-quality service delivery. Service providers are paid a capitation (or per head) payment according to a predetermined standard and can expect to experience surpluses or losses depending on their performance in delivering the capitated service.

case statement   A text or statement used in fundraising to describe or characterize the objectives or purposes of a fundraising campaign (or case).

cash basis   An approach to accounting in which transactions are entered in financial records only when cash is paid out or taken in.

cash flow   The movement of cash into and out of accounts associated with any center.

cash flow analysis   Examination or investigation of the amounts and patterns of cash moving into and out of a defined center, whether an enterprise, program, or other unit of analysis.

cash flow management   Coordination and direction of activities governing the flow of cash into and out of an entity (enterprise, department, or program).

categorical grant   A grant or transfer payment of federal money to a state or local government or nonprofit organization for a specific, narrowly defined program, goal, or purpose within a Congressionally defined range (or category) of activity.

center   A focal point, or *magnet* (objective, purpose, or activity), around which a group of related expenditures, costs, or transactions are or can be associated for purposes of analysis.

chart of accounts   A listing, table, or chart detailing, for reference purposes, the standard categories in which accounting data are captured, recorded, summarized, and reported.

chief executive officer (CEO)   Management terminology for the principal administrative or managerial person to whom all other employees of an entity report and who, in turn, reports to the governing board.

chief financial officer (CFO)   May also be known as the treasurer, chief accountant, comptroller, or by some other title. In smaller entities with no CFO, these duties may be divided among a treasurer (board member) and accountant (staff member).

chief information officer (CIO)   A position that emerged with the information revolution. The official with overall responsibility for computers, networking, and information technology.

chief operating officer (COO)   A position not found in all organizations. Generally, the highest-ranking official in an organization with overall responsibility for staff and supportive activities.

chief program officer (CPO)   The ranking official in an organization with overall responsibility for programs and services. In hospitals and medical settings, the CPO is usually known as the *chief of staff*. There is no comparable general term in social work or human services.

client   From an HSE financial perspective, a beneficiary, person, or organization receiving benefits.

client group   The set of actual clients served by an HSE.

client population   The client group plus the set of potential clients in the community who share the same characteristics or traits.

closing process   The ending phase of the annual (or other periodic) accounting process in which a variety of accounting procedures for "closing the books" are performed and final annual financial statements are prepared.

collection   The gathering and acceptance of gifts and donations. In religious organizations, collection and offerings are often performed in rituals that include giving thanks. In contemporary human services, collection of gifts and donations—when it occurs at all—is typically treated as a business practice.

commons   Pooled or shared resources, together with the association collectively controlling and managing them.

community accountability   The aspect of general accountability most concerned with the legitimacy and community impact of an HSE and its programs.

Community Chest   The national predecessor of United Way.

community effort   An indicator, especially a financial measure, of the effort that a city, neighborhood, or other community has invested in dealing with a particular problem

community organization   Associations, organizations, and groups whose actions define and enact a community through its norms, values, and especially practices.

confidentiality, client   An ethical standard detailing the circumstances and types of personal and private information about clients to be closely held by workers. Confidential information is not to be disclosed unless legally required or with a client's explicit permission.

contingency analysis   Investigations or planning to anticipate contingencies and prepare for them.

contingency fund   A pool of money or goods available for use only in the event of some unanticipated or unexpected development. Also known as *emergency funds* and *rainy day funds*).

contingency table   A 2×2 table used in descriptive statistics and hypothesis development to compare and contrast four alternatives (upper left, upper right, lower left, and lower right) on two dimensions (vertical and horizontal axes).

contract   Legally binding agreement between two or more parties. Implicit or explicit employment contracts govern or spell out terms for many jobs in HSEs. Purchase of service contracts are a major form—perhaps the major form—of public funding in contemporary human services.

contract management   The events and activities associated with negotiation, operation, and evaluation of one or more contracts.

cooperative   A type of enterprise characterized by cooperation and in which members share in the profits.

corporate solicitation   Fundraising efforts directed to corporations.

corporation   A legal individual composed of a collectivity (at minimum a board of directors or trustees) with legal standing to control assets; sue and be sued; and, most recently, under a controversial U.S. Supreme Court ruling, exercise First Amendment rights.

cost   The particular outlays or expenditures associated with some defined object, goal, or center.

cost accounting   Any system of accounting (originally developed for manufacturing) designed to assign income or expenditures or both directly to cost objects within the accounting system.

cost analysis   Information gathering and investigation to determine the cost of some cost object or cost center. Cost analysis is ordinarily supplemental to the accounting system, which provides raw data to be assigned to cost objects directly or indirectly.

cost–benefit analysis   A sophisticated form of economic ratio analysis in which costs are compared to monetized benefits and the result expressed as a decimal fraction.

cost center   A defined or prescribed object or unit to which costs can be assigned, particularly one associated with an organizational or program unit.

cost-effectiveness analysis   A form of economic analysis in which costs are compared with the benefits, results, effects, or impact of a program measured in quantitative but nonmonetary terms.

cost efficiency   In HSEs, an oxymoron used by people who appear to have little idea what they mean by the phrase. Cost and efficiency are usually both measures of some third object or quantity, and the relation between them is unknown or variable. Thus, saying "cost efficiency" is a little like saying "altitude color" or "time temperature."

cost elimination   An effort to reduce costs to zero. For example, with unallowable costs in a federal grant or contract, immediate cost elimination would be a high priority, unless other nonfederal funding existed to cover the unallowable costs.

cost measurement   The general purpose of cost study. Usually it involves definition of a cost object or center and identification of all the relevant expenditures associated with that object or center in order to determine its cost. This may be a one-time, periodic, or ongoing activity.

cost object   The unit of analysis in a cost study, particularly one associated with a goal, objective, or abstract principle.

cost of collecting receivables   Outlays associated with the recovery of actual income from accounts receivable. It is a financial consideration important in determining whether or not to pursue outstanding accounts receivable. As a general rule, the cost of collecting receivables (or any similar collection) should not exceed the amount collected. When it does, it is more cost effective for the enterprise to leave the amounts uncollected.

cost reduction   A more or less constant objective of modern financial management in human services. Managers are under nearly constant pressure to reduce costs.

cost reporting   The process of revealing, publicizing, or otherwise distributing information about costs.

cost study   The generic term for the set of investigative protocols that includes cost analysis, cost–benefit analysis, cost-effectiveness analysis, and other forms of cost measurement and reporting.

costing social problems   An activity of foundations, researchers, and others who attempt to express the severity or impact of a social problem in terms of its cost to society or the economy (for example, lost wages, missed productivity, or jobs lost due to the problem).

covert strategy   Unwritten, unstated, or unacknowledged strategy, usually found in highly competitive or conflictual situations where overt admission or acknowledgement of the strategy is perceived to place the HSE at a disadvantage.

credit   A term with multiple meanings. In accounting, it refers to entries made in the righthand column on a ledger page. It may also refer to a contractual agreement in which something of value is received now in exchange for agreement to repay its value in the future.

cultural capital   A type of human capital consisting of shared meanings, particularly those forms of knowledge, skills, and values that inform and give value to human services practice.

current restricted income   Also known as "current restricted funds." Donations or grants expendable only for the purposes specified by the donor or grant maker; income from investments of restricted funds, unless permitted by law to be used for general purposes; and investment income from restricted funds specifying that such income can only be used for restricted purposes.

cy pres **doctrine**   A legal doctrine that can be applied in cases where philanthropic purposes of restricted donations or gifts can no longer be honored. The Latin phrase means literally "as near as possible," and the law instructs restricted gifts that are legally found to be no longer appropriate to be reassigned by judicial ruling to purposes as close as possible to the original donor's intent.

dead hand of philanthropy   A phrase for the continuing, legally enforceable power of past donations and grants, particularly in cases where the intent of restricted donations is no longer appropriate or workable.

debit   A frequently misunderstood term; its only consistent meaning in accounting is the entries in the lefthand column on a ledger page.

debt management   That aspect of financial management concerned with the processing and handling of the debt of an HSE. It includes operations to monitor a debt (or total debts) and identify and carry out appropriate steps for repayment of the obligation.

debt management plan   A formal agreement between a borrower and creditor identifying terms for repayment.

decision   Determination (particularly of a course of action or plan) arrived at after review, analysis, or other consideration.

decision package   A bundle of coherent information supporting a decision or choice, including facts and data, possible alternatives, possible consequences, costs involved, and other considerations.

decision point   A particular event or moment in time at which a decision is, will be, or must be arrived at.

deficit   A deficiency, shortage, or negative balance. An incurred debt.

deficit financing   The support or financing of a program or activity through a deliberate course of action involving incurring debt. (Note: Simply anticipating or projecting greater expenditures than anticipated income is ordinarily not an acceptable course of deficit financing. Some provision must be made for how the debt will be managed.)

deficit spending   Modern theories of macroeconomics deal with the conditions under which the federal government can engage in deficit spending to the positive benefit of the economy (for example, counter-cyclical expenditures on the unemployed and underemployed). There are no comparable microeconomic theories justifying or explaining the conditions under which human services may undertake a program of deficit spending without a long-term plan for debt repayment.

delivery system   A system, network, or organization of service deliverers that is consistently available everywhere in the country and overseen by a national peak association, accrediting, or governing body. An example is the American Red Cross disaster services.

department   A suborganizational unit, particularly one with assigned or delegated program or functional responsibilities.

departmental budget   A financial plan for a department or subenterprise unit.

deposits   (a) Money placed in a bank or investment account and constituting a claim upon the bank. (b) The act of placing money into an account.

depreciation   A decrease in the value of an asset over time.

descriptive statistics   A branch of applied mathematics used to characterize a population by detailed examination of the characteristics of a sample drawn from that population.

direct cost   Any cost logically or intuitively associated with a cost center.

direct fundraising   A type of income generation in which a fundraiser is in direct or immediate contact with a group of potential donors (as opposed to working indirectly through a fundraising agent).

direct mail solicitation   A type of fundraising in which circulars, flyers, or other materials soliciting funds are mailed directly to potential donors.

disbursement   An outlay, obligation, or commitment of resources. The term is most often used in governmental contexts.

discretionary grant   A type of grant in which the grantor, grantee, or both may exercise considerable latitude in specifying the terms and conditions of the award.

dissolution of assets clause   A sentence or paragraph included in "articles of incorporation" of nonprofit corporations spelling out closing procedures for the distribution of remaining assets after all financial obligations are satisfied.

donation   A unilateral exchange. Donations to an HSE may be unrestricted (given without reservation or consideration), temporarily restricted (for a fixed period; for example, until the donor's death), or permanently restricted by conditions legally binding on the recipient of the donation.

donor   A person or organization making a monetary or in-kind gift to a public charity.

donor constituency   Those people or organizations with a shared interest in donations to a particular public charity.

donor relations   A task, assignment, or opportunity in a fundraising program. This refers to efforts to meet, communicate with, and report to donors on the activities of the HSE.

earmarking   A term for the process of dedicating or allocating income for specific purposes. (The term is traceable to practices in livestock sorting pens, where animals sorted into different groups or categories were marked on the ears.)

earned income   Monetary amounts or payments earned, that is, received as a result of effort expended. Examples include wages and salaries earned for services rendered; corporate earnings for output produced; and rents, interest, dividends, and other earnings on investments.

effectiveness   A much-contested term for a quality of desired outcomes that refers to the degree to which they have the desired effects. Effectiveness is logically prior to efficiency; unless some measure of effectiveness is achieved, the standard of efficiency is meaningless.

efficiency   A controversial and mostly unmeasured quality of the ratio of inputs to outputs. In some cases, decreases in cost can easily be mistaken for increases in efficiency.

employment contract   A legal agreement governing the relationship between an employer and an employee.

endowment   Generally, any set of gifts, qualities, or abilities usable as resources. In the nonprofit context, a set of gifts or resources established for a specific or dedicated purpose.

enterprise   Any undertaking or set of coordinated actions or related objectives involving risk, such as an organization established for a mission.

enterprise accounting   The standard form of accounting for all types of organizations (or enterprises) today. In enterprise accounting, the profit-making, nonprofit, or governmental organization as a whole is the basic entity.

entity   A set of related events, activities, or purposes.

evaluation   The act of establishing value.

executive   An official charged with administration or management oversight for execution or operation of a program or service.

executive director (ED)   The conventional title used for the CEO or COO of an HSE. The ED is usually also the COO reporting to the board on the state of the enterprise.

exempt entities division   The division of the IRS responsible for granting tax exemptions to qualifying nonprofit organizations; reviewing IRS Form 990s; and, increasingly, general financial oversight of the nonprofit sector.

expenditure   The process (or *throughput*) of spending. Expenditures are recorded as transactions in the financial accounts of an HSE.

expenditure control   One of a number of management control processes in which efforts are made to restrict, control, or eliminate activities that result in outlays beyond a predetermined level.

expenses   Monetized financial outlays incurred through the action of spending.

external audit   Audit by an outside auditor, that is, a qualified auditor (usually a CPA) who is not an employee or board member of an HSE.

face validity   In social science research, the determination that a variable actually measures what it appears to at first glance, or "on its face." Usually an assessment or determination not accompanied by detailed testing or elaborate procedures.

fair share of cost fees   Charges to clients based on a fair method of allocating the full cost of a program or activity to those participating in or benefiting from it.

FAS 116   Financial Accounting Standard 116 adopted by the Financial Accounting Standards Board (FASB), which details generally accepted financial accounting standards, notably the distinctions between permanently restricted, temporarily restricted, and unrestricted contributions.

FAS 117   Financial Accounting Standard 117 adopted by FASB, which details the required financial statements of nonprofit health and human services entities.

feasibility study   Assessment of the possibility or potential of completing an action successfully and the opportunity costs of a proposed action.

federal cost standards   An official set of 19 subsets of U.S. government standards defining allowable and unallowable costs under federal grants and contracts.

federal funds   A general term for monetized assets originating with the U.S. government and distributed to other organizations and firms through grants or contracts.

federated financing   A general term for fundraising operations such as those of United Way, that is, a group of related or federated member organizations voluntarily cooperate on a single fundraising campaign and agreed-upon procedures for allocation of the proceeds.

fee   Money charged to and collected from clients, significant others, or third-party payees as payment for a service.

fiduciary   A legal or ethical relationship of trust between two parties, in particular a principal and an agent.

finance   The discipline concerned with information about and knowledge of the circulation of money, the award of credit, investments, and banking. In nonprofit human services, the study of these topics as they relate to human services delivery includes special categories such as budgeting and fundraising and pays only minimal attention to investment and banking.

financial accountability   Legal and ethical obligations for the appropriate use of income to an enterprise, particularly to those from whom funding is received.

Financial Accounting Standards Board (FASB)   The official standards-setting body for all nongovernmental accounting in the United States.

financial control   Monitoring, regulating, and directing the internal flows of financial resources within an HSE, together with the rules, standards, criteria, policies, and contracts necessary to carry this out.

financial entity   A financial enterprise characterized by an accounting system, a budget system, an operating system, and perhaps a financial analysis system.

financial flow analysis   An examination or investigation of financial flows, particularly to determine problems or issues.

financial flowchart   A graphic presentation of a set of related steps in the flow of monetized resources into, through, or out of a financial entity.

financial impact analysis   An effort to track, monitor, or evaluate a financial impact.

financial intermediary   Technical term for a third-party funder.

financial management   The part of general administration or management of an HSE concerned with the accounting, budget, and financial analysis systems. This includes the control, direction, and related activities associated with generating necessary income and making expenditures to produce human services.

financial ratios   Decimal fractions constructed from financial statements and other relevant data as performance measurements of an HSE.

financial statements   After-the-fact reports of the financial position and financial activity of an enterprise. These may include both departmental budgets and departmental financial reports.

financial transaction   An event or activity resulting in a recorded entry in the accounting records of an HSE.

fiscal   Of or referring to governmental financing, especially a central government.

fiscal year   Also known as "financial year." Any 12-month or 365-day period determined by the accounting practice, known as the opening and closing of the financial records for audit, tax, and other purposes. It is probably called the "fiscal year" because "fiscal" is a government financial term and the IRS is a government agency.

fixed assets   Land, buildings, and other assets that are not ordinarily subject to sudden or dramatic changes over one or more fiscal years.

fixed budget   An assumption under which the budget of an HSE or any of its sub-budgets remains "fixed," or constant, throughout a budget period. The opposite type is a flexible budget.

flexible budget   Any budget subject to periodic revision or restatement during the course of the fiscal year.

formal organization   A network of enduring and rule-governed social relations, particularly one serving as a locale for employment, service delivery, and communications. Most human services organizations are formal organizations. In the model laid out in this book, a formal organization is analytically distinct from both a *corporation*, a legal persona with rights and responsibilities, and an *enterprise*, an organization of assets and associated liabilities, income, and expenses.

foundation   Nonprofit organization established by founders' gifts to operate programs or to make grants to other nonprofits for charitable and philanthropic purposes. Dwight MacDonald once defined the Ford Foundation as "a large body of money completely surrounded by the people who want some."

fourth sector   The set of social enterprises, or social businesses, including limited profit (Type B) corporations and an uncertain number of similar enterprises and activities.

free goods   Outputs that are available without charge or cost. Availability of a free good means that someone else is absorbing the cost of production. Human services offered without charge to the client are a form of free goods in which costs are absorbed by various third parties, either on a wide-spectrum basis, such as a grant, or case by case, as in unit-based contracts.

free riding   An economic phenomenon in which consumers use or consume a good without payment or charge (for example, riding on a bus or train or sneaking into an event without buying a ticket).

fringe benefit analysis   Examination of the benefit packages paid to employees. A clear understanding of which of these benefits are taxable and which are not is necessary.

fringe benefits   Benefits or rewards of employment in addition to wages and salaries, particularly those that are tied to the latter and reported on paycheck stubs, such as health insurance and retirement benefits.

front money   Liquid assets advanced ("fronted") to advance the development or implementation of a program or project.

full disclosure   A principle of financial accounting mandating that financial statements reveal or disclose all information important and necessary to an accurate understanding of the financial activities and position of the enterprise.

functional basis   Classification (of employees, expenditures, budget items, or anything else) based on the function performed for or within the HSE.

functional budget   A budget outlining proposed expenditures for a particular function or activity within an enterprise (for example, marketing, fundraising, or service delivery).

fund   An asset or group of assets designated for a specific purpose for which separate or distinct accountability is maintained. Within enterprise accounting, a way to account for restricted or currently restricted gifts.

fund accounting   A form of financial record keeping and reporting once widely used in nonprofit and government organizations. In fund accounting, the fund is the principle financial entity around which record keeping and reporting are organized. Fund accounting has been replaced by enterprise accounting.

fund balance   An anachronistic term in nonprofit accounting formerly used to describe total assets less total liabilities. The preferred term in contemporary accounting is "net income."

fund budget   A subenterprise budget developed to guide decisions about the handling of a fund. Because the source of funds (for example, a restricted gift) may be known, a fund budget may ordinarily consist only of expenses.

fundraising   The process or project of generating income, especially through an organized program for the solicitation of contributions or donations.

fundraising agent   A third party charged with responsibility for fundraising by the management of an HSE.

grant   A unilateral (one-way) voluntary transfer awarded on the basis of a usually detailed application. Two general types of grants are found in human services: categorical and discretionary grants.

grant maker, grantor   A person, group, or organization that receives and reviews proposals and awards grants of money.

grantee   The recipient of a grant award.

grants management   A component of financial management concerned with the pursuit of grants and the necessary administration that follows.

grant seeking   The pursuit of grants, particularly as a job assignment or career path.

grantsperson   Someone who writes grants or pursues grant funding.

group practice   A form of enterprise in which two or more practitioners organize into a single entity (usually a partnership). In human services, this refers to an HSE partnership formed by a group of two or more practitioners.

guidelines   Administrative rules governing or specifying the conditions governing an action, for example, the terms of grant applications or awards.

human capital   The knowledge, skills, and values of workers, volunteers, and clients, together with their social, cultural, and political capital, to the extent that these serve as resources for the delivery of human services.

human services   Any of a range of services delivered by professional social workers, particularly services designed to contribute to the socialization and development of people; provide social care for those incapable of full autonomy; offer counseling and guidance; and provide support for self-help and mutual aid activities, together with the planning, organizing, managing, financing, evaluation, and marketing of such efforts.

human services enterprise (HSE)   A set of organized financial arrangements, including solo and group practices, partnerships, or corporations, organized to facilitate the delivery of human services.

human services organization (HSO)   A set of formalized or routinized interpersonal relationships and communications associated to facilitate the delivery of human services.

in-kind donation   A gift of something of monetary value other than cash (for example, a painting, clothing, or an automobile).

income   The types and sums of all forms of financial inflows. In human services settings, the term is often used interchangeably with "revenue" and "funding."

income, net   In nonprofit enterprise accounting, the difference between assets and liabilities; an amount available for future use but not for distribution as profit.

income model   A general plan or schema outlining a program for where (and how) income will be received. Part of a strategic plan.

income sharing   Forms of financial realignment in which simplicity and improved accountability are introduced by eliminating a range of programs and consolidating discretionary funding for them into a single program.

incorporation   A legal process of forming a new legal entity. A corporation (whether nonprofit, for profit, or professional) is regarded as a separate entity (or "legal personality") from those who own or control it.

incremental decision   A choice or preference representing a small adjustment or change or the minimum change necessary. Managing the finances of human services is an endless and ongoing series of incremental decisions, no one of which will by itself resolve or settle things permanently.

indirect cost   Any portion of a cost primarily assigned to a particular cost center (for example, a center designated as a support center) that can logically be assigned in a secondary analysis to the full cost or true cost of another center. (For example, administrative cost and fundraising cost are cost centers in themselves, but some portion of each may be assigned to a particular program cost to determine its full cost.)

insurance   The transfer of risk from one party to another (or to a risk pool) in exchange for a fee.

insurance principle   The pooling of risks minimizes the threat to any individual member of the risk pool. There are other principles by which insurances are implemented, including good faith, indemnification, and loss minimization.

interest   A charge or payment for the use of money.

internal audit   A postclosure examination of a set of accounts performed by an employee or board member.

internal budget   A financial plan prepared for staff or board use only.

Internal Revenue Service (IRS)   The federal agency charged with overall responsibility for tax collection in the U.S. government. Within the IRS, the exempt entities division has particular responsibility for 501(c)(3) and 501(c)(4) nonprofit organizations and the IRS Form 990 filings.

internal subsidy   The intentional or planned redistribution within an organization from a surplus center to one or more cost centers.

inventory   Stocks of material on hand and available for use, sale, or donation. The monetary value of inventory is an asset. One of the financial characteristics of human services is that they cannot be inventoried.

inventory analysis   A set of techniques to determine the quantity, condition, quality, and monetary value of an inventory.

inventory control   Rules and procedures designed to enhance management control over an inventory.

investment   (a) A sacrifice of use of resources in the present in anticipation of a future benefit, gain, or return. (b) An expenditure made in anticipation of a benefit, gain, or return.

journal   Traditionally, one of two principal kinds of books used in accounting. Journals are defined as books of original entry, which are summarized in ledgers.

knowledge commons   Forms of shared knowledge used as resources. Examples include a library and practice wisdom shared by a group of practitioners.

land grant   A gift of natural resources properties. For example, the 1862 and 1890 Morrill Acts granted tracts of land to the states to support the establishment of various institutions of higher learning.

ledger   A book of accounts. In the Paciolian system of double-entry bookkeeping, each account is recorded on a separate page. Each page is divided in half, with debit entries on the left and credit entries on the right.

legal authority   (a) The binding quality of law. (b) An expert on law.

liabilities   Unfulfilled or owed obligations or financial commitments ("made but not yet paid").

line item   A functional expense item from a chart of accounts. (In the United Way schema, Items 7000–9990.)

line of credit   A limited authorization for borrowing. These are sometimes used in small businesses and HSEs for temporary borrowing to ease cash flow problems.

management   Top-level guidance and direction of a formal organization and enterprise (regardless of type), especially efforts to determine the policy, strategy, direction, and preferred outcomes of an enterprise or its programs.

management by exception   A management strategy that places heavy emphasis on management as an activity focused on dealing with problems arising from exceptions to policy.

management by objectives   A mission-oriented management strategy first laid out by Peter Drucker in which the first task or challenge of management is to define the mission, goals, and objectives of an organization. In human services, the next logical step was organizing the mission into one or more programs.

management by objectives and results   A management strategy introduced by George Morrisey that added identification of outcomes or outputs to the task of determining mission, goals, and objectives.

management decisions   Key or primary choices made by the board or top executives that determine the policy, strategy, direction, and preferred outcomes of an enterprise or programs.

management support organization   Any organization that answers questions or provides training, technical assistance, and other forms of support to an HSE or its employees. In financial management, MSOs include accounting and law firms, management consulting organizations, community foundations, grant maker associations, computer and information technology firms, investment counselors, and many others.

marginal analysis   Financial analysis, problem solving, planning, or policy making that is partial, sequential, recursive, and remedial. Includes selection of the first workable alternative, other constrained or limited considerations of alternatives, rational choice combined with persuasion, and various forms of strategic analysis.

marginal budget   A proposed form of budgeting forming part of a syncretic financial management system in which line-item budgets, program budgets, and performance budgets are developed as different but compatible output formats, using matrix budgets, contingency tables, scorecards, and other devices to link them to financial statements and one another. (See chapter 13.)

marginal cost   In economics, change in the total cost brought about by one additional unit of output.

marketing plan   The components or part of a business plan concerned with advancement of an HSE. (See Appendix C.)

matching funds   A term originating in the age of grants for a required proportion of income made available by a grantee to combine with (or match) the funding provided by a grant maker, as a sign of good faith or commitment to the grant project.

materiality   GAAPs used in auditing to assess relevance and reliability of financial statements. Information is said to be material if its omission or misstatement could adversely influence decisions made on the basis of the financial statements.

matrix budget   A budget showing an array of two dimensions simultaneously (for example, line items by departments; departments by programs; line items by administrative, fundraising, and program expenses, and so forth).

mission   Top-tier statements of an enterprise, activity, or program indicating in most general terms what is sought or to be accomplished. Nonprofit organization is said, by Peter Drucker, to be mission-driven rather than profit-driven enterprise.

monetize   To express or value in terms of money. In particular, to convert a non-monetary value to a monetary one.

multifunded agency   An anachronistic term for an HSE funded by more than a single source of income. The term "enterprise" as used here is intended to include such financial organizations.

net income   The residual financial value of a nonprofit enterprise. It is the computed term in the accounting equation of Assets − Liabilities = Net Income.

net present value   The current value of the sum of a series of cash inflows and outflows occurring over a specified period of time.

nonprofit corporation   A pool of assets and the board of governors or directors controlling them, recognized in state law as a legal person and subject to legal nondistribution constraints.

nonprofit organization   Any organization associated with a nonprofit corporation displaying (a) no distribution of financial surpluses to owners, (b) voluntary participation, (c) self-governance and control, (d) formal organization, and (e) voluntary participation.

National Taxonomy of Exempt Entities (NTEE)   A classification schema of nonprofit services and programs, currently managed by the Center for Charitable Statistics and used by the IRS and others to identify and classify nonprofit organizations and corporations.

object   In cost analysis, the target, center, or focal point of the analysis.

objective   A synonym for "goals," a third-tier and more specific detailing of mission and goals, and a preliminary step in the determination of outcomes.

old year/new year   A feature of financial reports and statements characterized by two columns with consecutive years of matching information.

OMB Circular A-21   Defines cost principles for educational institutions.

OMB Circular A-87   Defines cost principles for state, local, and Indian tribal governments.

OMB Circular A-122   Defines the meaning of direct and indirect costs for grants and contracts issued by the U.S. government.

OMB Circular A-128   Deals with audits of state and local governments.

OMB Circular A-133   Refers to two documents, both dealing with audits of federal grants in state and local governments and nonprofit organizations: OMB Circular A-133 and OMB Circular A-133 Compliance Supplement, a large and detailed audit guide used in the audits of federal grantees.

operations research   Interdisciplinary forms of quantitative analysis in which optimal solutions to management problems are sought. Pert-CPM, inventory analysis, and linear programming are among the most widely known operations research techniques. The general method of operations research is systems analysis. The original design for PPBS came from operations researchers.

organization   A system of ordered interactions or social relations operating or functioning within an ecosystem. A financial organization (for example, an HSE) is a collection of assets with associated liabilities and transactions for adding to (income) and subtracting from (expenses) the organization. A social organization (for example, a group), is a network of interpersonal relationships and interactions.

outcome   A quantitative measure of the results, consequences, or impact associated with a particular set of expenses.

outlay   A form of cost analysis in which costs are measured by expenses.

output   A quantitative measure (usually of the units of service produced or a particular set of related expenses).

overt strategy   A strategy that is open, public, or written.

patron–agent model   The legal and economic ideal-typical situation in which one party (the agent) acts on behalf of the interests of another (the principal or patron). Also known as the "principal–agent theory."

payback method   An approach to capital budgeting strategy in which the net present value and the internal rate of return are not considered. Instead, decisions are made by determining the length of time required to recover the cost of (or *pay back*) a capital budget expense.

payroll   Expenditures related to wages and salaries and associated benefits.

performance budget   A budget that relates expenses to programs by defining a performance measure using a metric of unit costs (Martin, 2001, p. 85).

performance contract   A contract or purchase of service contract that specifies outputs and outcomes of service provision and ties payments, extensions, and renewals to satisfactory performance in these areas.

performance management   A management strategy introduced by Peter M. Kettner and Lawrence Martin, in which primary emphasis is placed on determinations of performance, as measured by the quantity and quality of outcomes. (See also "program budget" and "performance budget.") Kettner and Martin (1996) defined *performance management* as the collection and reporting of information about the efficiency, effectiveness, and quality of human services programs at the state, community, enterprise, or program level.

permanently restricted income   Currently restricted income for which no time limits or expiration dates exist or are recognized. Permanent restrictions on gifts can ordinarily only be lifted or changed by court order.

PERT cost   A specialized PERT approach that determines not only the sequence of events but also the cost of each step in a process.

petty cash Small amounts of cash kept on hand in an office for minor purchases. The petty cash fund is periodically replenished to a fixed amount, and available cash and receipts together always total that amount.

philanthropic tree A taxonomy of philanthropic activity developed by George McCully and originating in the Aristotelian distinctions among nature, culture, and human service.

philanthropy Private action for the common good.

planned giving A program or schedule of repeated donations made according to a donor's plan. The term usually includes regularly scheduled annual gifts, pre-scheduled credit or debit card payments, deferred giving, various types of charitable remainder trusts, donor advised and donor managed funds, and several other possibilities.

policies and procedures manual Listings and statements of rules, guidelines, and practice procedures for reference by stakeholders of an HSE.

policies and procedures review An internal audit of existing rules, guidelines, and practice procedures to determine compliance with contracts, grants, restricted fund agreements, and other relevant documents.

politics Human activity that can occur anytime two conditions are met: uncertainty and the necessity of collective choice. When these conditions occur, B. R. Barber (1988) argued, politics becomes sovereign, taking priority over and under-cutting scientific, religious, rational, and other certainties.

postaudit An adjective describing accounting-related events and activities occurring following completion of a financial audit.

postbudget conference A recommended management meeting of all those responsible for the implementation of a budget in which understandings are reached as necessary, implementation priorities are agreed to, and tasks and tactics are assigned.

posting The bookkeeping activity of recording financial transactions.

practice wisdom A special form of practical knowledge built around knowledge and special insight gained in practice and held primarily by experienced practitioners.

price A monetary amount asked for or given in exchange for transfer of ownership of a tangible good or receipt of a service.

principle of effectiveness   Human and financial capital should be used to attain the best possible results with the minimum risk, harm, or waste.

principle of efficiency   Human and financial capital should be used in ways that achieve the most from a given investment of resources within the norms of humane and just practice.

principle of enforcement   Rules, guidelines, policies, and procedures should be stated in ways that compliance can be established and conformance enforced.

principle of feedback   Rules, guidelines, policies, and procedures should be periodically reviewed and revised as necessary based on their performance.

principle of transparency   Generally speaking, open awareness contexts are preferable to closed awareness and secrecy.

principle of individuality   Rules, guidelines, policies, and procedures should be closely tailored to the circumstances to which they are intended to apply.

principle of meaning   To be effective, rules, guidelines, policies, and procedures must be intelligible to those who are expected to comply with them or carry them out.

principle of productivity   When they come into conflict, the goals of service delivery (the ends) should generally supersede the goals of fiscal control (the means).

principle of quality   Human and financial capital should be used to obtain the highest-quality results.

private grants   Large donations or monetary gifts made by corporations, foundations, or other individuals without announcement, requests for proposal, or publicity.

private practice   Any form of social work or other professional practice enterprise not organized under public (governmental) or nonprofit auspices. Private practices may be profit seeking or not, depending on the choices made by the owners.

product   An outcome or result of service delivery.

production   The application of natural resources and human and financial capital to achieve desired results.

productivity   The ratio of outputs to inputs, especially labor or nonmanagement human capital. In a broader sense, "being productive" is also a moral ideal of those not wishing to waste their efforts.

professional services   Services provided by educated, licensed, or accredited professionals within the bounds and limits of their professional mandate.

professional services budget   A subenterprise budget detailing income and expenses related to professional services offered by an HSE.

profit   The return received on a business by owners or shareholders after all operating expenses have been met. A profit is not the same as a financial surplus but rather is one of several possible uses for a surplus. Public charities in the form of 501(c)(3) nonprofit organizations are prohibited by law from distributing financial surpluses as profits.

profit motive   A primary or principal motivation or impulse directed at personal acquisition of financial gains. It is often contrasted with a service motive, or the personal desire to be of assistance to others, independent of a desire for profit.

program   A coherent combination of mission, goals, and objectives with strategy and tactics, specifying the rationale, vision, and direction for a set of related, ongoing activities and identifying the human and financial resources necessary to achieve the desired results.

program budgets   Subenterprise budgets detailing or tracking the projected or anticipated income and expenses of specific programs.

program evaluation and review technique (PERT)   A project management and scheduling approach plotting links between events and activities in a project or program. It is closely associated with the statistical technique of the critical path method (CPM).

program matrix   A categorized listing of programs and some of their features (missions, goals, objectives, outcomes, funding levels, costs, and the like) organized in matrix (rows and columns) form.

program planning   Planning where the top priority is on issues, questions, and decisions regarding programs.

project   A time-limited program or group of events and activities, usually of narrow purpose or intent. Fundraising, community organization, grant writing, and program development often operate on a project-by-project basis. A project typically has identifiable beginning and ending events (for example, a decision to start and acceptance or rejection of the completed project).

project budget   A budget detailing anticipated expenses (and sometimes also income) for a project.

proposal   Any strategically oriented planning document proposing a program of activities and/or outlining the implications for the enterprise or others of what is being proposed.

proposal writing   Narrowly, the drafting of a proposal. More generally, the strategic and technical activities associated with preparing, submitting, negotiating, and revising a proposal.

prospect research   A term used in fundraising for the process of searching for potential donors or prospects, also known as *prospecting*, particularly using the Internet or publicly available financial information.

prospects   Potential future donors.

public sector   That portion of a national economy consisting of governmental production and consumption.

purchase of service   A term of art usually signifying bulk or large-scale purchases of services by a third party, such as a government body or insurance company.

purchase of service contract   Legally binding agreement between a government or another third party (payer) and an HSE provider (or vendor) specifying at least the volume of proposed output and unit price of the service to be provided, and possibly also mandating standards of efficiency, effectiveness, and quality.

quality   An assortment of characteristics of service delivery relating to a wide variety of possible conditions, including risks, safety, security, confidentiality, timeliness, friendliness of staff, physical and environmental conditions, success rate, and many other possible considerations, such as clients' subjective assessments of the quality of service received.

quality control   A dimension of financial management concerned with the art (and what science there may be) of maintaining or assuring that services delivered are of the highest quality.

quasi-nongovernmental organization (QUANGO)   Nonprofit created and sustained by public funding. This category includes many community human services.

rationality   A much discussed principle of management decision making suggesting that decisions must be logical, consistent with the available evidence, and congruent with one another; a choice with which all truly objective observers would concur. In much HSE budgeting, a more relaxed standard often applies: A rational decision must be compelling or persuasive to those making the decision and those affected by it.

ratios   Financial indices expressed as decimal fractions, especially those constructed from two terms taken from financial statements.

reconciliation   A form of financial analysis in which bank statements and checking account records are compared (reconciled).

redistribution   A general type of nonmarket economic distribution, in which funds are (re)distributed on a basis other than supply, demand, and price. Taxes, tax exemptions and credits, social insurance, and assistance programs are all redistributive.

reporting   Also known as *performance reporting*, which is an initiative of the Government Accounting Standards Board (GASB) directed toward state and local government reporting of information on the cost, quality, quantity, and timeliness of services.

residential centers   Programs and the organizations delivering services to live-in clients who reside at or very near the site of service delivery. Types of residential centers include nursing homes, intermediate care facilities, and residential hospices.

resource allocation   The assignment of resources to particular anticipated cost objects.

resources   A safety valve term in circumstances where both financial (monetized) and nonfinancial resources are discussed. In addition to money, other important types of resources in human services include material (in-kind) donations, volunteer labor, social capital, and more.

revenue concentration   A financial ratio measuring the extent to which an HSE is dependent on any particular income source.

risk   The potential for losing something of value or the possibility of suffering financial harm or loss. This is a quality of decisions or action strategies with a broad range of possible outcomes, including negative, undesired, or harmful ones.

risk assessment   The process of identifying the potential or plausible risks of an event or activity and the possible impact of each.

risk capital   Capital invested in new ideas or projects.

rolling budget   A budget that is continually updated and amended during the budget period.

rules   Prescribed norms or guidelines for acceptable behavior or allowable results.

sacrificial giving   A religious term denoting any gift that entails a sacrifice for the giver. In monetary terms, for example, this might entail a tax deduction or credit below the market value of the gift or a nondeductible donation.

salaries   Money payments to employees in exchange for work performed. Salaries are ordinarily fixed payments for a given period (for example, a week or month).

Note that in nonprofit organizations, the IRS is sometimes concerned with "excessive compensation," particularly in executive salaries.

sampling   Short for "statistical sampling." The practice in auditing, quality control, and survey research of examining the characteristics of a *sample*, or selected subset of cases, in order to reach conclusions about the population as a whole.

satisficing   A decision strategy focusing on acceptable or satisfactory rather than optimal or ideal outcomes.

scale economy   The tendency of some costs to increase less than proportionally with increases in output, due either to dilution of fixed costs (spreading the same cost across more units), to diminishing variable costs, or to both.

scope economy   The tendency of some costs to increase more slowly than expected in proximity to specific other cost centers, that is, due to shared indirect costs.

seed money   Funds granted in the early stages of a project, usually in anticipation of attracting additional future funds. (See also "risk capital" and "front money.")

self-study   A standard feature of accreditation processes in which an organization or program conducts a group self-examination or investigation, usually to determine its strengths, weaknesses, available opportunities, and threats from its environment.

self-dealing   A term used by the IRS to characterize situations in which one or more people (for example, staff or board members) are inappropriately taking advantage of their situation for their own financial advantage.

service   The act of providing aid, assistance, or benefit to another. In economics, this is any outcome other than a material or tangible good.

service delivery   Action to create or enact a benefit for another, including those secondary or supportive services that facilitate or enable the principal service acts. Also known as "production."

service efforts and accomplishments (SEA)   An initiative of the GASB mandating public HSEs and other public agencies to report their efforts and results in prescribed formats.

service matrix   A contingency table comparing types of basic volunteering, community service, community-based learning, and service learning on the dimensions of formal learning and value to the community.

simplicity   A condition of accountability.

situational assessment   Analysis or investigation of a set of circumstances.

skill   Proficiency or dexterity in the performance of a practice. This is a form of cultural capital.

sliding scale fee   A group or class of variable fees, especially those charged in proportion to clients' income, circumstances, or ability to pay.

social agency   An organization or firm employing social workers or delivering human services as an agent for others.

social capital   Forms of human capital consisting of trust and networks of relationships. Social capital is generally of two types: bridging capital and bonding capital.

social cost   Cost of an activity, output, or program borne by society as a whole. Social cost has both technical and euphemistic meanings, for example, for the broad consequences of economic action.

social economy   The portion of a total economy involving production (mostly of services) by nonprofits, cooperatives, foundations, mutual-benefit organizations, and social enterprises.

social enterprise   An organization or firm, whether nonprofit, public, for profit, or limited profit, engaged in production of services for philanthropic reasons or social or public good.

social planning   A concept that includes both the allocative planning of budgeting and the innovative planning of program development. Older notions from the 1930s and 1960s of a planned society appear to have gone by the wayside in the United States.

sole proprietor   Owner of any group of assets by a single person.

solicitation   The process of asking potential donors for donations, that is, an organized program of fundraising asks. Solicitations may be face-to-face, by direct mail, by e-mail, or by other means.

solo practice   Also known as "sole entrepreneurship." An HSE owned and operated by a single individual.

solopreneurship   Initiative or enterprise displayed by a single innovator, leader, or individual.

sources of income   A separate table or listing identifying or categorizing sources of income by type or individually.

special event   An event or activity, such as a dinner, ball, conference, or other nonroutine occurrence. In human services finance, special events tend to serve either one or both of two purposes: fundraising and donor or volunteer recognition.

There are generally three types of special events: the annual meeting, fundraising events, and constituency development events.

staff   The employees and volunteers of an enterprise.

staff fundraiser   An employee of the enterprise whose assignment or work contract specifies fundraising as a major or exclusive assignment.

stakeholder   A person or organization with an interest in or concern for (a stake in) an organization, program, or service.

standard   A formally stated and authoritative criterion, particularly one stating an anticipated or expected level of quality or excellence.

statements   In accounting, a general term for financial reports in tabular form. The two types of statements report on performance and financial position.

strategic planning   Allocative planning concentrated on key or strategic choices or innovative planning explicitly directed toward finding new ways to pursue established or novel ends.

strategy   The highest-level statement or understanding of the means of pursuing a mission to achieve a goal or result. Mission, goals, and objectives speak to the "what" and "why" of purposeful action. Strategy and tactics speak to the "how," "when," and "where."

subenterprise budget   A budget detailing projected expenses (and possibly associated income) of a component of an enterprise, including program, departmental, and all subprogram budgets.

subprogram budget   A budget detailing projected expenses (and possibly associated income) of any of the individual components of a program. This may include supplies, budgets, human capital budgets, special event budgets, and other components.

summarizing transactions   Numerical lumping, in which a group of separately entered transactions are added together.

sunset laws   Provisions in legislation providing for an end or termination date for a public program, beyond which it must be re-enacted or the program will expire.

supplies   A conventional category in the chart of accounts to summarize expenditures for easily consumable materials, such as paper, pencils, ink, printer cartridges, lightbulbs, paper towels, and the like.

supplies budget   A separate, supportive budget detailing anticipated expenditures for supplies. This is particularly useful in large organizations or cases where supplies require careful monitoring.

supply and demand   Key terms of the microeconomic model for determining the economic position of a firm.

supply side   A perspective or analytical technique examining only the purview of the organization or group providing or supplying a service. Break-even analysis, for example, is a supply-side perspective that does not consider demand or client perspectives.

support   Income received from some form of federated fundraising. Also known as "public support."

support services   Secondary and tertiary services necessary for the effective delivery of some primary service.

surplus   Funds remaining at the end of a financial period after all income has been collected and all obligations satisfied. In current accounting terminology, this is also known as "net income." This is sometimes incorrectly termed "profit," although legal and ethical constraints in nonprofit organizations preclude distribution to owners or shareholders.

synthesis   The opposite of analysis. Literally, recombining or putting things back together, especially in new and different combinations.

tax   An obligatory payment or charge assessed by a unit of federal, state, or local government for public purposes, to raise income for public programs, or to discourage certain types of behavior.

tax credit   A reduction in taxable income, particularly one granted by state and local tax authorities for certain charitable purposes (for example, homeowner's tax credits).

tax deduction   A reduction in tax obligation (taxes owed) granted to certain taxpayers in light of other actions they have taken during the tax period. The most relevant tax deduction for fundraising in human services is that granted for donations to certain public charities that qualify under Section 501(c)(3).

tax exemption   Legal release or freedom from obligation to pay certain taxes. The members of this class of tax-exempt organizations (referred to by the IRS as "public charities") are generally required to file annual exempt entities returns (IRS Form 990).

technical skills   A rather artificial term used here to mean something like "other people's professional skills." For financial management in human services, the list would include accounting and bookkeeping, database management, and corporate and tax law, among others.

theft   The illegal taking of money, property, information, or any other valuable resource from another.

third-party payments   Payments to an HSE (the first party), specifically for services rendered, made on behalf of a client (the second party) by another (the third) party, such as an insurance company or a contracted purchaser of service.

third sector   The set of all tax-exempt, tax-deductible 501(c)(3) nonprofit corporations. In some definitions, this group also includes 501(c)(4) corporations and other entities, such as voluntary associations. Also known as the "nonprofit sector."

time frame   An interval during which something takes place, especially one that brackets or frames an event, setting it in a context for better understanding.

time horizon   The outer limits of a time frame, bounded by the earliest and most recent (or future) events of interest.

transaction   A type of economic exchange. Key transactions in human services include purchases, delivery of services, donations, and transfer payments.

transaction cost   The cost of conducting a transaction. Transaction costs are ordinarily of three types: costs of negotiating the transaction, costs of search and information collection, and costs of monitoring and enforcing the transaction.

transfer payment   A contrast term with purchases or market transactions intended to highlight the unilateral nature of the monetary transaction and the redistributive result.

transparency   A much heralded and difficult to achieve quality or condition of information that is visible, open, public, and available for inspection.

travel journal   In accounting, a set of records separate from the general journal with notations of travel-related expenses and reimbursements.

trend analysis   Collection of data on a series of events or activities in order to try to identify patterns or trends in the data that explain or give insight into the underlying events or activities.

trial balance   A preliminary statement. For managers, a trial balance is often the most up-to-date source of information on current income, spending, and financial position.

triple bottom line   A term coined by John Elkington for a scheme of social accounting concerned with social, ecological, and financial results, also known as the "three p's"—people, planet, and profits.

true cost   A type of cost reflecting the true or full set of related expenses associated with a particular cost object or center. (Also known as "full cost.")

trust   (a) A legal financial arrangement under which a principal grants or awards a sum of money to an agent (the trustee) for some purpose specified in a trust agreement. (b) A quality or characteristic of interpersonal relations. (c) An important source of social capital (for example, trust is the quality that binds the members of a group together).

trust fund   A trust agreement under which the trustee manages a group of assets (the fund) for a principal, often a minor child or an incapacitated person, paying out income to the principal in a manner specified in the trust agreement.

two-class service system   System characterized by one level or quality of service for middle-class and/or affluent clients and another (often less available or lower quality) for low-income or poor clients.

uncollected fees   A type of account receivable, detailing fees or user changes assigned but not yet collected ("made but not paid").

unit cost   Outlay costs associated with production of a single unit of service.

unit cost budget   A specialized budget format in which total projected expenses are calculated by multiplying the anticipated unit of service by a standard unit cost estimate.

United Way International   The peak association for more than 4,000 local federated funding operations around the world operating under the United Way brand and mostly engaged in workplace fundraising.

United Way of American Service Information System (UWASIS)   The project unfolded in two phases during the 1970s: UWASIS I and UWASIS II.

unrelated business income tax (UBIT)   A tax payment developed by the IRS and assessed against some portion of the income of certain tax-exempt entities. UBITs acknowledge surplus-generating activities of nonprofit organizations not related to their legitimate tax-exempt public charity purposes. The UBIT is an intermediate sanction developed as an alternative to lifting the tax exemption of nonprofits when a limited portion of their activities are not charitable.

user fee   A charge levied against the user of a service, often corresponding to the level or amount of service consumed.

values   Forms of cultural capital, particularly those expressing standards of worthiness or importance.

variable cost   Cost that varies directly with the output of services. This is the opposite of fixed cost.

voluntary sector   A previously used term used to describe the set of noncommercial and nongovernmental human services.

volunteer labor   Term used by economists to describe the resource input from the effort and activities of volunteers.

wages   Payments to employees in exchange for work performed, especially work in which compensation is determined on a part-time or hourly basis.

war chest   A slang phrase describing discretionary funds reserved for a special purpose, particularly one involving conflict. Derived from the Liberty Fund campaigns of World War I, which served as the example for federated fundraising known as Community Chests and later United Way.

waste   Failure to take advantage of or make proper use of an available resource.

withholdings   Amounts withheld by employers and subtracted from gross wages or salaries, including the costs of fringe benefits and assorted tax withholdings.

workload   The total volume of employment-related events and activities expected from a worker during a given period of time.

write-off   A reduction of the value of an asset (such as a building or an account receivable) to zero, usually because of changing circumstances or a determination that it is not feasible to retrieve the value.

zero-base budgeting   A theoretical budget system designed to start each new budget from scratch, that is, with no prior assumptions regarding base commitments, earmarks, or past performance.

zero-sum budgeting   A budget system in which all projected expenses are justified by their projected benefits. The entire budget is presented as a set of decision packages rather than as conventional line items.

References

Abramson, C. M. (2009). Who are the clients? Goal displacement in an adult day care center for elders with dementia. *International Journal of Aging and Human Development, 68*(1), 65–92.

Adams, M., & Hardwick, P. (1998). An analysis of corporate donations: United Kingdom evidence. *Journal of Management Studies, 35,* 641–654.

Aft, R. N., & Aft, M. L. (2009). *Global vision and local action: The history of United Way International.* Cincinnati, OH: Philanthropic Leadership.

Alexander, C. (1977). Management of human service organizations. In J. B. Turner (Ed.), *Encyclopedia of social work* (17th ed., pp. 844–849). Washington, DC: National Association of Social Workers.

Alexander, G. D., & Carlson, K. J. (2005). *Essential principles for fundraising success: An answer manual for the everyday challenges of raising money.* San Francisco: Jossey-Bass.

Alexander, J. C., Smith, P., Norton, M., & Brooks, P. (2011). *Interpreting Clifford Geertz: Cultural investigation in the social sciences.* New York: Palgrave Macmillan.

Americans with Disabilities Act of 1990, P.L. 101-336, 104 Stat. 328 (1990).

Andreoni, J. (1990). Impure altruism and donations to public goods: A theory of warm-glow giving. *Economic Journal, 100*(401), 464–477.

Andreoni, J. (1993). An experimental test of the public-goods crowding-out hypothesis. *American Economic Review, 83,* 1317–1327.

Angelica, E., & Hyman, V. L. (1997). *Coping with cutbacks: The nonprofit guide to success when times are tight.* St. Paul, MN: Amherst H. Wilder Foundation.

Anheier, H. K., & Themudo, N. (2005). The internationalization of the nonprofit sector. In R. D. Herman & Associates (Eds.), *The Jossey-Bass handbook of nonprofit leadership and management* (pp. 102–128). San Francisco: Jossey-Bass.

Anthony, R. N., & Young, D. W. (2005). Financial accounting and financial management. In R. D. Herman & Associates (Eds.), *The Jossey-Bass handbook of nonprofit leadership and management* (2nd ed., pp. 466–512). San Francisco: Jossey-Bass.

Aranoff, G. (2003). Improving disclosure and transparency in nonprofit accounting. *Management Accounting Quarterly, 43,* 15–23.

Auslander, G. K. (1996). Outcome evaluation in host organizations: A research agenda. *Administration in Social Work, 20*(2), 15–27.

Austin, D. M. (1981). The political economy of social benefit organizations: Redistributive services and merit goods. In H. D. Stein (Ed.), *Organization and the human services* (pp. 37–88). Philadelphia: Temple University Press.

Austin, D. M. (1988). *The political economy of human service programs.* Greenwich, CT: JAI Press.

Austin, D. M. (2002). *Human services management: Organizational leadership in social work practice.* New York: Columbia University Press.

Austin, M. J., & Hopkins, K.M.A. (2004). *Supervision as collaboration in the human services: Building a learning culture.* Thousand Oaks, CA: Sage Publications.

Austin, M. J., Regan, K., Gothard, S., & Carnochan, S. (2013). Becoming a manager in nonprofit human service organizations: Making the transition from specialist to generalist. *Administration in Social Work, 37,* 372–385.

Baker, D. E. (1988). Accounting for restricted and unrestricted funds. *Journal of Accountancy, 165,* 68–76.

Banker, R. D., Janakiraman, S. N., & Konstans, C. (2001). *Balanced scorecard: Linking strategy to performance.* Morristown, NJ: Financial Executives Research Foundation.

Barber, B. R. (1988). *The conquest of politics: Liberal philosophy in democratic times.* Princeton, NJ: Princeton University Press.

Barber, G., Slavin, S., & Barnett, S. (1983). Impact of Reagan economics on social services in the private sector. *Urban and Social Change Review, 16,* 27–32.

Barman, E. (2006). *Contesting communities: The transformation of workplace charity.* Stanford, CA: Stanford University Press.

Barney, J. B., & Ouchi, W. G. (Eds.). (1986). *Organizational economics: Toward a new paradigm for understanding and studying organizations.* San Francisco: Jossey-Bass.

Becker, G. S. (1976). *The economic approach to human behavior.* Chicago: University of Chicago Press.

Beito, D. T. (2000). *From mutual aid to the welfare state: Fraternal societies and social services, 1890–1967.* Chapel Hill, NC: University of North Carolina Press.

Beito, D. T., Gordon, P., & Tabarrok, A. (2002). *The voluntary city: Choice, community, and civil society.* Ann Arbor: University of Michigan Press.

Berger, P. L., & Luckmann, T. (1966). *The social construction of reality: A treatise in the sociology of knowledge.* Garden City, NY: Anchor Doubleday.

Berman, E. M. (1995). Implementing TQM in state welfare agencies. *Administration in Social Work, 19*(1), 55–72.

Bernstein, L. (2000). *Creating your employee handbook: A do-it-yourself kit for nonprofits.* San Francisco: Jossey-Bass.

Best Practices. (2001). *Developing a balanced scorecard of performance measures.* Chapel Hill, NC: Author.

Bielefeld, W., & Corbin, J. J. (1996). The institutionalization of nonprofit human service delivery: The role of political culture. *Administration & Society, 28,* 362–389.

Billis, D. (Ed.). (2010). *Hybrid organizations and the third sector: Challenges for practice, theory and policy.* London: Palgrave Macmillan.

Blazek, J. (1996). *Financial planning for nonprofit organizations.* New York: Wiley.

Blazek, J. (2012). *Tax planning and compliance for tax-exempt organizations: Rules, checklists, procedures* (5th ed.). New York: Wiley.

Block, P. (2013). *Stewardship: Choosing service over self-interest* (2nd ed.). San Francisco: Berrett-Koehler.

Block, S. R. (2004). *Why nonprofits fail: Overcoming founder's syndrome, fundphobia, and other obstacles to success*. San Francisco: Jossey-Bass.

Boris, E. T. (2010). *Human service nonprofits and government collaboration: Findings from the 2010 National Survey of Nonprofit Government Contracting and Grants*. Washington, DC: Urban Institute Press.

Boris, E. T., & Steuerle, C. E. (2006). *Nonprofits and government: Collaboration and conflict* (2nd ed.). Washington, DC: Urban Institute Press.

Bourdieu, P., & Passeron, J. C. (1990). *Reproduction in education, society, and culture* (R. Nice, Trans.). London and Newbury Park, CA: Sage Publications in association with Theory, Culture & Society, Department of Administrative and Social Studies, Teesside Polytechnic.

Brager, G. A., & Specht, H. (1973). *Community organizing*. New York: Columbia University Press.

Braswell, R., Fortin, K., & Osteryoung, J. S. (1984). *Financial management for not-for-profit organizations*. New York: Wiley.

Braudel, F. (1986). *The wheels of commerce: Vol. 2. Civilization and capitalism, 15th–18th century*. New York: Harper & Row.

Braybrooke, D., & Lindblom, C. E. (1963). *A strategy of decision: Policy evaluation as a social process*. New York: Free Press of Glencoe.

Brewer, P. C., Garrison, R. H., & Noreen, E. W. (2016). *Introduction to managerial accounting* (7th ed.). Irwin, CA: McGraw-Hill.

Brilliant, E. L. (1990). *The United Way: The dilemmas of organized charity*. New York: Columbia University Press.

Brilliant, E. L. (2000). *Private charity and public inquiry: A history of the Filer and Peterson commissions*. Bloomington: Indiana University Press.

Brinckerhoff, P. C. (2004). *Nonprofit stewardship: A better way to lead your mission-based organization*. St. Paul, MN: Amherst H. Wilder Foundation.

Brooks, D. (Ed.). (1995). *Backward and upward: The new conservative writing*. New York: Vintage.

Brown, L. D., & Kalegaonkar, A. (2002). Support organizations and the evolution of the NGO sector. *Nonprofit and Voluntary Sector Quarterly, 31*, 231–258.

Bryce, H. J. (2000). *Financial and strategic management for nonprofit organizations: A comprehensive reference to legal, financial, management, and operations rules and guidelines for nonprofits* (3rd ed.). San Francisco: Jossey-Bass.

Buell, B. (1952). *Community planning for human services*. New York: Columbia University Press.

Burlingame, D. (2004). *Philanthropy in America: A comprehensive historical encyclopedia* (Vols. 1–2). Santa Barbara, CA: ABC-CLIO.

Buttrick, S. M., & Miller, V. (1978). An approach to zero-base budgeting. *Administration in Social Work, 2*(1), 45–58.

Caers, R., Bois, C. D., Jegers, M., Gieter, S. D., Schepers, C., & Pepermans, R. (2006). Principal-agent relationships on the stewardship–agency axis. *Nonprofit Management and Leadership, 17*, 25–47.

Carlson, M. (2002). *Winning grants step by step: The complete workbook for planning, developing, and writing successful proposals* (2nd ed.). San Francisco: Jossey-Bass.

Carnochan, S., Samples, M., Myers, M., & Austin, M. J. (2014). Performance measurement challenges in nonprofit human service organizations. *Nonprofit and Voluntary Sector Quarterly, 43,* 1014–1032.

Chabotar, K. J. (1989). Financial ratio analysis comes to nonprofits. *The Journal of Higher Education, 60,* 188–208.

Chambers, C. A. (1971). *Paul Underwood Kellogg and the survey: Voices of social welfare and social justice.* Minneapolis: University of Minnesota Press.

Chamlee-Wright, E. (2010). *The cultural and political economy of recovery: Social learning in a post-disaster environment.* London: Routledge.

Chamlee-Wright, E., & Storr, V. H. (2010). *The political economy of Hurricane Katrina and community rebound.* Cheltenham, UK: Edward Elgar.

Chang, C. F., & Tuckman, H. P. (1994). Revenue diversification among non-profits. *Voluntas, 5,* 273–290.

Chase, R. (2015, July 16). Bye, bye capitalism. We're entering the age of abundance [Web log post]. Retrieved from https://medium.com/backchannel/see-ya-later-capitalism-the-collaborative-economy-is-taking-over-34a5fc3a37cd

Chief Financial Officers Act of 1990, P.L. 101-576, 104 Stat. 2839 (1990).

Citizens United v. Federal Election Commission, No. 08-205, 558 U.S. 310 (2010).

Clark, S. J., & Jordan, C. E. (2001). Accounting for a not-for-profit organization's fund-raising costs. *Healthcare Financial Management, 55,* 62–65.

Clynch, E. J. (1979). Zero-base budgeting in practice: An assessment. *International Journal of Public Administration, 1*(1), 43–64.

Cnaan, R. A., & Milofsky, C. (2007). *Handbook of community movements and local organizations.* New York: Springer.

Cnaan, R. A., Wineburg, R. J., & Boddie, S. C. (1999). *The newer deal: Social work and religion in partnership.* New York: Columbia University Press.

Coase, R. (1937). The nature of the firm. *Economica, 12,* 386–405.

Coe, C. K., & Ellis, C. (1991). Internal controls in state, local, and nonprofit agencies. *Public Budgeting & Finance, 11,* 43–55.

Coleman, J. (1988). Social capital in the creation of human capital. *American Journal of Sociology, 94*(Suppl.), S95–S120.

Coley, S. M., & Scheinberg, C. A. (2008). *Proposal writing: Effective grantsmanship* (3rd ed.). Thousand Oaks, CA: Sage Publications.

Commission on Foundations and Private Philanthropy. (1970). *Foundations, private giving, and public policy report and recommendations of the Commission on Foundations and Private Philanthropy.* Chicago: University of Chicago Press.

Conlan, T. J. (1984). The politics of federal block grants: From Nixon to Reagan. *Political Science Quarterly, 99,* 247–270.

Connor, J. A., Kadel-Taras, S., & Vinocur-Kaplan, D. (1999). The role of nonprofit management support organizations in sustaining community collaborations. *Nonprofit Management and Leadership, 10,* 127–136.

Cordes, J. J., & Weisbrod, B. A. (1998). Differential taxation of nonprofits and the commercialization of nonprofit revenues. *Journal of Policy Analysis and Management, 17,* 195–214.

Cowger, C. (1979). Organizational considerations in the application of budgeting and cost-effectiveness systems to social welfare organizations. *Journal of Sociology and Social Welfare, 6,* 211–220.

Cox, S., Keith, J. G., Otten, G. L., & Raymond, F. B. (1980). Cost-effectiveness of primary and secondary prevention. *Health & Social Work, 5,* 56–60.

Dahl, R. A., & Lindblom, C. E. (1992). *Politics, economics, and welfare.* New Brunswick, NJ: Transaction.

Dalton, G. L., & Morelli, P. (1988). Casemix and caseload: Measurement of output of a social work agency. *Administration in Social Work, 12*(4), 81–92.

Davis, J. H., Schoorman, F. D., & Donaldson, L. (1997). Toward a stewardship theory of management. *Academy of Management Review, 22,* 20–47.

Davis, M. S. (1999). *Grantsmanship for criminology and criminal justice.* Thousand Oaks, CA: Sage Publications.

DeCock, C., & Hipkin, I. (1997). TQM and BPR: Beyond the beyond myth. *Journal of Management Studies, 34,* 659–675.

Demone, H. W., & Gibelman, M. (1984). Reaganomics: Its impact on the voluntary not-for-profit sector. *Social Work, 29,* 421–427.

Department for Business Innovation & Skills. (2011, November). *A guide to legal forms for social enterprise.* Retrieved from https://www.gov.uk/government/uploads/system/uploads/attachment_data/file/31677/11-1400-guide-legal-forms-for-social-enterprise.pdf

Dilley, S. C., & Weygandt, J. J. (1973). Measuring social responsibility: An empirical test. *Journal of Accountancy, 136*(3), 62–71.

Dirksen Center. (n.d.). *"A billion here, a billion there."* Retrieved from http://www.everettdirksen.name/print_emd_billionhere.htm

Djankov, S., La Porta, R., Lopez-de-Silanes, F., & Shleifer, A. (2008). The law and economics of self-dealing. *Journal of Financial Economics, 88,* 430–465.

Doelker, R. E. (1979). A multi-program cost analysis and planning model for social service programs. *Administration in Social Work, 3,* 477–488.

Dropkin, M., & Hayden, A. (2001). *The cash flow management book for nonprofits: A step-by-step guide for managers, consultants, and boards.* San Francisco: Jossey-Bass.

Drtina, R. (1982). Financial indicators as a measure of nonprofit human service organization performance: The underlying issues. *New England Journal of Human Services, 2*(3), 35–41.

Drucker, P. F. (1954). *The practice of management.* New York: Harper & Row.

Drucker, P. F. (1969, Winter). The sickness of government. *Public Interest, 14,* 3–23.

Dunham, A. (1970). *The new community organization.* New York: Thomas Y. Crowell.

Dykstra, A., & Aitken, I. (1984). Managing resource reduction in publicly operated facilities. *Journal of Health and Human Resources Administration, 6,* 450–475.

Ebaugh, H. R., Chafetz, J. S., & Pipes, P. F. (2007). Collaborations with faith-based social service coalitions. *Nonprofit Management and Leadership, 18,* 175–191.

Ebrahim, A. (2003). Making sense of accountability: Conceptual perspectives from northern and southern nonprofits. *Nonprofit Management and Leadership, 14,* 191–212.

Economic Opportunity Act of 1964, P.L. 88-452, 78 Stat. 508 (1964).

Edvinsson, L., & Malone, M. S. (1997). *Intellectual capital: Realizing your company's true value by finding its hidden brainpower.* London: Piatkus Books.

Elisha, O. (2008). Moral ambitions of grace: The paradox of compassion and accountability in evangelical faith-based activism. *Cultural Anthropology, 23,* 154–189.

Elkin, R. (1967). *A conceptual base for defining health and welfare services: An application to family and child welfare.* New York: Child Welfare League, Family Service Association of America, & Travelers Aid Association of America.

Elkin, R. (1985). Paying the piper and calling the tune: Accountability in the human services. *Administration in Social Work, 9*(2), 1–13.

Elkin, R., & Molitor, M. (1984). *Management indicators in nonprofit organizations: Guidelines to selection and implementation.* Baltimore, MD: University of Maryland, School of Social Work and Community Planning.

Elkin, R., & Molitor, M. (1985). A conceptual framework for selecting management indicators in nonprofit organizations. *Administration in Social Work, 9*(4), 13–23.

Elkington, J. (1998). *Cannibals with forks: The triple bottom line of 21st century business.* Gabriola Island, British Columbia: New Society.

Engdahl, R. L. (1991). Religious funding-raising: The theology of stewardship. *Nonprofit Management and Leadership, 1,* 345–356.

Eschman, J. R., Schwartz, S. L., & Austin, M. J. (2011). CompassPoint Nonprofit Services: Strengthening the capacities of nonprofits (1971–2008). *Journal of Evidence-Based Social Work, 8,* 143–159.

Estes, R. W. (1976). *Corporate social accounting.* New York: Wiley.

Ezell, M. (2000). Financial management. In R. J. Patti (Ed.), *Handbook of social welfare management* (pp. 377–393). Thousand Oaks, CA: Sage Publications.

Feit, M. D., & Li, P. (1998). *Financial management in human services.* New York: Haworth Press.

Ferreri, L. B., & Cowen, S. S. (1993). The university budget process: A case study. *Nonprofit Management and Leadership, 3,* 299–312.

Finch, W. A. (1982). Declining public social service resources: A managerial problem. *Administration in Social Work, 6*(1), 19–28.

Finke, R. (2003, October). *Spiritual capital: Definitions, applications, and new frontiers.* Paper presented at the Spiritual Capital Planning Meeting, Cambridge, MA. Retrieved from http://www.metanexus.net/archive/spiritualcapitalresearchprogram/pdf/finke.pdf

Finkler, S. A. (2013). *Financial management for public, health, and not-for-profit organizations* (4th ed.). Boston: Pearson Education.

Fishman, J. J. (2008). *The political uses of private benevolence: The statute of charitable uses* (Pace Law Faculty Publications Paper 487). Retrieved from http://digitalcommons.pace.edu/lawfaculty/487/

Fitzsimmons, J. A., Schwab, A. J., & Sullivan, R. S. (1979). Goal programming for holistic budget analysis. *Administration in Social Work, 3*(1), 33–43.

Forsythe, D. W. (2000). Financial management for nonprofit organizations. *Nonprofit and Voluntary Sector Quarterly, 29,* 488–490.

Fos, P. J., Miller, D. L., Amy, B. W., & Zuniga, M. A. (2004). Combining the benefits of decision science and financial analysis in public health management: A county-specific budgeting and planning model. *Journal of Public Health Management & Practice, 10,* 406–412.

Frankfather, D. L. (1981). Welfare entrepreneurialism and the politics of innovation. *Social Service Review, 55,* 129–146.

Franklin, C. (2001). Coming to terms with the business of direct practice. *Research on Social Work Practice, 11*(2), 235–244.

Freeman, R. E. (1984). *Strategic management: A stakeholder approach.* Boston: Pitman.

Freeman, R. J., Shoulders, C. D., Allison, G. S., Patton, T. K., & Smith, R. G. (2009). *Governmental and nonprofit accounting: Theory and practice* (9th ed.). Upper Saddle River, NJ: Pearson/Prentice Hall.

Fremont-Smith, M. R. (2004). *Governing nonprofit organizations: Federal and state law and regulation.* Cambridge, MA: Belknap Press.

Friedman, B. D. (1995). *Regulation in the Reagan–Bush era: The eruption of presidential influence.* Pittsburgh, PA: University of Pittsburgh Press.

Friedmann, J. (1973). *Retracking America: A theory of transactive planning.* New York: Anchor Doubleday.

Froelich, K. A. (1999). Diversification of revenue strategies: Evolving resource dependence in nonprofit organizations. *Nonprofit and Voluntary Sector Quarterly, 28,* 246–268.

Fry, R. P. (1998). *Nonprofit investment policies: Practical steps for growing charitable funds.* New York: Wiley.

Gambino, A. J., & Reardon, T. (1981). *Financial planning and evaluation for the nonprofit organization.* New York: National Association of Accountants.

Geever, J. C., & the Foundation Center. (2012). *The Foundation Center's guide to proposal writing* (6th ed.). New York: Foundation Center.

Gerrish, E. (2015). The impact of performance management on performance in public organizations: A meta-analysis. *Public Administration Review, 76,* 48–66.

Ghani, A., Carnahan, M., & Lockhart, C. (2006). *Stability, state-building and development assistance: An outside perspective.* Princeton, NJ: Princeton Project on National Security, Woodrow Wilson School of Public and International Affairs.

Gibelman, M., & Kraft, S. (1996). Advocacy as a core agency program: Planning considerations for voluntary human service agencies. *Administration in Social Work, 20*(4), 43–59.

Gidron, B., & Hasenfeld, Y. (2012). *Social enterprises: An organizational perspective.* New York: Palgrave Macmillan.

Giesen, P., Ferwerda, R., & Tijssen, R. (2007). Safety of telephone triage in general practitioner cooperatives: Do triage nurses correctly estimate urgency? *Quality and Safety in Health Care, 16*(3), 181–184.

Ginsberg, L. H. (2008). *Management and leadership in social work practice and education.* Alexandria, VA: Council on Social Work Education.

Glaser, J. S. (1994). *The United Way scandal: An insider's account of what went wrong and why.* New York: Wiley.

Glaser, R. G. (2014). Policy and procedures manual. In R. G. Glaser & R. M. Traynor (Eds.), *Strategic practice management: Business and procedural considerations* (pp. 335–356). San Diego: Plural.

Glazer, N. (1984, Spring). The social policy of the Reagan Administration: A review. *Public Interest, 75,* 76–98.

Global Reporting Initiative. (2010). *Non-governmental organizations*. Retrieved from https://www.globalreporting.org/standards/sector-guidance/sector-guidance/ngo/Pages/default.aspx

Goldberg, A., & Kovac, D. (1973). Implementing a fee system based on appropriate subsidy. *Social Casework, 54*, 233–238.

Goodman, N. (1960). Are there differences between fee and non-fee cases? *Social Work, 5*, 46–52.

Goodman, N. (1969). The catch in functional budgeting: To what end? *Social Work, 14*, 40–48.

Goodman, N. (1970). Fee charging. In R. Morris (Ed.), *Encyclopedia of social work* (16th ed., pp. 413–415). New York: NASW Press.

Government Performance and Results Act of 1993, P.L. 103-62, 107 Stat. 285 (1993).

Government Performance and Results Modernization Act of 2010. P.L. 111-352, 124 Stat. 3866 et seq. (2010).

Granovetter, M. S. (1973). The strength of weak ties. *American Journal of Sociology, 78*, 1360–1380.

Granovetter, M. (2005). The impact of social structure on economic outcomes. *Journal of Economic Perspectives, 19*, 33–50.

Grasso, A. J. (1994). Management style, job satisfaction, and service effectiveness. *Administration in Social Work, 18*(4), 89–105.

Greenlee, J. S., & Trussel, J. M. (2000). Predicting the financial vulnerability of charitable organizations. *Nonprofit Management and Leadership, 11*, 199–210.

Gröjer, J.-E., & Stark, A. (1977). Social accounting: A Swedish attempt. *Accounting, Organizations and Society, 2*, 349–385.

Grønbjerg, K. A. (1993). *Understanding nonprofit funding: Managing revenues in social services and community development organizations*. San Francisco: Jossey-Bass.

Gross, M. J. (1985). Budgeting. In S. Slavin (Ed.), *Social work administration* (2nd ed., pp. 11–25). Philadelphia: Temple University Press.

Gross, M. J. (1995). *Financial and accounting guide for not-for-profit organizations* (5th ed.). New York: Wiley.

Gruber, M. L. (1991). In and out of the rabbit hole with Alice: Assessing the consequences of efficiency prescriptions. *Administration in Social Work, 15*(1–2), 175–192.

Grundy, T. (1996). Cost is a strategic issue. *Long Range Planning, 29*, 58–68.

Gummer, B. (1992). Ready, aim, fire! Current perspectives on strategic planning. *Administration in Social Work, 16*(1), 89–106.

Gummer, B. (1996). Total quality management: Organizational transformation or passing fancy? *Administration in Social Work, 20*(3), 75–95.

Gunther, J. J., & Hawkins, F. (1996). *Total quality management in human service organizations*. New York: Springer.

Gunther, J. J., & Hawkins, F. (1999). *Making TQM work: Quality tools for human service organizations*. New York: Springer.

Hairston, C. F. (1981). Improving cash management in nonprofit organizations. *Administration in Social Work, 5*, 29–36.

Hairston, C. F. (1985a). Costing nonprofit services: Developments, problems, and issues. *Administration in Social Work, 9*(1), 47–55.

Hairston, C. F. (1985b). Using ratio analysis for financial accountability. *Social Casework, 66,* 76–82.

Hall, J. (1975). *Sliding scales of fees: Determining a rational basis for ability to pay.* Paper presented to the United Way of Tarrant County, Fort Worth, Texas.

Hall, M. D. (1981, Winter). Financial condition: A measure of human service organization performance. *New England Journal of Human Services, 2,* 29–34.

Hall, M. R., Sowell, M. L., & Institute for Governmental Service, University of Maryland at College Park. (1994). *Fundraising for leaders of nonprofits.* College Park, MD: Institute for Governmental Service.

Hammack, D. C. (1988). *The Russell Sage Foundation: Social research and social action in America, 1907–1947: An historical biography* [Microfilm]. Frederick, MD: University Press of America.

Hammack, D. C., & Wheeler, S. (1994). *Social science in the making: Essays on the Russell Sage Foundation, 1907–1972.* New York: Russell Sage Foundation.

Hanifan, L. J. (1916). The rural school community center. *Annals of the American Academy of Political and Social Science, 67,* 130–138.

Hardy, C., & Phillips, N. W. (1998). Strategies of engagement: Lessons from the critical examination of collaboration and conflict in an interorganizational domain. *Organization Science, 9,* 217–230.

Hargrove, D. S., & Melton, G. B. (1987). Block grants and rural mental health services. *Journal of Rural Community Psychology, 8,* 4–11.

Harper-Dorton, K., & Majewski, V. (2015, July). *Rural community sustainability: The anatomy of fourth sector corporations.* Paper presented at the 40th Annual National Institute for Social Work and Human Services in Rural Areas, Vermillion, South Dakota.

Harris, M. (1996). "An inner group of willing people": Volunteering in a religious context. *Social Policy and Administration, 30*(1), 54–68.

Hasenfeld, Y. (2010). *Human services as complex organizations* (2nd ed.). Thousand Oaks, CA: Sage Publications.

Hasenfeld, Y., & English, R. A. (1974). *Human service organizations: A book of readings.* Ann Arbor: University of Michigan Press.

Hasenfeld, Y., & Garrow, E. E. (2012). Nonprofit human-service organizations, social rights, and advocacy in a neoliberal welfare state. *Social Service Review, 86,* 295–322.

Hatry, H. P., Millar, A., & Evans, J. H. (1985). *Guide to setting priorities for capital investment.* Washington, DC: Urban Institute Press.

Haynes, K. S., & Mickelson, J. S. (1992). Social work and the Reagan era: Challenges to the profession. *Journal of Sociology and Social Welfare, 19,* 169–183.

Health Care and Education Reconciliation Act of 2010, P.L. 111-152, 124 Stat. 1029 (2010).

Heffernan, J. (1991). Efficiency considerations in the social welfare agency. *Administration in Social Work, 15*(1–2), 119–131.

Herzlinger, R. (1979). Managing the finances of nonprofit organizations. *California Management Review, 21*(3), 60–69.

Hess, C., & Ostrom, E. (2007). *Understanding knowledge as a commons: From theory to practice.* Cambridge, MA: MIT Press.

Hill, J. G. (1960a). Cost analysis in social work. In N. Polansky (Ed.), *Social work research* (pp. 223–246). Chicago: University of Chicago Press.

Hill, J. G. (1960b). *The Philadelphia time-cost study in a family service.* New York: Columbia University Press.

Hill, J. G., & Ormsby, R. (1953). *Cost analysis method for casework agencies.* Philadelphia: Family Service of Philadelphia.

Hill, W. G. (1971). Voluntary and governmental financial transactions. *Social Casework, 52,* 356–361.

Hodge, M. M., & Piccolo, R. F. (2005). Funding source, board involvement techniques, and financial vulnerability in nonprofit organizations: A test of resource dependence. *Nonprofit Management and Leadership, 16,* 171–190.

Hodges, R. L. (1982). Avoiding fiscal management problems in human service agencies. *Administration in Social Work, 6*(4), 61–67.

Holland, T. P., & Ritvo, R. A. (2008). *Nonprofit organizations: Principles and practices.* New York: Columbia University Press.

Hwang, G. H., & Aspinwall, E. M. (1996). Quality cost models and their application: A review. *Total Quality Management, 7,* 267–281.

International Association of Schools of Social Work. (n.d.) *Global definition of social work.* Retrieved from http://www.iassw-aiets.org/global-definition-of-social-work-review-of-the-global-definition/

Ivery, J. (2008). Policy mandated collaboration. *Journal of Sociology & Social Welfare, 35*(4), 53–70.

Jacobs, J. (1985). *Cities and the wealth of nations: Principles of economic life* (1st Vintage Books ed.). New York: Vintage Books.

Jacobs, J. (2002). *The death and life of great American cities.* New York: Random House.

Jacobs, J. (2004). *Dark age ahead.* New York: Random House.

Jamieson, B. S. (1982). Surviving the Reagan onslaught. *Public Welfare, 40,* 10–15.

Jansson, B. S., & Simmons, J. (1986). The survival of social work units in host organizations. *Social Work, 31,* 339–343.

Jegers, M. (1997). Portfolio theory and nonprofit financial stability: A comment and extension. *Nonprofit and Voluntary Sector Quarterly, 26,* 65–72.

Jegers, M. (2008). *Managerial economics of non-profit organizations.* New York: Routledge.

Johns, R. E. (1946). *The co-operative process among national social agencies.* New York: Association Press.

Johns, R. E., & De Marche, D. F. (1951). *Community organization and agency responsibility: Organizations as responsible participants.* New York: Association Press.

Johnson, W., & Clancy, T. (1991). Efficiency in behavior-changing social programs: The case of in-home child abuse prevention. *Administration in Social Work, 15,* 105–118.

Johnston, H. L. (1950). Rural health cooperatives. *Public Health Reports, 65*(43), 1383–1383.

Jones, B. D., True, J. L., & Baumgartner, F. R. (1997). Does incrementalism stem from political consensus or from institutional gridlock? *American Journal of Political Science, 41,* 1319–1339.

Kahn, A. J. (1969a). *Studies in social policy and planning.* New York: Russell Sage Foundation.

Kahn, A. J. (1969b). *Theory and practice of social planning.* New York: Russell Sage Foundation.

Kahn, J. (1993). Re-presenting government and representing the people: Budget reform and citizenship in New York City, 1908–1911. *Journal of Urban History, 19*(3), 84–103.

Kane, N. M. (1993). The financial capacity of nonprofit hospitals. *Health Affairs, 12,* 234–237.

Kaplan, A. (1964). *The conduct of inquiry: Methodology for behavioral science.* San Francisco: Chandler.

Kaplan, R. S. (1996). *The balanced scorecard for public-sector organizations.* Cambridge, MA: Harvard Business Press.

Kaplan, R. S., & Norton, D. P. (1993). Putting the balanced scorecard to work. *Harvard Business Review, 71,* 134–147.

Kaplan, R. S., & Norton, D. P. (1996). *The balanced scorecard: Translating strategy into action.* Boston, MA: Harvard Business School Press.

Kaplan, R. S., & Norton, D. P. (2001). *The strategy-focused organization: How balanced scorecard companies thrive in the new business environment.* Boston, MA: Harvard Business School Press.

Karski, R. L., & Barth, R. P. (2000). Models of state budget allocation in child welfare services. *Administration in Social Work, 24*(2), 45–66.

Karst, K. L. (1960). The efficiency of the charitable dollar: An unfulfilled state responsibility. *Harvard Law Review, 73,* 433–483.

Kautz, J. R., Netting, F. E., Huber, R., Borders, K., & Davis, T. S. (1997). The Government Performance and Results Act of 1993: Implications for social work practice. *Social Work, 42,* 364–373.

Kearns, K. P., Krasman, R. J., & Meyer, W. J. (1994). Why nonprofit organizations are ripe for total quality management. *Nonprofit Management and Leadership, 4,* 447–460.

Keating, B., & Keating, M. O. (2009). *Microeconomics for public managers.* Malden, MA: Wiley-Blackwell.

Keating, E. K., Fischer, M., Gordon, T. P., & Greenlee, J. (2005). *Assessing financial vulnerability in the nonprofit sector* (Faculty Research Working Paper RWP05-002). Cambridge, MA: Harvard University, John F. Kennedy School of Government.

Keating, E. K., & Frumkin, P. (2003). Reengineering nonprofit financial accountability: Toward a more reliable foundation for regulation. *Public Administration Review, 63*(1), 3–15.

Keener, T., & Sebestyen, D. (1981). A cost analysis of selected Dallas day care centers. *Child Welfare, 60,* 81–88.

Kelly, K. S. (1998). *Effective fundraising management.* Mahwah, NJ: Erlbaum.

Kettner, P. M., & Martin, L. L. (1985a). Issues in the development of monitoring systems for purchase of service contracting. *Administration in Social Work, 9*(3), 69–82.

Kettner, P. M., & Martin, L. L. (1985b). Purchase of service contracting and the declining influence of social work. *Urban and Social Change Review, 18,* 8–11.

Kettner, P. M., & Martin, L. L. (1986). Making decisions about purchase of service contracting. *Public Welfare, 44,* 30–37.

Kettner, P. M., & Martin, L. L. (1987). *Purchase of service contracting.* Newbury Park, CA: Sage Publications.

Kettner, P. M., & Martin, L. L. (1988). Purchase of service contracting with for-profit organizations. *Administration in Social Work, 12*(4), 47–60.

Kettner, P. M., & Martin, L. L. (1990). Purchase of service contracting: Two models. *Administration in Social Work, 14*(1), 15–30.

Kettner, P. M., & Martin, L. L. (1993a). Performance, accountability, and purchase of service contracting. *Administration in Social Work, 17*(1), 61–79.

Kettner, P. M., & Martin, L. L. (1993b). *Purchase of service contracting in the 1990s: Have expectations been met?* Paper presented at the Nonprofit Management Academy Research Conference, Morgantown, West Virginia.

Kettner, P. M., & Martin, L. L. (1995). Performance contracting in the human services: An initial assessment. *Administration in Social Work, 19*(2), 47–61.

Kettner, P. M., & Martin, L. L. (1996). The impact of declining resources and purchase of service contracting on private, nonprofit agencies. *Administration in Social Work, 20*(3), 21–38.

Kettner, P. M., Moroney, R. M., & Martin, L. L. (1990). *Designing and managing programs: An effectiveness-based approach.* Thousand Oaks, CA: Sage Publications.

Kingma, B. R. (1993). Portfolio theory and nonprofit financial stability. *Nonprofit and Voluntary Sector Quarterly, 22,* 105–119.

Kirwin, P. M., & Kaye, L. W. (1993). A comparative cost analysis of alternative models of adult day care. *Administration in Social Work, 17*(2), 105–122.

Kitsuse, J. I., & Spector, M. (1973). Toward a sociology of social problems: Social conditions, value-judgment and social problems. *Social Problems, 20,* 407–419.

Kleinman, M. L. (1985). Priority-setting for federations: An important tool for community planning and budgeting. *Journal of Jewish Communal Service, 61,* 283–288.

Kong, E. (2007). The development of strategic management in the nonprofit context: Intellectual capital in social service nonprofits. *International Journal of Management Reviews, 10*(3), 281–299.

Korten, D. C. (1999). *The post-corporate world: Life after capitalism.* San Francisco: Berrett–Koehler Press.

Krishman, R., Yetman, M. H., & Yetman, R. J. (2006). Expense misreporting in nonprofit organizations. *Accounting Review, 81,* 399–420.

Laidler-Kylander, N., Quelch, J. A., & Simonin, B. L. (2007). Building and valuing global brands in the nonprofit sector. *Nonprofit Management and Leadership, 17,* 253–277.

Lauffer, A. (1997). *Grants, etc.* (2nd ed.). Thousand Oaks, CA: Sage Publications.

Lee, P. (1937). *Social work as cause and function.* New York: Columbia University Press.

Leiby, J. (1991). Efficiency in social service administration: Historical reflections. *Administration in Social Work, 15*(1–2), 155–173.

Leontief, W. W. (1986). *Input-output economics.* New York: Oxford University Press.

LeRoux, K. M. (2005). What drives nonprofit entrepreneurship? A look at budget trends of metro Detroit social service agencies. *American Review of Public Administration, 35*, 350–362.

Levine, L. (1994). *Stewardship: Choosing service over self-interest*, by P. Block [Book review]. *Journal of Organizational Change Management, 7*(1), 74–76.

Levinthal, D., Meijs, L., & Hustinx, L. (2009). The third party model: Enhancing volunteering through governments, corporations, and educational institutes. *Journal of Social Policy, 39*, 139–158.

Lindblom, C. E. (1990). *Inquiry and change: The troubled attempt to understand and shape society*. New Haven, CT, and New York: Yale University Press and Russell Sage Foundation.

Lindeman, E. (1988). *Wealth and culture: A study of one hundred foundations and community trusts and their operations during the decade 1921–1930*. New Brunswick, NJ: Transaction Books. (Original work published 1936)

Lindsay, D. (2015). Nonprofit system is "chronically brittle," survey results suggest. *Chronicle of Philanthropy*. Retrieved from https://philanthropy.com/article/Nonprofit-System-Is/229679

Linzer, R., & Linzer, A. (2007). *The cash flow solution: The nonprofit board member's guide to financial success*. San Francisco: Jossey-Bass.

Linzer, R., & Linzer, A. (2008). *Cash flow strategies: Innovation in nonprofit financial management*. San Francisco: Jossey-Bass.

Lohmann, R. A. (1976). Break-even analysis: A tool for budgetary planning. *Social Work, 21*, 300–307.

Lohmann, R. A. (1980). *Breaking even: Financial management in human service organizations*. Philadelphia: Temple University Press.

Lohmann, R. A. (1992). *The commons: New perspectives on nonprofit organizations and voluntary action*. San Francisco: Jossey-Bass.

Lohmann, R. A. (2007). Charity, philanthropy, public service or enterprise: What are the big questions of nonprofit management? *Public Administration Review, 67*, 437–444.

Lohmann, R. A. (2015). *Voluntary action in new commons 1.2.1*. Morgantown, WV: Skywriters Press. Retrieved from http://works.bepress.com/rogerlohmann/4/

Lohmann, R. A. (2016). The Ostroms' commons revisited. *Nonprofit and Voluntary Sector Quarterly, 45*(S4).

Lohmann, R. A., & Lohmann, N. (2002). *Social administration*. New York: Columbia University Press.

Lohmann, R. A., & Lohmann, N. (2008). Management: Financial. In T. Mizrahi & L. E. Davis (Eds.-in-Chief), *Encyclopedia of social work* (20th ed., Vol. 3, pp. 163–173). Washington, DC, and New York: NASW Press and Oxford University Press.

Lowi, T. J. (1969). *The end of liberalism: Ideology, policy and the crisis of public authority*. New York: Norton.

Lowi, T. J. (1995). *The end of the Republican era*. Norman: University of Oklahoma Press.

MacMahon, A. W., Millett, J. D., & Ogden, G. (1941). *The administration of federal work relief*. Chicago, IL: Public Administration Service.

Maness, T. S., & Zietlow, J. T. (2005). *Short-term financial management* (3rd ed.). Mason, OH: South-Western/Thomson Learning.

Manser, G. (1960). A critical look at community planning. *Social Work, 5,* 35–41.

Martin, L. L. (1993a). *Total quality management in human services organizations.* Thousand Oaks, CA: Sage Publications.

Martin, L. L. (1993b). Total quality management: The new managerial wave. *Administration in Social Work, 17*(2), 1–16.

Martin, L. L. (1997). Outcome budgeting: A new entrepreneurial approach to budgeting. *Journal of Public Budgeting, Accounting and Financial Management, 9,* 108–126.

Martin, L. L. (2001). *Financial management for human service administrators.* Boston: Allyn & Bacon.

Martin, L. L. (2006). Improving financial management. *Nonprofit Management and Leadership, 17,* 129–130.

Martin, L. L., & Kettner, P. M. (1997). Performance measurement: The new accountability. *Administration in Social Work, 21*(1), 17–29.

Martin, L. L., & Kettner, P. M. (2010). *Measuring the performance of human service programs* (2nd ed.). Los Angeles: Sage Publications.

Marx, J. D. (2000). Online fundraising in the human services. *Journal of Technology in Human Services, 17,* 137–152.

Mason, J., Wodarski, J. S., Parham, T. M. J., & Lindsey, E. W. (1985). Agency directors and budget cuts. *Public Welfare, 43,* 26–32.

Mattocks, R. (2008). *Zone of insolvency: How nonprofits avoid hidden liabilities and build financial strength.* Hoboken, NJ: Wiley.

Mayers, R. S. (2004). *Financial management for nonprofit human services organizations* (2nd ed.). Springfield, IL: Charles C Thomas.

McCready, D. J., & Rahn, S. L. (1986). Funding human services: Fixed utility versus fixed budget. *Administration in Social Work, 10*(4), 23–30.

McCully, G. (2008). *Philanthropy reconsidered: Private initiatives — public good — quality of life.* Bloomington, IN: AuthorHouse.

McCully, G. (2015). On the unity of philanthropy, the humanities and liberal education. *Catalogue for Philanthropy.* Retrieved from http://www.philanthropicdirectory.org/blog/gmccully/unity-philanthropy-humanities-and-liberal-education

McGuirk, J. (2015, June 15). Urban commons have radical potential: It's not just about community gardens. *The Guardian.* Retrieved from http://www.theguardian.com/cities/2015/jun/15/urban-common-radical-community-gardens

McKinsey & Company. (n.d.). *Organizational Capacity Assessment Tool.* Retrieved from http://mckinseyonsociety.com/ocat/

McLaughlin, T. A. (2002). *Streetsmart financial basics for nonprofit managers* (2nd ed.). New York: Wiley.

McMillan, E. J. (1999). *Model accounting and financial policies and procedures handbook for not-for-profit organizations* (Rev. ed.). Washington, DC: American Society of Association Executives.

McMillan, E. J. (2000a). *Budgeting and financial management handbook for not-for-profit organizations* (Rev. ed.). Washington, DC: American Society of Association Executives.

McMillan, E. J. (2000b). *Essential accounting, tax, and reporting requirements for not-for-profit organizations* (Rev. ed.). Washington, DC: American Society of Association Executives.

McMillan, E. J. (2003). *Not-for-profit budgeting and financial management* (3rd ed.). Hoboken, NJ: Wiley.

McMullen, D. A. (1996). Audit committee performance: An investigation of the consequences associated with audit committees. *Auditing: A Journal of Practice & Theory, 15*, 87–103.

McNeal, A., & Michelman, J. (2006). CPA's role in fighting fraud in nonprofit organizations. *CPA Journal, 76*, 60–63.

Meezan, W., & McBeath, B. (2011). Moving toward performance-based, managed care contracting in child welfare: Perspectives on staffing, financial management, and information technology. *Administration in Social Work, 35*(2), 180–206.

Mester, L. J. (1987). Efficient production of financial services: Scale and scope economies. *Federal Reserve Bank of Philadelphia Economic Review, 73*, 15–25.

Meyer, D. R., & Sherraden, M. W. (1985). Toward improved financial planning: Further applications of break-even analysis in not-for-profit organizations. *Administration in Social Work, 9*(3), 57–68.

Meyer, J. A. (1997). The acceptance of visual information in management. *Information Management, 32*(6), 275–287.

Meyer, M. W. (2002). *Rethinking performance measurement: Beyond the balanced scorecard.* Cambridge, UK: Cambridge University Press.

Michalski, G. (2012). Accounts receivable management in nonprofit organizations. *Zeszyty Teoretyczne Rachunkowości, 68*, 83–96.

Mook, L. (2013). *Accounting for social value.* Toronto, Ontario, Canada: University of Toronto Press.

Mook, L., Quarter, J., Armstrong, A., & Whitman, J. R. (2015). *Understanding the social economy of the United States.* Toronto, Ontario, Canada: University of Toronto Press.

Mook, L., Sousa, J., Elgie, S., & Quarter, J. (2005). Accounting for the value of volunteer contributions. *Nonprofit Management & Leadership, 15*, 401–416.

Morris, R., Binstock, R. H., & Rein, M. (1966). *Feasible planning for social change.* New York: Columbia University Press.

Moynihan, D. P., & Kroll, A. (2015). Performance management routines that work? An early assessment of the GPRA Modernization Act. *Public Administration Review, 76*, 314–322.

Munson, C. E. (2012). *Handbook of clinical social work supervision.* New York: Routledge.

Murray, V. (2005). Evaluating the effectiveness of nonprofit organizations. In R. D. Herman (Ed.), *Jossey-Bass handbook of nonprofit leadership and management* (2nd ed., pp. 345–370). San Francisco: Jossey-Bass.

NAACP v. Alabama, 357 U.S. 449 (1958).

Nakamoto, D., & Altaffer, F. (1992). Cutback management using information and research. *Administration and Policy in Mental Health and Mental Health Services Research, 19*, 255–268.

Natarajan, R. (1996). Stewardship value of earnings components: Additional evidence on the determinants of executive compensation. *Accounting Review, 71*, 1–22.

National Association of Social Workers. (2008). *Code of ethics of the National Association of Social Workers.* Washington, DC: Author.

National Association of Social Workers. (n.d.-a). *NASW practice standards.* Retrieved from http://www.helpstartshere.org/about/nasw-practice-standards.html

National Association of Social Workers. (n.d.-b). *Social work profession.* Retrieved from https://www.socialworkers.org/pressroom/features/general/profession.asp

National Center for Charitable Statistics. (n.d.). National taxonomy of exempt entities. Retrieved from http://nccs.urban.org/classification/NTEE.cfm

National Conference of Commissioners on Uniform State Laws. (2011). *Revised Uniform Unincorporated Nonprofit Association Act (2008) (Last Amended 2011).* Retrieved from http://www.uniformlaws.org/shared/docs/harmonization_of_business_entity_acts/uunaa_draft%20final_received%20jan%202%202013.pdf

Nitterhouse, D. (1997). Financial management and accountability in small, religiously affiliated nonprofit organizations. *Nonprofit and Voluntary Sector Quarterly, 26*(Suppl.), S101–S123.

Niven, P. R. (2002). *Balanced scorecard step by step: Maximizing performance and maintaining results.* New York: Wiley.

Niven, P. R. (2003). *Balanced scorecard step-by-step for government and nonprofit agencies.* Hoboken, NJ: Wiley.

Nonprofit Finance Fund. (2015). *State of the sector surveys: 2015 survey.* Retrieved from http://www.nonprofitfinancefund.org/state-of-the-sector-surveys

Older Americans Act of 1965, P.L. 89-73, 79 Stat. 218 (1965).

Olve, N.-G., Roy, J., & Wetter, M. (1999). *Performance drivers: A practical guide to using the balanced scorecard.* New York: Wiley.

Ostrom, E. (1990). *Governing the commons: The evolution of institutions for collective action.* Cambridge, UK, and New York: Cambridge University Press.

Ostrom, E. (2002). *The drama of the commons.* Washington, DC: National Research Council, Committee on the Human Dimensions of Global Change.

Otten, G. L. (1977). Zero-based budgeting: Implications for social services? *Administration in Social Work, 1,* 369–378.

Palmer, P., & Randall, A. (2001). *Financial management in the voluntary sector: New challenges.* New York: Routledge.

Patient Protection and Affordable Care Act of 2010, 42 U.S.C. § 18001 (2010).

Patti, R. J. (2009). *The handbook of human services management* (2nd ed.). Los Angeles, CA: Sage Publications.

Pawlak, E. J., Jeter, S. C., & Fink, R. L. (1983). The politics of cutback management. *Administration in Social Work, 7*(2), 1–10.

Payton, R. L. (1988). *Philanthropy: Voluntary action for the public good.* New York: American Council on Education.

Pearce, J. L. (1993). *Volunteers: The organizational behavior of unpaid workers.* New York: Routledge.

Piketty, T. (2014). *Capital in the twenty-first century.* Cambridge, MA: Harvard University Press.

Poole, D. (2008). Organizational networks of collaboration for community-based living. *Nonprofit Management & Leadership, 18,* 278–293.

Pruger, R., & Miller, L. (1991a). Efficiency and the social services: Part A. *Administration in Social Work, 15*(1–2), 5–24.

Pruger, R., & Miller, L. (1991b). Efficiency and the social services: Part B. *Administration in Social Work, 15*(1–2), 25–44.

Purdy, L. (1921). The need and value of the budget system for social agencies. *Family, 1*(9), 10–13.

Putnam, R. D. (2000). *Bowling alone: The collapse and revival of American community.* New York: Simon & Schuster.

Pyhrr, P. A. (1970). Zero-base budgeting. *Harvard Business Review, 48,* 111–123.

Pyhrr, P. A. (1973). *Zero-base budgeting: A practical management tool for evaluating expenses.* New York: Wiley.

Pyhrr, P. A. (1977). The zero-base approach to governmental budgeting. *Public Administration Review, 37*(1), 1–8.

Quarter, J., Mook, L., & Armstrong, A. (2009). *Understanding the social economy: A Canadian perspective.* Toronto, Ontario, Canada: University of Toronto Press.

Quarter, J., Mook, L., & Richmond, B. J. (2007). *What counts: Social accounting for nonprofits and cooperatives* (2nd ed.). Medina, OH: Sigel Press.

Quarter, J., Mook, L., & Ryan, S. (2010). *Researching the social economy.* Toronto, Ontario, Canada: University of Toronto Press.

Quinn, J. B. (1980). *Strategies for change: Logical incrementalism.* Homewood, IL: R. D. Irwin.

Reed, R., Lemak, D. J., & Montgomery, J. C. (1996). Beyond process: TQM content and firm performance. *Academy of Management Review, 21,* 173–202.

Reider, R., & Heyler, P. B. (2003). *Managing cash flow.* New York: Wiley.

Reisch, M., & Taylor, C. L. (1983). Ethical guidelines for cutback management: A preliminary approach. *Administration in Social Work, 7*(3–4), 59–72.

Riahi-Belkaoui, A. (2003). *Accounting—By principle or design?* Westport, CT: Greenwood.

Rice, R. M. (1975). Impact of government contracts on voluntary social agencies. *Social Casework, 56,* 387–395.

Richmond, B. J. (1999). *Counting on each other: A social audit model to assess the impact of nonprofit organizations.* Unpublished doctoral dissertation, University of Toronto, Ontario, Canada.

Rimer, E. (1991). The impact of efficiency on social work administration education. *Administration in Social Work, 15*(1–2), 133–146.

Ritchie, W. J., & Eastwood, K. (2006). Executive functional experience and its relationship to the financial performance of nonprofit organizations. *Nonprofit Management and Leadership, 17,* 67–82.

Ritchie, W. J., & Kolodinsky, R. W. (2003). Nonprofit organization financial performance measurement: An evaluation of new and existing financial performance measures. *Nonprofit Management and Leadership, 13,* 367–382.

Rogers, E. M. (2003). *Diffusion of innovations* (5th ed.). New York: Free Press.

Rohter, L. (2015, August 7). New York Review of Books fills a niche by reviving forgotten works. *New York Times.* Retrieved from http://www.nytimes.com/2015/08/08/books/new-york-review-books-fills-a-niche-by-reviving-forgotten-works.html

Rosentraub, M. S., Harlow, K. S., & Harris, M. (1992). Uncompensated costs and indigent health care: Volunteers and a community services budget. *Nonprofit and Voluntary Sector Quarterly, 21*, 351–366.

Rosso, H. A. (1996). *Rosso on fund raising: Lessons from a master's lifetime experience.* San Francisco: Jossey-Bass.

Rothschild, J., & Whitt, J. A. (1986). *The cooperative workplace: Potentials and dilemmas of organizational democracy and participation.* Cambridge, UK: Cambridge University Press.

Russell Sage Foundation. (1919). *Statement on financial federation in New York City* [Unpublished document]. Rockefeller Archives Center, Sleepy Hollow, NY.

Ryan, R. M., & Washington, R. O. (1977). New patterns for organizing human services. *Administration in Social Work, 1*(3), 301–309.

Salamon, L. M. (2015). *The resilient sector revisited: The new challenge to nonprofit America* (2nd ed.). Washington, DC: Brookings Institution Press.

Salmon, F. (2010). The massive cost of underemployment [Web log post]. *Thomson Reuters.* Retrieved from http://blogs.reuters.com/felix-salmon/2010/02/11/the-massive-cost-of-underemployment/

Sarri, R., & Vinter, R. (1970). Organizational requisites for a socio-behavioral technology. In S. Harry (Ed.), *Social work administration: A resource book* (pp. 81–99). New York: Council on Social Work Education.

Sax, P. R. (1978). An inquiry into fee setting and its determinants. *Clinical Social Work Journal, 6*, 305–312.

Schick, A. (2007). *The federal budget: Politics, policy, process* (3rd ed.). Washington, DC: Brookings Institution Press.

Scott, W. R. (1998). *Organizations: Rational, natural, and open systems* (4th ed.). Upper Saddle River, NJ: Prentice Hall.

Sharkansky, I. (1980). Policy making and service delivery on the margins of government: The case of contractors. *Public Administration Review, 40*(2), 116–123.

Sherraden, M. W. (1986). Benefit–cost analysis as a net present value problem. *Administration in Social Work, 10*(3), 85–97.

Shireman, J. (1975). Client and worker opinions about fee-charging in a child welfare agency. *Child Welfare, 44*, 331–340.

Sills, D. L. (1957). *The volunteers, means and ends in a national organization; a report.* Glencoe, IL: Free Press.

Simon, H. A. (1997). *Administrative behavior: A study of decision-making processes in administrative organization* (4th ed.). New York: Free Press.

Sloan, M. F. (2009). The effects of nonprofit accountability ratings on donor behavior. *Nonprofit and Voluntary Sector Quarterly, 38*, 220–236.

Smith, S. R. (2014). Hybridity and nonprofit organizations: The research agenda. *American Behavioral Scientist, 58*, 1494–1508.

Smith, S. R., & Lipsky, M. (1992). *Nonprofits for hire: The welfare state in the age of contracting.* Cambridge, MA: Harvard University Press.

Snavely, K., & Tracy, M. B. (2000). Collaboration among rural nonprofit organizations. *Nonprofit Management and Leadership, 11*, 145-165.

Social Security Act of 1935, P.L. 74-271, 49 Stat. 620 (1935).

Sowers, K. M., & Ellis, R. A. (2001). Steering currents for the future of social work. *Research in Social Work Practice, 11*(2), 245–253.

Speckbacher, G. (2003). The economics of performance management in nonprofit organizations. *Nonprofit Management and Leadership, 13,* 267–281.

Steinberg, R. (2004). *The economics of nonprofit enterprises.* Northampton, MA: Edward Elgar.

Steinberg, R. (2008). *Principal-agent theory and nonprofit accountability* (Working Paper wp200803). Indiana University–Purdue University Indianapolis, Department of Economics. Retrieved from http://ideas.repec.org/p/iup/wpaper/wp200803.html

Stern, D. (1991). Efficiency in human services: The case of education. *Administration in Social Work, 15*(1–2), 83–104.

Stevens, C. (2004). Essential internal controls. *Association Management, 56,* 114–123.

Stewart, T. A. (1997). *Intellectual capital: The new wealth of organizations.* New York: Doubleday/Currency.

Stock, R. (1969, January). Societal demands on the voluntary agency. *Social Casework, 50,* 27–31.

Stoesz, D., & Karger, H. J. (1993). Deconstructing welfare: The Reagan legacy and the welfare state. *Social Work, 38,* 619–628.

Stretch, J. J. (1980). What human services managers need to know about basic budgeting strategies. *Administration in Social Work, 4*(1), 87–98.

Sumariwalla, R. D., & Levis, W. C. (2000). *Unified financial reporting system for not-for-profit organizations: A comprehensive guide to unifying GAAP, IRS Form 990, and other financial reports using a unified chart of accounts.* San Francisco: Jossey-Bass.

Taylor, H. A. (2015). *Wise giving Wednesday: Workplace giving.* Retrieved from http://give.org/news-updates/news/2015/07/wise-giving-wednesday-workplace-giving/#sthash.Pc6va2Yt.dpuf

Tinkelman, D. (1998). Differences in sensitivity of financial statement users to joint cost allocations: The case of nonprofit organizations. *Journal of Accounting, Auditing & Finance, 13,* 377–393.

Tinkelman, D. (2005). Nonprofit organizations' cost allocations. *CPA Journal, 75*(7), 50–54.

Tinkelman, D., & Donabedian, B. (2007). Street lamps, alleys, ratio analysis, and nonprofit organizations. *Nonprofit Management and Leadership, 18,* 5–18.

Title XX of the Social Security Act, P.L. 93-647, 42 U.S.C. 1397a–1397m5. (1975).

Tropman, J. E. (1972). Comparative analysis of community organization agencies: The case of the welfare council. In I. Spergel (Ed.), *Community organization* (pp. 93–121). Beverly Hills, CA: Sage Publications.

Trussel, J. M. (2002). Revisiting the prediction of financial vulnerability. *Nonprofit Management and Leadership, 13,* 17–32.

Tuckman, H. P., & Chang, C. F. (1991). A methodology for measuring the financial vulnerability of charitable nonprofit organizations. *Nonprofit and Voluntary Sector Quarterly, 20,* 445–460.

Turem, J. S. (1986). Social work administration and modern management technology. *Administration in Social Work, 19,* 15–24.

United Way of America. (1974). *Accounting and financial reporting: A guide for United Ways and not-for-profit service organizations.* Alexandria, VA: United Way of America, Systems, Planning, and Allocations Division.

United Way of America. (1975). *Budgeting: A guide for United Ways and not-for-profit human service organizations.* Alexandria, VA: United Way of America, Systems, Planning, and Allocations Division.

U.S. Government Printing Office. (2012). *2 CFR 230: Cost principles for non-profit organizations (OMB Circular A-122).* Retrieved from https://www.gpo.gov/fdsys/granule/CFR-2012-title2-vol1/CFR-2012-title2-vol1-part230/content-detail.html

Van Til, J. (1988). *Mapping the third sector: Voluntarism in a changing social economy.* New York: Foundation Center.

Vatter, W. J. (1947). *The fund theory of accounting and its implications for financial reports.* Chicago: University of Chicago Press.

Verheyen, P. (1998). The missing link in budget models of nonprofit institutions: Two practical Dutch applications. *Management Science, 44,* 787–800.

Vincent, A., & Plant, R. (1984). *Philosophy, politics and citizenship: The life and thought of the British idealists.* New York: Cambridge University Press.

Vinter, R., & Kish, R. (1985). *Budgeting in not-for-profit organizations.* New York: Free Press.

Vowell, S. S. (2000). *The complete guide to managing chapter funds: What you need to know about financial management, the law, tax issues, and working with the national organization.* Washington, DC: American Society of Association Executives.

Wacht, R., F. (1987). Analyzing financial statements: A new framework. *Nonprofit World, 5*(1), 23–26.

Walters, J. (2011, August 9). Human services meets capitalism. *Governing: The States and Localities.* Retrieved from http://www.governing.com/topics/health-human-services/human-services-meets-capitalism.html

Ward, D., & Hale, P. D. (2006). *Writing grant proposals that win* (3rd ed.). Sudbury, MA: Jones & Bartlett.

Warren, R. L. (1987). *The community in America* (3rd ed.). Lanham, MD: University Press of America.

Webb, N. J. (1996). Tax incentives for corporate giving programs: What measures increase funds available? *Administration in Social Work, 20*(3), 39–56.

Weber, M. C. (1991). The legal and policy implications of third party reimbursement for early childhood services. *Journal of Early Intervention, 15,* 298–303.

Wedig, G. J. (1994). Risk, leverage, donations and dividends-in-kind: A theory of nonprofit financial behavior. *International Review of Economics & Finance, 3,* 257–278.

Weil, M., Reisch, M., & Ohmer, M. L. (2013). *The handbook of community practice* (2nd ed.). Thousand Oaks, CA: Sage Publications.

Weiss, A. (2005). *Assessing nonprofit organizational capacity.* Retrieved from http://www.hfrp.org/evaluation/the-evaluation-exchange/issue-archive/evaluation-methodology/assessing-nonprofit-organizational-capacity

Wernet, S., Hulseman, F., Merkel, L., McMahon, A., Clevenger, D., Colletta, A., & Leeds, V. (1993). The fee for service schedule: A new formula. *Families in Society, 73,* 109–115.

White, R. C. (1940). *The administration of public welfare.* New York: American Book.

Whittaker, J. B. (2001). *Balanced scorecard in the federal government.* Vienna, VA: Management Concepts.

Wildavsky, A. (1967). *The politics of the budgetary process.* Boston: Little, Brown.

Wildavsky, A. (1973, Fall). Annual expenditure increment: Or how Congress can regain control of the budget. *Public Interest, 33,* 84–108.

Wildavsky, A. (1991). Efficiency as a function of culture. *Administration in Social Work, 15*(1–2), 147–153.

Wimpfheimer, S. (2004). Leadership and management competencies defined by practicing social work managers. *Administration in Social Work, 28*(1), 45–56.

Wineburg, R. J., Spakes, P., & Finn, J. (1983). Budget cuts and human services: One community's experience. *Social Casework, 64,* 489–496.

Wing, K., Gordon, T., Hager, M., Pollak, T., & Rooney, P. (2006). Functional expense reporting for nonprofits. *CPA Journal, 76*(8), 14–18.

Wolf, T. (2001). Financial statements and fiscal procedures. In J. S. Ott (Ed.), *Understanding nonprofit organizations: Governance, leadership and management* (pp. 298–309). Denver, CO: Westview.

Wooten, T. C., Coker, J. W., & Elmore, R. C. (2003). Financial control in religious organizations: A status report. *Nonprofit Management and Leadership, 13,* 343–365.

Worth, M. J. (2009). *Nonprofit management: Principles and practice.* Los Angeles: Sage Publications.

Wren, D. A. (1994). *The evolution of management thought* (4th ed.). New York: Wiley.

Wymer, W., Scaife, W., & McDonald, K. (2012). Financial planners and philanthropic planning. *Voluntas: International Journal of Voluntary and Nonprofit Organizations, 23,* 350–370.

Yates, B. T. (1995). Cost-effectiveness analysis, cost–benefit analysis, and beyond: Evolving models for the scientist–manager–practitioner. *Clinical Psychology: Science and Practice, 2,* 385–398.

Young, D. R. (1983). *If not for profit, for what? A behavioral theory of the nonprofit sector based on entrepreneurship.* Lexington, MA: Lexington Books.

Young, D. R. (2007). *Financing nonprofits: Putting theory into practice.* Lanham, MD: AltaMira Press.

Young, D. R., & Steinberg, R. (1995). *Economics for nonprofit managers.* New York: Foundation Center.

Young, D. W. (2005). Management accounting. In R. D. Herman & Associates (Eds.), *The Jossey-Bass handbook of nonprofit leadership and management* (pp. 513–559). San Francisco: Jossey-Bass.

Young, D. W., & Allen, B. (1977). Benefit–cost analysis in the social services: The example of adoption reimbursement. *Social Service Review, 51,* 249–264.

Zack, G. M. (2003). *Fraud and abuse in nonprofit organizations: A guide to prevention and detection.* Hoboken, NJ: Wiley.

Zald, M. N. (1967). *Organizing for community welfare.* Chicago: Quadrangle Books.

Zech, C. E. (2010). *Best practices in Catholic Church ministry performance management.* Lanham, MD: Lexington Books.

Zeitz, K. M., & Tucker, K. (2010). Capacity audit tool: Identifying inpatient delays to maximize service improvement. *Australian Health Review, 34,* 395–399.

Zietlow, J., & Seider, A. G. (2007). *Cash and investment management for nonprofit organizations.* New York: Wiley.

Zietlow, J., Hankin, J. A., & Seidner, A. G. (2007). *Financial management for nonprofit organizations: Policies and practices.* Hoboken, NJ: Wiley.

Zohar, D., & Marshall, I. N. (2004). *Spiritual capital: Wealth we can live by.* San Francisco: Berrett-Koehler.

Zunz, O. (2012). *Philanthropy in America: A history.* Princeton, NJ: Princeton University Press.

Index